DOCUMENTING DESEGREGATION

DOCUMENTING DESEGREGATION

Racial and Gender
Segregation in Private-
Sector Employment
Since the Civil Rights Act

Kevin Stainback and
Donald Tomaskovic-Devey

Russell Sage Foundation
New York

The Russell Sage Foundation

The Russell Sage Foundation, one of the oldest of America's general purpose foundations, was established in 1907 by Mrs. Margaret Olivia Sage for "the improvement of social and living conditions in the United States." The Foundation seeks to fulfill this mandate by fostering the development and dissemination of knowledge about the country's political, social, and economic problems. While the Foundation endeavors to assure the accuracy and objectivity of each book it publishes, the conclusions and interpretations in Russell Sage Foundation publications are those of the authors and not of the Foundation, its Trustees, or its staff. Publication by Russell Sage, therefore, does not imply Foundation endorsement.

Library of Congress Cataloging-in-Publication Data

Stainback, Kevin.
  Documenting desegregation : racial and gender segregation in private-sector employment since the Civil Rights Act / Kevin Stainback and Donald Tomaskovic-Devey.
     p. cm.
  Includes bibliographical references and index.
  ISBN 978-0-87154-834-4 (pbk. : alk. paper)   1. Discrimination in employment—United States.   2. Sex discrimination in employment—United States.   3. African Americans—Employment.   4. Minorities—Employment—United States.   5. United States—Social conditions—1945–   I. Tomaskovic-Devey, Donald, 1957–   II. Title.
  HD4903.5.U58S69 2012
  331.13'30973—dc23   2012013792

Text design by Genna Patacsil.

RUSSELL SAGE FOUNDATION
112 East 64th Street, New York, New York 10065
10 9 8 7 6 5 4 3 2 1

Contents

List of Tables and Figures   vii

About the Authors   xvii

Acknowledgments   xix

Introduction   xxi

PART I   NATIONAL EQUAL OPPORTUNITY POLITICS   1

Chapter 1   Documenting Desegregation   3

Chapter 2   Hyper-Segregation in the Pre–Civil Rights Period   50

Chapter 3   The Era of Uncertainty, 1966 to 1972   84

Chapter 4   The Short Regulatory Decade, 1972 to 1980   118

Chapter 5   Desegregation in the Neoliberal Era,
                1980 to 2005   155

PART II   LOCAL INEQUALITY REGIMES   179

Chapter 6   Local Labor Market Competition and New
                Status Hierarchies   181

Chapter 7   Sector and Industry Segregation Trajectories   211

Chapter 8   Contemporary Workplace Dynamics   250

Chapter 9   National to Local Segregation Trajectories   293

Methodological Appendix   323

Notes   339

References   345

Index   363

List of Tables and Figures |

Table 2.1	Distribution of Homogeneous EEOC-Reporting Workplaces, 1966	52
Table 2.2	Distribution of Race-Gender Groups Across Major Occupational Categories, 1966	52
Table 2.3	Regional Variation in Segregation Levels, 1966	56
Table 2.4	Sector Variation in Segregation Levels, 1966	57
Table 2.5	Percentage Over and Under Representation in Desirable Occupations Relative to Group Composition in the Local Labor Market Among Federal Contractors and Other EEOC-Reporting Workplaces, 1966	73
Table 2.6	Representation in Good Jobs Relative to the Local Labor Supply in Workplaces in States with and without Fair Employment Practice Laws, 1966	77
Table 3.1	Adjusted Average Yearly Black-White Desegregation Trajectories, by Gender, by Region, 1966 to 1972	101
Table 4.1	Supreme Court Rulings Clarifying and Strengthening Discrimination Law, 1972 to 1980	120
Table 4.2	Observed and Adjusted Segregation from White Men Trajectories in the Uncertainty (1966 to 1972) and Enforcement Periods (1973 to 1980)	129
Table 4.3	Observed and Adjusted Segregation Trajectories from White Women in the Uncertainty (1966 to 1972) and Enforcement Periods (1973 to 1980)	132
Table 4.4	Regression-Adjusted Segregation and Isolation Yearly Change by Contractor Types and Large Firm Size, 1973 to 1980	151
Table 5.1	Supreme Court Race/Gender Employment Discrimination Decisions, 1981 to 2011	165

Table 5.2   Regression Adjusted Yearly Desegregation Trajectories   170
by Political Era

Table 6.1   The Influence of a 10 Percent Increase in Group Size   190
on Local Labor Market Segregation from White Men,
1966 to 2005

Table 6.2   The Influence of a 10 Percent Gain in Group Size in   192
Local Labor Markets on Access to Managerial,
Professional, and Craft Jobs, 1966 to 2005

Table 6.3   Queuing Processes and Segregation Between White   195
Men and White Women at a 10 Percent Increase in
Group Size, 1966 to 2005

Table 6.4   Queuing Processes and Segregation Between White   196
Men and Black Men at a 10 Percent Increase in
Group Size, 1966 to 2005

Table 6.5   Queuing Processes and Segregation Between White   197
Women and Black Women at a 10 Percent Increase
in Group Size, 1966 to 2005

Table 6.6   Relative Managerial Representation in the Top Twenty   202
EEOC-Reporting Labor Markets, 2005

Table 6.7   Relative Managerial Representation in the Top Ten   203
African American EEOC-Reporting Labor Markets,
2005

Table 6.8   Relative Managerial Representation in the Top Ten   204
Hispanic EEOC-Reporting Labor Markets, 2005

Table 6.9   Relative Managerial Representation in the Top Ten   205
Asian EEOC-Reporting Labor Markets, 2005

Table 6.10   The Top Twenty Cities for White Male   207
Overrepresentation and White Female, Black Male,
and Black Female Underrepresentation in Managerial
Jobs, 2005

Table 7.1   Gender Segregation Levels by Sector, Ranked from   219
Lowest to Highest, 2005

Table 7.2   Race Segregation Levels by Sector, Ranked from   220
Lowest to Highest, 2005

Table 7.3   Managerial Representation Levels by Sector, Ranked   222
from Highest to Lowest, 2005

Table 7.4   Top Twenty Two-Digit Industries Ranked for   225
Employment Growth, Relative Income, and
Educational Requirements, 1973 to 1980

Table 7.5   Bottom Twenty Two-Digit Industries Ranked for   226
Employment Growth, Relative Income, and
Educational Requirements, 1973 to 1980

Table 7.6	Ten Steepest Yearly Desegregation Trajectories, 1973 to 1981	228
Table 7.7	Industries with Positive Segregation Trajectories, 1973 to 1981	230
Table 7.8	Ten Steepest Yearly Desegregation Trajectories, 2001 to 2005	231
Table 7.9	Industries with Positive Segregation Trajectories, 2001 to 2005	233
Table 7.10	Top Twenty Industries with Increasing White Female–Black Female Segregation Trajectories, 1973 to 1980 and 2001 to 2005	234
Table 7.11	Changes in Industry Employment and Segregation as a Function of Growth, Closure, and Credentialing Mechanisms, 1966 to 2005	237
Table 7.12	Changes in Managerial, Professional, and Craft Representation as a Function of Growth, Closure, and Credentialing Mechanisms, 1966 to 2005	239
Table 7.13	Ten Steepest Within-Workplace Industry Desegregation Trajectories, 1990 to 2005	243
Table 7.14	Within-Workplace Industry Resegregation Trajectories, 1990 to 2005	244
Table 7.15	Ten Best and Worst Industries for Managerial Employment	247
Table 7.15	(Continued)	248
Table 8.1	Direct OFCCP Regulation and OFCCP Industry Density Effects on Changes in Segregation, 1990 to 2005	263
Table 8.2	The Impact of OFCCP Regulation and OFCCP Industry Environment on Percentage Changes in Managerial Representation, 1990 to 2005	264
Table A.1	SIC Standardization Rules	329
Figure I.1	Hypothetical Employment Segregation Trajectories	xxviii
Figure 1.1	Whites Who Agree with the Statement "Negroes/Blacks/African Americans Have Less Inborn Ability," 1977 to 2006	22
Figure 1.2	Whites Who Agree with the Statement "Negroes/Blacks/African Americans Shouldn't Push Themselves Where They're Not Wanted," 1977 to 2002	23
Figure 1.3	Respondents Who Agree at Least Slightly That It Is Better for Men to Work and Women to Tend the Home, 1977 to 2006	24

Figure 1.4   Employment Segregation from White Men in EEOC-   31
              Reporting Private-Sector Workplaces, 1966 to 2005
Figure 1.5   Employment Isolation in EEOC-Reporting Private-   32
              Sector Workplaces, 1966 to 2005
Figure 1.6   Craft Employment Relative to Labor Market   34
              Participation in EEOC-Reporting Private-Sector
              Workplaces, 1966 to 2005
Figure 1.7   Managerial Employment Relative to Labor Market   35
              Participation in EEOC-Reporting Private-Sector
              Workplaces, 1966 to 2005
Figure 1.8   Professional Employment Relative to Labor Market   36
              Participation in EEOC-Reporting Private-Sector
              Workplaces, 1966 to 2005
Figure 1.9   Labor Force Composition, 1966 to 2005   38
Figure 1.10   Years of Education Relative to Average for White   40
              Males Among the Currently Employed, 1966 to 2006
Figure 1.11   College Education Achievement Relative to White   41
              Males, Currently Employed, 1966 to 2006
Figure 1.12   EEOC Reporting as Percentage of Total Private-Sector   42
              Labor Force, 1966 to 2000
Figure 1.13   Government Employment as Percentage of Total   43
              Labor Force by Race and Gender, 1966 to 2000
Figure 1.14   Small-Firm Private-Sector Employment, 1966 to 2000   44
Figure 1.15   EEOC Reporting of Private-Sector Labor Force   45
              Coverage by Region, 1966
Figure 1.16   EEOC Reporting of Private-Sector African American   46
              Employment Coverage by Region, 1966
Figure 1.17   EEOC Reporting of Private-Sector Coverage, by   47
              Industrial Sector, 1966
Figure 2.1   Employment Segregation, 1966   54
Figure 2.2   Employment Segregation in Single-Establishment   58
              Firms, Branch Plants, and Corporate Headquarters,
              1966
Figure 2.3   Employment Isolation from Intergroup Contact, 1966   59
Figure 2.4   Representation in Desirable Occupations Relative to   61
              Group Composition in the Local Labor Market, 1966
Figure 2.5   African American Protest Events, 1948 to 1964   67
Figure 2.6   Employment at Federal Contractors and Other   70
              EEOC-Reporting Firms, 1966
Figure 2.7   Segregation Levels Among Federal Contractors and   71
              Other EEOC-Reporting Firms, 1966

Figure 2.8   Average 1966 Isolation Index Among Federal   72
Contractors and Other EEOC-Reporting Workplaces

Figure 2.9   Fair Employment Practice Laws and Their Adoption,   75
1945 to 1964

Figure 2.10   Employment Segregation and Isolation by Fair   76
Employment Practice Laws, 1966

Figure 2.11   Employment Segregation and Isolation for Plans for   80
Progress Firms Compared to All Federal Contractors
and EEOC-Reporting Workplaces, 1966

Figure 3.1   Workplaces with No White Men, White Women,   93
Black Men, or Black Women, 1966 to 1972

Figure 3.2   Observed, Expected, and Net Employment Gains in   94
EEOC-Reporting Workplaces, 1966 to 1972

Figure 3.3   Employment Growth in EEOC-Reporting Workplaces,   95
1966 to 1972

Figure 3.4   Employment Growth in Working-Class Jobs, 1966 to   96
1972

Figure 3.5   Employment Growth in Other White-Collar Jobs,   97
1966 to 1972

Figure 3.6   Employment Growth in High-Skilled White-Collar   98
Jobs, 1966 to 1972

Figure 3.7   Employment Segregation Trends, Adjusted for   99
Industry, Organizational Characteristics, and Local
Labor Supply, 1966 to 1972

Figure 3.8   Regional Race Segregation Trends, Adjusted for   101
Industry, Organizational Characteristics, and Local
Labor Supply, 1966 to 1972

Figure 3.9   Race Segregation Trends by Fair Employment Practice   102
Laws, Adjusted for Industry, Organizational Characteristics, and Local Labor Supply, 1966 to 1972

Figure 3.10   Isolation Trends, Adjusted for Industry, Organizational   103
Characteristics, and Local Labor Supply, 1966 to
1972

Figure 3.11   Skilled Craft Production Representation Trends,   104
Adjusted for Industry and Organization Shifts, 1966
to 1972

Figure 3.12   Skilled Craft Production Occupation Trends by Fair   105
Employment Practice States, Adjusted for Industry and
Organization Shifts, 1966 to 1972

Figure 3.13   Managerial Representation, Adjusted for Industry and   106
Organization Shifts, 1966 to 1972

Figure 3.14   Professional Representation Trends, Adjusted for   107
               Industry and Organizational Shifts, 1966 to 1972
Figure 3.15   Segregation Trends by Federal Contractor Status,   109
               Adjusted for Industry, Organizational Characteristics,
               and Local Labor Supply, 1966 to 1972
Figure 3.16   Isolation Trends by Federal Contractor Status,   110
               Adjusted for Industry, Organizational Characteristics,
               and Local Labor Supply, 1966 to 1972
Figure 3.17   Males' Increased Access to Good Jobs in Plan for   111
               Progress Firms, Adjusted for Industry and
               Organizational Shifts, 1966 to 1972
Figure 3.18   Average Yearly Percentage Change of Plans for   112
               Progress Firms in Good Job Representation, Adjusted
               for Industry and Organizational Shifts, 1966 to 1972
Figure 4.1   African American Civil Rights and Feminist Social   122
               Movement Organizations, 1955 to 1985
Figure 4.2   Civil Rights and Women's Rights Protest Events, 1968   123
               to 1980
Figure 4.3   African American Protest Events, 1948 to 1996   124
Figure 4.4   Regression-Adjusted Trends in Segregation from   128
               White Men, 1973 to 1980
Figure 4.5   Regression-Adjusted Trends in Segregation from   131
               White Women, 1973 to 1980
Figure 4.6   Regression-Adjusted Trends in Employment Isolation,   133
               1973 to 1980
Figure 4.7   Regression-Adjusted Trends in Managerial   134
               Representation, 1973 to 1980
Figure 4.8   Regression-Adjusted Trends in Professional   136
               Representation, 1973 to 1980
Figure 4.9   Regression-Adjusted Trend in Craft Occupation   139
               Representation, 1973 to 1980
Figure 4.10   Regression-Adjusted Comparison of Black Male   142
               Segregation from White Men and from White Women
               by Federal Regulatory Status, 1973 to 1980
Figure 4.11   Regression-Adjusted Black Male Occupational   143
               Representation by Federal Reporting Status, 1973 to
               1980
Figure 4.12   Regression-Adjusted Comparison of Segregation from   145
               White Women by Federal Reporting Status, 1973 to
               1980
Figure 4.13   Regression-Adjusted Trends in White Women's Access   146
               to Professional Occupations by Federal Regulatory
               Status, 1973 to 1980

Figure 4.14   Regression-Adjusted Employment Race Segregation   147
               Among Black and White Women by Federal
               Regulatory Status, 1973 to 1980
Figure 4.15   Regression-Adjusted Isolation Trends by Regulatory   149
               Status, 1973 to 1980
Figure 5.1   EEOC and OFCCP Funding and Staffing, 1981 to   158
               1994
Figure 5.2   Human Resource Managerial Employment, 1968 to   161
               2006
Figure 5.3   Sexual Harassment Charges Filed with the EEOC,   162
               1980 to 2002
Figure 5.4   Regression-Adjusted Segregation from White Men,   168
               1980 to 2005
Figure 5.5   Regression-Adjusted Segregation from White Women,   169
               1980 to 2005
Figure 5.6   Regression-Adjusted Managerial Representation,   171
               1980 to 2005
Figure 5.7   Regression-Adjusted Professional Representation,   172
               1980 to 2005
Figure 5.8   Regression-Adjusted Craft Representation, 1980 to   173
               2005
Figure 5.9   Adjusted Isolation Trends, 1980 to 2005   174
Figure 5.10   Yearly Shifts in Segregation from White Men   174
               Associated with OFCCP Regulation, by Political Era
Figure 5.11   Yearly Shifts in Managerial Representation Associated   175
               with OFCCP Regulation, by Political Era
Figure 6.1   Rapid Regional Convergence in Racial Segregation,   184
               1966 to 2000
Figure 6.2   Continued Regional Differences in Employment   185
               Segregation Between White Women and Black Men
Figure 6.3   Odds Relative to White Men of Employment in a   186
               Managerial Job, 2000
Figure 6.4   Odds Relative to White Men of Being Employed in a   187
               Skilled Craft Job, 2000
Figure 6.5   White Males' Increased Access to Managerial Jobs   198
               with a 10 Percent Increase in Group Labor Market
               Presence, 2001 to 2005
Figure 6.6   White Males' Increased Craft Representation with a   199
               10 Percent Increase in Other Groups in the Local
               Labor Market, 2001 to 2005
Figure 6.7   White Males' Increased Professional Representation   200
               with a 10 Percent Increase in Other Groups in the
               Local Labor Market, 2001 to 2005

Figure 6.8   Increases in White Male Exposure to Intergroup   206
              Contact for a 10 Percent Increase in Group Labor
              Market Composition, 2001 to 2005
Figure 7.1   Segregation Between White Men and Black Men by   215
              Sector, 1966 to 2005
Figure 7.2   Segregation Between White Men and White Women   216
              by Sector, 1966 to 2005
Figure 7.3   Segregation Between White Women and Black   218
              Women by Sector, 1966 to 2005
Figure 7.4   White Male Managerial Representation by Sector,   221
              1966 to 2005
Figure 8.1   Contributions to Segregation Change from Shifts in   253
              Workplace Practices and the Founding of New
              Workplaces, 1990 to 2005
Figure 8.2   Total Variance in Segregation Associated with Time,   256
              Industry, Firm, and Establishment, 1990 to 2005
Figure 8.3   Trends in EEOC Complaints by Type of   258
              Discrimination, 1992 to 2009
Figure 8.4   Discrimination Charges Filed with the EEOC That   271
              Reported Employer Retaliation, 1992 to 2009
Figure 8.5   Influence of a 1 Percent Change in Managerial and   279
              Nonmanagerial Group Size on Workforce and
              Managerial Composition, Lagged Panel Models,
              1990 to 2005
Figure 8.6   Inertial and Dynamic Influences of a 1 Percent   280
              Change in Managerial and Nonmanagerial Group
              Size on Managerial Composition, 1990 to 2005
Figure 8.7   Influence of a 1 Percent Growth in Group Managerial   281
              Composition on Change in Managerial,
              Establishment, Craft, and Professional Workforce
              Composition, Establishment Fixed-Effects Panel
              Estimates, 1990 to 2005
Figure 8.8   Relative Declines in Managerial Representation with   282
              the Growth of Nonmanagerial Workforces, Dynamic
              Fixed-Effects Panel Estimates, 1990 to 2005
Figure 9.1   Employment Segregation from White Men in EEOC-   298
              Reporting Private-Sector Workplaces, 1966 to 2005
Figure 9.2   Density Plots of Organizational Variation in   300
              Segregation, 1966 to 2005
Figure 9.3   U.S. Labor Force Composition in 2005 and Projected   308
              in 2050

Figure 9.4   Distributions of Black Women in Management   312
               Relative to Their Representation in Local Labor
               Markets in EEOC-Reporting Private-Sector
               Workplaces, 1966, 1980, and 2005
Figure 9.5   EEOC and OFCCP Staffing, 1994 to 2010   316

About the Authors

KEVIN STAINBACK is associate professor of sociology at Purdue University.

DONALD TOMASKOVIC-DEVEY is professor of sociology at the University of Massachusetts Amherst.

Acknowledgments

THIS PROJECT WOULD not have been possible without the support, conversations, and guidance of many people. Sheryl Skaggs has pride of place in both understanding the value of the EEO-1 data as a research tool and figuring out how to gain access to them. At the Equal Employment Opportunity Commission (EEOC), Ronald Edwards and Bliss Cartwright have been consistently supportive of our inquiries about the data and production of research. For the last ten years or so, the EEOC has allowed restricted access to these data, and a community of researchers has grown up around them. We have shared information and insights with Frank Dobbin and Alexandra Kalev in particular, who have joined us in making these extraordinary data visible and accessible to the research community.

This book began, in many respects, with the formation of the EEOC research team at North Carolina State University. Some of the members were faculty, some worked in formal research assistant positions, and others volunteered. Regardless of their roles, they worked diligently to understand the strengths, weaknesses, and limitations of these data. Their contributions have been pivotal in developing the ideas put forth in this book. Foremost in this work was Corre Robinson, who was joined in weekly problem-solving and agenda-setting meetings by Cathy Zimmer, Tricia McTague, Tiffany Taylor, and Matthew "Zip" Irvin. At the University of Massachusetts Amherst, the project received important support from Karen Mason and Melissa Fugiero and extraordinary statistical support from Ken-Hou Lin.

The National Science Foundation has provided generous funding to this project over the years (SES-0216424 and SES-648491). The Russell Sage Foundation graciously provided financial support for Kevin Stainback's postdoctoral position at the University of Massachusetts Amherst, allowing us to begin this book. Purdue University also provided him with various forms of support during the writing of this book.

SULCIS and SOFI at Stockholm University provided Donald Tomaskovic-Devey with a supportive environment as the book neared completion, and the Rockefeller Foundation's Bellagio Center provided a most pleasant and supportive venue for the writing of chapter 8 and the editing of earlier chapters.

Over the years scholars have graciously shared their data with us. These data sources have been incorporated into this book in numerous ways. These scholars include Frank Dobbin, Paula England, Craig Jacobs, Jerry Jacobs, Debra Minkoff, Sarah Soule, and Sarah Wakefield.

Various aspects of this research project have been presented at professional conferences and seminars too numerous to count. We would like to thank in particular the seminar attendees at Yale University, Lund University, Duke University, Boston University, and University at Albany for listening and commenting on the work. Individuals who have been formative in diverse ways for the project include Richard Alba, David Brady, Michelle Barr, Michelle Budig, Philip Cohen, Donald P. Devey, Paula England, Elizabeth Hirsh, Randy Hodson, Matt Huffman, Jerry Jacobs, Alexandra Kalev, Robert Kaufman, Julie Kmec, Tricia McTague, Joya Misra, Corre Robinson, Vincent Roscigno, Sheryl Skaggs, Lewis Steel, Tiffany Taylor, Barbara Tomaskovic-Devey, George Wilson, and Cathy Zimmer. Frank Dobbin, Anna Branch, Ken-Hou Lin, and Mary Graham read and commented on the entire manuscript. We thank everyone for their contributions to this book. We also thank each other. This book is the culmination of several years of collaborative research, and we share equally in its production. Our contributions are equivalent, and our names are listed in alphabetical order.

Introduction

It shall be an unlawful employment practice for an employer—
(1) to fail or refuse to hire or to discharge any individual, or otherwise to discriminate against any individual with respect to his compensation, terms, conditions, or privileges of employment, because of such individual's race, color, religion, sex, or national origin; or
(2) to limit, segregate, or classify his employees or applicants for employment in any way which would deprive or tend to deprive any individual of employment opportunities or otherwise adversely affect his status as an employee, because of such individual's race, color, religion, sex, or national origin (Title VII of the Civil Rights Act of 1964).

IN 1964 THE U.S. Congress enacted, and President Lyndon Johnson signed, the Civil Rights Act. Although it was not the first or the last legislative moment of the civil rights movement, it was a pivotal one. The act outlawed segregation and discrimination by race, ethnicity, and religion in public education, public accommodations, voting, and federal assistance. Title VII of the act extended the equal opportunity principle to employment and for the first time explicitly mentioned "sex" as a protected category. It is this extension of rights to equal opportunity in employment, freedom from discrimination in employment, and the erosion of race and gender employment segregation as a legitimate and expected practice that is at the heart of this book.

The passage of the Civil Rights Act is without question one of the most monumental achievements in the history of the United States, perhaps even the world. The act made clear for the first time at a national level that the use of racial and gender status distinctions in employment was illegitimate and illegal. The passage of a law, however, does not automatically produce societal change. How did employers respond to this legal challenge? How much progress has the United States made as a nation since the Civil Rights Act of 1964? Which groups benefited, and who lagged behind? These are the questions we grapple with throughout the book. We answer them primarily with data on private-sector employment that were authorized by the Civil Rights Act to be collected by the then newly formed U.S. Equal Employment Opportunity Commission (EEOC). The data were to be used to monitor progress at both the workplace and societal levels. The EEOC has used these data as part of its enforcement activities, but no one has yet used them to systematically evaluate societal change. In this book, we utilize this remarkable historical record, analyzing the Employer Information Reports (EEO-1) that describe over 5 million workplaces from 1966 to 2005. We use our reading of the historical record and apply social science methods and theory to make sense of and organize our analyses of these remarkable workplace employment records.

Prior to this book, there have been almost no direct examinations of societal workplace desegregation since the Civil Rights Act. There is no shortage, however, of erroneous beliefs about what happened after the Civil Rights Act. One of the most common is that discrimination was eliminated or severely weakened by firms as they responded to the threat of discrimination lawsuits. We find this view naive in the extreme. Much research demonstrates that symbolic rather than real compliance was widespread and that contemporary discrimination lawsuits have very weak effects on firm behavior.

The extreme version of this belief is that equal opportunity policies somehow unfairly disadvantage white men, producing widespread reverse discrimination. In this somewhat amusing account, white men become the victims. Anecdotal evidence for this often comes in the form of stories about why a white man did not get a particular job but a racial minority or woman did. African American women have often been held up as particular beneficiaries of this reverse discrimination because they fulfill two "quotas" simultaneously. More objective evidence might be found in the decreased proportion of white men in the best jobs in the economy. In this book, we document that while white male advantages have been eroded, they remain the norm in nearly all workplaces. In stark contrast to the popular assumptions about black women's two-"quota" advantage in the labor market, our findings show that black women have benefited the least from equal opportunity policies. One remarkably stable finding in this book is that as firms hire a lower proportion of white men, white men are pushed up in organizational hierarchies. In other words, when racial minorities and women compete with white men for employment opportunities, white men's access to the best jobs increases. Ironically, perhaps as they become a smaller proportion of the labor force, white men are also more likely to work in integrated settings. Hence, even as white men's advantages grow, so too does the ability to tell a story about the racial minority or woman who got the good job.

Another widespread belief is that people are now less prejudiced, and so any remaining inequalities in racial or gender employment outcomes must represent racial or gender differences in the skills or preferences of individuals. The first problem with this story is that widespread cognitive and attitudinal bias associated with race and gender remains ubiquitous in the population. Another is that shifts in race and gender inequality in private-sector workplaces do not track closely the shifts in skills in the population. In fact, we find that white women, black men, and black women make the strongest progress into good-quality jobs in workplaces that screen for educational credentials. The more workplaces select on merit-linked criteria, the lower the racial and gender inequalities. The most fundamental problem with the individualist account is that organizational change is never simply a response to the individuals employed in a workplace. More than simply aggregations of people, organizations develop their own logics, routines, and goals. Moreover, they structure internal social relations and expectations in order to meet those goals and replicate those routines.

The view that individual-level discrimination by employers and their agents is the core problem and is widespread suffers from its own problems. The commonsense notion of discrimination as arising from individual prejudice and bias does not help us understand the movement away from institutionalized inequality and probably not much about contemporary workplace variation. Change in organizational behavior requires change in practices, not preferences. In addition, most consequential decisions in even moderately large organizations are made by a set of interconnected actors, including coworkers, supervisors, management at one or more levels, and often human resource personnel. Even if racial or gender bias is declining or becoming rare, group-level decision-making makes the probability of some type of individual prejudice or bias being present in the group skyrocket. Thus, the prevention of bias is not about changing social psychology but about changing organizational behavior and practice.

One of the fundamental contributions of this book is to show that equal opportunity gains are reversible—progress is neither inevitable nor continuous. For instance, we find that, after 1990, white men's advantage strengthened in quite a few industries and their employment segregation from white women, black men, and black women actually increased. Changes in law may be necessary, but they are simply not sufficient to motivate change in organizational behavior. High-wage industries are the most likely to show patterns of resegregation after the waning of the political pressure generated by the civil rights and women's movements. Women and minority progress into equal-status contact with white men and into the most desirable jobs is now most likely to occur in low-paying workplaces.

What we discover in this book is that desegregation trajectories away from the near-total white male privilege observed prior to the 1964 Civil Rights Act have been responsive primarily to pressures for change from the environment and from internal constituencies. When these pressures are absent, so is progress. We document the important environmental pressures that came from the civil rights movement and federal legislation in the 1960s and from the women's movement, judicial rulings, and federal regulation in the 1980s. After 1980, the pace of change slowed considerably as racial employment inequality faded from the political discourse and gender-based politics slowly withered.

The first half of this book centers on these national trajectories away from institutionalized white male privilege and is organized by the historical eras that motivated either change or stability in workplace practices. We identify the period between 1960 and 1972 as particularly important in producing employment advancement for African Americans, particularly for black men. The period from 1972 to 1980 produced widespread equal opportunity progress for white women, black men, and black women. The post-1980 period was characterized by very limited aggregated gains for black men and black women, while gains for white women continued through about 2000.

As white males' institutionalized privilege began to weaken, organizational variation in inequality regimes emerged. Prior research has tended to ignore this organizational variation, preferring to ask questions about societal progress toward or away from equal opportunity. This tendency reflects the preference of much of social science for examining individuals and nations, not the set of social relations in which people are embedded. But it is those social relations that guide behavior and generate opportunities. In 1964, ignoring organizational variation in the discrimination or inequality associated with race or gender made perfect sense. It was normatively sanctioned and behaviorally ubiquitous.

In contemporary U.S. labor markets, it makes much more sense to look for local inequality regimes. The second half of the book does just this. Workplaces vary in their labor market, legal, political, and normative environments, and these produce contemporary variability in racial and gender hierarchies at work. Workplaces also vary in their human resource practices. We find stronger equal opportunity trajectories in more formalized workplaces that utilize merit-based screening and hold managers accountable for racialized and gendered employment outcomes. Contemporary workplaces can be expected to vary tremendously in their degree of inequality and bias.

Workplace-level studies of desegregation since the Civil Rights Act are rare, and none are framed as an analysis of historical change. This is at first surprising, until we remember that, with the exception of the EEO-1 reports we analyze here, no systematic data on workplace segregation exist for the United States. The EEO-1 data have only recently become available to the research community, and this is the first book-length presentation of desegregation dynamics.

One of our central contributions is to reveal variation in the pace and direction of equal employment opportunity (EEO) change. Across this book, we contrast the desegregation trajectories of white men, white women, black men, and black women at different time points and in different spatial, industrial, and organizational contexts. As we do this, we discover that there were a multitude of desegregation and resegregation trajectories across time, geography, and organizational contexts, as well as for each demographic group. In effect, the question is not so much how well has the United States done, but which types of firms have responded to the moral and legal mandates of the Civil Rights Act and for whom?

EQUAL OPPORTUNITY NARRATIVES

Most social science proceeds analytically either through examining the statistical linkages among variables or by documenting how events and emergent processes transform specific cases. Both of these analytic approaches can be powerful in revealing the structure and process that produce social states. Social life tends to evolve as a sequence of events that are not preordained in their outcome or content. Andrew Abbott (1992) refers to these sequences as "narratives" to highlight that, once strung together as a sequence, events form a story of what happened and why. In other words, a narrative is a causal explanation of how and why some social condition was achieved. Analytically, we organize this book to produce such a narrative approach to the study of employment desegregation.

Given the multitude of actors moving through history, we should not expect them to produce a single desegregation story. On the other hand, we do expect that when a social process is institutionalized, through a deep cultural or organizational embedding of action, there will be a limited number of narratives both potential and actual. The more a status distinction such as race or gender is taken for granted—that is, is institutionalized—the fewer the stories. In this book, we observe the movement away from a single story of white male privilege and toward multiple historically, spatially, and organizationally contingent narratives. No longer exhibiting a national inequality regime, the United States has shifted to multiple local inequality regimes.

Before the Civil Rights Act of 1964, both racial and gender employment segregation and inequality were deeply institutionalized in U.S. workplaces. That is, all or almost all people in all or almost all workplaces, unions, corporate headquarters, and other organizations that had an impact on workplace behavior assumed that white males would hold authority over others and that women of all races and nonwhites of all genders would tend to hold lower-rewarded and subordinate positions. This is not to say that class distinctions among white men did not exist, but rather that there would nearly always be status differences between white men and all others in face-to-face interaction. It makes sense to look for and observe a single inequality narrative in 1964, at least in terms of white male advantage, because of the deep institutionalization of racial and gender hierarchies in U.S. society at that time.[1]

The Civil Rights Act concretized a set of bitter struggles against this deep-seated cultural constant. These struggles were born out of the civil rights movement for equal rights by and for African Americans but were extended to include formal equal rights based not only on race but also on gender, ethnicity, religion, and even national origin. In this way, the Civil Rights Act was an event that potentially destabilized the highly institutionalized and highly unequal status quo. Of course, the Civil Rights Act was one event in a sequence of events: the strategy of the Congress of Industrial Organizations (CIO) of organizing unions across racial lines in the 1930s; the civil rights movement of the 1950s and 1960s; the formation of the EEOC and the Office of Federal Contract Compliance (OFCC, later the Office of Federal Contract Compliance Programs, or OFCCP) in the mid-1960s; the emergence of a vibrant and aggressive women's movement in the early 1970s; the development of employment discrimination case law; and the institutionalization of equal opportunity and subsequently diversity in corporate human resource practices. Collectively, this sequence of events undermined the totalizing narrative of white men's employment dominance and opened the door for multiple new equal employment opportunity story lines to develop.

Across the twentieth century, presidential administrations, Congress, and the courts all displayed both support for and opposition to civil rights legislation and regulatory enforcement. African Americans' civil rights advancement received occasional support from the executive and judicial branches from the 1940s through the early 1960s, and then through legislative action in the 1960s and early 1970s. This support slowed dramatically in the decades that followed. For the women's movement, political influence was established in the late 1960s. Although most pronounced in the 1970s and 1980s, when the women's movement was most active and visible, public and political debate surrounding women and work continued into the 1990s. Moreover, specific issues kept women's rights dynamically evolving: pregnancy discrimination in the late 1970s and into the 1980s;

comparable worth policies in the 1980s; sexual harassment in the 1980s and 1990s; and "sex-neutral" family leave policies throughout the 1990s.

As the firmly institutionalized character of racial and gender inequality fragmented in the face of political, legal, and organizational challenges, the historical trajectory of equal and unequal employment opportunity became uncertain. That is, numerous possible stories were unleashed. At one extreme might have been a simple re-creation of white males' privileged position, as occurred in the 1890s when Jim Crow segregation reinstituted black subordination after a brief period of movement toward equal rights for African Americans following the Civil War. At the other extreme, the story might have been race and gender disappearing altogether as status distinctions, eclipsed perhaps by meritocratic distinctions based on individual workers' talents and abilities and the acquisition of education and job skills. Although such a story may seem far-fetched, it did in fact happen to both Jewish and Irish immigrants during the twentieth century—both immigrant groups were thought of as "not-white" when they were incorporated into U.S. society but have since become socially very much "white." By documenting the paths of employment desegregation and the emergence of a more equal, but yet still segregated and incomplete, set of employment practices, this book reveals which of the many potential narratives about the period since the passage of the Civil Rights Act came to fruition.

In the absence of an institutionalized status order, the array of potential trajectories of change after the Civil Rights Act could have been vast, and in this book we document multiple trajectories for different groups, labor markets, industries, and firms. But of course, the Civil Rights Act and other events associated with the goal of equal employment opportunity took place within still-institutionalized racial and gendered orders (Bonilla-Silva 1997; Martin 2004). Even as racial and gender hierarchies were challenged, weakened, or blurred, social actors continued to recognize these status distinctions as consequential, and organizations have preserved and sometimes extended preexisting racialized and gendered divisions of labor. The closer we are in time to the Civil Rights Act, of course, the more durable the initial condition of near-total status hierarchy across workplaces, labor markets, and firms. As we move forward in time we find more diversity, but we also still expect to find a limited number of narratives constrained and enabled by the emerging sequence of consequential actors, events, and social relations. Figure I.1 displays several hypothetical trajectories that might have taken place after the Civil Rights Act outlawed employment segregation and discrimination.

A period of sharp desegregation followed by resegregation is exactly what happened to African Americans between the end of the U.S. Civil

Figure I.1   Hypothetical Employment Segregation Trajectories

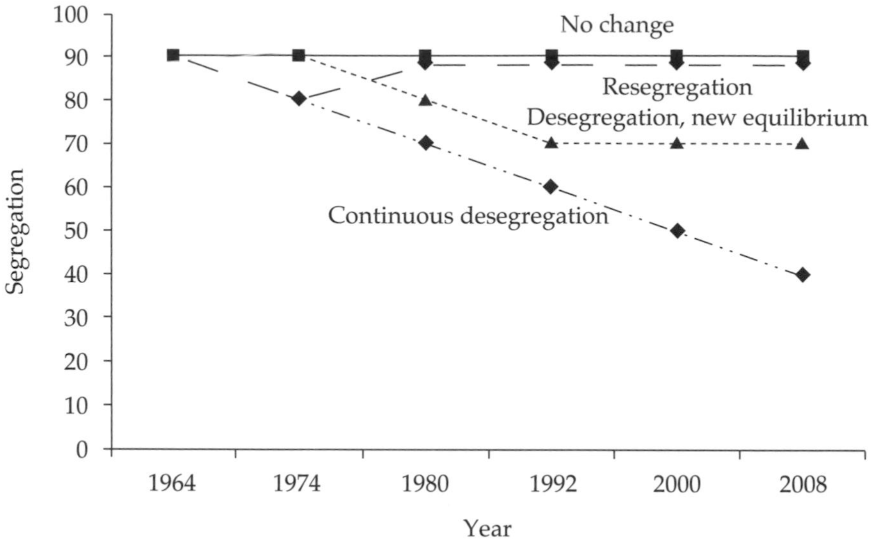

Source: Authors' compilation.

War in 1865 and the installation of Jim Crow segregation in the 1890s. The pattern of continuous desegregation happened to the Irish and Jews across the twentieth century. In this book, we observe all of the patterns (and more) suggested in figure I.1.

Key Actors and Mechanisms

Which events, actors, and social relations matter? If the potential set of stories is indefinite, perhaps the consequential events, actors, and social relations are as well. This is certainly true at the most abstract level, but concretely both history and social theory give us ample guidance as to where we might expect to find powerful social forces for both stability and change in employment-linked inequalities.

Some choices are simple. The central assumption of the book is that the primary actors in the process of employment desegregation are within workplaces. Without question, many other actors are likewise important in shaping the contours of the narrative we describe. Indeed, social movements, EEO advocates in political positions, political parties exploiting white racial fear, and the human resource profession all played prominent roles in the trends we document. Our primary focus throughout most of this book is on the response of organizations to these actors and to the pressures in their environments.

Employment desegregation is about employers changing the status composition of their employees in various jobs and occupations. The influential work of James Baron and William Bielby (1980) made this point directly: they argued that workplaces are central to both the allocation of social and economic resources and the preservation of group-linked stratification. We know from decades of research and theory that workplaces, like other organizations, tend not to change unless some set of pressures encourages change. We also know that organizational decision-makers hire, fire, pay, promote, supervise, and manage—that is, they create the distribution of people across jobs and the rewards associated with employment. Workplaces are the fields on which equal or unequal employment opportunity struggles are waged.

Organizational theory helps identify the conditions under which workplace inertia and change are likely to occur. The key insight is that organizations are purposively created to regulate and stabilize behavior. Organizations, by design, resist change. For organizational actors to change their employment practices, both motivation (spurred by either leadership or coercion) and an alternative model of behavior and practice are typically required. We highlight the *environmental uncertainty* associated with social movement and political pressure, the *institutionalization* of models of equal opportunity compliance and regulatory oversight, and *pressure from workplace constituencies* as catalysts for organizational stability and change in race and gender workplace inequality.

The Civil Rights Act altered the relationship between private-sector firms and the federal government. In so doing, the federal government changed how employers could use race and gender distinctions to match workers to jobs. Suddenly, racial minorities and women as both job applicants and employees could aspire to better jobs; workers and lawyers could mobilize the law to challenge employment discrimination; and the purview of personnel managers expanded from staffing and administering benefits to responsibility for equal employment opportunity.

After the Civil Rights Act, one might say that the game was no longer fixed to ensure white male dominance, but it would be naive to say that the rules were suddenly made fair. Rather, the rules were suddenly up for negotiation. Institutionalized racism and sexism were no longer simply assumed to be legitimate, but the practices that might lead to different distributions of opportunity were yet to be invented. Our historical and theoretical account is primarily about the resources that various actors have available to negotiate and challenge the assumption of white male employment prerogatives as well as the role of organizational inertia and resilient status hierarchies in preserving them.

From the abundant history of equal employment opportunity efforts we can, with fair precision, document the events and actors that drove changes in the rules of the game. We know that equal employment legislation preceded a series of historical events, mostly across the 1960s and 1970s. We also know that regulatory enforcement of these laws by the U.S. federal government emerged primarily in the 1970s and waned across the 1980s and that corporate human resource management (HRM) practices that reacted to these regulatory efforts defined the practical limits of legal and administrative regulation. We also know that effective pressure from the civil rights movement on both legislators and employers faded after 1980, while the women's movement continued to have an impact on legislation and human resource managers well into the 1990s. In 1964 it looked as if the civil rights movement had won equal employment opportunity only for black men; just a few decades later it would appear that its primary beneficiaries were white women.

THE PLAN OF THE BOOK

This book is organized into two parts. The first part examines the organizational change that results from historical shifts in the political and legal environments of workplaces. Our core argument is that the effectiveness of equal opportunity law, its interpretation, and its regulation are jointly contingent on the ebb and flow of political pressures for change and uncertainty as to what will eventually be endorsed as a legitimate, good-faith managerial response by regulators and the jurisprudence established by the courts. In the second part, we turn our attention to more proximate contexts affecting racial and gender workplace segregation. In particular we explore local labor markets, industries, and organizational dynamics.

The two parts of the book complement each other. Part I charts the shift from a monolithically race- and gender-segregated labor market to one with significant variability across labor markets, industries, and workplaces. This part focuses on macroprocesses of societal change. The second part of the book focuses on the emergent variation in racial and gender hierarchies across local labor markets, industries, and workplaces. These chapters uncover the contemporary mechanisms that encourage desegregation as well as those that obstruct progress.

Social movement and federal political pressure are shown to be important for generating EEO progress in the early period following the Civil Rights Act. Part I proceeds historically and shows that the pressure of national equal opportunity politics on private-sector racial progress had dissipated by 1980. Gender progress continued, but by the beginning of this century seemed to have reached a new status quo.

Part II focuses on contextual variation in equal opportunity trajectories, emphasizing that the important factors shaping equal opportunity narratives have shifted from national to more local contexts. This part pays particular attention to labor supply and competition in local labor markets, to industry as a normative field producing segregation and desegregation, and to the organizational processes that maintain and erode segregation.

Outline of the Chapters

In chapter 1, we outline our analytic tools. First and foremost, this chapter introduces an organizational approach to employment dynamics. We begin by discussing why workplaces tend to resist change and then highlight the crucial role of organizational environments in encouraging experimentation with new work arrangements, human resource practices, and leadership goals. External pressures stemming from social movements, politics, and fear of legal intervention and federal regulation produce not only laws, like the Civil Right Act, but also uncertainty as to reasonable human resource practices. We distinguish between the coercive pressures for equal opportunity associated with lawsuits and federal regulation and the institutionalization of new human resource practices tied to organizational fields. The potential importance of the responses of internal constituencies—including both white males' resistance to equal opportunity in their workplaces and other groups' pressure to expand opportunities—is discussed as well. This chapter outlines other potential influences on employment desegregation, such as competitive markets, and our analytic strategy for disentangling the various narrative streams we are trying to isolate.

Chapter 2 begins in 1941, the year President Franklin Roosevelt issued executive order 8802, which prohibited racial discrimination in the federal government and among federal contractors and created the Fair Employment Practices Commission. We outline the pre–Civil Rights Act history of federal and state antidiscrimination statues, a history primarily concerned with racial inequality and the international embarrassment of U.S. racial apartheid in the postcolonial cold war era. We begin our data analysis in this chapter with 1966, the year the Equal Employment Opportunity Commission began collecting data on the race-gender-occupational composition of private-sector workplaces. We document the near-total monopoly of white males in the most desirable jobs in the private sector at that time and the near-total segregation in roles between white men and others. We also document marginally lower racial inequality in states that had adopted their own fair employment practice laws prior to 1964.

In chapter 3, we outline the key historical events and actors of the early post–Civil Right Act period. The key lesson from this history is that the period from 1964 to around 1972 was characterized by a great deal of social movement and legislative pressure for equal opportunity, but almost no regulatory, legal, or even human resource capacity to monitor or coerce change. We refer to this as the "period of uncertainty" and go on to describe the national patterns of employment stability and change. We find that black men in particular made rapid gains during this period, especially in federal contractor firms. Women, both white and black, did not.

Chapter 4 continues the historical narrative, focusing on what we call the "short regulatory decade" from 1973 to 1980. This is an era of relatively strong federal regulatory oversight, increased legislative, judicial, and regulatory emphasis on women's employment rights, effective legal challenges to employer discrimination, and the institutionalization of equal opportunity human resource practices. The central findings for this period are that there were strong gains in access to professional and managerial jobs among white women as well as continued although weaker gains in those jobs among black men, who also saw gains in craft production jobs. We find that federal contractors, who were required to have affirmative action plans on file, became particularly good contexts for the employment gains of black men and white women. The extremely limited post–Civil Rights Act gains of black women in the large-firm private sector become evident during this period. In fact, we find that black and white women were already experiencing an increase in employment segregation by 1980 as white women made strong gains in managerial and professional roles once dominated by white men.

Chapter 5 takes up the story after Ronald Reagan was elected president of the United States and the federal commitment to equal employment opportunity was dramatically reduced. During this period, the women's and civil right movements diverge, and we see a marked decline in civil rights movement activity even as women's movement organizations continue to grow in both size and influence. We tie this to the Republican electoral strategy of using racial politics to lure voters away from the Democratic Party, while simultaneously trying to distance itself from civil rights claims and struggles. We see in the 1980s and 1990s continued legislative and legal gains by actors trying to expand women's rights in the workplace. During the same period, the human resource profession became a white women's profession and HR practices shifted away from race-based affirmative action to a focus on race-neutral celebrations of diversity. Black employment desegregation stalled, and white women's gains in the workplace continued on a positive, if not as rapid, trajectory. In the 1980s, being a government contractor—and thus required to have an affirmative action plan—benefited only white women in terms of further advances into good jobs and employment integration with white men.

Although this final section of the historical narrative spans the relatively long period from 1981 to 2005, there is very little variation in the pattern across presidential eras in this period: neither party aggressively supported the agenda of civil rights advocates, and both parties, in a passive play for white women's votes, quietly supported "family-friendly" workplace legislation. Rather, the period since 1981 can be characterized as "neoliberal" in the sense that the government no longer played a vigorous regulatory role in promoting equal opportunity in employment.

In the second part of the book, we turn to the local contexts that shape equal opportunity trajectories. Chapter 6 focuses on local labor market desegregation and the influence of changes in labor supply on segregation trajectories. We show that regional differences in segregation, especially racial segregation, eroded quickly following the passage of the 1964 Civil Rights Act and were replaced by local labor market processes of ethnic competition and queuing. We find that white men have benefited from both processes and that their access to good-quality jobs rises when other groups make up a larger proportion of the local labor market. We do not find distinct queues for good-quality jobs among white women, black men, and black women, nor among the growing Hispanic and Asian labor forces. We do find that the growth of both the Hispanic and the Asian labor forces is associated with increased black-white employment segregation.

Chapter 7 explores the effects of industrial shifts on desegregation trends, highlighting three core processes—industrial employment growth, social closure from desirable jobs, and meritocratic selection processes. We highlight which industries display patterns of continued desegregation, resegregation, and stabilization into a new segregation equilibrium. Since 1964, there have been large shifts in the composition of the economy. Growth itself does not produce desegregation or increased opportunity. The gains that did happen tended to be in industries with low wages, suggesting that white male defense of these jobs was correspondingly weaker. We also find that education-based screening encourages equal opportunity gains.

Chapter 8 explores the organizational dynamics associated with desegregation trajectories. We show through the literature and with our own analyses that shifts in race and gender segregation patterns are often not the result of direct regulatory or lawsuit pressure, but instead reflect the reaction of firms to the behavior of other firms in their immediate environment. Thus, lawsuits, EEOC fines, and OFCCP reporting all seem primarily to operate indirectly through their influence on normative expectations in organizational fields.

In this chapter, we also use the EEO-1 reports to highlight the influence of the race and gender composition of both the firm and the local labor force on internal organizational practices. We find that large, visible firms have more positive equal opportunity outcomes. However, we also reveal that while white males are still commonly found in managerial roles supervising all groups, white women increasingly occupy segregated managerial roles supervising other women. Black men typically manage black men, and black women typically manage black women. Both black men and black women are the least likely to be found in managerial roles supervising white men or white women. We also show that increased managerial diversity leads to female and minority employment gains. One of the most important findings in this chapter is that in the current period equal opportunity progress is unlikely in the absence of managerial accountability. In fact, in the absence of accountability, backlash and resegregation are common and a new, still-high inequality equilibrium becomes the norm.

Our efforts conclude in chapter 9. The United States is no longer on a path to equal employment opportunity. Even for white women, in the absence of new political and social pressure we predict that a new inequality equilibrium with white males will be—perhaps already has been—established. We explore a set of possible futures for U.S. equal employment opportunity efforts, focusing in particular on the role of the contemporary ethnic complexity associated with Hispanic and Asian immigration, human resource practices, regulatory opportunities, and political leadership. We emphasize the crucial role of political uncertainty and managerial accountability if there are to be future equal opportunity gains. In their absence, or in the absence of new social movement pressure, the future is most likely to hold a new inequality inertia or even resegregation.

PART I | National Equal
Opportunity Politics

Chapter 1 | Documenting Desegregation

TITLE VII OF the Civil Rights Act of 1964 was intended to reduce U.S. status-based employment discrimination. Its passage has been praised as one of the central moments in the extension of social, economic, and political rights to all adult citizens in the United States. Ironically, it also stands, historically, as one of the U.S. government's most controversial actions, because it was arguably the most extensive attempt to regulate the behavior of private-sector organizations. Nearly fifty years later, remarkably little is known about how that law and associated political, legal, and administrative shifts affected racial and gender inequality in U.S. workplaces. Although the law targeted the behavior of employers, its efficacy has been gauged almost entirely through the study of either individual wages and promotions or aggregate national trends in occupational segregation and access to desirable occupations. Although some contemporary scholarship has explored the effects of workplace context and variation in equal opportunity practices on racial and gender inequality, most of our knowledge of equal employment opportunity (EEO) change simply does not address the organizational responses to the fundamental legal, political, and social changes surrounding civil rights law and its regulation.

The central goal of this book is to describe the trajectories of U.S. private-sector employment opportunities for white men, black men, white women, and black women. In this chapter, we assemble our analytic tools, both theoretical and methodological, for accomplishing this task. First we explain why the simple enactment of equal employment opportunity law will not automatically produce EEO progress. There are compelling historical and scientific reasons that suggest that EEO progress requires much more than simple legal change. Analytically, we contrast the causal forces that encouraged stability in racial and gender stratification with those that encouraged equal opportunity. Because our field of observation is large and heterogeneous—large private-sector U.S. firms since 1966—we confront the analytic problem of combining historical analysis with large-

3

sample statistical demography. We proceed by first identifying the historical moments in which racialized and gendered assumptions and practices were challenged and then observing the linked change in the trajectories of organizational behavior. We use theory, previous research results, and some elegant statistical techniques to strategically narrow and expand our field of observation.

There is a tension in our work between a holistic model of social change and a theory-guided approach that highlights the most probable or important causes. Our work is holistic in that we incorporate insights about the continued importance of the past in the present, the need to see social change as partial and localized, and the insidious insertion of inequality practices, both new and old, into the psychology and social relations of everyday life. From this perspective, we approach our subject like students of history, assuming that the past is always present and the present is always at least potentially dynamic with the ability to move away from any particular past. We also describe as completely as possible the key moments and distributions in the march away from institutionalized employment segregation. On the other hand, we incorporate contemporary scientific understandings of cognitive psychology, organizational behavior, workplace relations, and political processes as the simplifying frames through which change and stability in racial and gender employment inequality are observed. It is this combination of history, demography, and causal analysis that is both empirically and theoretically powerful for simplifying such a large amount of data and so long a period of observation.

THE LIMITS OF LAW

Scholars have linked the development and passage of U.S. equal employment opportunity laws to the political mobilization of disadvantaged groups, changes in public opinion, and political party alignment. Another influential literature, largely historical in nature, seeks to isolate the pivotal historical actors who shaped not only the meaning of EEO and the larger cultural discourse of equality and inclusion but also the response of organizations to these legal shifts in the implementation of recruitment, evaluation, promotion, and termination policies. Surprisingly little research examines how well these public and private policy initiatives brought about the intended social change. We use these literatures and our own analyses of data collected by the Equal Employment Opportunity Commission (EEOC) since 1966 to examine a series of questions related to EEO progress in the post–Civil Rights Act era. How much change has taken place since the passage of the Civil Rights Act, and for whom? In which industrial, occupational, and spatial contexts have EEO gains been made, progress stymied, and losses endured? Under what conditions might we expect continued progress? These are the central questions explored in this book.

In general, scholars disagree about the importance of policy for improving social, political, and economic opportunities for African Americans and women. Some commentators conclude that the Civil Rights Act of 1964 was effective in desegregating the American workplace and promoting access to quality jobs for racial minorities and women. The underlying assumption of what we may call a "legal determinist perspective" is that once formal barriers are removed, progress is inevitable. This is not to say that many scholars were naive enough to think that the abolition of *unequal* opportunity laws and the passage of *equal* opportunity laws would be enough to redress long-standing categorical inequalities overnight, but much like scholars of the Enlightenment, they held the belief that although the historical residue of inequality might persist, it would decline and equal opportunity would continue to improve with time.

Others tend to have a view of sustained progress based on changes in beliefs and attitudes. They suggest that changes in racial and gender inequality at work are likely to track normative changes in support for racial minorities and women in the workforce. Paul Burstein (1998), for example, suggests that equal opportunity policies are implemented when the public supports the measures and that public support grew across the 1960s and 1970s. A stronger version of this "normative perspective" stresses an evolutionary process, suggesting that policy measures designed to bring about gender equality would provide no additional benefits because change would come about with or without legal change (Jackson 1998; Strauss 2001). These perspectives generally agree that equal opportunity progress primarily occurs through durable changes in public opinion. Hence, declines in white racism and sexism are the primary mechanisms promoting equal opportunity. These notions are consistent with the increasingly egalitarian movement of public attitudes since 1960. Stephen and Abigail Thernstrom (1997) go even further, suggesting that equal opportunity policies are counterproductive in that they may reduce white tolerance and lead to racial backlash.

Most perspectives on the driving force of equal opportunity employ a taken-for-granted assumption that once public opinion relaxed and legal equality in opportunity was granted under the Civil Rights Act, EEO progress would unfold—perhaps not immediately, but in an incremental, evolutionary, and reasonably predictable direction. Beginning from a legal or public opinion framework, this assumption might make sense, but from an organizational perspective it does not. We argue that it is at best a naive view to expect that after civil rights laws were enacted, organizational behavior would respond and equal employment opportunity would flourish. Others have noted the continued significance of race and gender in employment and suggest that these categorical distinctions are resilient, if not immutable. This approach is less naive, but also less likely to come to grips with the real changes that have transpired.

Our position is different. We believe that social, cultural, and political struggles over the enactment, enforcement, interpretation, and managerial commitment to EEO laws and mandates are ongoing, even as the social relationships that constitute organizational divisions of labor, chains of authority, and reward structures tend to reinforce and reproduce existing status distinctions. Indeed, both the stall—or even reversal—in black-white equality observed over the 1980s and the "end of the gender revolution" in the 1990s suggest that change is not linear and progress is not inevitable. It is precisely the outcomes of these social, cultural, and political battles that shape the contours of the equal opportunity narratives for white and black men and women that we describe in this book.

Comparing Race and Gender

In this book, we consistently compare the progress made by white women to the progress made by black men and black women relative to white men. The Civil Rights Act provided equal protection under the law to both blacks and women. In 1964 the nation had already experienced decades of struggle for African American equal opportunity and an even longer period of incorporation of new immigrant groups into the white mainstream. The more radical act was the extension of rights to women, which produced rather than followed a social movement for gender equality. In 1964 the political capacity of the women's movement was very low. On the other hand, women—or at least white women—had some strong advantages over racial and ethnic minorities. Importantly, they had the same social class distribution as white men, and thus, in the 1960s, educated and affluent women were available to lead the growing women's movement for equality. Moreover, because they lacked the class handicaps inherited by African Americans from the long period of U.S. racial apartheid, white women could quickly take full advantage of the new educational opportunities that became available. Thus, while in 1964 black men clearly held the political momentum, in retrospect it was white women who were better positioned to take advantage of the new environment created by the acrimonious struggle for civil rights. From the vantage point of the present, the reversal of fortunes is quite striking. In the next section, we discuss the organizational practices and processes that are likely to maintain status inequalities in the workplace and those that might be catalysts for change.

PRESSURES TO PRESERVE RACE AND GENDER STRATIFICATION

Prior to the civil rights movement, racial employment segregation was nearly absolute. It was legally required and vigorously enforced under Jim Crow laws in most southern states and normatively legitimate in most American workplaces regardless of region. More generally, the status subordination of all groups to white men was simply taken for granted. Although we do not have workplace-level estimates of black-white employment segregation prior to 1966, we can assume not only that it was uniformly high but that it also might already have seen some declines among federal contractors and in states that had adopted antidiscrimination laws prior to the passage of the Civil Rights Act (Stainback, Robinson, and Tomaskovic-Devey 2005). One fairly good estimate of workplace gender segregation in California for around 1970 (Bielby and Baron 1986) suggests that men and women almost never worked together in the same job in the same workplace. In the next chapter, we will produce our own estimates of workplace segregation in 1966, two years after the Civil Rights Act and the first year in which the Equal Employment Opportunity Commission began to collect workplace-level data. These estimates suggest that race and gender segregation were nearly universal and that white males' monopolization of the most desirable white- and blue-collar jobs was similarly widespread.

The United States entered the post–Civil Rights Act period with an employment structure that was for most actors entirely segregated by both race and gender. In the next chapter, we examine the initial movements away from total segregation. We believe that it is critically important to understand that the movement to incorporate black men, black women, and white women into new employment roles happened in organizational contexts in which all of the status expectations, divisions of labor, and interactional habits were predicated on either the total exclusion of these groups from employment or a system of strictly segregated roles. In 1966, 93 percent of managers in the regulated private sector were white males. Nearly everyone worked in race- and gender-segregated jobs.

Segregation is no longer monolithic. Today racial and gender inequality at work is generally understood to be the result of cognitive, interactional, and organizational processes, including employer and coworker prejudice, cognitive biases, statistical discrimination, social closure, and the personnel policies and practices governing the allocation of jobs to individuals, as well as the social and economic rewards attached to these positions (Stainback, Tomaskovic-Devey, and Skaggs 2010). These interactional and organizational mechanisms tend to be mutually reinforcing and lead to status expectations about both the appropriateness of different types of people for different jobs and the value of those jobs to the organization (Ridgeway 1997).

Today we see the impact of these microlevel mechanisms on the reproduction of workplace inequality. In 1964 the only mechanism that mattered was the near-total, societywide exclusion of racial minorities and women from desirable jobs. At that point in history, exclusion on the basis of race and gender was ideologically and legally legitimate. The human resource practices that have since been developed to short-circuit cognitive bias and control the pernicious effects of prejudice on employers' hiring, promotion, evaluation, and termination decisions did not yet exist. Thus, the microlevel mechanisms producing status inequalities that we now take for granted were invented or installed in the post–Civil Rights Act period as African Americans and women struggled to gain access to more desirable jobs and white men and old organizational habits resisted the erosion of their monopolies of privilege and power.

We mention these mechanisms here to make explicit that the relation between legal shifts in EEO law and the production of intended social change is not path-dependent; instead, there are considerable countervailing pressures in society and in workplaces that encourage continued and even expanded discrimination and bias. It is also the case that when segregation and white men's advantage were practically institutionalized prior to the Civil Rights Act, there was no need to evaluate the various mechanisms that produced discrimination against white women, black men, and black women. Rather, discrimination was so powerfully produced and enforced that variation in individual psychology or organizational power was largely irrelevant.

Formal Structure, Informal Culture, and Organizational Inertia

The "dead weight of history" is difficult to shrug off. Indeed, movements for social change, sometimes even in the face of striking political or legal success, are often confronted by frustrating resistance. After fifty years of continuous black African rule since gaining its independence from Great Britain, Zimbabwe finds itself repeatedly confronting the contradiction of having relatively rich white farmers who are both a source of national income and an irritating reminder of the limits of postcolonial black power.

In the United States, the continued primacy of white men in most positions of power and influence, fifty years after the civil rights and women's rights movements, is even more striking. In Zimbabwe, land confiscation and white emigration have undermined white economic power. In the United States, as we will see, increased opportunities for white women and to a lesser extent black men and black women generally did not come at the expense of white men. On the contrary, white men's collective access to positions of power in workplaces expanded.

The "dead weight of history" confronts organizations in the present not only through changes in law and regulatory enforcement but also through organizational histories and workplace cultures, past rules and practices, and the organization of work. All of these factors hold important implications for workplace stratification and equality.

Since Max Weber's early treatise on bureaucracy, sociologists have continued to observe that organizational routines, structures, and practices are stubbornly resistant to change once established. Organizational rules and procedures define jobs in terms of the tasks that need to be performed and specify the job responsibilities, the span of authority, and the resources and rewards attached to these positions. Organizations that are successful are able to reproduce behavior in positions regardless of the individuals who populate them.

In addition to the formal division of labor, less formal organizational cultures arise as an emergent process negotiated through social interactions and relational dynamics within workplaces. These dynamics are shaped by the broader set of societal-level cultural understandings that people bring to work. Informal culture scripts expected behaviors for people in different jobs, including expectations for competence, power, and status composition. At the level of jobs, social relationships and divisions of labor knit the basic architecture of production together and generate relatively stable organizations and status hierarchies. Because status and task structure tend to be reproduced from one day to the next, organizational stability is maintained even as individuals come and go.

The combination of the formal structure of positions and the informal culture of practice ensures that organizational behaviors are relatively static. Hence, organizational theory predicts that change is the exception rather than the rule (Stinchcombe 1965). Even when innovation is required—perhaps owing to new technologies, or legal uncertainty, or product market competition—the typical behavioral response of most organizations is to copy organizational practices from existing firms in the same organizational field (DiMaggio and Powell 1983). Prior research has shown that this is exactly what U.S. firms did. They copied older personnel practices to satisfy equal opportunity mandates (Edelman 1990). The implication of this line of reasoning is that eliminating discrimination or reaching EEO goals does not simply follow from legal change. This is not to say that organizations never change and that EEO progress is impossible. Rather, the point is that changes in employment practices are far from mechanical responses to law.

PRESSURES FOR EQUAL OPPORTUNITY

Equal employment opportunity law faces a powerful set of countervailing forces that both reinforces existing employment segregation and sets the stage for new rounds of discrimination and bias in employment decision-making. Given organizational tendencies toward inertia, EEO change is not likely to arise simply because of the enactment of law, but rather when there are significant uncertainties or coercive or normative pressures for change originating within workplaces or from their environments. Progress after the Civil Rights Act can be expected to have been most rapid when the regulatory future was unknown, costs to white men were small, the relative power of status groups was strong, and environmental pressures for change were strong.

Uncertainty

We suggest that *uncertainty* is one of the most powerful forces shaping equal opportunity trajectories. Uncertainty in the most basic sense is the lack of clear information about the future. It is a sense that current practices no longer fit the environment and might need to change. When organizational actors are unsure of what action to take or what the consequences of that action will be, we can say that a state of uncertainty exists. Moreover, while actors may be aware of alternative routines of action, and may even have the capacity to rehearse potential outcomes of these various lines of action in their minds, there are probably myriad alternatives that are not deployable owing to a lack of preexisting models and real or perceived opposition from powerful stakeholders. Because of the lack of prescribed routines of action, environmental uncertainty is likely to produce a variety of innovative responses. As behavioral models emerge, some come to be defined as solutions to the problem of reducing uncertainty, diffuse across organizational fields, and eventually tend to promote a new set of legitimate practices.

Organizational scholars often use the term "uncertainty" to refer to dynamic shifts in organizational expectations or resources, especially those circumstances in which there is no prescribed organizational response to external pressure (Meyer and Rowan 1977). The Civil Rights Act was clearly a source of uncertainty in the political environment of workplaces with regard to the development and implementation of equal opportunity policy. Organizational uncertainty also emerges from a variety of other sources, including social movement pressures (Collins 1997), the courts (Guthrie and Roth 1999), ambiguous laws (Edelman 1990, 1992), and lawsuits (Skaggs 2009). Although capturing all of these environmental pressures is beyond the scope of a single study, the historical record indicates that there are specific periods of social movement pressure and political support for EEO, and therefore variation in organizational uncertainty. Our core argument is that the efficaciousness of equal opportunity law, its interpretation, and its regulation are jointly contingent on the ebb and flow of political pressures for change and uncertainty as to what will eventually be endorsed as a legitimate, good-faith managerial response by regulators and the courts.

When there is greater uncertainty in dynamic environments, organizations are particularly likely to invent or seek new practices. The early years after the Civil Rights Act—when firms were unsure of the demands or sanctions they would face from the Equal Employment Opportunity Commission, the Office of Federal Contract Compliance, or other actors— qualifies as such a period. When organizations are uncertain about normatively appropriate behavior, the fear of public embarrassment and eventual regulation prompts experimentation with new personnel practices. As we discuss in the next chapter, Frank Dobbin (2009) has documented how a handful of corporations experimented with equal opportunity policies during the 1960s and early 1970s, eventually defining "best practices" before the federal government developed any regulatory capacity.

Chapters 2 through 5 document the rise and demise of EEO uncertainty in firms' political environments, showing that employment progress for African Americans and white women happens most quickly when uncertainty is high and stalls when the political environment becomes more certain.

Regulatory Coercion

Another source of organizational change is *coercion* by powerful actors in the environment. This may be because certain organizational forms or practices are viewed as legitimate and so become required by powerful actors, such as the EEOC. On the other hand, actors that are relatively powerful in their environments are better able to resist coercive pressures emanating from their regulators and may go so far as to co-opt the regulatory apparatus.

Organizations comply or resist based on their relative power in resource exchange relationships (Pfeffer and Salancik 1978). Organizational theory recognizes this process with the concept of "coercive isomorphism," in which a position of exchange or regulatory dependence leads to changes in routines to match the expectations of the more powerful actor (DiMaggio and Powell 1983). These power relations become particularly evident when interdependency is paired with uncertainty in the ability to predict the actions of the more powerful organization. To ensure its viability, the weaker organization strategically adapts to or even anticipates demands from the more powerful organization. Asymmetrical interdependence not only allows more powerful organizations to effectively influence weaker organizations within the resource exchange relationship but also allows powerful organizations to resist the influence of weaker organizations (Salancik 1979).

Past research has shown that after the Civil Rights Act job opportunities for minorities, and to a lesser extent for white women, improved in firms and industries that depended on government support and were subjected to the most extensive regulatory pressure (Baron, Mittman, and Newman 1991; Beller 1982; Leonard 1984a, 1989; Salancik 1979). John Sutton and his colleagues (1994) find that close proximity to the federal government increases the adoption of policies and practices associated with due process (such as grievance procedures). On the other hand, Frank Dobbin and his colleagues (1993) do not find that federal contractors are more likely to adopt internal labor market practices, which are often associated with EEO plans. We suspect that the inconsistent findings in this literature reflect real historical changes in federal regulatory activity. We explore this theme extensively in the following three chapters. We find that regulatory coercion of federal contractors had a brief life, ending in 1980 for African American men and by the 1990s for white women. Black women rarely benefited from OFCCP oversight.

Normative Isomorphism

Paul Burstein (1985) and others have suggested that general societal normative change has driven EEO progress (see also Jackson 1998; Thernstrom and Thernstrom 1997). This explanation is inconsistent with most organizational theory, which sees institutional norms as emanating from much more proximate organizational environments. "Mimetic isomorphism"—the copying of organizational practices—is typically conceptualized to happen within an organizational field (DiMaggio and Powell 1983). Normative pressures for change inhere in social relationships and the legitimate practices within an organizational field. Within organizational fields, generally conceived as industries, the adoption of organizational practices is not deemed obligatory as much as obvious and proper. For this reason, we expect that organizational change typically tracks change in organizational fields rather than societal norms. Practically, this suggests that when prominent firms in an industry begin to employ more African Americans or to move women into management roles, we should see the behavior generalizing across the industry. Some industries change on one dimension (race) but not another (gender), and some may never change at all. Some very recent research suggests that equal opportunity workplace change is more strongly tied to federal regulation or lawsuits in an industry than to the equal opportunity audits of federal contractors, EEOC discrimination charges, or lawsuits targeted at specific firms (Hirsh 2009; McTague, Stainback, and Tomaskovic-Devey 2009; Skaggs 2009). The interpretation is that coercive regulation or legal action changes behavior in an industry rather than in the target firm. Target firms are just as likely to show backlash behavior, punishing racial minorities or women who make discrimination charges. Thus, EEO gains happen through the diffusion of newer, less discriminatory practices through the industry.[1] We find strong evidence of industry-based diffusion of organizational practices. Unfortunately, these include contemporary patterns of resegregation in addition to responsiveness to pressures to create more equal opportunity workplaces.

Internal Constituencies

Change can also be driven by *internal workplace constituencies*, particularly the dominant coalition in the organization, but other groups may produce pressure for change as well (Edwards 1979). Status-based processes of exclusion and usurpation over scarce or valuable opportunities are central to the production of workplace inequality (Reskin 1988; Tomaskovic-Devey 1993). Although the specific mechanisms producing exclusion and inclusion vary as a function of human inventiveness and historical context, status groups dynamically attempt to preserve their advantages by limiting access to others outside of the status group (Tilly 1998). Excluded groups tend to devise means to usurp status monopolies, either by directly challenging advantages or by monopolizing alternative resources (Parkin 1979).

When the dominant coalition—typically comprising top management and professional staff—is committed to EEO goals, we would expect stronger pressures for EEO change. James Baron (1991) cites considerable anecdotal evidence that leadership commitment is required to advance EEO agendas. Likewise, Cynthia Cockburn (1991) finds that EEO initiatives are most likely to be successful when supported by top management.

As such, women and racialized minorities in leadership roles may be particularly important sources of change.

The literature has primarily focused on women in leadership roles. For example, Frank Dobbin, Soohan Koo, and Alexandra Kalev (2011) find that firms are more likely to adopt diversity policies when women are better represented among managers. Mia Hultin and Richard Szulkin (1999, 2003), in a study of Swedish workplaces, find that women's wages are higher in firms with more women managers. Other studies tend to find lower male-female wage inequality with increases in women in management (Cardoso and Winter-Ebmer 2010; Cohen and Huffman 2007a; but see Penner and Toro-Tulla 2010; Penner, Toro-Tulla, and Huffman 2010). Multiple studies find that gender segregation is lower in organizations with more women in managerial roles (Baron et al. 1991; Cohen, Broschak, and Haveman 1998; Huffman, Cohen, and Pearlman 2010; Stainback and Kwon 2012). Other studies find that the presence of women in higher-level leadership roles increases women's access to authority positions at lower levels of the organization (Cohen et al. 1998; Skaggs, Stainback, and Duncan 2012). We find evidence that the status composition of management influences desegregation trajectories in this study as well.

Equal opportunity goals may have more support when women or minority constituencies become large enough to press for access to better jobs within the organization. Rosabeth Moss Kanter (1977) argued that when a minority group rises to above 15 percent of employees, stereotyping is reduced because of the cognitive availability of individual-level variation among employees in the stereotyped group. Another model predicts that women and minorities are most likely to attain supervisory roles in workplaces where they are large proportions of the nonmanagerial workforce. Some authors have argued that this is a basic mechanism of political appeasement through which dominant status groups diffuse political pressure and maintain control of both the labor force and the most coveted jobs in the organization (Elliott and Smith 2001, 2004; Smith and Elliott 2002; Stainback and Tomaskovic-Devey 2009). The process of bottom-up ascription can be interpreted as a limited reaction to demands for inclusion by ethnic minorities and women. We find that when racial minorities or women gain access to supervisory or managerial positions, it is often in the segregated sphere of supervising others within the subordinate status group.

Human Resource EEO Practices

It is fairly clear that EEO law has encouraged the adoption of formalized human resource practices to demonstrate legal compliance. This has been primarily interpreted by social scientists as a legitimating device, a symbolic adoption to forestall regulatory or legal action. There is evidence, however, that race and gender segregation and inequality are lower in organizations with more formalized personnel practices. Formalization has been hypothesized to reduce inequality because it reduces the influence of the basic interactional mechanisms that produce status segregation and inequality (Szafran 1982; Bielby 2000). In other words, formalization tends to moderate particularistic behavior on the part of managers and hiring agents (Anderson and Tomaskovic-Devey 1995). For example, Barbara Reskin and Debra McBrier (2000) show that women's access to managerial jobs increases when firms use formal recruitment strategies. Formalization may encourage employers to search for candidates qualified for specific jobs rather than select candidates with whom they are simply socially comfortable or familiar. When the jobs themselves have clear skill requirements, we might expect to see more progress for minority workers. Professions have exactly this character. Because professions typically require specific educational credentials, they have strong formal criteria that trump race and gender in the selection of most applicants. Desirable jobs with more diffuse hiring criteria, such as managerial roles, are more likely to resist equal opportunity integration.

We find that white women's, black men's, and black women's access to professional jobs has grown much more rapidly than their access to managerial positions. In addition, we discover that in industries that screen employees based on ability, minority and female integration is much more rapid.

The literature on the formalization of human resource practices has pointed out that by the early 1980s the key set of practices that signaled regulatory compliance had diffused across most U.S. workplaces that were large enough to face regulatory threats. The influence of these practices on the managerial representation of minorities and women was not yet visible in 1966, but by 1980 it had become institutionalized. After 1980, blacks and women gained access to managerial jobs in larger, more formalized workplaces with internal managerial labor markets; typically, they supervised other racial minorities and women (Stainback and Tomaskovic-Devey 2009).

Another potentially important change in corporate human resource practice was the shift in the composition of human resource managers from white men to white women. In the 1960s, human resource managers (then called personnel managers) were overwhelmingly white men. Today the human resource managerial occupation is primarily a white woman's occupation. To the extent that pressure for inclusion is a political process within organizations, human resource managers are potential allies for minorities and women making claims for better jobs or pay. The fact that these professionals are increasingly white women suggests that they may be particularly important allies for white women. It is certainly the case that after 1980 it was primarily white women who made sustained progress in terms of desegregation and access to good jobs.

EEO progress is not likely to be a simple result of legal change. Rather, organizational theory leads us to expect that change will happen as experimental changes in human resource practices become legitimate and diffuse across organizations. This experimentation is likely to happen during periods of regulatory uncertainty, when legal sanctions and enforcement criteria are still in flux. Some of these new human resource practices will become legitimate and diffuse more rapidly because of coercive and mimetic pressures from a firm's environment. At the same time, resistance to equal opportunity progress should be expected. Resistance will be generated by not only the bias processes that operate at the individual and group level but also the basic tendency toward inertia in organizational practices.

THE CHANGING FACE OF DISCRIMINATION

After passage of the Civil Rights Act, both legal and interactional expectations shifted. The goal of both the intervention of the Civil Rights Act and all the subsequent regulatory, legal, and human resource practices was the eradication of discrimination. Although discrimination did not disappear, it became possible for actors, whether federal regulators, personnel managers, unions, or employees, to challenge practices that appeared to be discriminatory. To use Samuel Lucas's (2008) language, the era of "condoned exploitation" was replaced by one of "contested prejudice." One way of thinking about this transition is to note that discrimination and bias went from a near-constant across firms to a variable both across and within firms. Some workplaces changed their organizational routines around race and gender segregation faster than others. Some did not change at all. Some integrated working-class jobs but left managers untouched. Some new workplaces were founded in which interactional routines were less strongly tied to the pre–Civil Rights Act era divisions of labor and status expectations. Some firms, regions, and industries were subject to stronger regulatory or legal pressure to shift toward equal employment practices. Some workplaces began to hire women or minorities into lower-level jobs and then were faced with the demands of these new employees for increased access to higher-level jobs.

When the Civil Rights Act outlawed discrimination, it defined discrimination simply as differences in treatment and segregation in roles.

Because differences in treatment were nearly universal, as was employment segregation, the simple language fit the simple reality. As the assumption of discrimination withered, it was gradually replaced by an assumption of equal employment opportunity, and both the courts and the social sciences became concerned about defining when discrimination was present. At first, the courts saw inequality in outcomes as evidence of discrimination, and the burden of proof was put on employers to demonstrate that inequalities in their workplaces were not produced by discrimination. Later the burden of proof shifted to employees, who were required to show specific acts or practices that were discriminatory in intent. Essentially the judicial presumption switched from a presumption of discrimination in the presence of inequality to a presumption of nondiscrimination despite inequality of outcomes (Nelson, Berry, and Nielsen 2008).

The social sciences have been much better at identifying meritocratic practices than discriminatory ones. Discrimination is often inferred from the residual inequalities after statistically accounting for individual traits that are taken as legitimate bases for allocating opportunity. These typically include education and both general labor market and firm-specific experiences, but can also include on-the-job training, personality, intelligence, and even the stable aspects of individuals' careers that are unobserved but treated as "personality" rather than discrimination.

In economics, this approach was based on human capital theory, which harbored strong assumptions that hiring, pay, and promotions should follow individual productivity and that in the long run competitive markets made discrimination on the basis of race or gender expensive (Becker 1957/1971). In sociology, the empirical approach was similar, but the expectation was that legitimate merit-based criteria were strengthening over time as a function of the diffusion of legal rational expectations for organizational behavior (Davis and Moore 1945). Although sociologists were somewhat skeptical of market-only explanations, they tended to agree with economists that discrimination was observable as the race or gender wage (or hiring or promotion) gap after relevant controls for merit- or productivity-based criteria (Tomaskovic-Devey et al. 2005).

Even as the courts became more restrictive in accepting evidence of discrimination, sociology and economics increasingly relied on restrictive statistical methodologies that conceptualized discrimination as the outcome of individual acts of discrimination. Thus, discrimination was defined as the residual wage gap in a sample of individuals after statistical controls for observable merit-related traits (such as education, job tenure, and work experience), unobservable differences in productivity and personality (presumably captured in stable individual average wages), and sometimes even the industry, occupation, and firm in which people were employed. The possibility that discrimination occurs earlier in the career in terms of access to employment, skills, and training or through differential sorting across industries, occupations, and firms was downplayed, if not ignored, in the quest for increasingly conservative statistical models. Similarly, the possibility that large inequalities are produced by the accumulation of relatively small acts of bias in decision-making was typically ignored.

Oddly, neither sociologists nor economists have spent much effort in the intervening years trying to conceptualize when and how discrimination varies across workplaces. This made perfect sense in 1964, when discrimination was a constant, but has increasingly missed the point. As racial- and gender-based discrimination became contested rather than condoned, we should expect that variation in discrimination across workplaces would increasingly be the thing to be explained. The question is not, is there discrimination? Rather, the question has become, *where* is there discrimination? Or perhaps more interestingly, where is there *no* discrimination?

Conventional social science models have not been very good at identifying where we can expect higher or lower levels of discrimination. To accomplish this we need to conceptualize discrimination as something that is expected to vary across workplaces. In this book, we do this primarily by focusing on the environmental pressures on firms to practice equal opportunity policies as well as on the internal pressures to preserve or erode race- or gender-linked biases in employment practices.

Some economists have proposed that the profit motive should undermine discrimination because it artificially inflates the cost of white male labor. Prior research suggests, however, that minorities and women have made the most progress in workplaces that lacked a profit motive (Tomaskovic-Devey 1993). On the other hand, some recent research suggests that firms that face product market competition may reduce status-linked inequalities within their workplaces. For example, Dustin Avent-Holt and Donald Tomaskovic-Devey (2010) find that organizations embedded in more competitive environments are more likely to stress education than gender in allocating wages. Other studies show that gender segregation is lower in workplaces in more competitive markets (McTague et al. 2009; Stainback and Kwon 2012). We suspect that to the extent that market pressures undermine status distinctions, it is a weak causal agent. Political pressures either from the organizational environment or from internal constituencies within the firm are simply stronger causal agents.

Next, we review three plausible explanations of the conditions under which discrimination may vary across workplaces: statistical discrimination, social closure, and cognitive biases. Although we cannot observe these processes directly in our data, we see the theories of statistical discrimination from economics and social closure from sociology as producing useful theoretical expectations as to where desegregation trajectories will be steep or absent. Psychological biases, on the other hand, are so widespread that we doubt that they can add much to an explanation of organizational variation in discrimination or desegregation.

Employers and Statistical Discrimination

The theory of statistical discrimination explains why employers in particular might *consciously* exclude minority or female job candidates or demand higher credentials before hiring them. Statistical discrimination refers to employers using expected differences in competencies between groups to discriminate against all members of the less-favored group (Tomaskovic-Devey and Skaggs 1999a). When statistical discrimination is occurring, the employer relies on stereotypes about status group productivity or reliability to justify making discriminatory hiring decisions against all individuals from that group. Although in some accounts this behavior is described as economically rational, it is clearly discrimination under the law, since individuals are denied employment because of their race or gender. We have no idea how prevalent this type of direct, self-conscious discrimination by employers is, but there is ample evidence from studies of employer hiring decisions that it is widespread (Browne and Kennelly 1999; Kirschenman and Neckerman 1991; Holzer 1996; Moss and Tilly 1996; Pager 2003; Correll, Benard, and Paik 2007). There is also substantial quantitative and qualitative evidence from contemporary validated discrimination claims of active self-conscious bias in workplace hiring, firing, promotion, and harassment (Roscigno 2007).

The statistical discrimination account links stereotypical reasoning to employers' motive to discriminate. Employers are predicted to discriminate when the economic costs of a hiring error are potentially high. Thus, statistical discrimination should be expected to produce variation both within and across firms in the level of discrimination. When training time is long or responsibility for the resources of the firm is high, employers have increased economic motives to discriminate. Employers with no active prejudice or taste for discrimination might still discriminate, simply because they are trying to avoid costly employment errors. Thus, the theory of statistical discrimination points to jobs with a long period of employer-borne training and the potential to make costly mistakes as the most likely reasons for discrimination against minority or female job applicants. We find that in both management and craft production jobs, both of which have long periods of on-the-job training, white men are most consistently advantaged.

Social Closure and Opportunity Hoarding

Social closure theory suggests that when people share a salient group identity, they tend to use those identities to hoard opportunities and rewards. Shared ethnicity, nationality, race, and gender can be the basis for pride and a sense of mutual obligation, justifying discrimination in favor of people with similar traits and the exclusion of others from those opportunities (Parkin 1979; Tilly 1998). Status identities enable groups to organize to both make resource claims and create the political will to struggle against other groups that do not share the same identity (Murphy 1988; Schwalbe et al. 2000).

Collective struggles and routine interaction draw on these identities to legitimate both the exploitation of out-groups and opportunity hoarding for socially similar others (Ridgeway 1997). Social closure is often linked within divisions of labor to economic exploitation. In other words, when groups dominate ownership, managerial, or skilled positions, they can use those positions to extract a larger share of the economic resources produced by their firm. Relatively weak, subordinate groups of workers tend to receive lower wages. There is documentation that when jobs or occupations are dominated by racial minorities or women, wages are depressed (see, for example, Carrington and Troske 1995, 1998; Cohen and Huffman 2003; Huffman and Cohen 2004; Kmec 2001; Stainback and Tang 2012; Tomaskovic-Devey 1993).

When social closure processes are in play, a white manager who hires his friend's or current employee's white son rather than a racial minority applicant may not be discriminating against the minority candidate so much as discriminating in favor of the son of someone he already knows. He may also know that if he had hired the minority candidate he would have had to justify to his friend or employee why the son was not hired. Discrimination based on social closure not only is concerned with protecting opportunities for the dominant group but also acts to preserve the status distinctions between in-group and out-group. The key shift in the post–Civil Rights Act era has been that social closure is now contested because it is no longer socially legitimate.

Like statistical discrimination theory, the social closure model predicts organizational variation in the degree of discrimination and thus in desegregation trajectories. Because social closure is about the exclusion of out-groups from desirable opportunities, a social closure approach to discrimination predicts that social boundaries and segregation will be less strongly defended when rewards are low. Thus, we would expect that low-pay jobs will integrate earlier and more completely. Desirable jobs will integrate more slowly, if at all. White men may attempt to maintain their access to good jobs, even as they lose the ability to control all jobs. The same is true for workplaces: high-wage, high-opportunity workplaces will integrate more slowly than low-wage workplaces because these are the most lucrative positions to monopolize. Consistently, we find strong evidence that when women or minorities gain access to managerial jobs, they typically do so in low-wage industries and supervise other minorities or women. We also find that segregation remains highest in high-wage industries.

Although we focus in this book on EEO narratives and trends, mention should be made of two other major trends that were occurring simultaneously and had strong implications for social closure pressures. First, the rapid postwar expansion of incomes and manufacturing employment came to an end in the mid-1970s and was followed by lower rates of economic growth and increased employment insecurity. Second, after the late 1970s income inequality rose rapidly in the United States and wages for most of the population stagnated. Both trends no doubt increased the pressures for social closure as economic opportunities for everyone, even white men, became constrained and employment risk was heightened. Thus, the 1960s and early 1970s were periods when equal opportunity for racial minorities and women may have been perceived as less threatening; later, as opportunities to find good jobs became increasingly scarce, pressures to secure and defend white male employment prerogatives may well have expanded. Although we will never know, we can speculate that African Americans' stalled progress after 1980 might not have occurred if white men were not faced with declining opportunities in the overall economy.

Stereotypical Beliefs and Psychological Biases

It is clear that many employment decisions are influenced by social psychological processes of cognitive bias, stereotyping, and in-group preferences tied to race and gender (for reviews, see DiTomaso, Post, and Parks-Yancy 2007; Stainback et al. 2010). The psychological tendencies to accept stereotypes, make errors in employee evaluations, and prefer people like ourselves all encourage employers and managers, as well as employees, to resist efforts to promote equal employment opportunity and to accept the inequalities they encounter as the legitimate result of individual or group differences in capabilities.

Although there is clear evidence of secular decline in classic racial and

Figure 1.1   Whites Who Agree with the Statement "Negroes/Blacks/
African Americans Have Less Inborn Ability,"
1977 to 2006

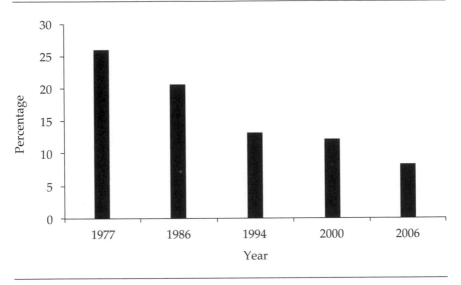

Source: Authors' calculations based on the General Social Survey (Smith, Marsden, and Hout 2011).

gender bigotry in the United States since the civil rights era (Schuman et al. 1997), it is also clear that cultural prejudice and the more subtle processes of cognitive bias against minority group members and in favor of whites remain prevalent and influential (Nosek et al. 2007). Figure 1.1 displays this decline in classical white prejudice, but also makes clear that 8 percent of the white population still expresses explicit, old-fashioned racist thinking. It is clear that these beliefs, though far from extinguished, have declined, but it is also likely that there is considerable underreporting of what are now socially unacceptable beliefs. Because most employment decisions, especially in large firms, are made collectively by a number of coworkers and managers, it is reasonable to expect that at least one individual in these groups will often be an old-fashioned bigot (for the mathematical proof of this conclusion, see Lucas 2008).

But traditional racist and sexist beliefs do not pose the only problem of employment integration. Social closure processes do not require meritocratic explanations for people to prefer to work with other people like themselves. In-group preferences and the defense of privilege can be based on any number of explanations and emotional reactions (see Roscigno

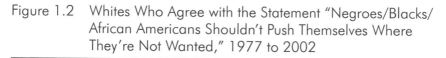

Figure 1.2   Whites Who Agree with the Statement "Negroes/Blacks/African Americans Shouldn't Push Themselves Where They're Not Wanted," 1977 to 2002

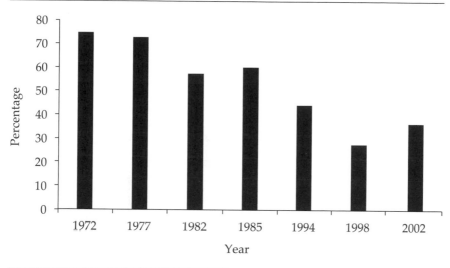

Year

Source: Authors' calculations based on data from the General Social Survey (Smith, Marsden, and Hout 2011).

2007; Stainback 2008). Figure 1.2 makes clear that while dropping over the years, almost 40 percent of whites are still willing to tell interviewers that they are uncomfortable with integration. One imagines that in the real world that more than half of whites remain self-consciously uncomfortable with racial integration.

The scientific literature on stereotypes and bias is clear that the levels of implicit, cognitively automatic bias in the population are typically higher than the levels of self-consciously endorsed stereotypes. About three-quarters of the white population have prowhite, antiblack biases. A similar proportion, of both men and women, associate paid work in the labor market with men's work and unpaid domestic responsibilities with women's work (Nosek et al. 2007). Although explicit prejudice is correlated with implicit bias, they are not the same thing (Cunningham, Nezlek, and Banaji 2004). A person can be self-consciously bigoted and not have automatic cognitive biases. Many people who have implicit biases in terms of race and gender are not actively prejudiced. Nancy DiTomaso and her colleagues (2007) suggest that most bias in employment situations is generated by a normative preference, shared across many subpopulations, for whites and men rather than by bias against any particular out-group.

Figure 1.3   Respondents Who Agree at Least Slightly That It Is Better
for Men to Work and Women to Tend the Home,
1977 to 2006

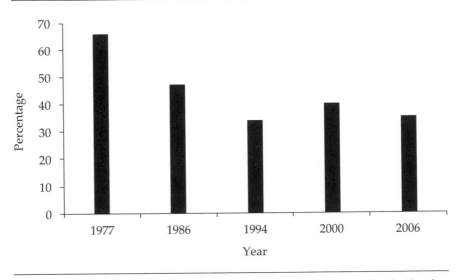

Source: Authors' calculations based on data from the General Social Survey (Smith, Marsden, and Hout 2011).

Given that cognitive biases are much more prevalent than active prejudice, most people do not perceive themselves as acting in a discriminatory
fashion, even if they are consistently giving the benefit of the doubt to
white or male job applicants and coworkers.

Gender stereotypes remain widespread. The notion that motherhood
should take priority over employment for women is even more widespread than white resistance to integration. Figure 1.3 displays these
trends and also shows a secular decline in gender essentialism into this
century, though levels remain fairly high. Importantly, although both explicit and implicit gender bias is widespread, there are only small gender
differences in these biases (Nosek et al. 2007). Both men and women tend
to think men are more competent.

Stereotypes are not limited to people—they can extend to work as well.
Occupations or jobs that become associated with a particular race or
gender lead decision-makers and applicants to expect race- or gender-
appropriate job matches (Gorman 2005; Ridgeway 1997). In this most
basic way, race and gender employment segregation is self-reinforcing. It
takes some cognitive effort to break out of stereotypes about appropriate

job candidates. One finding in the literature is that gender bias in wage-setting is higher when decisions are not monitored by some meritocratic human resource practice (Anderson and Tomaskovic-Devey 1995; Castilla 2008; Elvira and Graham 2002; Hultin and Szulkin 1999). To make matters worse, when candidates are judged competitively for hiring or promotion, even very small racial or gender bias in evaluations can lead to large cumulative differences in selection (Martell, Lane, and Emrich 1996). The same must be true for job titles, as small biases in pay or respect accumulate over many years to create larger differences in the pay and opportunities associated with race- or gender-typed jobs (Tilly 1998).

Because psychological biases remain widespread, they provide a weak explanation for variability in discrimination across contemporary workplaces. If discrimination is an act contaminated by some sort of bias and the bias is widespread in the population, then the probability of encountering powerful actors who harbor some level of prejudice, stereotyping, cognitive bias, or even simple in-group preference is very high, probably close to unity. In any reasonably complex division of labor in which job applicants and employees interact with multiple decision-makers, the probability of encountering biased individuals in decision-making roles is very high (Lucas 2008; Tomaskovic-Devey 1993). As such, we see the psychological tendencies to devalue racial minorities or women or to extend preferential evaluations and treatment to white men as stronger explanations for inertia in organizational practices, but less likely to produce variation in equal opportunity and segregation across contemporary workplaces.

In any particular workplace, or for any particular employment decision, cognitive bias in the evaluation of job candidates and in-group preferences among decision-makers is likely to be present. This does not, of course, mean that cognitive bias is the only influence on decision-making. In most consequential employment decisions, criteria such as education, past experience, and personality are likely to loom large in the evaluation of job candidates. But even small levels of bias in the evaluation of employees can lead to large differences in outcomes (Martell et al. 1996). Although it is possible that over time there has been some decline in the level of out-group bias in the population, it seems unlikely that in-group preferences have declined similarly. It is also the case that even a small proportion of prejudiced individuals in the population generates a high rate of exposure for individual employment decisions (Lucas 2008). Research suggests that what is decisive in explaining workplace variation in equal opportunity is not variation in psychological states, but variation in the management practices that control bias. Much of chapter 8 is devoted to this topic.

Evidence of Contemporary Discrimination

We know that the experience of discrimination remains widespread. In one survey of three U.S. cities conducted in the early 1990s, 20 percent of African Americans and 10 percent of both Hispanics and Asians reported an experience of racial discrimination in the last year in their current job (Hirsh and Lyons 2010). A 2002 nationally representative survey of U.S. workers provides similar estimates of workplace racial discrimination experiences for African Americans (17 percent) and Hispanics (13 percent) (Stainback and Irvin 2012). In the same 2002 survey, approximately 11 percent of women reported experiencing gender discrimination in their current job (Stainback, Ratliff, and Roscigno 2011).

A study conducted by Ronald Kessler, K. D. Mickelson, and David Williams (1999) examines lifetime reports of discrimination. They find that more than one-quarter of African Americans reported one or more lifetime experiences of not getting a job and not receiving a promotion because of discrimination. Further, 10 percent reported being fired. Among women, most of whom were white, the proportions were much smaller and not significantly different from men. In the same study, 70 percent of African Americans reported sometimes or often experiencing discrimination in their daily life. Again, for women the numbers were much smaller and not gender-differentiated. Among women, half of those who had experienced any discrimination in their life described the source as linked to their gender. Among African Americans, race was the perceived source of discrimination 90 percent of the time (Kessler et al. 1999).

Laura Neilsen and Robert Nelson (2005) estimate that less than 1 percent of the time do employees who believe that they have experienced discrimination actually file a discrimination complaint with the EEOC. Thus, discrimination is much more socially widespread than it is formally litigated.

Perceptions of discrimination, of course, do not match the legal or social scientific definitions, but are reactions to actual encounters, reflecting an individual's legal consciousness as well as the sense of personal efficacy required to find fault with his or her employer or coworkers. Thus, people with more knowledge of the law and a stronger sense of entitlement are more likely to interpret behaviors or comments as discrimination (Hirsh and Kmec 2009; Neilsen and Nelson 2005; Stainback and Irvin 2012; Stainback et al. 2011). Moreover, much discrimination is not visible to the victim or the perpetrator and goes unrecognized by all parties. In fact, working in organizations with formalized screening practices tends to reduce perceptions of discrimination (Hirsh and Lyons 2010), even though there is evidence that such policies may actually increase biases in favor of white men (Dobbin, Schrage, and Kalev 2010).

The best set of studies we have on the actual practice of discrimination comes from Vincent Roscigno and his colleagues (Roscigno 2007; Roscigno, Garcia, and Bobbitt-Zeher 2007). They analyzed both statistically and through qualitative accounts over 60,000 discrimination complaints received by the Ohio Civil Rights Commission. Focusing on the legally verified cases, they find that discrimination is typically produced through a relational process in which social closure and psychological bias processes are the central causal mechanisms. The distribution of verified primary charges was similar for race- and gender-based claims. Firing was most common, followed by harassment. Promotion and hiring discrimination was less common. Firing, hiring, and promotion are central mechanisms of social closure. However, it is important to note that harassment is widespread, and while it takes different forms by race and gender, it always serves to establish a status hierarchy in the workplace (Roscigno et al. 2007). Thus, social closure has both a material component (the focus in this book on segregation and integration) and an interactional component—the hierarchy of worth tied to race and gender that influences everyday interaction.

Of course, these discrimination charges happened because plaintiffs were willing to file a claim and make their way through the legal process. Most hiring and promotion discrimination is typically not visible to the person who has been passed over because the decision is made elsewhere.

Roscigno and his colleagues (2007) find that the actual content of discrimination claims is different for black men, black women, and white women. White women are often the victims of sexual harassment and are fired for pregnancy or motherhood or when employed in typically male jobs or workplaces. Thus, the gender typicality of employment and the interactional accomplishment of gender are central to reconstructing gender at work and generating gender discrimination (Ortiz and Roscigno 2009; Padavic 1991; Stainback et al. 2011).

Black men are often the victims of racial stereotyping, managerial discretion in the interpretation of skills (Moss and Tilly 1996), and the selective enforcement of bureaucratic rules that hold black men to higher performance standards and subject them to harsher policing of rule violations. They are also subject to substantial harassment, much of which is explicitly racialized (Mong and Roscigno 2010). Black men employed in mostly white workplaces also report isolation as a form of social closure from networks, training, and the like (Light, Roscigno, and Kalev 2011).

Although black women conceivably could claim either race or gender as the basis for their discrimination charges, about three-quarters of their primary charges allege racial discrimination. Black women are more likely than white women to be discriminated against in terms of hiring, firing, and general harassment. Compared to white women, black women are much less likely to experience discrimination based on pregnancy. Like black men, black women are subject to higher rates of differential treatment and disparate policing of behavior. Importantly, black women often report being discriminated against or harassed by white female supervisors or coworkers. Throughout this book, we find that progress has been slowest and most easily reversed for black women. At the interactional level, they are the most disadvantaged because they are at risk of social closure and stereotyping not only from white men but also from black men and white women. White women, of course, are far more numerous than black men in the work lives of black women, as both coworkers and managers.

As a matter of law, the Civil Rights Act was unlikely to create equal opportunity in U.S. workplaces. Rather, psychological biases and stereotypes about the proper race or gender of job incumbents as well as past recruitment and promotion practices were all likely to reproduce prior workplace hiring patterns. In addition, pressures for social closure by the already advantaged and statistical discrimination by employers have tended to preserve and even enhance white and male privileges in employment. On the other hand, uncertainty generated by political pressures, formalization and accountability in employment practices, and pressure for equal opportunity from racial minorities and women inside the firm may all have encouraged employment integration and equal opportunity progress.

DOCUMENTING DESEGREGATION

The data on which we have built this book are derived from workplace surveys that were authorized to be collected from private-sector employers by the Civil Rights Act of 1964. Title VII created the EEOC and granted it limited powers of investigation and enforcement of the employment provisions of the Civil Rights Act. The act also required employers to submit annual reports to the EEOC on their employment distributions. Since 1966, the EEOC has been collecting data from U.S. employers on occupation by race-ethnic and gender employment. These data are to be used to monitor progress both at the workplace and societal levels.

Measuring EEO Trends

Our core goal in what follows is to document trends in access to private-sector employment since the 1964 Civil Rights Act, contrasting trajectories in different political periods, labor markets, industries, and organizations for white men, black men, white women, and black women. Progress has been far from uniform for different race-gender groups. Nor have patterns been consistent across time, local labor markets, industries, or workplaces.

The Civil Rights Act specifically prohibited employment segregation. The end of slavery led to a short period of legal equality between whites and blacks, which ended with the implementation of Jim Crow laws in the South and segregated employment and housing practices across the country. Segregation was one of the central tactics used by whites to reinstitute their social, economic, and political advantages over African Americans across the twentieth century. Until the 1970s, race and gender segregation in employment was both normative and nearly absolute. There has been a great deal of research on housing segregation trends in the United States, but almost no research on workplace-level segregation trends. Equal opportunity in workplaces requires employers to not simply hire minority or female employees but to hire them in the same jobs that go to similarly skilled whites and males, and on the same terms.

Gender   The EEOC asks employers to identify the "sex" of employees as either male or female. The EEOC continues to use the term "sex" to not only count people in the EEO-1 form but also to describe segregation and discrimination processes. The social science literature and some government agencies (such as the Office of Federal Contract Compliance Programs and the General Accounting Office) have moved toward referring to processes that create male and female difference in terms of "gender" rather than "sex." The word "sex" is increasingly confined to biological persons. In common language, "sex" and "gender" tend to be used interchangeably. Social scientists have come to realize that almost all social practices can be described in terms of individuals with different phenotypes behaving in gendered ways. In this book, we prefer to use the word "gender" given that people, jobs, and interactions are typically gendered.

Race   This book contrasts the employment fates of African and European Americans. The EEOC initially used a set of distinctions that they termed "racial"—Asian/Pacific Islander, black, Hispanic, Native American—to count employment distributions. Whites were not counted before 1980 except as part of employment totals.[2] We take racial distinctions to be socially constructed, rather than biological, and so the term "race," like "gender," refers to social distinctions and practices rather than biology. When the Civil Rights Act was passed, the polite term for African Americans was "Negro." Today "black" and "African American" are used more commonly; we adopt that convention in this book and use the terms interchangeably. We use lower-case spellings of "black" and "white" for consistency and to emphasize that these are social constructions. We use upper-case spellings for "African American," "European American," "Asian," and "Hispanic" for consistency with common usage. We analyze Asian and Hispanic data from the EEO-1 reports after 1980 because by then immigration had increased the size of these two heterogeneous groups considerably. The EEO-1 data do not distinguish between natives and immigrants, and so neither do we.[3]

Segregation   We measure segregation in our analyses with the conventional index of dissimilarity (D). The index equals 100 when groups are completely segregated from each other. The level of the index suggests what percentage of a group would have to switch occupations in order to end segregation in a workplace. Because these data refer to occupations within workplaces, rather than job titles within workplaces, we underestimate actual workplace segregation.[4]

Figure 1.4 displays the national trends in private-sector workplace segregation reported to the EEOC from 1966 to 2005. As we examine these trends in this book, one of our most important findings should be evident immediately. Racial desegregation was mostly complete by 1980, but the integration of white women in the same jobs in the same workplaces with white men continued at least into this century.

Isolation   We also estimate the degree to which groups are isolated from cross-group interaction. In a completely integrated workplace, numerically larger groups can still be socially isolated. Increased equal-status contact was envisioned by the Civil Rights Act and has been consistently linked to reductions in both prejudice and cognitive biases (Pettigrew and Tropp 2006), primarily because such contact disrupts stereotypes, increases out-group empathy, and reduces contact-generated anxiety. Our measure of isolation is simply the percentage of equal-status interactions within one's own group.[5] As integration increases, social isolation should decrease, but larger groups will still tend to be socially isolated simply because of group size. For example, in 1966 white men were 60 percent of the EEOC-reporting private-sector labor force. If segregation had been zero, we would expect the isolation measure to be 60 percent, because 60 percent of white male interactions would have been with other white men. By 2005, white men were only 38 percent of the labor force, and so in a perfectly integrated world we would expect the white male isolation index to have fallen to 38 percent.

Figure 1.5 displays the trends in workplace isolation from out-group contact since 1966. Black men and black women have been much more likely to interact at work with peers of a different race and gender than

Figure 1.4   Employment Segregation from White Men in EEOC-
Reporting Private-Sector Workplaces, 1966 to 2005

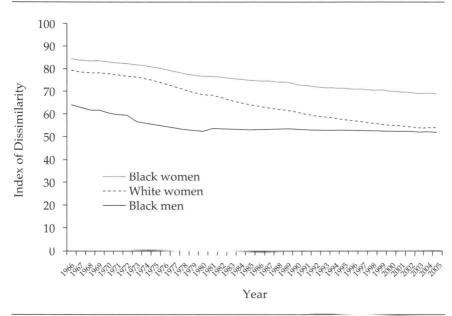

Source: Authors' calculations based on data from EEO-1 surveys (EEOC, various years).

whites. Black men's out-group contact plateaued, while black women's isolation grew after 1980. White men and white women continue to have increased intergroup contact, primarily owing to increased exposure to one another.

Representation in Good Jobs   Segregation is a measure of the movement toward a socially equal organization of employment. Isolation is a measure of exposure to others. Isolation and segregation tell us about shifts in the social distance between status groups, but nothing about the quality of employment. To assess trends in access to desirable jobs, we examine trends in access to craft production, managerial, and professional occupations within EEOC-reporting workplaces.

When comparing the relative probability of individuals being in specific occupations, we must be particularly careful to control for the labor market supply of different groups. White men's proportion of the labor force has declined tremendously since the enactment of the Civil Rights Act, even as white women and Hispanic and Asian men and women have

Figure 1.5   Employment Isolation in EEOC-Reporting Private-Sector
              Workplaces, 1966 to 2005

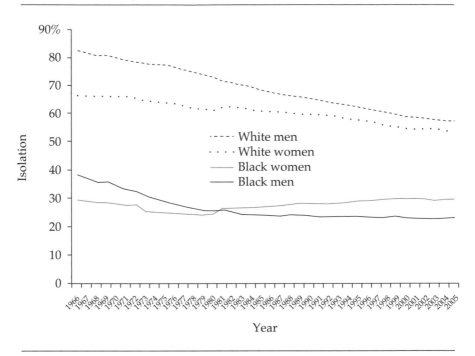

Source: Authors' calculations based on data from EEO-1 surveys (EEOC, various years).

grown in labor market representation. Hence, we would expect the number of white men in desirable jobs to decline simply as a function of their
declining proportion of the labor force. To make matters more complicated, the distribution of both employment and ethnic groups has changed
across places over time; thus, comparing relative employment frequencies
requires adjustment for both temporal and spatial changes in labor supply. We do this in our analyses of occupational representation by calculat-
ing employment representation as the proportion of craft employment in
a workplace (for example, the percentage of craft jobs held by black men)
divided by the proportion of all employment in the local labor market in
that group (for example, the percentage of black men employed in the local labor market).[6] Thus, our comparisons are the workplace occupational
difference from labor supply.[7] To make the measure more interpretable,
we subtract 1 from the observed representation measure and multiply it

by 100. This allows us to interpret the measure in terms of under- and overrepresentation. A score of zero indicates that a group is represented on average at the same rate at which its members are employed in local labor markets. A score of 40 indicates that a group is overrepresented by 40 percent, and a score of −40 means that the group is underrepresented by the same percentage relative to its relative labor force size. Positive scores suggest net advantage in access to jobs compared to the baseline for each race-gender group's labor market representation.

Craft occupations include the skilled manual trades such as carpenters, plumbers, and machinists. These jobs typically require only a high school degree but have substantial autonomy, require a high degree of skill, and pay relatively high wages. Traditionally the most desirable working-class jobs, they are also traditionally male jobs. Managerial and professional jobs are typically the best paid, most respected, and most self-directed jobs in workplaces. They differ in the degree to which they require educational certification. Managerial jobs tend to require a diffuse set of background characteristics and can often be attained through experience, even in the absence of a generalist college degree. In contrast, professional jobs typically require quite specific college or professional degrees (for example, a B.S. in engineering, a B.A. in accounting, or a J.D. in law). We center our attention on these three occupational destinations because they clearly represent the most desirable employment destinations and because we have different expectations as to the degree of difficulty that African Americans and women may experience in attaining these jobs.

White males' representation in skilled working-class jobs in medium-size and large private-sector firms jumped after 1966 and has been stably high ever since. Black men made even stronger progress through the early 1980s, when they were employed at about the same rate as they were hired in this labor force overall. Women remain almost entirely excluded from these jobs to this day, although there has been occasional progress (see figure 1.6).

Craft jobs are the most valuable working-class jobs. In addition, because skills are largely transmitted from the current generation of workers to the next, through either apprenticeships or on-the-job training, craft jobs should be relatively difficult for minorities and women to gain access to in the presence of status exclusion based on social closure. It is in these jobs that workplace formalization is likely to be at its weakest, and the opportunity for incumbents to select similar others and exclude out-groups the highest. In addition, these jobs are strongly associated with male labor, and so it is not surprising to see that gains have largely been confined to white and black men. White men have had slowly increasing access to

Figure 1.6   Craft Employment Relative to Labor Market Participation
in EEOC-Reporting Private-Sector Workplaces,
1966 to 2005

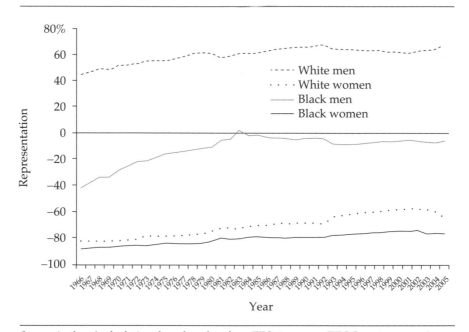

Source: Authors' calculations based on data from EEO-1 surveys (EEOC, various years).

these skilled working-class jobs across the entire post–Civil Rights Act period. Black men had increased access through 1980 and have experienced
small declines since then (see figure 1.7).

Managerial jobs should show similar barriers to integration and are
even more likely to be hoarded by powerful decision-makers because of
their high pay and power. Managerial jobs, however, are more likely to be
subject to formal internal labor market policies and to be the object of discrimination lawsuits and external regulatory attention, and so they should
show some integration, at least in regulated or highly visible organizational environments. We would also expect the integration of women and
minorities into managerial occupations to be more frequent when managerial jobs are relatively poorly paid and when incumbents manage minorities and women. After an initial surge, white male managerial employment has been quite stable since about 1980. Black male managerial
employment surged in the 1960s, continued to grow through the early

Figure 1.7   Managerial Employment Relative to Labor Market
Participation in EEOC-Reporting Private-Sector
Workplaces, 1966 to 2005

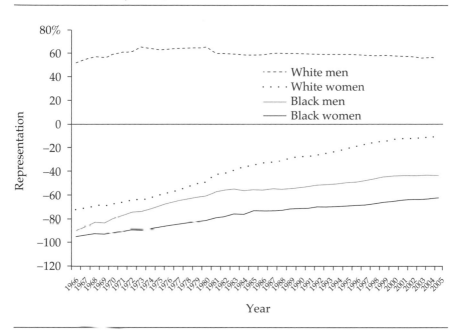

Source: Authors' calculations based on data from EEO-1 surveys (EEOC, various years).

1980s, and has been relatively stable ever since. The small upward trend
for black men visible in figure 1.7 after 1980 is entirely produced by
changes in the industrial structure rather than changes in employer behavior (Stainback and Tomaskovic-Devey 2009). White women's access to
managerial jobs has grown steadily since the early 1970s. Like white
women, black women did not make gains in managerial employment until the 1970s. Like black men, their progress ended around 1980, except for
small gains in relatively low-wage managerial positions generated by employment shifts into the service sector.

Entrance into professional jobs—which, as clearly desirable positions,
are potentially discriminatory targets from a social closure perspective—is
at least initially governed by objective educational requirements. It is here
that we would expect to see the most EEO progress, because specific educational certifications should dominate and status-based discriminatory
decision-making should be at its weakest. We know from other research

Figure 1.8   Professional Employment Relative to Labor Market
             Participation in EEOC-Reporting Private-Sector
             Workplaces, 1966 to 2005

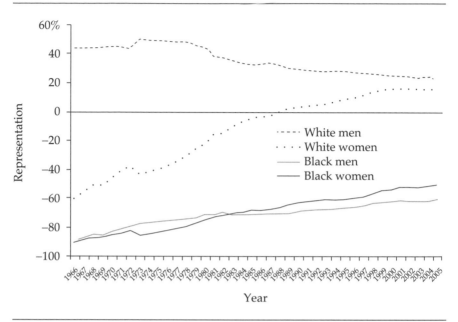

Source: Authors' calculations based on data from EEO-1 surveys (EEOC, various years).

(Jacobs 1995; England 2010) that educational desegregation, particularly
in the professions, has been rapid, at least compared to workplace desegregation. Through increased access to university enrollment in professional degree programs, racial minorities and women have been able to
achieve the formal educational credentials necessary to enter many professional occupations. Figure 1.8 confirms these intuitions. It is in professional jobs that white women, black men, and black women have had the
most sustained gains, and it is only in these educationally certified jobs
that white men have seen any aggregate decline in access to good-quality
jobs since the Civil Rights Act.

Analytic Strategy

In the next four chapters, we focus on the influence of shifts in the political
and regulatory environment on workplace equal opportunity trends, cen-
tering our attention especially on one set of environmental influences on

organizational change. Although this is a normal analytic strategy for historians and historically oriented social scientists, it risks false inference if there are other historical processes occurring simultaneously that might obscure or confound our field of vision. We know that even as the EEO political terrain shifted, other fairly substantial and consequential transitions were under way in the economy. The ones we are most concerned with—because they are directly implicated in any story of employment opportunity and exclusion—are shifts in the populations of firms and employees, as well as shifts in race- and gender-linked human capital characteristics. There is another way to think about this analytic problem: political pressures for equal employment opportunity were waxing and waning at the same time as the composition of firms and workers was also changing, and we statistically control for these compositional dynamics in the next four chapters. We examine their influence more directly in subsequent chapters.

Industrial and Regional Shifts

Over the half-century since the Civil Rights Act, there has been a fundamental shift in the composition of the economy. New firms have been born, while others have died. Employment in some industries has grown, while in others it has declined. Because we have good theoretical reason to expect that firms tend to copy divisions of labor and human resource practices within their industry, we run the risk of conflating politically inspired change with industrial shifts. This is a particular risk because of the direction of industrial shifts over time. As the economy has moved from a goods-producing economy to a service-oriented economy, it has also shed higher-wage jobs as low-wage employment has expanded. Because social closure theory tells us that equal opportunity progress is most likely in low-wage jobs and firms, it is important to take shifts in the economy into account before analyzing the influence of political environments. We do this in the next four chapters by statistically removing the influence of industrial shifts in the economy from segregation trajectories.[8]

Simultaneously, U.S. population and employment shifted from the Northeast and Midwest to the South and West across the late twentieth century. As we will see, regional segregation contrasts were at their highest in 1966, but then converged rapidly. We adjust all models to control for regional shifts in employment.

Labor Force Shifts

The labor force today is quite different from the labor force of 1964. When the Civil Rights Act was passed, the vast majority of the U.S. labor force

Figure 1.9   Labor Force Composition, 1966 to 2005

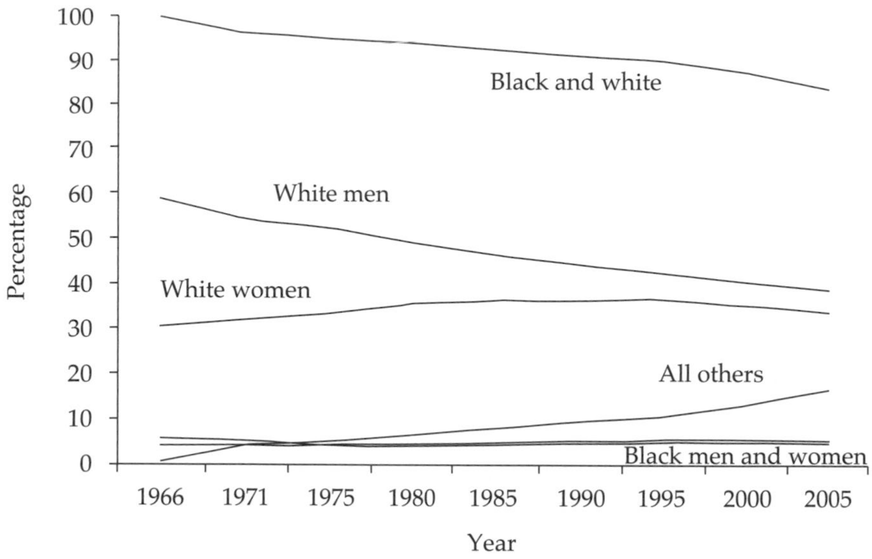

Source: Authors' calculations based on IPUMS-Current Population Survey (King et al. 2010).

was either black or white, and white men made up nearly 60 percent of the total labor force. By 2006, 17 percent of the labor force was neither black nor white (it was mostly Hispanic and Asian), and white men made up only 38 percent of the labor force. Across the period, black men and black women were a fairly constant 5 percent each of the labor force, and white women rose from 30 percent in the mid-1960s to 36 percent in the 1980s and 1990s, dropping back to 33 percent in the twenty-first century (see figure 1.9).

These shifts in the race and gender composition of the labor force have crucial implications for workplace integration. We expect to see increased workplace integration—and to some extent increasingly integrated jobs within workplaces—simply because white men have dropped dramatically as a proportion of the labor force. In addition, these shifts are geographically uneven: major increases in both Hispanic and Asian populations have taken place primarily on the East and West Coasts, at least prior to the 1990s. After the 1990s, the Hispanic labor force grew in many parts of the country. To observe the influence of political processes on employment shifts for white men, white women, black men, and black women, we also employ in the next four chapters a statistical adjustment to condition out the effect of labor force shifts from our time trend estimates.

PARALLEL NARRATIVES

All analyses are partial. In this section, we point out what we do not observe in these data and the possible implications for conclusions based on EEO-1 surveys of private-sector workplaces.

Human Capital Trends

Conventional discussions of labor market inequality highlight group differences in educational attainment and labor market experience as potential explanations for continuing status-based inequalities. This makes perfect sense in any analysis of individuals, because human capital differences between people tend to be more influential determinants of which jobs people are hired into and the earnings they receive than either race or gender. In individual-level analyses, we typically observe the influence of race or gender on employment or earnings after controlling for human capital resources. The EEO-1 reports provide no information on the human capital credentials of workers, so a direct statistical control is not possible. If our goal was to predict individual careers, this would be a substantial weakness.

Our primary aims in this book are different; we are much more interested in unpacking the aggregate trajectories of workplace segregation and desegregation since 1966. Our evidence is largely based on comparisons of trajectories across race-gender groups in different political eras, labor markets, industries, and firms. Thus, to explore our substantive questions we do not need individual-level human capital data. However, even though the EEO-1 data preclude such an examination, we do think it is important to compare our observed trajectories to shifts in the relative human capital of race-gender groups.

Figure 1.10 displays trends in the ratio of average educational credentials of employed white men to those of white women, black men, and black women. The basic trends are clear. White women have the same average educational credentials as white men across the entire period of this study. Black women and black men have lower average education, but also show a continual convergence with white men across the period. Figure 1.11 provides the same trends for college degrees. Here white men have an advantage over all other groups, but there are strong patterns of linear convergence from 1966 to 2006. By 2006, employed white women's college degree attainment is nearly identical to white men's. Although

Figure 1.10   Years of Education Relative to Average for White Males
Among the Currently Employed, 1966 to 2006

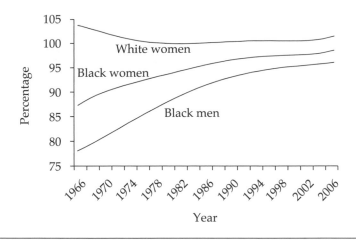

Source: Authors' calculations based on IPUMS-Current Population Survey (King et al. 2010).

black women and black men continue to lag considerably behind white men, they both show patterns of convergence. Hence, while differences in education may explain some of the differences in occupational success between African Americans and white men, particularly for jobs that require college degrees, these differences are consistent only with linear trends of employment convergence. Thus, trends in race-gender–specific education are consistent only with linear convergence patterns at the aggregate level. These trends also suggest that we should expect to observe the most progress relative to white men in jobs that require educational credentials. That, of course, was the pattern we observed for professional occupations in figure 1.8.

In the standard models in sociology and economics, there is always a concern that some unmeasured human capital or labor supply characteristics are producing race and gender gaps in employment opportunity. For race, the unmeasured characteristic is often imagined to be the quality of education or cultural skills. For gender, it is women's presumed preferences for family work or for gender-typical employment. In a dynamic analysis such as this one, to invoke such explanations requires some heroic assumptions. We document that black women and white women, after a period of rapid integration, became more segregated after 1970; that after a twenty-year period of rapid integration with white men, black men, and black women made little further progress after 1980; and that after 2000 white women's integration with white men slowed to a near-

Figure 1.11 College Education Achievement Relative to White Males, Currently Employed, 1966 to 2006

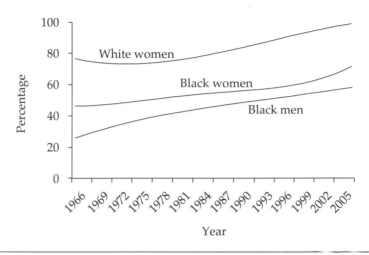

Year

Source: Authors' calculations based on IPUMS-Current Population Survey (King et al. 2010).

standstill. Although all of these shifts are easily understood in terms of political and organizational dynamics, they would require implausibly sudden shifts in race-gender-specific labor supply preferences or human capital quality.

Small Firms and the Government Sector

Under Title VII of the Civil Rights Act, the EEO-1 data collection was limited to private-sector firms with one hundred or more employees to report on workplaces with fifty or more employees. William Bielby and James Baron (1984) showed that gender segregation tends to be higher in smaller workplaces. Donald Tomaskovic-Devey (1993) showed that this was true for race segregation as well. Thus, estimates of equal opportunity progress in EEOC-reporting private-sector organizations are probably higher than in the entire private sector. Because average establishment size declined somewhat after 1985 among EEOC-reporting firms, it is also possible that our trend analyses are particularly conservative relative to the entire private-sector economy in these later years.

Figure 1.12 displays the percentage of total U.S. employment in EEO-1-reporting workplaces. What we see is that the regulated private sector represented between 30 and 35 percent of total employment from 1966 onward. We also see that white males were slightly overrepresented in

Figure 1.12   EEOC Reporting as Percentage of Total Private-Sector Labor Force, 1966 to 2000

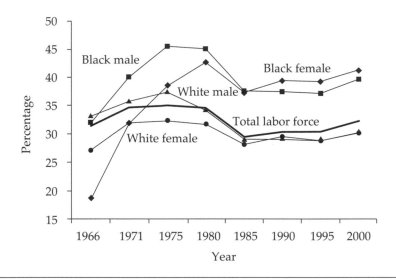

Source: Authors' calculations based on EEO-1 surveys (EEOC, various years) and IPUMS-CPS (King et al. 2010).

EEOC-reporting firms in 1966 and slightly underrepresented by late century. We also see surges in black male, white female, and black female employment in EEOC-reporting firms immediately after 1966. All groups, but particularly white men, display slow continued employment growth in EEOC-reporting firms after 1985.[9] Most striking is that black men and black women were strongly overrepresented in that part of the private sector that had been historically subjected to employment discrimination law and EEOC reporting requirements.

Prior research has suggested that the public sector was more effective than the private sector in implementing EEO and affirmative action (AA) policies (Wilson 1997a, 1997b). Thus, our focus on large private-sector firms may miss positive changes that are likely to be occurring in the public sector. Figure 1.13 reports government-sector employment across our observation period. Three things stand out: First, white men are less likely to find or seek government employment, and other groups are more likely to do so. Second, although government employment is considerably smaller than EEOC-reporting private-sector employment, it employs a disproportionate share of black men, white women, and especially black women.

Figure 1.13   Government Employment as Percentage of Total Labor Force by Race and Gender, 1966 to 2000

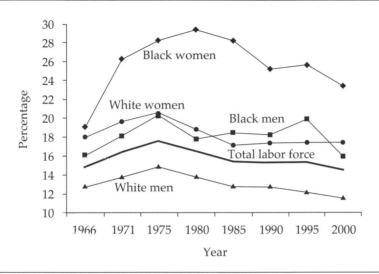

Source: Authors' calculations based on IPUMS-CPS (King et al. 2010).

These trends strongly suggest that since 1966 that white male employment has shifted to the small-firm private sector. Figure 1.14 confirms this expectation. As soon as 1975, white men became consistently overrepresented in the small-firm private sector. For the purposes of this figure, this line is defined as the non-EEOC-reporting private sector. These are the firms with little or no federal oversight of their equal employment opportunity behavior. The other striking finding in figure 1.14 is that after 1966 African Americans were consistently underrepresented in the small-firm, nonregulated private sector. This shift of white men into this sector and black men and black and white women out of it suggests that some new sorting mechanism is at play. Although we do not explore this mechanism in this book, it is not unreasonable to suspect that African Americans found that employment in the more regulated private and government sectors was easier to find and perhaps easier to live with.

This book focuses on EEO trends in large private-sector workplaces. These are exactly those private-sector firms where we expect progress to be most dramatic. The sorting of black men, black women, and white women into these firms suggests that this may be the case. In addition, about 50 percent of the firms we track are government contractors and so are required to have affirmative action programs. All must report to the EEOC, and so are both aware of government monitoring and forced to

Figure 1.14   Small-Firm Private-Sector Employment, 1966 to 2000

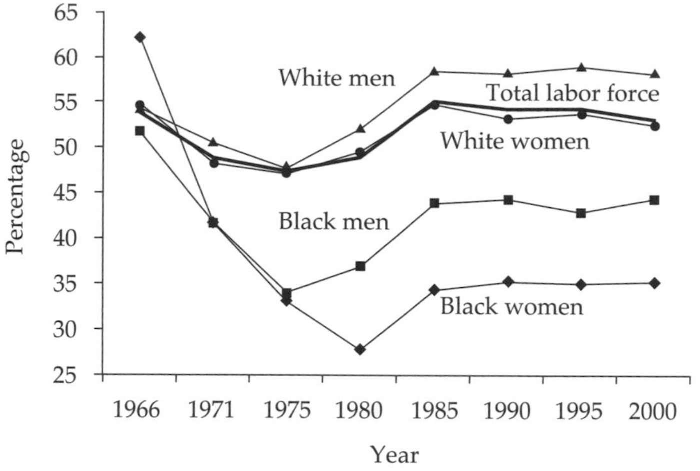

Source: Authors' calculations based on EEO-1 surveys (EEOC, various years) and IPUMS-CPS (King et al. 2010).

collect yearly statistics on their employment distributions down to the workplace level. Because these are also the largest firms in the economy, they are the ones most likely to be targeted for high-profile race and gender discrimination lawsuits. These are precisely the firms that were the intended targets of the 1964 Civil Rights Act.

On the other hand, our data prohibit us from documenting EEO progress among small private-sector firms, which comprise approximately 60 percent of private-sector employment across the entire period of this study. Most civil rights law has reporting exclusions for small firms, and very small firms (typically less than fifteen employees) are not even subjected to most EEO law. We have seen that white men have been moving out of both the government sector and the regulated private sector since the 1960s and into this nonregulated private sector. To the extent that this reflects white men's flight from both affirmative action and direct employment competition with white women, black men, and black women, we will overestimate societal desegregation trends.

Region and Sector Differences in EEOC Coverage

The legislated firm and workplace size limitations in EEO-1 reporting have had implications for both regional and sectoral coverage. For most of

Figure 1.15   EEOC Reporting of Private-Sector Labor Force Coverage by Region, 1966

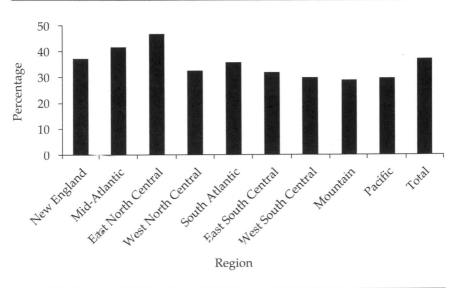

Source: Authors' calculations based on data from EEO-1 surveys (EEOC, various years) and IPUMS-CPS (King et al. 2010).

the private sector, the only potential equal opportunity intrusion of the federal government was through EEOC reporting. We have already seen that about two-thirds of private-sector firms were excluded because of these size limits. Because size is strongly associated with economic sector and regions vary fairly dramatically in their industrial structure, the reach of the EEOC into private-sector firms was uneven from the moment the Civil Rights Act became law.

Region is, of course, important because of the centrality of black labor and employment segregation to the southern political economy prior to the Civil Rights Act. As figure 1.15 shows, EEO-1 coverage in 1966 was quite a bit lower in the more agricultural South than in much of the rest of the country and quite a bit higher in the more industrial Midwest and Northeast. Not only did African Americans make up large proportions of the total population in many parts of the South, but because of the sharecropping agricultural system they were the primary labor force for southern agriculture.[10] In addition, African Americans' near-exclusion from the manufacturing economy forced many African Americans to either immigrate north, remain in slavelike agricultural conditions, or, for women, work as domestics in white homes. Replacement by black labor was often used as a potent threat by employers to forestall white unionization in the South.

Figure 1.16   EEOC Reporting of Private-Sector African American
Employment Coverage by Region, 1966

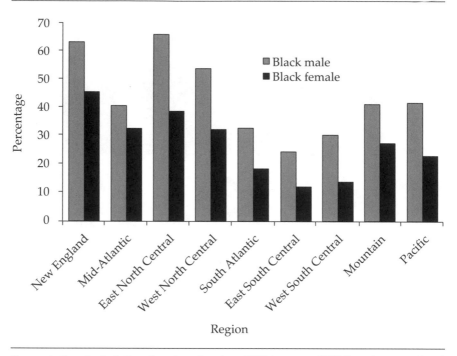

Region

Source: Authors' calculations based on data from EEO-1 surveys (EEOC, various years) and IPUMS-CPS (King et al. 2010).

As figure 1.16 shows, in 1966 African Americans were vastly underrepresented in southern EEO-1 reports. While in 1966 nationally, 40 percent of black men employed in the private sector worked in EEOC-reporting firms, coverage was 33 percent in the South Atlantic, 30 percent in the West South Central, and only 25 percent in the East South Central states. For black women, the coverage was even worse. Nineteen percent of black women in the private sector were employed in EEOC-reporting firms in the South Atlantic, and coverage was only 12 percent and 14 percent in the East and West South Central regions, respectively. One can look at this pattern in at least two ways. On the one hand, the size restrictions, which were the result of political manipulations by southern congressmen to protect southern employers from federal oversight, can be seen as an extension of the same racial politics that exempted agriculture and domestic labor from wage and hour laws, Social Security, and unemployment insurance in the 1930s. On the other hand, in 1964 in the South a large popula-

Figure 1.17   EEOC Reporting of Private-Sector Coverage, by
Industrial Sector, 1966

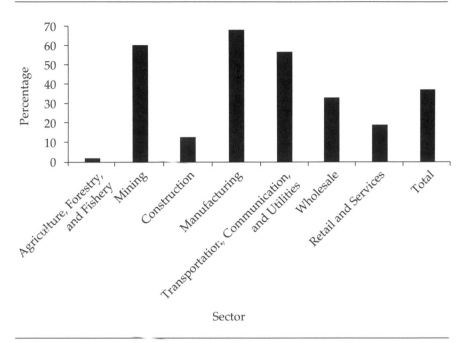

Sector

Source: Authors' calculations based on data from EEO-1 surveys (EEOC, various years) and
IPUMS-CPS (King et al. 2010).

tion of employed black men and black women was available to move into
the large-firm private sector, which was newly subject to both regulatory
and legal sanctions for discrimination.

While the fight for civil rights necessarily implied a regional confronta-
tion, which sectors of the economy were covered by EEOC reporting had
regional implications as well. The argument that large firms should be
regulated, or at least monitored, was linked to the notion that these firms
could absorb the costs of change. In addition, the largest firms had come
to occupy the central place in the economy, becoming in many ways the
symbolic face of American capitalism. The largest firms were mostly in the
manufacturing, transportation, and utility industries. At the time there
were no Wal-Mart retail stores trading in every town across the country,
and banks were prohibited from operating across state lines. Thus, large
firms were reasonable targets because they were the national firms. Figure
1.17 shows that it was exactly in these sectors that firms tended to be large
enough to be regulated by the EEOC. Mining was similarly high in cover-

age, although it comprised less than 1 percent of national employment. Agriculture, construction, services, and retail trade were covered by EEOC reporting requirements at very low rates. The service and retail trade industry represented a large proportion of the economy in 1966 at 44 percent of employment. Agriculture and construction were much smaller at 5 and 6 percent, respectively.

Unemployment, Incarceration, and the Neoliberal Era

To the extent that discrimination toward African Americans leads to lower labor force participation and raises unemployment rates, we are underestimating minority disadvantage in access to all jobs when using employment data. Across the period of this study, the black unemployment rate has tended to hover at about twice the white unemployment rate. Black labor force participation was slightly higher than white labor force participation in the 1960s, reflecting black women's higher rates of labor force participation. By 1980, white labor force participation increased slightly, reflecting both the growth of discouraged workers among African Americans and the strong surge in white women's employment.

During the period of our study, the most dramatic trend that excludes people from employment has been the rapid rise in imprisonment, particularly of young black men (Western and Pettit 2010). Thus, because our estimates are based on employment, we will tend to overestimate black progress in the labor force, particularly after 1980, because we have no information on the high rates of black exclusion from the labor force. Because one of the most dramatic and disturbing findings in this book is that black equal opportunity progress in EEOC-reporting firms essentially stopped after 1980, the exclusion of the non-employed suggests that many of the real employment gains encouraged by the Civil Rights Act have been eroded by black exclusion from the labor force because of the public policy of mass imprisonment after 1980.

There were also changes in the organization of American capitalism during the period of investigation. In the 1970s, the dominant role of U.S. manufacturing in the world economy was eroded and private-sector firms went on an offensive against government regulation and unionization (Miller and Tomaskovic-Devey 1983). Financial pressures on corporations arising from global competition may have served as a distraction from equal opportunity goals. After 1980, the new neoliberal ideology of limited employer or government responsibility for the welfare of working people became dominant in the United States (Harvey 2005). It is not unlikely that these ideological and policy shifts also influenced the historical and institutional narratives we develop in this book. We leave it to future scholars to link both major trends more explicitly to equal opportunity trajectories.

CONCLUSION

The EEO-1 reports from medium-size and large private-sector firms are a remarkable resource for examining trends in desegregation since the Civil Rights Act of 1964. The Civil Rights Act itself mandated the collection of these data with the goal of monitoring progress toward equal opportunity in employment. That is exactly the task at hand. Has employment segregation declined since the Civil Rights Act? If so, when and for whom? Where has progress been most rapid? Where has it been most disappointing? Did all jobs desegregate or only the least desirable? These are the questions we turn to in the remainder of this book. Across the next four chapters, we begin with an emphasis on the effects of political and legal shifts on equal opportunity. We then move into a consideration of the more localized dynamics operating at the level of labor markets (chapter 6), industries (chapter 7), and workplaces (chapter 8).

Chapter 2 | Hyper-Segregation in the Pre–Civil Rights Period

PRIOR TO THE passage of the Civil Rights Act of 1964, employment segregation was deeply institutionalized in U.S. workplaces. During this historical moment, people in the United States understood that white men would occupy the most desirable jobs and hold authority over other groups. It was also assumed that women of all races and nonwhites of all genders would tend to occupy marginally rewarded jobs with little or no authority over others. These ongoing, society-wide patterns of social relations were both legally codified and normatively sanctioned, ensuring the maintenance of rigid race and gender hierarchies.

The purpose of this chapter is to highlight the high levels and relative homogeneity of employment segregation in 1966—the first year the EEOC began collecting data on private-sector employment patterns. The Civil Rights Act of 1964 mandated this data collection effort in order to monitor progress toward an equal employment opportunity society. The fact that the data were collected only two years after the passage of the act is remarkable testimony to the speed with which the EEOC was created and set into motion. This data collection effort was the first serious intrusion of the federal government into private-sector employers' personnel policies, at least with respect to race and gender. Although wage and hour laws and laws relating to unionization had existed since the 1930s, neither required systematic reporting by employers of the demographic attributes of their employees. Most corporate personnel managers were oriented more toward unions than the federal government prior to the initiation of EEOC data collection (see Dulebohn, Ferris, and Stodd 1995; Kaufman 2008).

Requiring private-sector employers to submit annual reports to the EEOC was arguably one of the federal government's most controversial actions from the point of view of employers. Certainly, employer organizations had long resisted equal opportunity and fair employment practice laws and regulations (Chen 2009). It was not, however, the first time the U.S. government sought to influence the employment practices of private-sector firms. Indeed, each president since Franklin D. Roosevelt had issued an executive order to federal contractors to practice affirmative action in hiring black Americans. Regulatory enforcement, however, was limited at best. Frank Dobbin (2009) concludes that President John F. Kennedy's 1961 executive order was different from previous presidential mandates, because the Kennedy administration was ostensibly more serious about racial equality than previous administrations and because the civil rights movement made the need for change in behavior more salient to employers. Thus, there are reasons to expect that by 1966 employer behavior toward African Americans may have already begun to change as a result of the civil rights movement as well as federal and local politics. There is no reason to expect similar shifts around gender segregation. In what follows, we document race and gender segregation in private-sector employment in 1966 and discuss the historical narrative shaping the patterns we observe.

WHAT DID EMPLOYMENT SEGREGATION LOOK LIKE IN 1966?

Workplace-level estimates of race and gender employment distributions prior to the first 1966 EEO-1 surveys do not exist. Therefore, we will primarily gauge progress toward equal employment opportunity from the available 1966 baseline. There is reason to believe, given the current literature, that some EEO progress might already have been made in states that had already implemented pre-1964 fair employment practice (FEP) laws, as well as among federal contractors and perhaps among the largest U.S. employers.

We begin with the simplest of statistics. What percentages of private-sector EEOC-reporting workplaces were racially or gender homogeneous? Table 2.1 provides two approaches to this question: How common was *complete* exclusion from private-sector workplaces? And how common were race-gender homogeneous workplaces? In other words, to what extent did employers maintain separate workplaces for different race-gender groups?

The EEO-1 reports show that very few workplaces employed no white men (7.8 percent) or no white women (11.3 percent). However, complete exclusion was a much more common experience for black men and black women. In 1966 half of EEOC-reporting workplaces employed no black men, and almost two-thirds (63 percent) employed no black women. Table

Table 2.1   Distribution of Homogeneous EEOC-Reporting
            Workplaces, 1966

	White Men	Black Men	White Women	Black Women
Percentage without ...	7.8%	50.2%	11.3%	63.0%
Percentage entirely ...	7.5	0.05	0.7	0.01

Source: Authors' calculations based on data from EEO-1 surveys (EEOC, various years).

2.1 also reveals that while more than one-third of workplaces were all-white, they tended to be gender-integrated: only 7.5 percent were all white male, and fewer than 1 percent of workplaces employed only white females. Of course, this does not indicate that white men and white women were integrated in the sense that they worked in the same jobs—only that they tended to be found in the same workplaces. Despite the extremely high levels of between-job employment segregation that we observe later, private-sector employers did not maintain separate workplaces for African Americans. In fact, among the 103,644 EEO-1 workplace reports in 1966, only 159 employed black workers exclusively. In contrast, there were nearly 40,000 all-white workplaces.

The EEO-1 reports also contain race-gender employment distributions across nine occupational categories (see table 2.2). In 1966 there were clear

Table 2.2   Distribution of Race-Gender Groups Across Major
            Occupational Categories, 1966

Occupation	White Men	Black Men	White Women	Black Women
Officials and managers	20.5%	1.3%	2.6%	0.4%
Professionals	6.6	1.8	1.5	1.2
Technical	4.0	2.6	2.0	2.5
Sales	13.0	2.1	5.5	3.9
Clerical	7.4	6.7	62.4	27.4
Skilled craft	13.9	7.8	1.8	2.7
Operative	18.8	28.9	10.8	22.8
Laborers	8.5	25.6	4.9	11.9
Service	7.3	23.2	8.5	27.3
Total	100	100	100	100

Source: Authors' calculations based on data from EEO-1 surveys (EEOC, various years).

distinctions across the private-sector economy as to which occupations were available to whom. Not surprisingly, only two years after the passage of the Civil Rights Act white men were concentrated in the more desirable and highly rewarded managerial, professional, and skilled craft occupations. In 1966 black men were concentrated in unskilled manual labor and service occupations. In fact, fully 78 percent of all black male employment was in operative, laborer, and service occupations. White women were even more occupationally concentrated. Approximately 62 percent of white women were found in just one major occupational group—clerical. Black women were found in the same occupations as black men (operative and service) and white women (clerical).

Because the distributions in table 2.2 are for the entire EEOC-reporting private sector, they do not tell us how segregated these groups were from each other within workplaces. They only provide a snapshot of the concentration of race-gender groups within aggregate occupational categories. Prior to the Civil Rights Act, employment segregation was very high. Figure 2.1 displays how segregated black men, white women, and black women were from white men and white women within workplaces in 1966. Recall that the segregation index varies from 0 to 100, with 100 indicating total segregation—groups never being found together in the same occupation in the same workplace. Although we have adjusted these measures upward to take into account the potential mismatch between the EEOC's occupational categories and actual workplace-level divisions of labor (see the methodological appendix), we are still underestimating workplace segregation. This is because we observe only broad occupational groups, not the actual job titles that employers use to distinguish between different types of jobs. Indeed, previous research conclusively demonstrates that status segregation between detailed job titles is always higher than segregation between occupations (Bielby and Baron 1986; Tomaskovic-Devey 1993; Petersen and Morgan 1995). As such, the very high level of average segregation in 1966 is consistent with an interpretation that segregation was practically total across these private-sector workplaces. White men were almost entirely segregated from all others. Their average segregation level from black men was 71.2, from white women 85.2, and from black women 86.8. Black men were equally segregated from white women (85.4). White women and black women were more likely to work together in the same major occupational group in the same workplace, with a segregation index of 54.2. In other words, in 1966 in the average workplace, 54.2 percent of black women would have needed to switch jobs to have equal employment outcomes with white women. For all of these comparisons, the modal workplace is completely segregated.

In 1966 the most common workplace practice was nearly complete

Figure 2.1   Employment Segregation, 1966

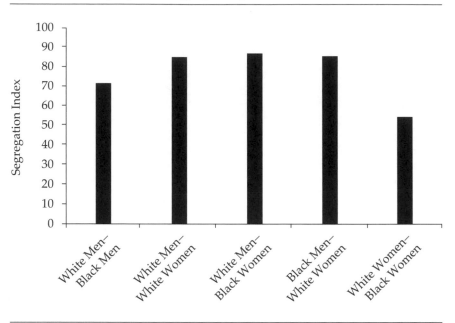

Source: Authors' calculations based on data from EEO-1 surveys (EEOC, various years).

race-gender employment segregation—gender segregation was nearly total. Race segregation was extraordinarily high and, because blacks were a
relatively small proportion of employees in most workplaces, complete
racial segregation was just less practical, particularly at the level of major
occupational distinctions. Most workplaces simply did not have enough
black employees to create totally segregated workplaces. On the other
hand, the level of race segregation among men was quite a bit higher than
among women. White men in particular were most likely to work in socially homogeneous jobs.

It is also possible that the lower level of racial segregation in 1966 reflects progress inspired by the civil rights movement. If EEO progress did
occur for black Americans, we expect that it was most pronounced in
states with fair employment practice laws, among federal contractors, and
among the largest corporations. We examine these possibilities shortly.
But first we examine variation in employment segregation across regions,
industry sectors, and workplace types. The homogeneity in segregation
across these comparisons is striking.

Table 2.3 explores regional variation in employment segregation in 1966.

As one might expect, race segregation tends to be higher in the South, but even here the contrasts are relatively small. The South Atlantic and the East South Central—the core southern regions with large black populations, histories of chattel slavery, and plantation agriculture in the eighteenth and nineteenth centuries, as well as Jim Crow segregation in the twentieth century—had white male–black male segregation levels of 75.0 and 74.0, respectively. The West North Central states and the Mountain states were only slightly lower, at 73.3 and 73.8, respectively. The West South Central stands out as the most race-segregated region among men, at 78.2.

Race segregation among women, however, is strikingly higher in all three southern regions. In 1966 the New England region stood out for having the lowest level of race and gender segregation across all regional comparisons. It is also the case that black men almost never worked in equal-status employment with white women in the South. In the previous chapter, we learned that EEOC-reporting firms in the South employed a much smaller proportion of private-sector black workers than firms in other regions. In 1966 the South was more strongly associated with total race-based exclusion from medium-size- and large-firm private-sector employment than it was with segregation within EEOC-reporting workplaces.

Table 2.4 documents levels of racial and gender segregation across industry sectors. There are only a few notable sector contrasts in 1966 segregation levels. White male–black male employment segregation is noticeably lower in durable manufacturing, the sector in which many federal contractors were concentrated. White female–black female segregation is also relatively lower in this sector, but also in nondurable manufacturing, wholesale trade, and producer services. White male–white female segregation is nearly total in mining, construction, transportation, utilities, and communication, wholesale trade, and producer services, and visibly lower in the low-wage retail, social services, and personal services sectors of the economy. Gender segregation is most extreme in the traditionally male-dominated construction and mining industrial sectors. Race and gender segregation tend to be lower in private social services (such as hospitals and schools) and in retail trade workplaces. By a large margin, black men were most likely to be in equal-status contact with white men in durable manufacturing.

We suspect that some of this sector variation represents measurement error introduced by the absence of job titles and that some of it is real. In the next few chapters, we control for detailed industry when evaluating desegregation trends. In chapter 7, we return to sector in its own right as a context for understanding desegregation.

Although the differences are not dramatic, we also explore variation in

Table 2.3 Regional Variation in Segregation Levels, 1966

	New England	Mid-Atlantic	East North-Central	West North-Central	South Atlantic	East South	West South	Mountain	Pacific
White men–black men	65.9%	67.4%	68.2%	73.3%	75.0%	74.0%	78.2%	73.8%	69.3%
White women–black women	46.0	47.7	50.6	55.1	62.3	63.9	66.5	53.8	49.1
White men–white women	81.7	83.8	85.2	86.2	85.4	87.8	86.8	86.1	85.7
White men–black women	84.0	86.0	86.4	86.1	87.9	87.8	90.0	85.1	87.1
Black men–white women	81.8	81.7	84.4	86.2	87.2	89.7	88.7	85.3	85.1

Source: Authors' calculations based on data from EEO-1 surveys (EEOC, various years).

Table 2.4   Sector Variation in Segregation Levels, 1966

	White Men– Black Men	White Women– Black Women	White Men– White Women
Agriculture, forestry, fishery	72.8%	72.4%	86.1%
Mining	71.0	60.8	96.1
Construction	77.3	72.6	97.1
Nondurable manufacturing	71.3	52.8	81.2
Durable manufacturing	64.1	50.6	85.2
Transportation, utilities, communications	74.6	58.8	92.8
Wholesale trade	76.8	48.2	92.5
Retail trade	74.3	57.6	76.2
Producer services	76.2	46.5	90.6
Social services	69.6	60.7	72.0
Personal services	72.3	66.2	75.6

Source: Authors' calculations based on data from EEO-1 surveys (EEOC, various years).

segregation across organizational type, contrasting single-establishment workplaces with branch plants and corporate headquarters in multi-location firms. We suspected that large, multi-plant corporations would have been more visible and that equal opportunity pressures therefore would have already encouraged desegregation in these firms. Figure 2.2 provides this comparison.

The key distinctions we see are that in 1966 white men's segregation from black men and black women was at its height in the headquarter establishments of large corporations. In contrast, white women were most integrated with black men and black women in corporate headquarters. These same three groups were most likely to work together in the same occupation in the same workplace in single-establishment firms. Branch plants tended to be in between their headquarters and single-establishment firms on most comparisons. We doubt that these small differences reflect a special reaction to equal opportunity pressures. To the extent that they do, they suggest that corporate headquarters initially desegregated white women into jobs with black men and black women but not into equal-status contact with white men.

We do not want to overdramatize these sector, regional, and organizational differences. They are by and large small and may be artifacts of unobserved firm differences on other dimensions. Our primary conclusion is that there was little systematic variation in segregation across these dimensions in 1966. Even the regional differences in race segregation between southern and northern states are not as marked as one might ex-

Figure 2.2   Employment Segregation in Single-Establishment Firms,
              Branch Plants, and Corporate Headquarters, 1966

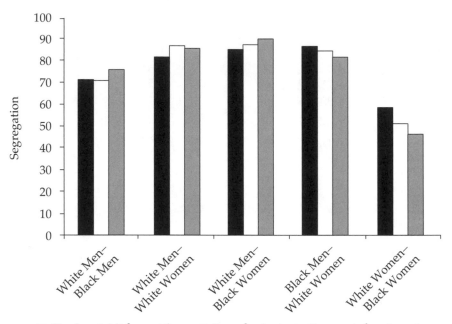

■ Single establishment firms □ Branch plants ▥ Corporate headquarters

Source: Authors' calculations based on data from EEO-1 surveys (EEOC, various years).

pect. Instead, we observe a pattern in 1966 of very high employment segregation everywhere.

WHO WAS SOCIALLY ISOLATED IN 1966?

Another way to think about employment segregation is to look at the extent to which workers are interactionally exposed to equal-status workers
of a different race or gender. One of the key social psychological findings
in the study of racial and gender prejudice is that bias tends to decline with
equal-status contact (Pettigrew and Tropp 2006). We measure isolation
from other groups as the percentage of coworkers in the same occupation
of the same race and gender averaged across each workplace. Figure 2.3
displays the degree of isolation from other groups. The central finding is
that in 1966 white men were nearly totally isolated from cross-group contact. Barely 18 percent of their equal-status interactions were with anyone

Figure 2.3   Employment Isolation from Intergroup Contact, 1966

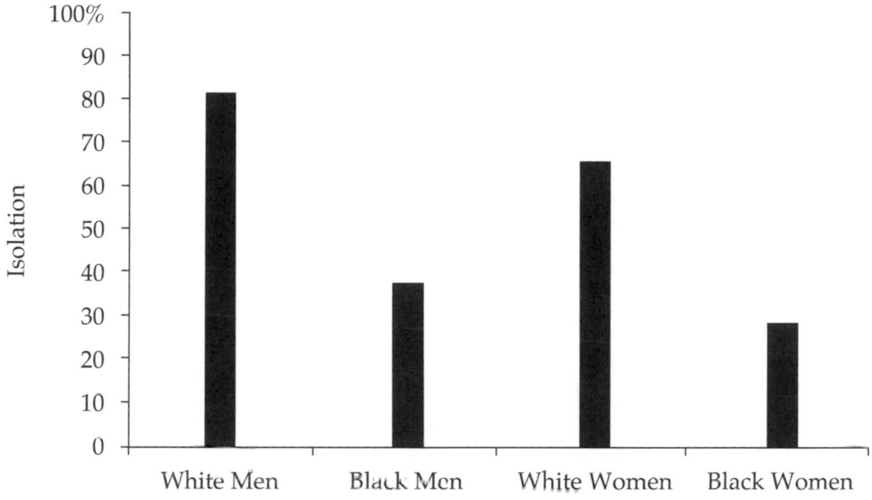

Source: Authors' calculations based on data from EEO-1 surveys (EEOC, various years).

who was not a white man. Because these are occupations, not job titles, we can expect that at the job level isolation was even higher. African Americans, on the other hand, routinely interacted with whites. Black women, who were only 2.5 percent of employees in the EEO-1 workplaces, interacted routinely with others 79 percent of the time. Black women worked on average in work groups that were only 21 percent other black women, reflecting in part what a small proportion of EEOC-reporting employment they were. Black men comprised 5.9 percent of EEO-1 employment; with an isolation score of 38 percent, they were almost twice as isolated as black women in 1966. On average, white women worked with other white women 66 percent of the time; presumably, given the 1966 segregation levels reported here, much of the exposure they had beyond their own group was to black women. White men stand out as almost completely isolated from other groups. In 1966, 82 percent of the time white men encountered only other white men in equal-status employment contacts.

WHO WAS EMPLOYED IN GOOD JOBS IN 1966?

In 1966 black men, white women, and black women were nearly totally excluded from both managerial and professional jobs, and nearly all women were excluded from skilled craft production jobs. We examine race-gender representation in these jobs in 1966. Our representation measure is designed to take into account differences in labor market participation for each race-gender group across geography. In large parts of the country there are no or very few African Americans, and this was even more the case in 1966 than it is today. Thus, it makes sense to standardize representation to account for the pool of potential workers who might be employed in a particular labor market. It is also the case that women's labor force participation grew over time, as did that of other ethnic groups, particularly Asians and Hispanics. As a result, white men have been a declining proportion of the labor force over time, and their diminishing representation needs to be taken into account if we wish to determine if equal employment opportunity progress is taking place. For example, in 1966 white men held 91 percent of all managerial jobs in EEOC-reporting workplaces. By 2000, the white male share of EEO managerial jobs had fallen to only 57 percent. It would be premature, however, to interpret this as a decline in white males' privileged access to managerial employment, because white males dropped from 62 to 38 percent of total employment across this same time period. As we will see, white male managerial representation adjusted for labor supply actually has increased since 1966 (see also Stainback and Tomaskovic-Devey 2009).

Figure 2.4 reports group representation in managerial, professional, and skilled craft occupations in 1966. Because this statistic standardizes representation at the workplace level by group representation in the local labor market, any value above zero indicates the percentage to which a group is overrepresented relative to local labor supply. Values below zero indicate the percentage of underrepresentation within these jobs. Zero indexes proportional representation.

In 1966 white men were overrepresented in all desirable occupations. White men's managerial representation was 52 percent higher than their participation in the labor force. The comparable overrepresentations for white men in professional and skilled craft occupations were 45 and 42 percent, respectively. The other groups were all underrepresented in these desirable occupations. This is hardly unanticipated. Black women were the most underrepresented in managerial positions (95 percent), followed by black men (89 percent), and white women (73 percent). In 1966, although they still rarely filled managerial jobs, white women, black men, and black women were all more likely to be managers in single-establishment firms than in major corporations. White male managers were ubiquitous, but particularly in the South Atlantic states.

The patterns for professional workers are remarkably similar. In 1966 white men were overrepresented in these high-skilled, educationally cer-

Figure 2.4   Representation in Desirable Occupations Relative to
Group Composition in the Local Labor Market, 1966

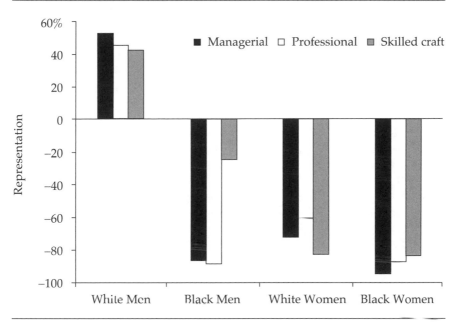

Source: Authors' calculations based on data from EEO-1 surveys (EEOC, various years).

tified jobs by 45 percent relative to their labor force representation. White
women were underrepresented by 61 percent. Although not as extremely
excluded from professional occupations as from managerial jobs, black
men and black women were still nearly totally excluded from professional
jobs in the EEO-regulated private sector. In 1966 almost all black men and
black women in the United States had gone through segregated educational systems. Prior to the Civil Rights Act, most black men and black
women with college degrees were limited to professional jobs serving the
black community as teachers, doctors, lawyers, and the like. Thus, they
were unlikely to be employed in professional jobs in EEOC-reporting
firms. As we will see later, this pattern changed over time with the erosion
of race and gender as a basis of social closure exclusion from educationally
certified jobs.

Skilled craft jobs are the most desirable working-class occupations: typically they require long periods of training and deliver high wages and
substantial workplace autonomy. Within these valued jobs, we again find
that white men were the only overrepresented group, at 42 percent, but in

1966 black males showed at least some access to these jobs. They remained underrepresented relative to their employment in EEOC-reporting firms, but at 25 percent underrepresentation, we cannot conclude that they were barred from these jobs. In 1966, while the most talented black men were nearly totally excluded from managerial and professional jobs, they did have some access to skilled production jobs. White women and black women, on the other hand, were practically absent from managerial, professional, and skilled working-class jobs. These patterns reveal the interesting race-gender dynamics that shaped the contours of workplace segregation in 1966.

It is fair to say that in 1966 EEOC-reporting workplaces were typically hyper-segregated. By comparison, Baron and Bielby (1986) report that male-female segregation at the job title level in California around 1971 was 96.3 percent. Even though we lack job title information, our estimates of gender segregation are all above 85 percent; this suggests that our estimates are reasonable, but that they still underestimate true segregation.[1] Based on Baron and Bielby's results, our estimates are probably about ten points lower than what they might have been if we observed segregation at the level of job titles.

While race segregation is somewhat lower than gender segregation, the analyses of other outcomes suggest that this largely reflects the relative rarity of black employees among private-sector EEOC-reporting workplaces. Because the degree of segregation is sensitive to group size, it may be that the lower level of race segregation than gender segregation we observe is simply a function of the small size of the black population in many communities. As we saw in chapter 1, in 1966 black men were employed in EEOC-reporting firms at about their representation in the national labor force. This was not the case for black women, who were severely underrepresented in the EEOC-reporting firms.

It is clearly the case that in 1966 the normal employment pattern was hyper-segregation of black men and black women from white men. Many black men and black women, however, would routinely interact across race and gender boundaries even in 1966, and black women and white women were the most likely to work together in the same occupational group in the same workplace. Black men and black women were severely underrepresented in desirable jobs relative to their representation in local labor markets. On the other hand, the civil rights political struggles against racial segregation were already over ten years old in 1966. Thus, the uncertainty around race generated by the civil rights movement may have already changed employer behavior by 1966. We now turn to some strategic comparisons to gauge how likely it is that EEO progress had already begun prior to 1966.

POLITICS, UNCERTAINTY, AND INITIAL SEGREGATION LEVELS

In the remainder of this chapter, we examine changes in federal and state employment politics from 1941 to 1963, paying particular attention to the development of equal employment opportunity legislation, regulatory bodies and enforcement, and the impact of changes in organizations' political and legal environments on the erosion of the near-total exclusion of black men, black women, and white women from desirable employment opportunities prior to 1966. As emphasized in the preceding chapter, although organizational change is not legislatively preordained, organizations are likely to respond to changes in their political and legal environments.

Scholars interested in the effects of Title VII on changes in employment opportunities have gauged its influence by examining rates of change in earnings inequalities, employment, and occupational advancement before and after the passage of the act. This area of research has questioned whether the changes that took place after the passage of the Civil Rights Act resulted from the act itself or had already been put in motion (see, for example, Collins 2001; Donohue and Heckman 1991; Leonard 1984a, 1989, 1990; Smith and Welch 1977, 1984). These researchers have generally discovered that progress for African Americans began prior to the Civil Rights Act, and they conclude that change was inevitable, typically because of presumed market forces, and not a result of social movement activity in general or the Civil Rights Act in particular. We think that this line of reasoning, because it focuses on law rather than uncertainty, may miss the actual mechanisms of change that are not law but rather uncertainty as to what will be deemed legitimate organizational behavior.

One problem with the research exploring the efficacy of the Civil Rights Act is that it has tended to ignore both the fact that both federal- and state-level antidiscrimination laws and mandates existed for quite some time prior to the passage of the Civil Rights Act of 1964 and that the civil rights movement had become increasingly visible after the mid-1950s, producing political pressure on elected officials as well as corporations. Overlooking these previous pressures for desegregation leads some researchers to conclude that the Civil Rights Act did not produce change because progress was observed before 1964. But the act itself was the product of a political process that had begun after World War II and accelerated through the early 1960s. Thus, there was uncertainty in the political environments of firms regarding the future of race relations in employment long before the Civil Rights Act became law.

A second problem is the way in which laws are treated by this line of research. Laws, once implemented, are assumed to exert continuous pressure for change. Laws in themselves, however, do very little. It is the uncertainty that laws introduce, the new constituencies that law mobilizes and legitimates, and the level of regulatory enforcement that promote change in organizational behavior. From our perspective, EEO progress, by its very nature, is a politically mediated process (Collins 1997). Hence, the effects of laws on organizational action are politically contingent.

Finally, this research tends to assume that organizations respond only to direct coercive pressures. In this scenario, organizations subject to additional federal pressures, such as federal contractors, are more likely to comply with EEO law and mandates. This view suggests that organizations are rationally responding to the threat of losing a government contract. Although this seems likely to be the case, organizations are probably just as likely to respond to environmental uncertainty emanating from ambiguous state and federal mandates as they are to direct coercive pressures, especially in the initial years following the passage of the Civil Rights Act when the definitions of "equal opportunity" and "compliance" were highly ambiguous. Firms may even resist EEO demands because of the possibility that these demands will mobilize resistance at both the work-group and legal levels. Anthony Chen (2009) has documented private-sector firms' long history of resistance to fair employment practice laws and to the establishment of the EEOC, further weakening any assumption that legal mandates or regulation are likely to elicit enthusiastic or even polite compliance.

Following various strands of organizational theory, our sense is that after the creation of law, organizations seek to find solutions to EEO/AA compliance in order to stabilize the regulatory environment. In other words, they seek to reduce uncertainty. Although many innovative organizational responses may take place, eventually a legitimate form of compliance emerges, other firms mimic this form, and the number of adoptees increases. The regulatory environment then reaches stability as policies, programs, practices, and offices that demonstrate regulatory compliance diffuse across organizational fields. Our basic position is that EEO change begins when enforcement of EEO laws is strong or new uncertainty enters the regulatory environment.

Although the Civil Rights Act of 1964 was important for increasing the political space to struggle for equal employment opportunities for racial minorities and women, it was not the only significant antidiscrimination mandate that had occurred since the post–Civil War Reconstruction Era. Starting in the 1940s, a series of federal mandates and state-level laws emerged that encouraged firms to provide employment opportunities for blacks, primarily black men. Women, on the other hand, received scant attention in antidiscrimination movements and legislation until the passage of the Equal Pay Act of 1963.

The primary goal of most early legislation was to increase employment opportunities for racial and ethnic minority men. Early legislative efforts arose in the 1940s in response to World War II labor shortages, and these efforts would continue through the 1970s as civil rights and liberal social movements took hold (Bloom 1987; Chen 2009; McAdam 1982). The political pressures exerted by these movements led the federal government to develop and implement antidiscrimination legislation and enforcement, not necessarily to improve racial minorities' opportunities or quality of life, but to pacify the civil rights movement (Burstein 1979, 1985; Dahl 1967; Morris 1984, 1999) and control the public image of the United States abroad during the cold war (Sitkoff 1993; Skrentny 1996). The importance of political environments for changes in race and gender inequality is illustrated in the following section through a brief historical overview of social movements, early federal and state antidiscrimination legislation, court rulings, the economy, and the political environment since the 1940s.

ANTIDISCRIMINATION POLICIES AND THE FEDERAL POLITICAL ENVIRONMENT, 1941 TO 1963

The politics of racial labor market inequality were present long before 1964. In January 1941, civil rights leader A. Philip Randolph began organizing a movement to pressure President Franklin D. Roosevelt to intervene at the federal level to improve black employment opportunities, especially among large federal contractor firms in the defense industry, as well as to integrate the U.S. military. The unresponsiveness of the Roosevelt administration led Randolph to organize a mass march on Washington to take place on July 1, 1941, if the president did not implement an antidiscrimination policy for the defense industry (Garfinkel 1969; Kesselman 1948; Reed 1980). The Roosevelt administration made numerous unsuccessful attempts to stop the march well into June, but finally, on June 25, 1941, days before the march was to take place, Roosevelt issued executive order 8802, which restricted employment discrimination on the basis of race and religion—but not gender—in the federal government and in firms and unions with government contracts.

This order created the Fair Employment Practices Committee (FEPC), which was overseen by the War Manpower Commission (WMC). The FEPC was created as a temporary wartime agency charged with receiving and processing discrimination complaints and overseeing compliance by federal agencies and defense contractors. Merl Reed (1980, 44) notes that the War Manpower Commission was chiefly concerned with "production for the war effort, [and was] indifferent and sometimes hostile to the problems of job discrimination." In the first few years, the committee held little power and received little political support, materially or rhetorically.

The FEPC became somewhat more effective in advancing black employment opportunities after its reorganization in 1943 under executive order 9346, which reconfigured the FEPC as an independent agency, removing it from the WMC's control and placing it under the control of the executive office of the president. Several historians have noted the increased capacity and efficiency of the organization after 1943 as a result of improvements in funding, which allowed the organization to set up regional offices across the country (Reed 1980; Norgren and Hill 1964; Ruchames 1953). This enhanced the FEPC's ability to monitor and investigate organizations, although it tended to focus especially on federal agencies. The federal agencies, while far from willingly compliant, were more responsive than private-sector government contractors.

Because it had no regulatory power over private-sector firms, the FEPC's method of gaining compliance from private-sector federal contracting firms was public embarrassment. This was somewhat helpful for pressuring organizations to hire African Americans. For these organizations, however, the social legitimacy imperative did not instill a desire for a positive public image as an equal opportunity employer, as it might today; rather, federal contractors were avoiding a negative public image, which might carry the accusation of impeding the war effort and hence being unpatriotic. We suspect that some racial integration occurred as an unintended consequence of organizations seeking legitimacy. This was more likely to have happened in the federal government than in the private sector, and in the private sector, to the extent that there was any pressure at all, it was directed at federal contractors.

In 1945 the war was coming to an end, wartime production was beginning to slow, and fewer defense contracts were being issued. As the wartime economy waned and black Americans were no longer needed for production, the FEPC halted compliance checks on government contractors and federal offices. Vehement opposition to the FEPC from southern Democrats in Congress and a lack of support among the vast majority of whites ensured the program's demise in 1946 (Reed 1980).

During Truman's presidency (1945 to 1953), some civil rights advances did transpire. On July 26, 1948, Truman issued executive order 9981, which called for the gradual racial integration of the U.S. military. Although this had been one of the demands from Randolph's 1941 call to march on Washington, the last all-black military unit was not disbanded until Sep-

Figure 2.5   African American Protest Events, 1948 to 1964

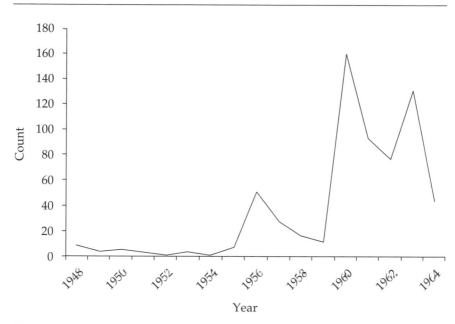

Source: Data provided by Professor Craig Jenkins as originally published in Jenkins, Jacobs, and Agnone (2003).

tember 30, 1954. At the end of the Truman administration, the Office of Government Contract Compliance, begun under Roosevelt, urged the Bureau of Employment Security to act affirmatively toward African Americans and end employment discrimination. There do not appear to have been any material consequences.

The Eisenhower administration (1953 to 1961) witnessed more fundamental challenges to the racial apartheid system in the United States. The 1950s saw an increasingly mobilized and effective movement for the civil rights of black Americans. The Supreme Court's ruling on *Brown v. Board of Education* (1954) was the turning point in terms of successful political and legal mobilization against entrenched racial segregation. Figure 2.5 visually displays the number of black protest events from 1948 to 1964. It is clear that the political pressures built rapidly after 1954.

Eisenhower reiterated Truman's call to desegregate the military. In 1953 he issued executive order 10479, which prohibited government contractors from discriminating on the basis of race or religion. Federal contractors were required to post nondiscrimination statements in their workplaces. In 1955 Eisenhower issued another executive order: executive order 10590 prohibited racial discrimination in the federal civil service. Many researchers claim that these were largely symbolic gestures to improve the negative civil rights image of the United States in Europe, Russia, and Africa (McAdam 1982; Morris 1984; Piven and Cloward 1977; Skrentny 1996), rather than reflecting real political will to end racial employment segregation.

These executive orders banning discrimination in the federal government and among federal contractors were primarily responses to social movement pressure and lacked any regulatory capacity, with the exception of a couple of years during World War II. In the Democratic Party–controlled Congress, equal opportunity legislation was met with massive resistance by southern Democrats and quiet resistance by most Republicans (Chen 2009). Similarly, *Brown v. Board of Education* (1954) was resisted in all of the South and much of the North. In 1957 Eisenhower sent one thousand Army troops to desegregate Central High School in Little Rock Arkansas. This event captured the attention of not only the U.S. public but the world. On September 24, 1957, in an internationally broadcast public speech, Eisenhower commented on the situation in Little Rock:

> In the South, as elsewhere, citizens are keenly aware of the tremendous disservice that has been done to the people of Arkansas in the eyes of the nation, and that has been done to the nation in the eyes of the world.
>
> At a time when we face grave situations abroad because of the hatred that Communism bears toward a system of government based on human rights, it would be difficult to exaggerate the harm that is being done to the prestige and influence, and indeed to the safety, of our nation and the world.
>
> Our enemies are gloating over this incident and using it everywhere to misrepresent our whole nation. We are portrayed as a violator of those standards of conduct, which the peoples of the world united to proclaim in the Charter of the United Nations. There they affirmed faith in fundamental human rights and in the dignity and worth of the human person, and they did so without distinction as to race, sex, language or religion. (Eisenhower 1957, as quoted in Lawson and Payne 1998)

Robert Burk (1984) examines the Eisenhower presidency and civil rights and claims that Eisenhower was quite reluctant to take a strong stand on civil rights issues and that the majority of his actions were symbolic and largely in the interest of fighting communism.

In 1961 President Kennedy issued executive order 10925, which was more expansive in scope than Roosevelt's executive order 8802. It required all government contractors to take "affirmative action" in hiring and promoting racial minorities. Frank Dobbin (2009) has concluded that Kennedy's executive order was different from those of the preceding three presidents. It was issued as the civil rights movement was becoming increasingly successful in capturing the sympathy of whites outside of the South and embarrassing the United States around the world. The Kennedy administration, although it did not create any regulatory capacity to support the executive order, was also signaling a stronger commitment to the civil rights of African Americans.

Surprisingly, one piece of legislation passed just prior to 1964, the Equal Pay Act of 1963, applied to "sex." The core component of the law was the idea of paying for work equally, regardless of gender, and specifically providing equal compensation to men and women who held the same job and had comparable skills and experience. Equal employment opportunity (access to jobs) was not yet on the table. Businesses were largely unsupportive of an equal pay law because they felt that the federal government should not be involved in market processes and because pay differences between men and women were seen as legitimate. Organized labor, however, was more supportive of an equal pay law because such a law would strengthen union power by precluding women's ability to undercut men's wages (Blankenship 1993). The law passed with so many exemptions that it probably applied to fewer than 5 percent of employed women.[2]

The history of repeated executive orders mandating that federal contractors employ black workers suggests that federal contractors might have shown comparatively lower levels of race segregation than other employers in 1966. On the other hand, four presidential executive orders with little or no enforcement capacity might have signaled exactly the opposite to federal contractors. That is, by the time Kennedy's executive order—the fourth in a series from four different presidents—was issued, it may have been understood by most firms as a symbolic act to which there was no need to respond. Thirty years of toothless executive orders may have produced anything but uncertainty.

Did Federal Contractors Desegregate Early?

By and large, federal contractors seem not to have desegregated early. In 1966 federal contractor firms were more likely than other EEOC-reporting workplaces to employ at least one black man or black woman (figure 2.6). Twenty-four percent of other EEOC-reporting workplaces, but only 13 percent of federal contractors, did not have a single black male employee.

Figure 2.6   Employment at Federal Contractors and Other EEOC-Reporting Firms, 1966

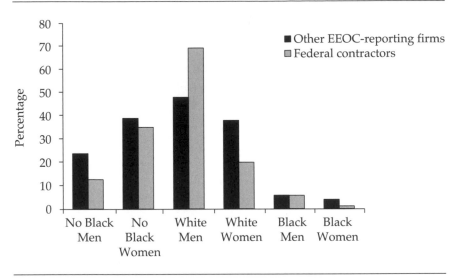

Source: Authors' calculations based on data from EEO-1 surveys (EEOC, various years).

The difference was less dramatic for black women: 35 percent of federal contractors employed no black women in 1966, which was 4 percent less than other EEOC-reporting workplaces. Hence, there is some evidence that federal contractors may have taken affirmative action, at least for black men, earlier than other firms. On the other hand, federal contractors had a much higher proportion of white male employees and a lower proportion of both white and black female employees than did other workplaces. In 1966 there was essentially no difference between federal contractors and other firms in the proportion of their workforce comprising black men. If federal contractors began hiring black men in response to Kennedy's executive order to take affirmative action, they were certainly not hiring very many.

Figure 2.7 suggests that in 1966 racial segregation at federal contractor firms was slightly lower than at other private-sector firms. Although these differences are modest for white male–black male segregation (73.1 percent versus 69.9 percent), they are about twice as large for white female–black female segregation (57.4 percent versus 50.1 percent). This pattern of lower segregation would be consistent with workplaces hiring just a few African Americans.

Figure 2.7   Segregation Levels Among Federal Contractors and Other EEOC-Reporting Firms, 1966

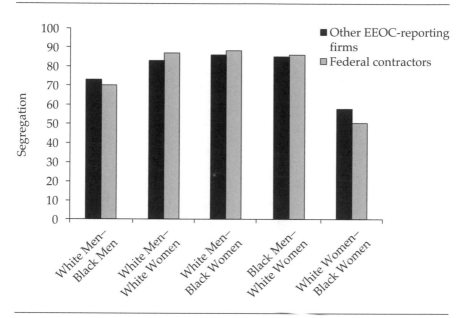

Source: Authors' calculations based on data from EEO-1 surveys (EEOC, various years).

Of course, we cannot tell from these 1966 estimates when federal contractors began to desegregate. Was it during World War II? Or was it under the Eisenhower administration as the civil rights movement became a mass movement with considerable public support? Or, as Frank Dobbin (2009) suggests, was it after President Kennedy's 1961 executive order?

At first glance, this appears to be a clear indicator of progress—an erosion of white male dominance of employment within federal contracting firms. However, a closer inspection reveals a more creative reaction of federal contractors to affirmative action mandates. Figure 2.8 reports the isolation index for contractors and noncontractors in 1966. Black men, black women, and white women are all, as one would expect in integrating workplaces, less isolated when they work for federal contractors. White men, on the other hand, are *more* isolated when working for federal contractors! This suggests that even as blacks were hired by federal contractors, presumably in response to executive orders to take affirmative ac-

Figure 2.8   Average 1966 Isolation Index Among Federal Contractors and Other EEOC-Reporting Workplaces

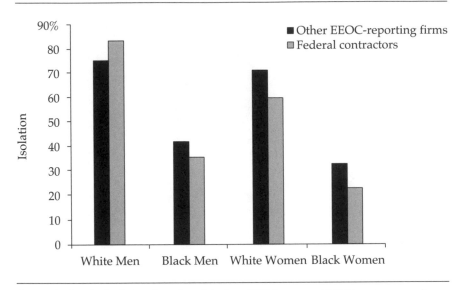

Source: Authors' calculations based on data from EEO-1 surveys (EEOC, various years).

tion, they were not hired into positions that put them in increased equal-status contact with white men.

When we examine the representation of groups in the most desirable occupations, the reason for the higher social isolation of white males among federal contractors becomes clear (table 2.5). White males' monopoly of the most skilled, most powerful, and best-paid jobs was consistently higher in federal contracting firms than in other EEOC-reporting firms. Black men, black women, and even white women were in every comparison less likely to be employed in managerial, professional, and skilled craft production jobs by federal contractors.

It is clear that federal contractors did not achieve slightly lower rates of racial segregation by integrating the most desirable jobs. Rather, some black men were hired alongside white men in operative, laborer, and service positions, and to an even greater extent black women were hired alongside white women in clerical positions. The fact that black employment was not higher among federal contractors than among other EEOC-reporting firms suggests that whatever integration was produced by the twenty years of racial politics preceding the Civil Rights Act, it was weak and left privileged white men largely untouched.

Table 2.5 Percentage Over and Under Representation in Desirable Occupations Relative to Group Composition in the Local Labor Market Among Federal Contractors and Other EEOC-Reporting Workplaces, 1966

	Managerial Representation		Professional Representation		Skilled Craft Representation	
	Other EEOC-Reporting Workplaces	Federal Contractors	Other EEOC-Reporting Workplaces	Federal Contractors	Other EEOC-Reporting Workplaces	Federal Contractors
White male	44	57	32	53	39	49
Black male	–86	–97	–90	–91	–37	–46
Black female	–93	–98	–81	–97	–81	–94
White female	–55	–88	–33	–80	–72	–90

Source: Authors' calculations based on data from EEO-1 surveys (EEOC, various years).

STATE FAIR EMPLOYMENT PRACTICE LAWS, 1941 TO 1963

Prior to the passage of the Civil Rights Act of 1964, many states reacted to the civil rights movement by passing more or less enforceable EEO legislation, collectively called fair employment practice laws (Chay 1998; Chen 2009; Collins 2000, 2001; Heckman 1976; Landes 1968; Moreno 1997). Nearly half of all U.S. states enacted laws restricting racial discrimination in employment opportunities prior to the implementation of Title VII (see figure 2.9). In 1964 these state-level laws provided formal legal protections to approximately 40 percent of black workers and practically all blacks outside of the South (Collins 2001; Moreno 1997).

With only a few exceptions, previous research on employment trends emphasizes the effects of federal civil rights legislation while ignoring the reality that, in addition to federal mandates, many states enacted potentially enforceable laws restricting racial discrimination prior to the passage of Title VII. These exceptional articles devote their attention to the pre–civil rights period of 1940 to 1960 and find that states with FEP laws provided greater employment, wage, and occupational opportunities to blacks than states without such laws (Collins 2001; Heckman 1976; Landes 1968). The oldest laws were enacted before 1950 in the Middle Atlantic states, the Northwest, and New Mexico. California, much of the industrial Midwest, Colorado, Nebraska, and Kansas adopted FEP laws between 1950 and 1964. Distinguishing between the first and second round of state laws, Anthony Chen (2009) concludes that the first-round state laws tended to be the product of a more cohesive liberal–civil rights movement coalition and so may have had a broader institutional impact on employers.

We can compare the early- and late-adopting FEP states to the non-FEP states to see whether these state-level policies are associated with lower racial segregation. To the extent that firms responded to local laws, we might expect that the earliest-adopting states would have the lowest levels of segregation in 1966, both because there had been more time to respond by 1966 and because the political coalition behind the early adopters, as Chen (2009) suggests, was broader-based. On the other hand, if real change is produced by political uncertainty, we might expect that those states that adopted FEP laws during the rise of the civil rights movement would display the lowest rates of racial employment integration because of the higher levels of mass struggle.

Figure 2.10 provides the necessary comparisons. Here we find that in 1966 race segregation was lower in FEP states and lowest in those states in which FEP laws had existed since the World War II era. Again, the pattern

Figure 2.9   Fair Employment Practice Laws and Their Adoption,
              1945 to 1964

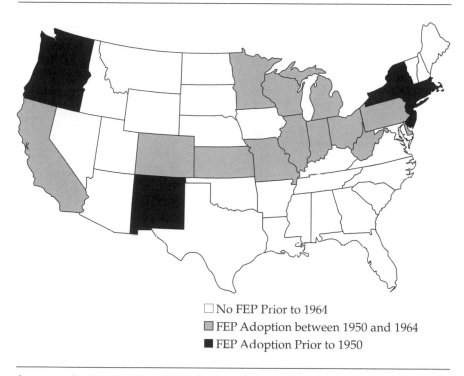

☐ No FEP Prior to 1964
▨ FEP Adoption between 1950 and 1964
■ FEP Adoption Prior to 1950

Sources: Authors' compilation of data from Landes (1968); Heckman (1976); Collins (2000).

is most dramatic for white female–black female segregation, which was 15.2 points lower in the earliest-adopting FEP states. By comparison, in 1966 white male–black male segregation was only 7.9 points lower in the early-adopting FEP states. Although the pattern for non-FEP states is similar to the segregation patterns we saw earlier for the southern region, the comparison of earlier- and later-adopting FEP states suggests that some of the higher race segregation in the South we observe in 1966 was a function of the earlier civil rights politics in the Northeast and Pacific states.

Although FEP laws seem to be associated with lower segregation, we see that, as with federal contractor status, segregation was not lowered by increasing white male exposure to other groups (figure 2.10). In 1966 white males' social isolation from intergroup contact was very high, regardless of the presence of FEP laws. The same cannot be said of the other groups.

Figure 2.10   Employment Segregation and Isolation by Fair
Employment Practice Laws, 1966

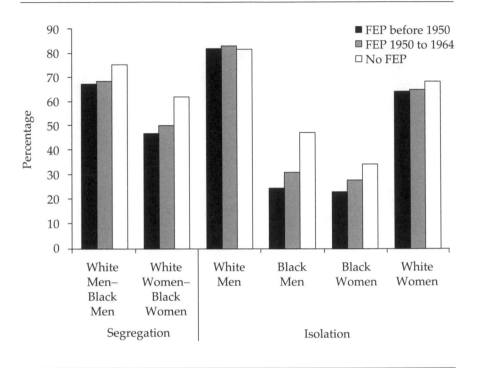

Source: Authors' calculations based on data from EEO-1 surveys (EEOC, various years).

Black male and black female isolation from other groups were higher in non-FEP states and lowest in the states that adopted FEP laws prior to 1950.

Table 2.6 examines FEP-linked variation in occupational representation relative to labor market participation in the best-quality jobs. White males' privileged access to managerial, professional, and skilled craft positions, while still substantial, was 6 to 7 percent lower in the post-1950 FEP states than in those with no FEP laws at all. That this was the case during the more recent FEP era suggests that legal change during a period of social movement activity may have led to some erosion of white males' monopolies over the very best jobs.[3] This result is in contrast to the data on federal contractors, among whom integration did not challenge white males' control over the best employment opportunities. Earlier FEP laws did not substantively undermine white males' privileged access to the best jobs, at least compared to their access in states without FEP laws. Unfortunately,

Table 2.6 Representation in Good Jobs Relative to the Local Labor Supply in Workplaces in States with and without Fair Employment Practice Laws, 1966

	Managerial Representation			Professional Representation			Skilled Craft Representation		
	FEP Before 1950	FEP 1950 to 1964	No FEP	FEP Before 1950	FEP 1950 to 1964	No FEP	FEP Before 1950	FEP 1950 to 1964	No FEP
White male	55%	49%	56%	46%	43%	49%	44%	39%	46%
Black male	–92	–87	–91	–83	–91	–94	–2	–31	–32
Black female	–94	–96	–94	–84	–92	–91	–82	–85	–87
White female	–74	–73	–75	–61	–60	–64	–81	–84	–83

Source: Authors' calculations based on data from EEO-1 surveys (EEOC, various years).

because the data do not exist, we cannot make over-time comparisons prior to 1966 within states.

In 1966 black males were faring best in the early-adopting FEP states. In fact, they approached labor market parity in skilled craft production jobs in states with World War II–era fair employment practice laws. FEP laws do not appear to have helped black women gain access to managerial jobs prior to 1966, although their professional and craft representation was somewhat higher in early-adopting states. White female representation did not vary by FEP status—as it should not, because all of these laws targeted racial (and religious) employment fairness. Hence, there is some evidence that FEP laws may have decreased segregation and increased the quality of employment opportunities for black men and black women. There is even some indication that white men in states that adopted FEP laws during the initial phases of the civil rights movement may have actually experienced some limits on their near-total control over the best jobs.

That state FEP laws were more effective than federal mandates on government contractors makes sense to us. In FEP states the state legislature actually had to pass antidiscrimination laws, and employers no doubt feared that regulation might follow, because support had been broad-based enough to prevail in the legislative arena. Until the 1964 Civil Rights Act, only halfhearted executive orders had been issued to produce symbolic affirmation of equal opportunity. The exception may have been Kennedy's 1961 executive order, which seemed to be backed by a higher level of political commitment and a civil rights movement that clearly was not giving up easily.

DID KENNEDY'S 1961 EXECUTIVE ORDER MAKE A DIFFERENCE?

We have been examining variation in segregation along the two dimensions most often identified by prior scholars as early sources of equal employment opportunity. In general, we are skeptical of accounts that suggest a strong influence of FEP laws or of presidential executive orders to federal contractors to practice affirmative action in the hiring and promotion of blacks. Our skepticism arises from the weakness of the enforcement authority involved in both sets of regulatory efforts. That FEP laws seem to have been more effective comes somewhat as a surprise to us. We suspect that there were sources of uncertainty in these state environments that did not exist in the context of federal contractors.

Frank Dobbin (2009), whose prior work is associated with a profound skepticism of the efficacy of equal opportunity law, has recently suggested that, for the largest federal contractors, Kennedy's 1961 executive order that federal contractors take affirmative action in the hiring of minorities produced real change. Although Dobbin does not directly observe shifts in employment composition, he does thoroughly document a shift in the public behavior of large federal contractors after the executive order was issued. In his account, Kennedy's affirmative action order was different from earlier executive orders for two reasons. First, the Kennedy administration was more firmly committed to racial equality than previous administrations, and the leading contractor firms responded by demonstrating good-faith efforts to recruit black workers, including managers, in order to forestall direct regulation. In addition, the 1960s were different from the 1940s and 1950s in that protests in support of the civil and economic rights of blacks had grown in intensity and garnered increased support among whites. Private-sector firms were also directly targeted for protest by civil rights activists (Collins 1997). Dobbin does not suggest that movement among contractors toward a new, more open model for hiring black workers was immediate or universal. On the contrary, his work suggests that it was diffused among federal contractors, beginning with the largest.

Kennedy's executive order did not explicitly outline how compliance would be judged, but it did create a committee of government and private-sector leaders to oversee the order. One subcommittee, called Plans for Progress (PFP), is singled out in Dobbin's account as particularly influential in both recruiting voluntary compliance among federal contractors and helping to diffuse new recruitment and hiring practices to increase black employment. Lockheed Aircraft's plant in Marietta, Georgia, is identified as the first mover in 1961: Lockheed desegregated its massive Marietta airplane plant in order to protect an equally massive new federal contract to purchase airplanes. To signal its compliance with the executive order, Lockheed created a nondiscrimination policy, began recruiting employees at black high schools and colleges, pledged to train blacks for supervisory positions, and ended the union-enforced exclusion of blacks from apprenticeships for skilled craft jobs.

It was this basic recipe that became the model for the Plans for Progress committee. By July 1961, eight major defense contractors in addition to Lockheed Aircraft had signed on to this plan: Western Electric, Boeing, Douglas Aircraft, General Electric, Martin Marietta, North American Aviation, RCA, and United Aircraft (Dobbin 2009, 46). By the end of 1961, the plan had been generalized from the largest defense contractors to all of the fifty largest federal contractors (Braestrup 1961). By 1962, there were eighty-five PFP firms, and that figure skyrocketed to over three hundred by 1965. Newspaper reports suggested that by 1963 PFP firms were hiring ten times the number of blacks they had hired in 1960 and that up to 25

Figure 2.11   Employment Segregation and Isolation for Plans for
Progress Firms Compared to All Federal Contractors and
EEOC-Reporting Workplaces, 1966

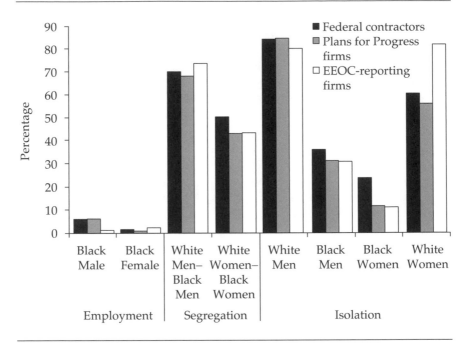

Source: Authors' calculations based on data from EEO-1 surveys (EEOC, various years).

percent of all new hires in PFP firms in 1963 were black (Dobbin 2009, 49). These were impressive claims, made via the newspapers by Robert Troutman, the director of the PFP initiative, but as far as we can see, these claims have never been verified independently. We turn here to an analysis of the largest federal contractors in 1966 to see if we can find evidence of the dramatic progress claimed at the time.

In figure 2.11, we provide 1966 employment segregation and isolation estimates for Plans for Progress firms compared to all federal contractors and to other large firms that were not federal contractors. PFP firms employed slightly more black men than other federal contractors, as well as slightly fewer black women than other federal contractors and substantially fewer than noncontractors. In 1966, among the PFP firms, white male–black male segregation was two points lower than it was for all federal contractors and five points lower than for other large EEOC-reporting firms. Race segregation among women was similarly low in both PFP firms and large EEOC-reporting firms. Hence, there is only weak evidence of PFP firms hiring more African American men, and no evidence that they hired more African American women. Segregation between white men and African American men was marginally lower, however, in PFP firms. There is no evidence that white men were less isolated in PFP firms, so if these firms were actually trying to hire and integrate black men, they did it with very little cost to white men. In terms of isolation, white women stand out in PFP firms for their much lower levels of isolation than in large EEOC-reporting firms or federal contractors in general. We also examined representation in good jobs, and here again, PFP firms were either no different from other firms or in some cases worse.

By 1966, at large federal contractors that had voluntarily joined Plans for Progress, men were marginally less race-segregated than in other firms. Of course, segregation at federal contractors may have been worse than among their peers in 1961, when Dobbin documents the change in corporate personnel practices among these firms. In this case, what appears to be a slightly lower level of race segregation among men and no difference among women might reflect more rapid progress from an initially more highly segregated workforce. On the other hand, the strong reaction of these firms to Kennedy's executive order might have been merely symbolic posturing to forestall regulation and manage public relations. We may never know unless companies have internal records from that period that they might now be willing to share. In the next chapter, we examine the post-1966 trajectories of the Plans for Progress firms.[4]

Although we know that President Kennedy's 1961 executive order prompted large federal contractors to create affirmative action plans and affirm equal opportunity policies, there is no good evidence that by 1966 these early steps had produced lower levels of segregation than prevailed at other firms. This may be because they were much worse than other firms to begin with, or because Plans for Progress was a largely symbolic enterprise.

IMPLICATIONS

In 1966 most private-sector workplaces were hyper-segregated along the lines of both race and gender. White men were disproportionally employed in the most powerful, prestigious, and skilled jobs. As a result, white men almost exclusively worked with other white men in equal-status jobs in the same workplace. While both were very high, gender segregation was consistently higher than race segregation in 1966. This is not surprising considering that the civil rights movement had already been active since World War II, state-level laws outlawing racial discrimination had been enacted, and numerous presidential executive orders banning discrimination had been issued. Providing legal protection to women, on the other hand, was not a government priority, and in 1966 there was no social movement around women's rights to put pressure on corporations. The overwhelming pattern was of high segregation regardless of geographic region, industrial sector, or firm governance status. The exceptions to this pattern were few: all forms of segregation were noticeably lower in the retail trade and social service sectors, gender segregation was more extreme in mining and construction, and race segregation was marginally higher in the South, especially in the West South Central states (Texas, Missouri, Oklahoma, and Arkansas).

These data precluded us from observing change in segregation before 1966. However, we did compare federal contractors, firms in states that adopted fair employment practice laws prior to the Civil Rights Act, and the original Plans for Progress firms, reasoning that if such change had occurred, it would most likely have started in firms in those contexts.

We found that race segregation was lower in FEP states and among federal contractors, especially among women, but we also found that this integration did not reduce the social isolation of white male employees from contact with nonwhites and women. There is some evidence that in states that had adopted FEP laws prior to 1950 black men gained a higher level of access to managerial, professional, and craft jobs than in non-FEP states. Among federal contractors, white male monopolies of managerial, professional, and skilled craft jobs were actually more extreme than in other EEOC-reporting private-sector workplaces. The contrast between FEP states where equal opportunity mandates were successfully legislated and the response of federal contractors to executive orders that were primarily symbolic suggests that symbolic changes in the absence of a real political threat produced limited change in organizational behavior.

Dobbin (2009) shows that after 1961 the largest federal contractors publicly embraced affirmative action and the equal opportunity policies stemming from the Plans for Progress initiative. There is little evidence, however, that by 1966 PFP firms were less segregated than smaller federal contractors or other large firms. Of course, if they were more segregated to begin with, any progress that they had made since 1961 would not be visible in the 1966 estimates. On the other hand, they may have simply been good at public relations.

In the next chapter, we turn to desegregation trends between 1966 and 1972. This is the period of maximum uncertainty around law, regulatory enforcement, and racial segregation for these firms. At this historical moment, racial protest on the streets of U.S. cities had accelerated and employers had become aware that racial segregation was both illegal and likely to be policed. They were not at all sure, however, how compliance would be judged, because neither the Equal Employment Opportunity Commission nor the Office of Federal Contract Compliance Programs had established any case law or issued any regulatory positions.

Chapter 3 | The Era of Uncertainty, 1966 to 1972

IN 1966 WORKPLACES were extremely segregated by race and gender. We suspect that there had already been some minor declines in race segregation as a reaction to the civil rights movement, the passage of fair employment practice laws in many northern and western states, and President Kennedy's 1961 executive order admonishing federal contractors take affirmative action in the hiring of African Americans. We now examine changes in the political landscape as well as in corporate employment practices between 1964 and 1972. How did private-sector employers respond to the changing contours of the political and legal landscape following the passage of the Civil Rights Act of 1964?

The Equal Employment Opportunity Commission was created to monitor progress toward an equal employment opportunity economy. The EEO-1 forms that private-sector firms have been submitting to the EEOC since 1966 are ideal for this purpose: they provide population-level coverage of workplace employment distributions by race and gender.[1] In this regard, they are akin to a census of federal contractors with more than twenty-five employees and other workplaces that are not federal contractors and have more than fifty employees. Although this amounts to only about half of all private-sector employment, it is the half of the economy populated by all of the large and medium-size corporations that were the primary targets of the expanding regulatory enforcement efforts.

The 1966 to 1972 period is one of maximum uncertainty around racial integration. On the one hand, employers were certain that the law had changed and that there was substantial political pressure on them to incorporate black workers into their firms. On the other hand, they had no clear idea as to what behaviors would be acceptable to regulators and the courts. They also faced internal resistance from their current workforces, as well as the inertia of past practice, and no doubt they were asking themselves: How many black workers would be enough? How many black employees would satisfy the EEOC, the OFCCP, and the courts when they began to examine corporate employment practices? Because of the deep-seated cultural reality of race relations in the United States, employers were also deeply concerned that hiring too many blacks might produce a backlash among their current workforces and disrupt production.

Because the law was vague as to how desegregation should be accomplished and no regulatory guidance or court rulings had emerged yet to clarify what was expected under the law, firms were aware that they should do something, but not what. They certainly did not know what was sufficient to inoculate themselves against regulatory or social movement intrusions on their business practices. Resistance, on the other hand, was predictable and local. The resulting uncertainty made this period from the late 1960s to the early 1970s the worst time to look like a racist firm even as it remained a time when most employees knew, and many white employees expected, that racial segregation was the normal course of affairs. Moreover, no one was quite sure what a nonracist firm looked like. If uncertainty is an important motivator of innovation in equal employment opportunity (EEO) practice, we should expect to see widespread, but contained, desegregation during this early period, despite the lack of regulatory guidelines or enforcement.

For gender discrimination, this was not a period of uncertainty, at least not at so high a level. As we saw in the previous chapter, all social movement activities and the resulting changes in law were targeted at race. As we will see shortly, the leaders of the newly established regulatory agencies (EEOC and the Office of Federal Contract Compliance [OFCC]) made clear that they saw their jobs as promoting racial progress, but not progress for women. Although the Civil Rights Act made employment discrimination on the basis of "sex" illegal, it was not until later that corporations and the courts began to take EEO progress for women seriously. Hence, this period is one in which the law was the same for race and gender, but uncertainty as to the proper corporate response was high only for race. In fact, although gender discrimination in employment was now illegal, newspapers continued posting separate "help wanted" columns for women and men (Pedriana and Abraham 2006). The Supreme Court did not rule this practice illegal until 1973.

As we have already seen, the passage of the Civil Rights Act of 1964 extended equal nondiscriminatory access to employment to previously excluded groups and created the Equal Employment Opportunity Commission to monitor EEO progress in private-sector U.S. firms. Shortly thereafter, the Johnson administration issued executive order 11246 establishing the Office of Federal Contract Compliance (later the Office of Federal Contract Compliance Programs, or OFCCP) to monitor and enforce

EEO in firms with federal government contracts. Similar to executive orders issued by previous presidents, 11246 required federal contractors to "take affirmative action" in the hiring and promotion of racial minorities. In another signal that women's rights were not yet on the EEO agenda, affirmative action among federal contractors did not apply to women's employment opportunities until a subsequent executive order was issued in 1967.

It was not until 1968 that the OFCCP notified government contractors and subcontractors that they needed to develop and maintain annual affirmative action reports with employment goals, plans, timetables, and progress reports for achievement. Importantly, these reports were not to be submitted to regulators but were to be stored by the firm in case the OFCCP chose to conduct a compliance review. Federal contractors potentially faced penalties for noncompliance, including the loss of federal contracts and possible debarment from future federal contracts. But even here, contractors were assured that this would happen only if a discernible pattern of noncompliance could be detected over time. Compliance was not defined, and so the strong signal to federal contractors was that they should keep records and develop plans and then regulators might someday ask to see them and evaluate them on the basis of an ill-defined "progress" metric. In the late 1960s, federal contractors had to imagine what a compliance review might entail and what penalties might actually be applied.

Despite the vagueness of these regulatory requirements, past research suggests that federal contractors were responsive to EEO/AA laws, especially those that experienced compliance reviews (Leonard 1984a, 1984b). As we will see later in this chapter, race segregation among men did decline rapidly at federal contractors during this post-1964 period of regulatory uncertainty.

The EEOC was created as an independent regulatory agency in 1964, and much like the Fair Employment Practices Committee created in the early 1940s, it has always been influenced in its policies and enforcement philosophy by the political environment. Political processes, of course, influence the regulatory capacity of all U.S. executive branch agencies charged with monitoring and enforcing legislation. For the EEOC, political influence emanates not only from the general political environment but also from negotiations over budget allocations and leadership. Although the EEOC is officially a nonpartisan agency, changing presidential administrations and their orientation toward equal opportunity law and goals have over time deeply influenced the effectiveness of the EEOC as the chief antidiscrimination enforcement agency. Importantly, the top administrators dictating the EEOC's enforcement and litigation philosophies are presidential nominees, and they serve at the pleasure of the administration (Boris and Honey 1988; Wood 1990). Historically, the appointees' enforcement philosophies have mirrored the presidential administration's position on EEO/AA law. The same is true, of course, for the OFCCP.

Although presidential influence affects the regulatory orientations of these organizations, the EEO narrative is not shaped by presidential tenure alone. It is the relative power of the presidential administration vis-à-vis both Congress and the courts that ultimately shapes the trajectories of the EEO patterns we document. Prior to 1972, the EEOC's power was largely limited to collecting data and issuing symbolic statements. It was only after 1972 that Congress granted the EEOC the power to file lawsuits and their coercive power over corporate EEO behavior was strengthened. On the other hand, the EEOC was born as an activist agency with significant political and social movement support for advancing the employment opportunities of African American men.[2]

Next, we provide a brief review of the historical record concerning politics and race and gender workplace inequality in the immediate post–Civil Rights Act era. This chapter highlights changes in equal employment opportunity during a significant historical period following the passage of the Civil Rights Act of 1964. We first foreground important changes in the political and legal environments confronting private-sector employers, then present an analysis of the trends in organizational behavior from 1966 to 1972.

POLITICAL PARTIES AND THE POLITICS OF RACE AND GENDER IN THE POST-1963 PERIOD

Historically, the Republican Party, the party of Lincoln, was more supportive of civil rights than the Democratic Party, the party of the segregated South. The civil rights protests and political events occurring from the 1940s through 1960 led to a public convergence of Republican and non-South Democratic ideologies concerning civil rights issues. Issues of race relations were at the center of the 1960 presidential election between John Kennedy and Richard Nixon, but both candidates espoused positive rhetoric concerning the advancement of civil rights in the United States. The cold war had made America's racial apartheid system embarrassing to both parties. In the House, 80 percent of Republicans, but only 63 percent of Democrats, voted for the Civil Rights Act. The Senate was similar, with 82 percent of Republicans and 69 percent of Democrats supporting the measure. Practically all of the opposition to the Civil Rights Act came from southern congressmen of both parties.[3]

The post–Civil Rights Act period led to a sharp break in the historical narrative regarding the relationship between political parties and support for civil rights (Carmines and Stimson 1989). President Lyndon Johnson maintained a pro–civil rights rhetoric and publicly asserted that the federal government should intervene in matters of racial inequality, such as the desegregation of public schools. His opponent in the 1964 presidential race, Barry Goldwater, in a break from past Republican stances, rejected the use of federal force to promote racial desegregation. Senator Goldwater voted against the Civil Rights Act of 1964, stating that the act violated the appropriate reach of the federal government. His staunch states' rights approach to civil rights issues gained him a large following in the South and led to a gradual power shift in southern politics away from the Democratic Party to the Republican Party.

Goldwater was, at the time, considered too conservative for most Americans, and Johnson won the election, taking over 60 percent of the popular vote. Goldwater, however, won his native state of Arizona and the five Deep South states. These previously solidly Democratic states had not voted Republican since the Reconstruction Era after the Civil War. This began a strong shift in the ideological position of Republicans; the ushering in of a neoconservative, racially intolerant rhetoric for the party also led to the end of Democratic Party dominance in the South among white voters. This shift will become important in subsequent chapters when we see that both parties became keenly competitive over the votes of white women and white men.

During the Johnson presidency (1963 to 1969), the executive and legislative branches of government maintained a strong public commitment to civil rights advancement, spurring the most active round of legislative activity in U.S. history. A host of legislation and executive orders were passed and issued concerning civil, voting, and housing rights for African Americans (for example, the Civil Rights Act of 1964, the Voting Rights Act of 1965, and the Fair Housing Act of 1968). Title VII of the Civil Rights Act of 1964 outlawed employment discrimination on the basis of race, color, religion, sex, and national origin in hiring, promotion, and compensation practices.

Paradoxically, the inclusion of "sex" as a distinction protected from employment discrimination was not a commitment to extend rights to women but rather was a failed tactic employed by southern Democrats to thwart the passage of the Civil Rights Act (Bryner 1981; Burstein 1985). Contemporary accounts document that the mere suggestion of including "women" as a protected category in proposed legislation invoked laughter from members of Congress (Deitch 1993). Because supporters of the initial legislation were not supportive of the inclusion of "sex" in the law, opponents attempted to prevent its passage by including "sex" in the proposed legislation, claiming that, without it, "white, Christian women would be treated unfairly" (Deitch 1993, 190). Others note that the opponents of the act were concerned that the addition of "sex" "would have far-reaching implications for the place of women in society" (Morris 1999, 528). Ironically, as we will see later in this book, the clearest beneficiaries in terms of employment from the Civil Rights Act have turned out to be white women.

Although discrimination on the basis of "sex" was now illegal, women were not the intended targets of the initial legislation and subsequent enforcement was largely directed toward increasing opportunities for minority men. The inclusion of women in the Civil Rights Act of 1964 provided the prerequisites for the women's movement that would emerge in the late 1960s and flourish during the 1970s. The unintended consequences of the addition of "sex" to the act provided the political context that allowed women to later make legitimate claims on a variety of equality issues. But in the mid-1960s, gender equality was not on the agenda of either party. The women's movement would not develop the capacity to demand EEO change until the early 1970s.

THE POWER OF UNCERTAINTY

By the late 1960s, although the EEOC and OFCCP were the primary regulatory agencies, the responsibility of EEO/AA enforcement fell to more than twenty different federal agencies. These agencies often had overlapping regulatory functions, but interestingly, they also had different views on what constituted legal compliance and what signaled EEO violations. We suspect that the welter of agencies, born as a reaction to the civil rights movement and often staffed by people from that movement, was a confusing threat to most large corporations, particularly since neither the corporations nor these new regulators had a clear sense of what constituted nondiscrimination or equal opportunity. During these early years, employer behavior could be deemed compliant by the EEOC and noncompliant by the OFCCP (Bryner 1981), which probably produced great uncertainty within firms as to how far they needed to go to demonstrate compliance. Blumrosen (1993) describes the movement from legislation to regulatory implementation as the "law transmission system." We see the period after 1964 and before 1972 as the moment when this system was still very much in flux and employers were left to their own devices in defining compliance.

Upon its creation, the EEOC was given neither legal nor rule-writing powers. Instead, it was intended to be a bureaucratic apparatus for collecting data, providing guidelines for firm behavior, and accepting discrimination complaints, though it lacked the power to sue or to impose sanctions on employers in violation of EEOC guidelines. If an employer did not willingly comply with EEOC guidelines, the only recourse for the aggrieved party was to initiate a private lawsuit. Considering the weakness of regulatory agencies, it seems unlikely that the federal government was successful in coercing progressive change in employer behavior through either legal or administrative threat.

Although numerous scholars have commented on the federal government's inability to discipline employers in order to bring about equal employment opportunity during these early years, coercion is not the only force that prompts organizations to act; uncertainty can also be a driving force for change. The years from 1964 to 1972 witnessed the initiation of what would eventually become landmark private lawsuits, EEOC negotiations with companies, and the requirement that employers maintain and submit annual governmental reports; it was also a time that witnessed some of the highest levels of public support for EEO measures. At the same time, social movement pressure for African Americans' economic and civil rights was still high. These factors may have led some organizations to demonstrate good faith by adopting EEOC guidelines, experimenting with them, or perhaps even seeking to define regulatory compliance. And their experimentation may have led organizations to alter the race and gender composition of their workforces.

Nicholas Pedriana and Robin Stryker (2004) have suggested that the EEOC was effective during this historical moment despite its "weakness." They contend that while the EEOC did not have the organizational capacity to coerce change, at least not in the traditional sense, it was able to develop capacity through "broad statutory construction," which resulted in part from social movement pressures. Blumrosen (1970) describes the importance of activists within the EEOC to interpret the EEOC mandate as broadly as administratively possible. In effect, while the EEOC had little coercive power to bring about intended social change, its power came from issuing guidelines regarding what constituted discriminatory behavior; these guidelines were essentially seen as law in the eyes of both firms and eventually the courts. In this sense, the creation of guidelines and their interpretation in the courts helped to constitute the normative environment of organizations. This perspective is consistent with institutionalist claims that the state can be "administratively weak yet normatively strong" (Dobbin and Sutton 1998).

Women were not a priority of EEO/AA enforcement strategies. On November 23, 1965, a *Wall Street Journal* article on the EEOC's new guidelines with respect to job gender discrimination clearly revealed the commission's apathetic response to gender discrimination. According to the article, "Franklin D. Roosevelt, Jr., commission chairman, talking about sex segregation said he didn't believe the guidelines 'will cause a revolution in job patterns.' . . . He emphasized that the commission will be occupied primarily with problems of race discrimination." The EEOC's 1965 guidelines explicitly stated that "the commission does not believe that Congress intended to disturb such laws and regulations which are intended to, and have the effect of, protecting women against exploitation and hazard" (John Herbers, "New Guidelines on Job Sex Discrimination," *Wall Street Journal*, November 23, 1965). During the 1966 to 1972 period, the enforcement of gender antidiscrimination measures was portrayed as especially problematic. EEOC executives showed great ambivalence concerning exactly how the EEOC would process "sex" discrimination claims. Franklin D. Roosevelt Jr., the first EEOC chair, was optimistic about reducing racial discrimination, but when a reporter asked, "What about sex?" Mr. Roosevelt replied with a laugh, "I'm all for it" (John Herbers, "Bans on Job Bias Effective Today," *New York Times*, July 2, 1965). In Blumrosen's (1970) description of the initial formation of the EEOC internal agenda, any mention of gender discrimination is conspicuously absent.

The EEOC's lack of response to gender discrimination was partially responsible for the creation of the National Organization for Women (NOW) in 1966 (Brauer 1983; Harrison 1988). One specific goal of NOW was to eliminate separate help-wanted advertisements for women and men—a clear violation of equal opportunity law under the Civil Rights Act, but still standard practice in most U.S. newspapers. The EEOC had declared racial criteria in job advertisements to be in violation of Title VII, but had exempted "sex"-segregated advertisements, stating that maintaining separate male and female job columns was for the "convenience of the reader . . . because some occupations are considered more attractive to persons of one sex than the other" (John Herbers, "Help Wanted: Picking the Sex for the Job," *New York Times*, September 28, 1965).

The National Organization for Women filed a formal petition with the EEOC to outlaw separate job advertisements for women and men. With continued pressure from NOW, the EEOC reversed its earlier position and in 1968 issued guidelines stating that sex-segregated job columns were in violation of Title VII. The Supreme Court upheld the EEOC guidelines in 1973, and newspapers finally discontinued sex-segregated job advertisements ten years after the Civil Rights Act had made them clearly illegal (Pedriana and Abraham 2006).

The OFCCP was equally reluctant to enforce sex discrimination provisions among federal contracting firms. In fact, sex was omitted from the 1965 executive order (11246) requiring federal contractors to take affirmative action (although it was added through an amended executive order

[11375] issued in October 1967). The Labor Department, which houses the OFCCP, did not issue guidelines prohibiting sex discrimination in federal contracting firms until June 1970. Furthermore, the federal government's coercive pressures on federal contractors to address sex discrimination did not begin until 1972, after the secretary of labor, James D. Hodgson, issued an order stating that federal contractors that continued to underutilize women would face the possibility of losing contracts and possible debarment ("U.S. Bids Contractors End Sex Discrimination," *New York Times*, December 3, 1971).

EQUAL EMPLOYMENT OPPORTUNITY, 1966 TO 1972

The historical record suggests that uncertainty as to what qualified as a nondiscriminatory workplace was high and legal enforcement was low in the period initially following the Civil Rights Act. Importantly, this uncertainty surrounded the employment of African Americans. Although "sex" was now a legally protected category, the nascent regulators denied its importance, and the law existed without federal or social movement political pressure to motivate changes in managerial behavior toward women. So what happened?

Workplace Integration

By 1966, firms had already had a few years to respond to the uncertainty produced by the civil rights movement, including Kennedy's 1961 executive order to federal contractors to take affirmative action. It was only two years after passage of the Civil Rights Act, so little time had passed. By 1972, the period of uncertainty was over and it had begun to become clear what compliance with the new equal opportunity mandates might look like.

We begin by examining the incidence of complete exclusion. Figure 3.1 shows the percentage of workplaces with no white men, no white women, no black men, and no black women. In 1966 there were almost no firms that employed no white men or white women, and not surprisingly, this remained the case in 1972.

The percentage of EEOC-reporting workplaces with no black men dropped only slightly, from 16.8 to 15.1 percent. This suggests that much of the initial hiring of black men to desegregate workplaces had already happened by 1966, when data collection by the Equal Employment Opportuity Commission began. The story for black women is quite different.

Figure 3.1   Workplaces with No White Men, White Women, Black Men, or Black Women, 1966 to 1972

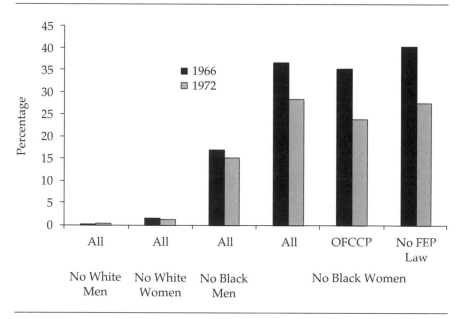

Source: Authors' calculations based on data from EEO-1 surveys (EEOC, various years).

In 1966, 36.5 percent of EEOC-reporting workplaces had no black female employees. This dropped to 28.2 percent by 1972.

Among federal contractors, the integration of black women into the workplace was even more dramatic, with workplaces dropping from 35.1 to 23.7 percent with no black women employees. Most dramatic of all was the change in the states that had no fair employment practice laws, mostly in the South, where the integration of black women across workplaces grew very rapidly. In 1966 these states that had previously resisted the enactment of equal oportunity law had much higher incidences of total black female exclusion, but by 1972 the proportion of workplaces with no black women employees had dropped to about the national average.

When we look at absolute employment growth, we see dramatic employment composition shifts. EEOC-reporting workplaces added nearly 6.3 million jobs to the U.S. economy between 1966 and 1972. During this period, white men dropped from 62 to 55 percent of total EEOC-reporting employment. At the same time, both relatively and absolutely the employment of white women, black men, and especially black women surged.

Figure 3.2   Observed, Expected, and Net Employment Gains in
             EEOC-Reporting Workplaces, 1966 to 1972

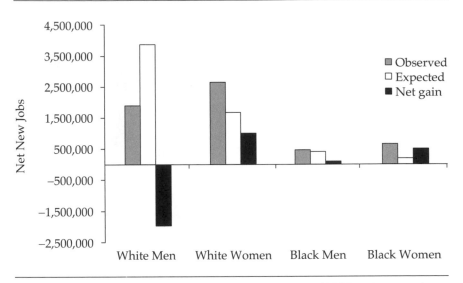

Source: Authors' calculations based on data from EEO-1 surveys (EEOC, various years).

Absolute white male employment grew by 13.7 percent—in contrast to white women's employment, which grew by 44.2 percent, and black men's, which grew by 31.6 percent. Most strikingly, black women's employment in EEOC-reporting workplaces grew 108 percent from 1966 to 1972. With 606,000 new jobs, black women still accounted for only 4.1 percent of total employment in 1972, but this was an enormous increase in black women's employment compared to 1966 levels (2.5 percent).

Figure 3.2 displays the employment shift from 1966 to 1972, decomposing shifts that were a function of the change in group employment share rather than simple growth. Because total employment grew by 6.3 million jobs, we expect job growth for all groups. But white male employment growth lagged considerably behind the growth in overall employment. If white men had maintained their 1966 share of total employment in 1972 in EEOC-reporting firms, they would have held 1.9 million more jobs than they actually did. On the other hand, employment opportunities expanded in EEOC-reporting firms for white women (nearly 1 million net new jobs), black men (500,000), and black women (450,000). Some of the growth in white women's employment represented their growing labor force participation during this period.

Employment shifts differed between federal contractors and other

Figure 3.3   Employment Growth in EEOC-Reporting Workplaces, 1966 to 1972

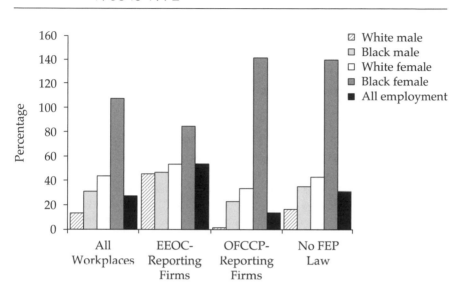

Source: Authors' calculations based on data from EEO-1 surveys (EEOC, various years).

firms and between states with and without FEP laws. Figure 3.3 compares the percentage change in employment from 1966 to 1972 for all employees and for our comparison groups. Overall employment among noncontractors surged (by 53 percent), but grew more slowly among contractors (up by 14%). Employment in the non-FEP states also grew a bit faster (32 percent) than the national average (28 percent).

Clearly, black female employment grew strongly in all comparisons, but it was among federal contractors and in the non-FEP, primarily southern states that black women saw the most dramatic gains. Conversely, white women and black men made the most dramatic gains among firms without federal contracts. We assume that black male hiring in the South and among federal contractors had already been taking place prior to the passage of the Civil Rights Act. We also suspect that the new uncertainty around gender prompted both federal contractors and southern employers to extend the notion of race-based affirmative action to black women.

At the level of workplace integration, we can see that black women made the most dramatic gains, and these gains were particularly strong among federal contractors and in the South. Black men and white women made gains that were stronger than secular employment growth in firms without federal contracts. Because the Civil Rights Act was the first legal shift to extend employment rights to women and minorities in private firms without federal contracts, it appears that these firms began by hiring more black men and white women than they had historically. Although their job growth was not as dramatic, black males, similar to black females, were hired in increased numbers in the non-FEP states.

OCCUPATIONAL INTEGRATION

Of course, hiring black men, black women, and white women in increased numbers is not the same thing as equal opportunity. Employers primarily hired these new employees into lower-status and segregated jobs. If we focus first on working-class jobs, we can see that both black men and white men experienced absolute declines in laborer jobs, even as they were replaced by white women and black women (figure 3.4). Conversely, both black men and white men made substantial gains in skilled craft jobs. White men, white women, and black women all experienced strong employment growth in service occupations, although black men did not. White women and black women saw particularly strong employment

Figure 3.4   Employment Growth in Working-Class Jobs, 1966 to 1972

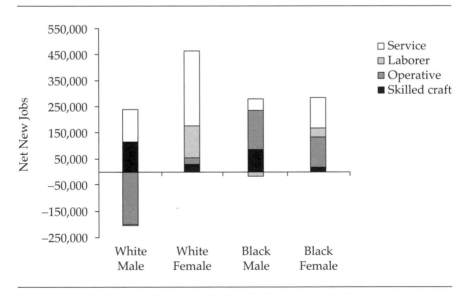

Source: Authors' calculations based on data from EEO-1 surveys (EEOC, various years).

Figure 3.5   Employment Growth in Other White-Collar Jobs,
1966 to 1972

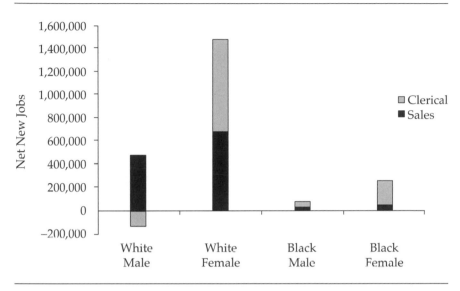

Source: Authors' calculations based on data from EEO-1 surveys (EEOC, various years).

growth within operative occupations. The dominant pattern is that white working-class men in semiskilled production jobs were replaced by white women, black men, and black women. While white men were hired into an additional 115,000 craft production jobs between 1966 and 1972, they lost almost 200,000 operative jobs during this period. Although this means that there was a clear upgrading of white men's employment, at least for working-class jobs, some white men were clearly displaced by the employment shifts that happened in response to the Civil Rights Act.

Among lower-level white-collar jobs, white women and black women also made strong employment gains (figure 3.5). This was particularly true for clerical positions, which grew quite rapidly. Black men made only modest absolute inroads into clerical or sales jobs during this initial period, although they made strong relative gains. This is not surprising because they were almost totally excluded from both occupations in 1966. Black men's and black women's gains for both occupations were particularly strong in the South. Black women were hired at dramatically increased rates in clerical and sales occupations among federal contractors. White men, however, experienced absolute declines in clerical employment as these jobs were further feminized.

When we turn to the most desirable white-collar jobs, the basic story of

Figure 3.6   Employment Growth in High-Skilled White-Collar Jobs, 1966 to 1972

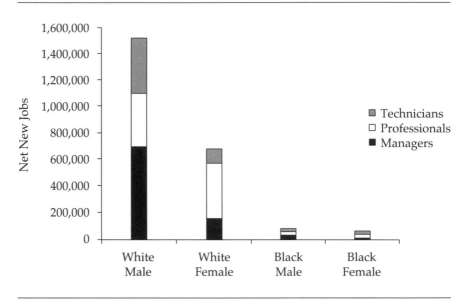

Source: Authors' calculations based on data from EEO-1 surveys (EEOC, various years).

occupational integration switches to favor white men (figure 3.6). While all groups made gains, white male gains dwarfed those of the other groups. White men made their strongest gains within managerial jobs. White women did so in the professions. Black men made real gains in managerial jobs, while black women's largest gains were among technicians. Although the numbers are smaller, we see the same pattern of particularly strong gains for black males and black females in the South and for black women among federal contractors.

In terms of occupational integration, we see a general pattern of occupational upgrading for white men into high-skilled white-collar jobs. In fact, 36 percent of all job gains by white men were in managerial positions. This was a tremendous upgrading of the employment status of white men in EEOC-reporting private-sector workplaces. Even as white male total employment declined, their access to managerial jobs soared. In contrast, white women (30.2 percent) and black women (34.2 percent) made their strongest job gains in clerical jobs. Black men made their strongest gains—34.7 percent of new jobs—in machine operator positions.

From here forward, we present estimates of race and gender segregation and employment trends that statistically control for two important shifts in the labor market.[4] The structure of the economy changed radically from a society with a large manufacturing sector to one dominated by the provision of services to people, households, and businesses. In chapter 7, we examine variations in desegregation trajectories associated with sector and industry, but for the time being we hold this source of change constant. We do the same for changes in labor supply, which are equally dramatic. In chapter 6, we look at the influence of labor supply shifts on desegregation trends, with particular attention to the importance of the decline of white men and the dramatic employment growth of white women, as well as of Hispanics and Asians in the labor force in more recent years.

Segregation Trends

Figure 3.7 reports segregation trends from 1966 to 1972 after adjusting for changes in labor supply and industrial composition. Gender segregation is exceptionally high and remains so across the period, with a constant dissimilarity index around 88. We can say that gender segregation was

Figure 3.7   Employment Segregation Trends, Adjusted for Industry, Organizational Characteristics, and Local Labor Supply, 1966 to 1972

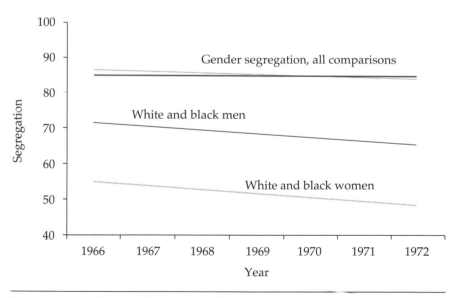

Source: Authors' calculations based on data from EEO-1 surveys (EEOC, various years).

nearly total for all cross-gender comparisons (white men–white women, white men–black women, black men–white women) and that at the aggregate level of the EEOC-reporting private-sector economy there is no evidence that employers reacted at all to the cynical inclusion of "sex" as a protected category in the Civil Rights Act.

The same cannot be said for racial segregation. Workplace race segregation among both men and women dropped rapidly between 1966 and 1972. Among men, our estimate of black-white segregation was 71.4 in 1966 and fell to 64.5 in 1972, averaging more than a one-point drop per year. Among women, the decline in race segregation was even more marked, starting at 54.2 and ending in 1972 at 44.8, averaging 1.6 points per year. The previous literature has shown that black-white segregation fell more rapidly among women than among men (King 1992; Robinson et al. 2005; Stainback et al. 2005), but we lack a clear explanation as to why. Given the results in the previous chapter, we suspect that it was simply easier for personnel managers, who were hesitant to anger male workers, to experiment with integrating female jobs than male jobs.

What About the South?

Figure 3.8 reveals that there was considerable variation in the intensity of the trends in different regions of the country. The South, where race segregation was generally highest in 1966, shows the most rapid decline in race segregation. The Mountain states, which have very small African American populations, also had very high race segregation among men in 1966.

There was a sharp regional convergence in racial employment segregation by 1972. In 1966, race segregation was clearly higher in the South, particularly among women. By 1972, there were fairly small regional differences in race segregation. This is particularly remarkable because there was not yet any effective regulatory enforcement, and the South was the region in which the fight for African Americans' civil and economic rights had been resisted most fiercely. Again, we see that racial desegregation was steeper among white women and black women than among white men and black men in most regions; however, this is not true in all regions.

Table 3.1 compares the average yearly decline in racial segregation by gender across the period. In the South, race segregation fell more quickly among women than among men. In the North and West, race segregation dropped more quickly among men than among women. Strikingly, race integration was less pronounced in New England and the Pacific states, which in 1966 had the lowest levels of segregation. Black women made no gains in jobs working alongside white women in either the New England

Figure 3.8   Regional Race Segregation Trends, Adjusted for Industry,
              Organizational Characteristics, and Local Labor Supply,
              1966 to 1972

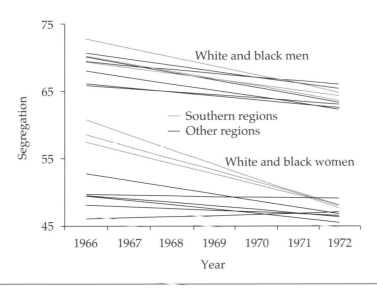

Source: Authors' calculations based on data from EEO-1 surveys (EEOC, various years).

Table 3.1   Adjusted Average Yearly Black-White Desegregation
             Trajectories, by Gender, by Region, 1966 to 1972

	Men	Women
New England	−0.467	0.170[a]
Mid-Atlantic	−0.587	−0.253
East North Central	−0.941	−0.658
West North Central	−1.135	−0.996
South Atlantic	−1.101	−1.569
East South Central	−0.829	−1.736
West South Central	−1.322	−2.188
Mountain	−0.896	−0.524
Pacific	−0.568	−0.079[a]

Source: Authors' calculations based on data from EEO-1 surveys (EEOC, various years).
[a]Trend is not statistically significant. Trajectory estimates are made after statistically controlling for industry, organizational characteristics, and local labor supply.

Figure 3.9 Race Segregation Trends by Fair Employment Practice Laws, Adjusted for Industry, Organizational Characteristics, and Local Labor Supply, 1966 to 1972

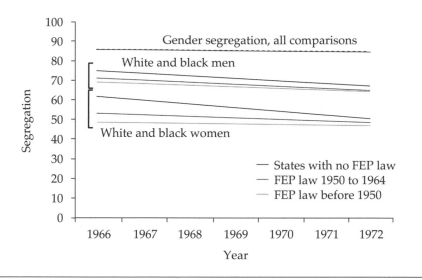

Source: Authors' calculations based on data from EEO-1 surveys (EEOC, various years).

or Pacific states, a pattern that would spread to other states in the late 1970s.

What About Fair Employment Practice States?

Another way to look at this regional shift is through a comparison of FEP states with all others. Figure 3.9 shows the same trends as in figure 3.8, organized now to examine the presence or absence of FEP laws. We see the same pattern of regional convergence, with the non-FEP states, which were mostly in the South, rapidly converging with the states that adopted FEP laws prior to 1964. Gender segregation did not decline in any region.

Because there is such a close overlap between non-FEP states and southern states, it is difficult to conclude definitively whether the FEP laws produced change earlier in FEP states or the defense of racial segregation by whites precluded change in the South. The rapid convergence certainly suggests that EEOC-reporting employers in the South quickly came to behave like employers elsewhere. In either case, it is clear that the

Civil Rights Act, even though it lacked clear guidelines and enforcement mechanisms, produced sufficient political uncertainty to prompt rapid change in southern states, particularly in the segregation of white women and black women. It is important to remember that these estimates control for both labor supply and industrial composition, so the results do not simply reflect the decline of southern agriculture and domestic labor (Branch 2011).

Did Racial Desegregation Lead to More Cross-Race Interaction?

Because gender segregation was unchanged between 1966 and 1972, any increased interactional exposure would have been produced by the racial integration trends we have explored. When we extend our analysis to examine whether desegregation led to increased interaction, we find that, regardless of region, white men's and white women's intergroup contact did not change appreciably, if at all, nor did it vary by region. This is not true for black men and black women, who were increasingly exposed to interaction with whites, particularly in the South (figure 3.10). The racial integration of EEOC-reporting workplaces changed the everyday life of

Figure 3.10   Isolation Trends, Adjusted for Industry, Organizational Characteristics, and Local Labor Supply, 1966 to 1972

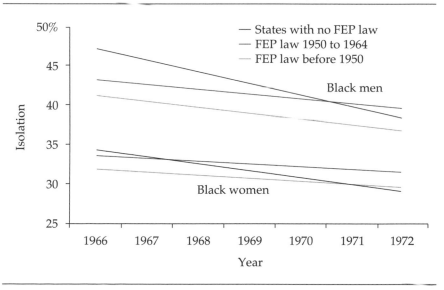

Source: Authors' calculations based on data from EEO-1 surveys (EEOC, various years).

Figure 3.11   Skilled Craft Production Representation Trends, Adjusted
               for Industry and Organization Shifts, 1966 to 1972

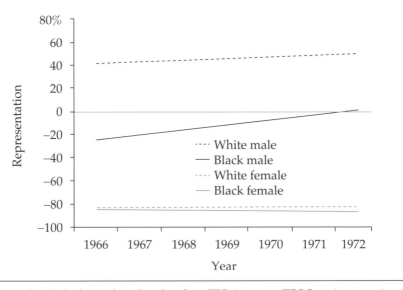

Source: Authors' calculations based on data from EEO-1 surveys (EEOC, various years).

black men and black women, but most whites were left unaffected. This
reflects, of course, the small size of the black population in most places
and the incorporation of black labor into the lowest-status jobs in these
now monitored, if not regulated, companies.

Did Racial Desegregation Include Good Jobs?

Social closure theory suggests that the easiest way to integrate a workplace is by granting previously excluded groups access to the least desirable jobs. Total segregation, at least on the basis of race, was no longer
a politically viable way to organize work, but what level of integration
would indicate legal compliance was completely unknown. Personnel
managers had to deal with resistance to integration from managers and
current employees. Figure 3.11 displays the trends in access to craft production jobs. These were the best working-class jobs and ones in which
African American men already had some representation in 1966. If there
was to be any progress in valuable jobs in this initial period, it should have
been within these occupations. As figure 3.11 shows, black men did, in
fact, make progress in skilled working-class jobs during this period.

Figure 3.12   Skilled Craft Production Occupation Trends by Fair
Employment Practice States, Adjusted for Industry and
Organization Shifts, 1966 to 1972

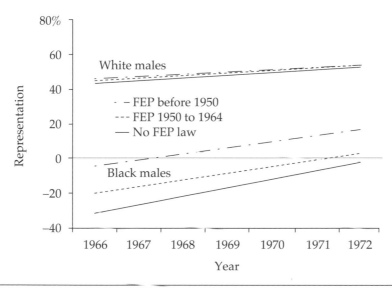

Source: Authors' calculations based on data from EEO-1 surveys (EEOC, various years).

Because our measure adjusts for change in labor supply and workplaces were hiring black labor into low-skilled jobs during this period, this
shift is particularly impressive. In this initial period of regulatory uncertainty, black men were either hired or promoted into these skilled jobs at a
noticeable rate. White male representation in these jobs increased as well.
This is less surprising, because with the influx of black men and black
women into lower-level jobs, the relative representation of white men
who kept control of most of these jobs had to increase almost by definition
in order to maintain privilege and status differences. While white males'
overrepresentation in skilled craft jobs grew by 1.5 percent per year, black
male underrepresentation declined by an impressive 3.5 percent per year.
This is a clear indicator of strong progress for black men, even as white
males' traditional advantaged access to skilled jobs grew. Not surprisingly, women made no gains at all in skilled working-class jobs during the
1966 to 1972 period. These jobs remain overwhelmingly male to the present. Susan Eisenberg (1999) provides a series of striking accounts of how
male work groups have effectively excluded all women from skilled crafts
jobs.

Figure 3.13   Managerial Representation, Adjusted for Industry and
Organization Shifts, 1966 to 1972

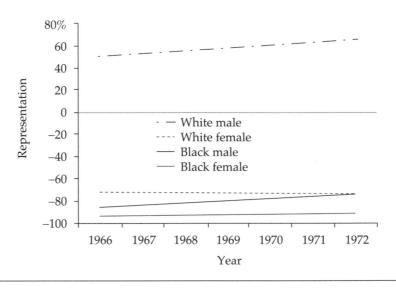

Source: Authors' calculations based on data from EEO-1 surveys (EEOC, various years).

In figure 3.12, we examine the geographic distribution of skilled craft representation. Because women were effectively excluded from these jobs, we examine only trends for black and white men's access to skilled working-class jobs. In all regions, white men were overrepresented in these jobs by about 40 percent in 1966, and this advantaged access grew between 1966 and 1972. Black men had very different levels of access to craft production jobs in 1966. In the earliest FEP states (New York, New Jersey, Connecticut, Massachusetts, Rhode Island, Washington, Oregon, and Arizona), black men were already in craft production jobs in 1966, at slightly lower levels than their presence in the EEOC-reporting labor force. This representation was produced by a combination of real access to skilled jobs and the near-total gender segregation that excluded women from competing for these skilled working-class positions.

In all three regions, black men made real gains in craft production jobs between 1966 and 1972. Recall that the non-FEP states were primarily in the South as well as the Mountain states. Only the southern states had substantial black populations, so the trend line for non-FEP states effectively represents black men's employment experiences in the South. In the South, black male representation in skilled working-class jobs grew by 4.8

Figure 3.14   Professional Representation Trends, Adjusted for Industry and Organizational Shifts, 1966 to 1972

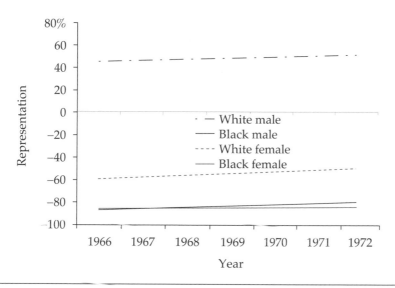

Source: Authors' calculations based on data from EEO-1 surveys (EEOC, various years).

percent a year between 1966 and 1972. In the FEP states, representation grew slightly more slowly, at 3.5 percent and 3.9 percent per year during the same period. Both racial desegregation and access to good-quality working-class jobs grew faster in the South than outside the South during this initial period.

Figure 3.13 displays national trends for access to managerial jobs. As other groups were granted access to low-level jobs in the corporate sector of the economy, white men's privileged access to managerial jobs grew fairly rapidly, at about 2.5 percent per year. Black men's access grew as well, but at a slower rate, about 1.9 percent a year. By 1972, black men's representation in managerial jobs remained at 75 percent below their labor force representation, but this was still a gain from their near-total exclusion from management in 1966. White women and black women made no real managerial gains in the initial post–Civil Rights Act desegregation of the private sector. When we examine these same trends by region, we find that the pace of change was fairly constant across regions.

When we examined professional representation trends, we found an exception to the otherwise overwhelming pattern of initial post–Civil

Rights Act desegregation being about race but not gender (figure 3.14). We see the same pattern of increased white male and black male representation in professional jobs that we saw for craft and managerial jobs. Black male representation in professional jobs grew by about 1.2 percent a year, about the same as the white male growth rate. Most strikingly, however, white women's representation grew by 1.6 percent a year in professional jobs. Black women, on the other hand, made almost no gains at all, net of shifts in the structure of the economy and labor market. These trends, similar to those for managers, are essentially constant across regions.

The big winners when it came to access to good-quality jobs in the initial post–Civil Rights period were white men. White men's privileged access to skilled working-class, professional, and managerial jobs grew as black men, white women, and black women were hired into lower-level jobs. Black men made strong gains as well in all three valuable job destinations after 1966. In skilled craft jobs, their gains were even stronger than those of white men; thus, there was actually a decline in white men's advantage over black men in the best working-class jobs. This was not the case for managerial jobs, where white males' access to managerial employment surged. In general, women made no gains in good-quality jobs during this period. The one exception was that white women made gains in professional jobs. There was also no difference across regions in these basic trends, with one exception: black male employment in skilled working-class jobs grew particularly quickly in the South.

DID FEDERAL CONTRACTORS DESEGREGATE MORE QUICKLY?

It is clear that federal contractors had more pressure on them to desegregate than did other private-sector firms. Prior to 1961, federal contractors had repeatedly been exposed to federal executive orders to increase African American employment opportunities, but it is probably safe to say that they understood these orders to be largely symbolic and without consequence. Consistently, Blumrosen (1970) describes the predecessor agency of the OFCCP as essentially passive relative to federal contractors as late as 1965. On the other hand, Dobbin (2009) suggests that President Kennedy's 1961 executive order was different, and his historical account leads us to expect that at least among the largest federal contractors that signed up as "Plans for Progress" firms, equal opportunity progress should have happened most quickly. In the last chapter, we saw that in 1966 federal contractors, and even Plans for Progress firms, were undistinguished in this regard. This does not mean that they made no progress; they may have been making progress from a worse starting point. In this section, we pres-

Figure 3.15   Segregation Trends by Federal Contractor Status,
Adjusted for Industry, Organizational Characteristics,
and Local Labor Supply, 1966 to 1972

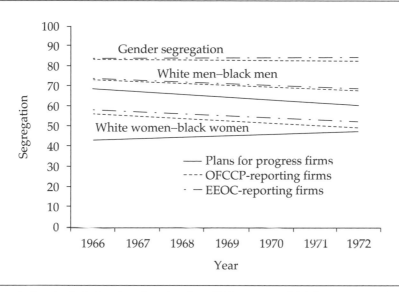

Source: Authors' calculations based on data from EEO-1 surveys (EEOC, various years).

ent estimates of trends after 1966. Because our estimates adjust for local labor supply, industrial composition, and workplace size, it is possible for us to provide cleaner estimates of both the initial levels of segregation and their trends.

After 1966, we find the expected near-absence of progress, irrespective of contractor status, for gender segregation. During the 1966 to 1972 period, gender discrimination and segregation were clearly not yet on most employers' radar screens.

The desegregation patterns implied by Dobbin's (2009) analysis of the immediate reaction of federal contractors to Kennedy's executive order are supported (figure 3.15). In 1966, after adjusting for between-workplace industry, labor market, and size composition, the largest federal contractors had lower levels of race segregation among men and among women than did other firms, and there was essentially no difference between other federal contractors and firms that were not subject to federal affirmative action mandates. In 1966 race segregation among men was six points lower in Plans for Progress firms and thirteen points lower among women. Although we cannot observe the trends during the five preceding

Figure 3.16   Isolation Trends by Federal Contractor Status, Adjusted
               for Industry, Organizational Characteristics, and Local
               Labor Supply, 1966 to 1972

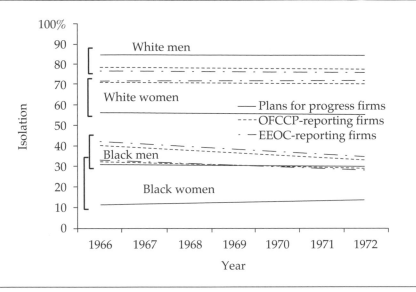

Source: Authors' calculations based on data from EEO-1 surveys (EEOC, various years).

years, these estimates do adjust for other likely influences on segregation levels. The similarity between other federal contractors and noncontractors further supports an interpretation that PFP firms had acted more aggressively to reduce racial segregation than other firms in the early 1960s.

When we examine the trends between 1966 and 1972, however, the pattern is gender-specific. Adjusted for compositional changes in labor supply and firm composition, race segregation among men declined in Plans for Progress firms by 1.3 points per year. Federal contractors in general saw a decline of one point per year, and noncontractors of 0.7 points per year. Race segregation among women hardly changed for most firms. In contrast, race segregation among women actually increased by four points between 1966 and 1972 in PFP firms. It is the smaller federal contractors that exhibited declines in racial segregation among women in the 1966 to 1972 period.

The most striking result in figure 3.15, however, is the racial resegregation among women that took place among the Plans for Progress firms. Although the 1966 result suggests that these firms experimented first and most aggressively with integrating black women into white women's jobs,

Figure 3.17   Males' Increased Access to Good Jobs in Plan for
Progress Firms, Adjusted for Industry and Organizational
Shifts, 1966 to 1972

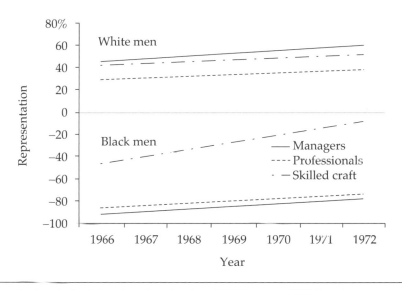

Source: Authors' calculations based on data from EEO-1 surveys (EEOC, various years).

the trend after 1966 strongly implies that they either abandoned those experiments or instituted some new distinctions between white women's and black women's employment destinations. Among the largest federal contractors, segregation between white men and black men, however, declined strongly between 1966 and 1972.

Figure 3.16 allows us to see what these desegregation trends meant at the level of routine social interaction. The general pattern is that black men, black women, and white women who worked for federal contractors were all exposed to interaction with out-groups at somewhat higher rates. For white men, however, not only were they the most socially insulated in these same firms, but their cross-race and cross-gender contact barely changed among federal contractors during the late 1960s and early 1970s. Plans for Progress firms racially integrated relatively quickly among men while isolating the average white male from equal-status cross-race contact. What is most striking in figure 3.16 is that white men and white women in all three types of firms did not have appreciably greater cross-race, cross-gender contact over time, even as black men and black women increased their cross-race, cross-gender contact.

Figure 3.18   Average Yearly Percentage Change of Plans for Progress
Firms in Good Job Representation, Adjusted for Industry
and Organizational Shifts, 1966 to 1972

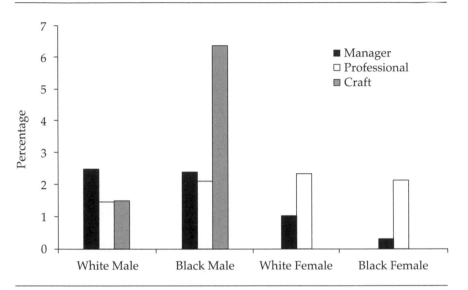

Source: Authors' calculations based on data from EEO-1 surveys (EEOC, various years).

Plans for Progress firms were notable for improving black men's access to good jobs during the 1966 to 1972 period. Black men's increased access to managerial, professional, and especially skilled craft jobs in these leader firms was dramatic across this early period prior to the establishment of a regulatory regime (figure 3.17). The strong growth in black male access to craft jobs may have been helped along by President Nixon's "Philadelphia Plan" (1969), which called for the use of a quota system to ensure black male access to skilled unionized jobs in OFCCP-reporting firms. This strikes us as the likeliest explanation because black men's increased access to craft jobs in PFP firms was about twice that observed in the rest of the private-sector EEOC-reporting economy. Although black men ended the period still very much underrepresented in good jobs, they also had clearly closed the gap with white men, even as white men's overrepresentation in these jobs was growing. Importantly, the gains of black men were not at the expense of white men in these jobs, but at the expense of white men in lower-level jobs, where the majority of black male employment expansion occurred.

This is not to say that black women did not make gains in Plans for

Progress firms, but by comparison these gains were small and seemed to come more at the expense of white women. Figure 3.18 makes the overall trends across the period clear.[5] Black men made the strongest gains in good jobs. White males made strong gains as well. Among large federal contractors, black women made weak gains; white women made weak managerial employment gains and experienced small professional losses. Earlier we saw that during this period, across all firms, white women made gains in professional jobs. It turns out that these gains were limited to firms that were not federal contractors. Although we do not know for sure, this may represent the hiring by federal contractors of more white men, black men, and even black women professionals from these noncontractor firms, leaving vacancies for white women to fill.

Our ability to distinguish between federal contractors has helped produce a new understanding of the early post–Civil Rights Act period. Although the executive branch had been encouraging federal contractors to take affirmative action since the 1940s, it would appear that these firms did not respond until the 1960s, and then only the largest federal contractors did so. Even among these Plans for Progress firms, it appears that after an initial period of experimenting with racial integration among women, there was sustained progress primarily for black men.

IMPLICATIONS

The period immediately following the passage of the Civil Rights Act was one in which U.S. corporations became aware that they might soon be held accountable for their long-standing preference for white male labor. The Civil Rights Act prohibited discrimination and segregation on the basis of race and gender. Until this point, discriminatory employment practices had been taken as normal and perhaps even natural. In much of the South, racial segregation practices were legally required. But the mere fact of racial discrimination's illegality was for many employers a weak threat. After all, presidents had at that point been instructing federal contractors to take affirmative action in the hiring of African Americans for twenty-five years. Moreover, about half of U.S. states had already instituted fair employment practice legislation with similar injunctions to stop racial discrimination.

The 1960s were different. After John F. Kennedy's election, for the first time both the Republican and Democratic Parties supported the extension of civil rights to African Americans. The racial apartheid that typified U.S. society was an international embarrassment as the United States battled the Soviet Union for leadership among the newly emerging countries in Africa and Asia. Most importantly, African Americans had mobilized into an effective social movement, gaining white allies as their moral and organizational power grew. The civil rights movement was not going away, and many whites sympathized with the call for equality under the law.

It was clear that business as usual would not do, but it was equally unclear what business should do. Nobody knew what equal opportunity might mean in practice. In a world where white males were routinely deferred to in interactions on the streets and in the workplace by women of all races and by all nonwhite men, certainly few imagined workplaces of real equality. When faced with uncertainty and no real road maps as to what to do next, it appears that many firms hired black men, black women, and white women in increased numbers. Many black men were hired into operative jobs, particularly among federal contractors and in the South. Many workplaces hired black women for the first time as clerical and operative employees. White women made stronger gains among firms that were not federal contractors, primarily gaining access to clerical jobs.

This is not to say that no progress was made in the very best jobs. Forty percent of the increased black male employment between 1966 and 1972 was in managerial, professional, and high-skilled craft jobs. This rate was almost identical to the growth of all new jobs in these three occupations (39.7 percent). Black men garnered just about their per capita share of new high-skilled jobs in this initial period of uncertainty. White women made weaker gains: 29 percent of their job growth was in professional and managerial positions. Black women made anemic gains, with 13 percent of their job growth in the most desirable occupations. White men, by contrast, became increasingly employed in the very best jobs in the economy. Sixty-nine percent of new white male employment in EEOC-reporting firms was in managerial, professional, and skilled craft jobs. Because these jobs provided 39 percent of all new positions and white men saw weak or no gains in other occupations, this was a substantial upgrading of the average white male's workplace advantage over other groups. Although it is clear that working-class and clerical occupations became particularly open to black men and black women after 1966, it is also clear that the consequence for many white men seems to have been a promotion. All of these trends were exaggerated among federal contractors and in the southern states.

The Civil Rights Act was modeled after legislation that had been floating around since the 1940s. For decades federal legislation banning racial discrimination in the workplace was proposed but not enacted. In addition, state-level fair employment practice laws outlawing employment discrimination on the basis of race, religion, and national origin had been adopted by many states beginning in the mid-1940s. Hence, although many employers may not have supported the passage of a law banning racial discrimination, such an idea was not unheard of.

In 1964, in a desperate attempt by some legislators to stop the passage of the Civil Rights Act, "sex" was added as an additional status to be granted equal employment opportunity. The notion that women should have equal employment opportunities with men was so far off the political agenda that congressmen laughed at the idea. During the 1960s, leaders at the EEOC and OFCC made clear that they saw their job as enforcing racial, not gender, progress, and that is precisely how it turned out.

So what happened? Racial employment segregation declined, but it did so mostly in the South and among the largest federal contractors—exactly the social locations that came under the most political pressure from the civil rights movement, the media, and the federal government. Early in the period, both in the South and among large federal contractors, racial segregation typically declined most quickly in female jobs. After the EEOC and OFCC made clear that it was black men they cared about, we see sustained improvement in the employment of black men, with real gains in their access to high-skilled and autonomous jobs in the skilled trades, professions, and managerial ranks.

These gains did not, however, come at the expense of white men, who solidified and expanded their advantaged access to the best working- and middle-class jobs in the economy. Black men and black women made their strongest gains in the lowest-skilled jobs, pushing white men into the higher ranks. That white women did not reap similar benefits suggests that it was the intersection of racial and gender privilege, not race alone, that was preserved in the face of black gains. From 1966 to 1972, there is no evidence that the average white man had increased equal status contact with African Americans net of shifts in labor supply and the population of firms. What this finding means is that some white men were increasingly isolated in high-status jobs while others were increasingly in equal-status contact with African Americans in working-class jobs. For white women, the same racial integration was happening in clerical jobs, but they lacked any race advantage that would have propelled them into more desirable managerial and professional roles. All women were excluded from skilled production jobs across the period.

In the 1960s, there was no uncertainty propelling organizational change when it came to gender. Gender segregation did not budge. Even though women now had the same legal protection as racial minorities, gender was not yet socially or politically recognized as a legitimate basis for equality claims. Even though the Civil Rights Act was nearly two years old when President Johnson issued his executive order for federal contractors to take affirmative action, the order omitted "sex." Although this was remedied a few years later, the fact that a politician, presumably dependent on the female vote for reelection, could omit "sex" is a strong indicator of the low salience of "sex" as a protected category in the mid-1960s.

One of the most important findings of this chapter is that it was among the very largest federal contractors that we see widespread and sustained desegregation before and after 1966. That this desegregation was confined to black men after 1966 and included access to high-quality occupations is strong evidence that these were the firms that felt the most threatened by the uncertainty of the time. They suspected correctly that when the federal government eventually developed the capacity to monitor and enforce equal opportunity laws, it would be the largest firms, particularly the largest federal contractors, that would be held accountable first.

Dobbin (2009) has pointed to these Plans for Progress firms as the first movers—the ones that embraced nondiscrimination policies and affirmative action recruitment policies as early as 1961. Dobbin points to newspaper articles, mostly based on press releases by PFP chairman Robert Troutman, that suggest that these firms made rapid strides in the employment of African Americans in the 1960s. Until now, we might have suspected that these press releases were exaggerated. Certainly the firms had every incentive to promote the appearance of racial progress in order to avoid social movement and federal regulatory attention. It appears, however, that racial progress at these firms was not merely symbolic. The largest federal contractors did increase equality of opportunity, integrating black men into their workforces, including into the ranks of skilled craft, management, and professional jobs. They also seem to have been the first to experiment with the racial integration of women, although they backed off that initiative when the EEOC and OFCC signaled that equal opportunity was primarily to be gauged by the progress of black men.

An important aspect of these early attempts to desegregate corporate America was that it was done without threatening white male access to the very best jobs. Skilled white males remained socially segregated, with almost no equal-status contact across race or gender lines. Impressively, hiring minorities and women into lower-level jobs only increased white men's privileged access to the skilled trades and elite professional and managerial jobs. It was low-skilled working-class white men and women who experienced racial integration as both a loss of jobs in the corporate private sector and increased equal-status contact with African Americans.

POLITICAL TRANSITIONS

The early 1970s saw two contradictory trends relative to civil rights. The period of regulator uncertainty for employers ended as case law around employment discrimination started developing and both the EEOC and OFCC began to flex their muscles. At the same time, Republicans, the party of racial equal opportunity since the presidency of Abraham Lincoln, shifted their electoral strategy to become the party of states' rights and racial division.

Even as Nixon and his party were crafting an electoral strategy of racial divisiveness, the courts and federal regulators were defining what constituted employment discrimination. The Griggs v. Duke Power (1971) case at this time was an important advance for workplace equal employment opportunity. In this case, the Supreme Court maintained that employers could be held responsible for unintentional, as well as intentional, discrimination, broadening the definition of discrimination to include unequal employment outcomes. Under this ruling, the Court maintained that employers were liable for policies, practices, and procedures that led to differential outcomes ("disparate impact") for different status groups, whether intentional discrimination was implicated or not. Thus, ostensibly race-neutral practices could be deemed discriminatory in the eyes of the courts. Soon after, the Democratic-controlled Congress passed the Equal Employment Opportunity Act of 1972, which Nixon supported and then signed. The act strengthened the capacity of civil rights enforcement agencies, especially the EEOC and OFCCP, to monitor and enforce Title VII. The EEOC gained the power to bring lawsuits against employers.

The period from 1972 until the early years of Ronald Reagan's presidency was one in which the capacity of the state to regulate and monitor equal employment opportunity strengthened, even as the political backlash against the gains of African Americans grew and was nurtured by a Republican Party in search of electoral success in the South. At the same time, the women's movement entered the scene as an increasingly important force in both civil society and electoral politics. In the next chapter, we examine the influence of this new political environment on equal opportunity progress.

Chapter 4 | The Short Regulatory Decade, 1972 to 1980

A GREAT DEAL changed after 1972. The federal regulatory apparatus became much more clearly defined and active. The women's movement emerged as a powerful political force. In response, Congress and the courts made clear that Title VII of the Civil Rights Act prohibited "sex"-based discrimination and segregation in employment. Companies now knew that they needed to take seriously women's employment opportunities. They knew that if they did not, they risked embarrassing and potentially expensive lawsuits from their employees or even from the federal government. If they were federal contractors, they were now at risk of being audited on the content of their affirmative action plans and their progress toward equal opportunity for women as well as African Americans.

In the 1970s, white women in particular were well situated: there were lots of them, they were entering the labor force in increased numbers, and they were nearly as well educated as white men. Importantly, the women's movement gained strength, making electoral, legislative, and legal gains. Predictably, the segregation of white women from white men plummeted. Women, particularly white women, made rapid gains in managerial and professional jobs in EEOC-reporting workplaces.

Conversely, the political pressure for equal opportunity for African Americans weakened considerably as the civil rights movement lost momentum and the Republican Party pursued an electoral agenda of dividing the country along racial lines. Black male employment advances continued, but at a slower pace. Black women made some gains in jobs working with white men, but surprisingly, disturbingly, became more segregated from white women in the short decade of emerging gender uncertainty and regulatory oversight from 1972 to 1980.

118

REGULATORY CAPACITY

The original Civil Rights Act limited the enforcement capacity of the Equal Employment Opportunity Commission to responding to complaints and was unclear even there as to the breadth of the EEOC's mandate to respond to citizen complaints. The Equal Employment Opportunity Act of 1972 strengthened the capacity of civil rights enforcement agencies, including the EEOC and OFCCP, to monitor and enforce Title VII. The EEOC gained the power to initiate lawsuits against employers, whereas prior to 1972 the organization could only receive and process complaints. The EEOC in its own history refers to itself as "toothless" prior to 1972 and as "growing teeth" after the 1972 EEO Act. Broadening the reach of EEO law, the act also extended Title VII protections against discrimination to students in educational institutions and employees of state and local governments, and it reduced the size of employers subject to equal opportunity law from twenty-five to fifteen.

Thus, the capacity of the EEOC and OFCCP to regulate private-sector employers grew substantially after 1972. In 1974 the OFCCP and EEOC agreed to share information on discrimination complaints with each other. Later in the decade, Congress passed the Civil Service Reform Act of 1978, which gave the EEOC responsibility for enforcing antidiscrimination laws applicable to the civilian federal workforce and to coordinate federal equal employment opportunity programs. Significant changes in the structure of EEO/AA enforcement resulted, which reduced the number of government organizations responsible for the administration of equal opportunity policies from over twenty to just three (Bryner 1981), with the vast majority of responsibility falling to the EEOC and OFCCP. Typically seen by historians as a favorable improvement in equal opportunity regulation, this consolidation reduced many of the incongruities of EEO enforcement between different regulatory agencies. If, however, uncertainty is what motivates corporate innovation and empowers human resource personnel to propose and enforce new policies and practices, then having fewer regulatory agencies might produce less ambiguity and make it easier to settle for symbolic compliance rather than real progress. We have no good evidence of this effect, but suspect that as firms began to encounter fewer federal voices pressuring for equal opportunity progress, the urgency of change probably weakened.

Importantly, the contours of equal opportunity law began to be clarified by the Supreme Court. In Griggs v. Duke Power (1971), the Supreme Court maintained that employers could be held responsible for unintentional, as well as intentional, discrimination. Under this ruling, the Court maintained that employers were liable for policies, practices, and proce-

Table 4.1   Supreme Court Rulings Clarifying and Strengthening
Discrimination Law, 1972 to 1980

Year	Case	Ruling
1971	Griggs v. Duke Power	Intentionality not necessary to prove discrimination
1973	McDonnell Douglas v. Green	Failure to hire can be discrimination
1974	Alexander v. Gardner-Denver Co.	Broadened right to sue for discrimination
	Corning Glass Works v. Brennan	Equal pay for "substantially" similar work
1975	Albemarle Paper Co. v. Moody	Back pay for discrimination
1976	General Electric Co. v. Gilbert	Pregnancy discrimination is not sex discrimination
	Franks v. Bowman Transportation Co.	Retroactive seniority to remedy past discrimination
1977	Teamsters v. United States	All members of a class entitled to relief
	Hazelwood School District v. United States	Discrimination is underrepresentation relative to local labor market
	Occidental Life Insurance. v. Equal Employment Opportunity Commission	Discrimination cases need not be filed quickly
	McDonald v. Santa Fe Transport	Whites covered by race discrimination prohibition
1978	Los Angeles v. Manhart	Gender equality in pension contributions mandated
1979	United Steel Workers of America v. Weber	Voluntary affirmative action legal
1980	General Telephone Company of the Northwest v. Equal Employment Opportunity Commission	EEOC authority to seek class action relief upheld

Source: Authors' compilation.

dures that led to differential outcomes ("disparate impact") for different
status groups, whether or not intentional discrimination was present.
This put employers on notice that good intentions and symbolic compliance might not be sufficient. Across the rest of the 1970s, a series of decisions by the Supreme Court both clarified and extended EEO law (see table 4.1). This new law in all cases was interpreted to apply to women as well as to racial minorities and tended to reinforce the authority of the EEOC in particular.

The late 1970s saw a series of more conservative Supreme Court inter-pretations of Title VII; for instance, the Court deemed affirmative action to potentially be "reverse discrimination" against whites in employment (see McDonald v. Santa Fe Transport [1977], and for college admissions, Regents of the University of California v. Bakke [1978]).

Gender: The New Corporate Uncertainty

The women's movement emerged again during this time. With the new protections afforded in the Civil Rights Act of 1964 and the Equal Pay Act of 1963, supporters of gender equality were poised for progressive change. Many women's rights groups were formed for the purpose of acting col-lectively to achieve gender equality on a variety of social, political, and economic dimensions. Although employment discrimination on the basis of "sex" was illegal after 1964, women had not been the intended targets of the initial legislation and enforcement, as we saw in the last chapter. The law and its enforcement were largely directed toward increasing op-portunities for minority men. The National Organization for Women formed specifically in reaction to the exclusion of "sex" from the EEOC's active regulatory agenda (Ferree and Hess 1985). The women's movement would develop the capacity to make gender equality a visible corporate HR problem across the 1970s.

The women's movement became increasingly active during the early 1970s, especially around the Equal Rights Amendment (ERA). This pro-posed amendment to the U.S. Constitution would guarantee gender equal-ity under the law. Congress passed the ERA in 1972, with support from la-bor unions (most notably the UAW and AFL-CIO), and then sent it to the states for ratification; the passage of the ERA as a constitutional amendment required ratification by thirty-eight states. The addition of an equal rights amendment to the U.S. Constitution never took place; however, many states implemented their own ERAs beginning in the early 1970s, ensuring that political uncertainty around gender remained high across the entire decade.

Although the women's movement was more oriented toward legisla-tion and the courts than the civil rights movement had been, across the 1970s protest events supporting women's rights became more common than events supporting the cause of racial justice. This is not surprising given the increased organizational capacity of the women's movement (see figure 4.2).

The EEOC used its new power to file discrimination suits to initiate a series of high-profile cases against some of the largest employers in the United States, including AT&T, Ford Motor Company, and the entire steel industry. In the 1970s, newspapers stopped running separate help-wanted

Figure 4.1   African American Civil Rights and Feminist Social
              Movement Organizations, 1955 to 1985

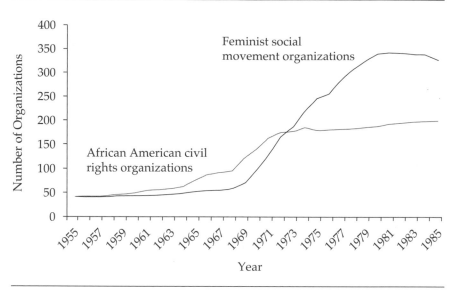

Source: Authors' presentation based on data provided by Professor Debra Minkoff, as originally published in Minkoff (1997).

ads for men and women, a practice that had been suspended for race soon
after the passage of the Civil Rights Act (Pedriana and Abraham 2006). In
1972 the EEOC began a pattern of extending the reach of equal opportunity regulatory practice and law ever further into the realm of gendered
social relations when it issued guidelines asserting that pregnancy discrimination was a form of "sex" discrimination.

    After the Supreme Court ruled in 1976 that pregnancy was not protected
by Title VII of the Civil Rights Act (General Electric Co. v. Gilbert, 429 U.S.
125), Congress responded in 1978 by passing the Pregnancy Discrimination Act, affirming that pregnancy discrimination was a form of sex discrimination. In 1980 the EEOC released guidelines on sexual harassment,
affirming that both quid pro quo and hostile-environment harassment constituted "sex" discrimination under Title VII. This was the beginning of a
long expansion of what had originally been narrowly construed "sex" discrimination law to include associated gender-related biases. Although
most of this shift occurred in the 1980s and 1990s, it was in the 1970s that
both pregnancy and sexual harassment began to be defined as part of the
broader concept of what we now think of as gender discrimination.

Figure 4.2   Civil Rights and Women's Rights Protest Events,
          1968 to 1980

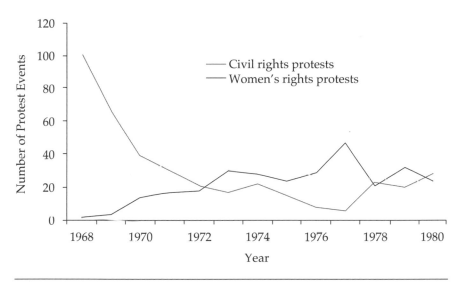

Source: Authors' presentation based on data provided by Professor Sarah Soule (personal communication, 2010).

The End of the Civil Rights Era

Only four years after the passage of the Civil Rights Act, race became a polarizing factor in the 1968 presidential election. The Democratic Party was bitterly divided on the future of civil rights. Surrounded by protest over the Vietnam War, Vice President Hubert Humphrey, a longtime civil rights advocate, was nominated as the Democratic presidential candidate at the Democratic National Convention in Chicago. The Republican candidate, Richard M. Nixon, would win the election with promises to end the war and reduce support for many civil rights measures developed during the Johnson administration. The staunch segregationist and former governor of Alabama George Wallace ran as an independent in this presidential race. His strong views against civil rights measures gained him support from many southern whites, who traditionally voted for the Democratic Party. He received over 13 percent of the popular vote but won outright in five southern states. Nixon's successful election was due, in part, to Wallace's ability to take away white Democratic votes from Humphrey in the South. The electoral weakening of the Civil Rights Act had begun.

Even as the electorate began to become polarized around race, the civil

Figure 4.3   African American Protest Events, 1948 to 1996

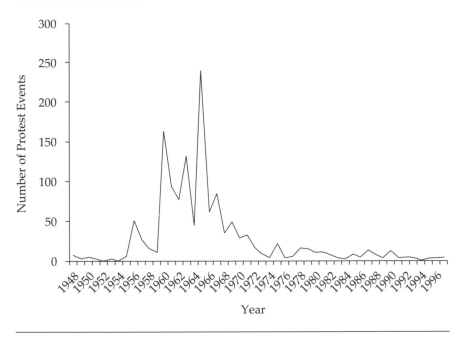

Source: Data provided by Professor Craig Jenkins as originally published in Jenkins, Jacobs, and Agnone (2003).

rights movement began to falter. In 1968 Martin Luther King Jr. was assassinated, as was civil rights supporter and Democratic presidential hopeful Robert F. Kennedy. Hubert Humphrey lost the presidency partly because he supported the extension of civil rights to African Americans. As we saw in figure 4.1, the founding of new civil rights social movement organizations had essentially stopped by 1972, even as foundings of women's rights organizations surged. Fundamentally for the creation of uncertainty around race in the United States, African American social movement activity declined precipitously in the late 1960s and had essentially ended by 1980 (see figure 4.3).

The 1968 election was followed by the consolidation of Nixon's "Southern Strategy" when he realized that if he could harness the growing white backlash to African American gains, he could capture the votes of the conservative southern whites who had historically voted Democrat. Under this new strategy, President Nixon—and Republicans in general—could concede the newly enfranchised African American vote in the South altogether (Sitkoff 1993). Nixon focused on framing the election around the war in Vietnam, civil rights issues, and crime. Specifically, Nixon sought to capitalize on the rhetoric of equal opportunity while invoking the image of African Americans, not as peaceful protesters being attacked by police, which may have led to positive sentiment toward racial equality among whites in the early 1960s, but rather as undeserving and unappreciative of the changes produced by federal legislation.

After entering office, President Nixon began to seek support from the white southerners who had voted for Wallace. In his attempt to gain reelection in 1972, he opposed many civil rights measures, such as busing, and tried to "defeat the fair housing enforcement program and the extension to the Voting Rights Act of 1965" (Sitkoff 1993, 213). Nixon did support measures that would aid in providing access to skilled jobs for African American men in the construction industry. The "Philadelphia Plan" (1969) called for the use of quotas to ensure access to trade unions for black males in OFCCP-reporting firms.

During this period, we also witness a shift in how politicians began to more subtly attack previous civil rights legislation, setting the stage for the continuing ideological polarization between Democrats and Republicans in the United States. The issue of polarization would be cast as color-consciousness among Democrats and as color-blindness among Republicans. Nixon's rebuke of color-conscious programs and policies would be particularly well received by many white Americans.

> Black Americans—no more than white Americans—do not want more Government programs which perpetuate dependency. They don't want to be a colony in a nation. They want the pride and the self-respect and the dignity that can only come if they have an equal chance to own their own homes, to own their own businesses, to be managers and executives as well as workers, to have a piece of the action in the exciting ventures of private enterprise. (Nixon 1968)

In the presidential election of 1976, Gerald Ford tried to use Nixon's strategy of capturing the conservative white southern vote. Jimmy Carter, a born-again Christian from Georgia, narrowly won the election for the Democrats, winning most of the southern electoral votes. Unlike earlier southern Democrats, Carter did not use racial politics to spread fear and inflame whites, and he publicly embraced the ideals of racial equality. In practice, however, his rhetorical and legislative support for civil rights measures was muted. For instance, in his 1976 campaign he supported the maintenance of racially segregated residential areas, claiming that the government should not try to dissolve "ethnic purity" and that some areas should have the right to remain segregated on the basis of race (Lydon 1976a). He later issued a formal apology, but concurrently stated that he would never "use federal force" to desegregate neighborhoods (Lydon 1976b). In addition, Carter did not take firm positions on issues such as affirmative action or school busing to achieve racial integration, but he did appoint many African Americans to cabinet positions and federal judgeships and hire them as White House aides.

In the late 1970s, the Republican Party seized upon the remedy of "affirmative action," as recently redefined by the Supreme Court, as the new crime of "reverse discrimination." This was an opportunity to antagonize and capture the white vote. Prior to Ronald Reagan's election to the presidency in 1980, the Republican race strategy was largely electoral rather than legislative or regulatory. In fact, the regulatory apparatus organized through the EEOC and OFCCP were strengthening across the decade. Although the regulatory attack on racial equal opportunity had not yet begun and the legal retreat was only just beginning, the electoral war was in full fight. Political pressure to promote racial employment opportunity withered, a casualty of the renewed race-baiting politics of the Republican Party, emerging party competition for the white vote, the Democratic Party's retreat from a civil rights agenda, and the declining efficacy of the civil rights movement.

DESEGREGATION IN THE SHORT REGULATORY DECADE

After 1972, the political environment that confronted private-sector corporations changed. The regulatory and legal definition of discrimination became more clearly defined, although it was still a moving target. It was now clear not only that discrimination included prohibitions on gender discrimination, but that other forms of bias associated with gender were also potential bases for successful discrimination complaints. The powers of the EEOC were expanded, and both the EEOC and OFCCP became more active as regulators. The women's movement began to gain strength, both organizationally and politically. Although the movement's main focus was on the Equal Rights Amendment and abortion rights, it had notable successes in employment law, abetted by Congress, federal regulators, and the Supreme Court.

African American social movement organizations, on the other hand, weakened considerably, and an aggressive political backlash against civil rights gains became the centerpiece of the Republican Party's national electoral strategy. The Democratic Party, while still formally supporting civil rights, moved into a reactive and protective stance as its electoral position became tied to its dwindling ability to attract white southern voters. Regulatory pressure for both race and gender equal employment opportunity was probably at its peak, but the uncertainty as to what was discrimination, as well as the political pressure, had clearly shifted from race to gender.

Immediately after the passage of the Civil Rights Act, there was rapid racial desegregation, especially for black men, but few shifts in gender segregation. During the 1970s, gender-linked discrimination became a focus of both regulatory and corporate attention. At the same time, most large companies established regulatory and human resources apparatus to enforce prohibitions on race discrimination. Uncertainty was high for gender segregation, but direct enforcement had been developed primarily around racial discrimination.

Since this was the period of peak federal enforcement, it was also the period in which we would expect the greatest gains for black men, black women, and white women. If enforcement was the main mechanism, we might expect weaker gains for women, because both enforcement and human resource routines aimed at eradicating gender-linked discrimination were only beginning to be established. On the other hand, if uncertainty is a primary motive for action, we would have the opposite expectation: that gender desegregation would proceed more dramatically than race desegregation.

Figure 4.4 reports trends in white male segregation from 1973 to 1980. As in the last chapter, these estimates are adjusted to remove the influence of labor supply as well as organizational and industry shifts in the composition of the economy. All three groups—black men, black women, and white women—show strong desegregation relative to white men. Although most black men, black women, and white women were still insulated from equal-status contact with white men, some were hired into the same jobs in the same workplaces. This was a fairly radical shift in employment practices. Perhaps for the first time, equal employment opportunity was simultaneously advancing briskly for all protected groups relative to white men.

The contrast with the earlier period is instructive. Table 4.2 reports the difference in segregation shifts between the two periods, both absolutely and after adjustments for compositional changes in the economy. Desegregation can come from many sources, most prominently from changes in labor supply and changes in the types of firms that populate the economy. Increases in white women's labor force participation and the rise of the relatively low-segregation service sector (Tomaskovic-Devey et al. 2006) are no doubt the most powerful of these changes in this period. This also

Figure 4.4   Regression-Adjusted Trends in Segregation from White
Men, 1973 to 1980

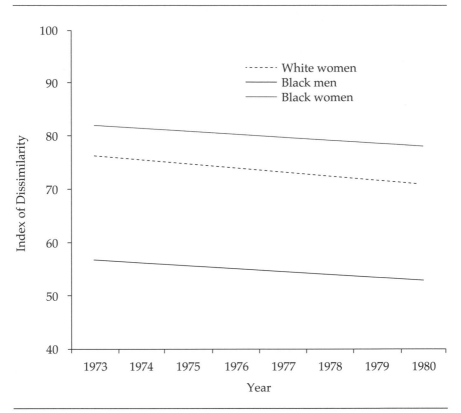

Source: Authors' calculations based on data from EEO-1 surveys (EEOC, various years).

means that absolute shifts in segregation can be misleading, especially if the goal is to isolate the influence of political and enforcement eras, as it is here. For these reasons, we treat the regression-adjusted shifts as the better indicator of change associated with political uncertainty and regulatory enforcement.

In the immediate post–civil rights period, we see a strong annual decline in the segregation of black men from white men. The decline was nearly one point per year, and only 6.3 percent of this dramatic desegregation trend was produced by shifts in the composition of the economy and changes in labor supply. White women also show a strong decline (–0.716 per year) from near-total segregation from white men, but almost all of this decline (82.1 percent) was produced by their increased labor supply

Table 4.2 Observed and Adjusted Segregation from White Men Trajectories in the Uncertainty (1966 to 1972) and Enforcement Periods (1973 to 1980)

	1966 to 1972: Uncertainty Period			1973 to 1980: Enforcement Period		
	Observed	Adjusted	Percentage of Change Compositional	Observed	Adjusted	Percentage of Change Compositional
White women	-0.716	-0.128	82.1%	-0.900	-0.733	18.6%
Black men	-0.950	-0.890	6.3	-0.529	-0.514	2.8
Black women	-0.183	-0.331	-80.1	-0.543	-0.539	0.7

Source: Authors' calculations based on data from EEO-1 surveys (EEOC, various years).

Note: Adjusted trends are based on regression adjustments for shifts in labor supply and the geographic, organizational, and industry composition of the economy.

and shifts in the industrial structure. Black women show the smallest absolute gains, but their gains net of shifts in the economy and labor supply are stronger than those observed for white women, with a drop of about one-third of a point per year in measured segregation. Race desegregation, especially among men, was the dominant pattern immediately after the Civil Rights Act.

After 1973, the pattern shifted strongly in favor of gender-linked desegregation. White women's segregation from white men dropped nearly a point (−0.90) a year, and very little (18.6 percent) of this integration was a result of compositional shifts. The political winds had shifted, and employers were increasingly hiring white women into the same jobs as white men. Although not as dramatic, the same pattern held for black women and black men. For black women, this represented an increased pace of integration with white men, but for black men there was a clear deceleration relative to the initial period of rapid post–Civil Rights Act progress.

During the same period, the pattern of desegregation from white women was much more race-specific. In figure 4.5, we see that, net of compositional shifts in the economy and labor market, white women were increasingly likely to work side by side with both white and black men. Of course, the level of employment segregation from both black men and white men was still extremely high; thus, few women and men actually experienced equal-status work. On the other hand, compared to the hyper-segregation of the pre–civil rights period, these were clear, if not revolutionary, gains. On the contrary, white women became markedly *more segregated* from black women across the period.

Table 4.3 repeats the comparison of observed and adjusted trends for segregation, in this case from white women. In the first period, black women increasingly worked in the same jobs as white women, with a decline in segregation of over a point per year . Almost 80 percent of white female–black female integration was caused by change in workplace hiring patterns. Although there were some declines in segregation between white women and both white men and black men, almost all of it was caused by compositional changes in the labor force and the population of workplaces. Again, the immediate post–civil rights period was primarily characterized by workplace race—but not gender—desegregation.

Dramatic shifts occurred between 1973 and 1980. White women increasingly worked with white men and black men in equal-status contact, and the majority of this desegregation was driven by real changes in organizational behavior. In this period of EEO enforcement and gender uncertainty, white women joined white men in equal-status employment particularly rapidly.

Figure 4.5   Regression-Adjusted Trends in Segregation from White
Women, 1973 to 1980

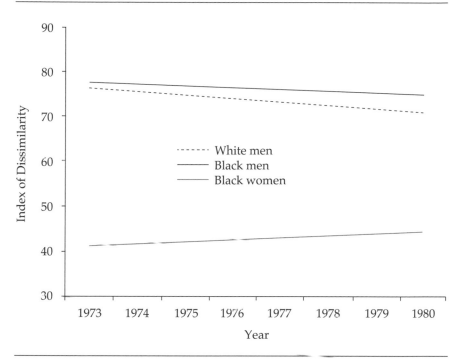

Source: Authors' calculations based on data from EEO-1 surveys (EEOC, various years).

The shocking trend, however, was the resegregation of black women
and white women in this period. Race segregation among women actually climbed 0.371 point per year. After controlling for compositional
change, the increase in race segregation among women was even steeper.
The U.S. women's movement has repeatedly been accused of being a
white women's movement. Although we do not think that this was in any
way the intent, apparently a perverse result of this period of strong social
movement activity was white women gaining access to equal-status employment with men and becoming increasingly segregated from black
women.

Not surprisingly given these segregation trends, we see that, while still
high, white male isolation dropped across the period (figure 4.6). This was
also true for black women and especially for black men. White women, on
the other hand, showed the least increase in intergroup contact. On the
one hand, they were exposed to more interactions with white men and to

Table 4.3 Observed and Adjusted Segregation Trajectories from White Women in the Uncertainty (1966 to 1972) and Enforcement Periods (1973 to 1980)

	1966 to 1972: Uncertainty Period			1973 to 1980: Regulatory Period		
	Observed	Adjusted	Percentage of Change Compositional	Observed	Adjusted	Percentage of Change Compositional
White men	−0.716	−0.128	82.1%	−0.900	−0.733	18.6%
Black men	−0.317	−0.015	95.3	−0.557	−0.343	38.4
Black women	−1.10	−0.848	22.9	+0.371	+0.458	−23.5

Source: Authors' calculations based on data from EEO-1 surveys (EEOC, various years).
Note: Adjusted trends are based on regression adjustments for shifts in labor supply and the geographic, organizational, and industry composition of the economy.

Figure 4.6   Regression-Adjusted Trends in Employment Isolation, 1973 to 1980

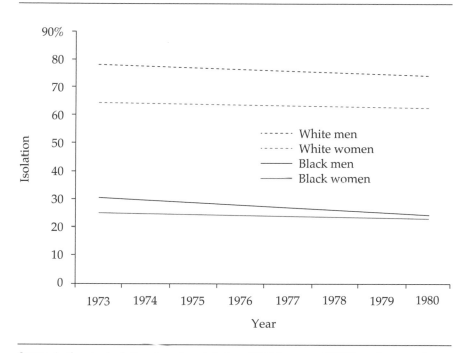

Source: Authors' calculations based on data from EEO-1 surveys (EEOC, various years).

a lesser extent black men, but this was counterbalanced by their increasing isolation from black women.

OCCUPATIONAL REPRESENTATION

In this section, we examine trends in access to the most desirable jobs. Our reasoning is that indicators of increasing equal employment opportunity include not only increased hiring but also increased hiring into the best working- and middle-class jobs. We define "equal opportunity" as representation in these good jobs at the same rate as participation in the local labor market. When representation is zero, we have equal opportunity relative to the supply of labor in the local labor market. When it is positive (which happens only for white men in the analyses to follow), a group has privileged access to good jobs. Negative numbers represent underrepresentation in good jobs. As in the last chapter, we examine access to managerial, professional, and skilled craft jobs.

Figure 4.7 Regression-Adjusted Trends in Managerial Representation, 1973 to 1980

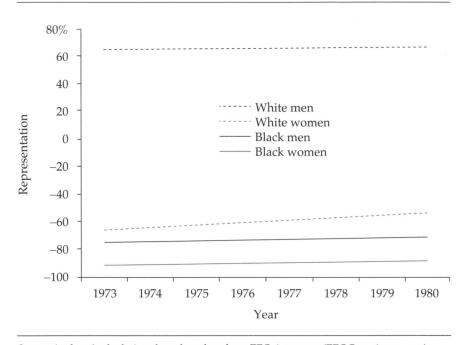

Source: Authors' calculations based on data from EEO-1 surveys (EEOC, various years).

Managerial Jobs

Figure 4.7 charts access to managerial jobs across this period. Adjusting for the shifting population of firms and shifts in labor supply, white male managerial overrepresentation held steady at around 65 percent across the period. Black men made gains, although weak ones. They ended the period 70 percent less likely to be managers than their representation in the local labor markets, only a very slight improvement over their 74 percent underrepresentation in 1973. This was about half the observed rate of gain in managerial jobs that black men enjoyed between 1966 and 1972. Black women made even weaker gains and remained practically invisible in managerial roles. Black women's anemic gains, of about one-half percent per year, were about the same as those that they experienced in the earlier period.

In striking contrast to the slow progress of black men and black women, white women made rapid gains in managerial jobs in private-sector firms during this period of peak uncertainty regarding what constituted gender discrimination. Although they were still underrepresented in 1980 at 53 percent below parity relative to their numbers in the EEOC-reporting labor force, women saw a remarkable improvement of eleven points in only seven years. This is twice the rate of managerial gains by white women in the immediate post–civil rights period, and it also explains, in part, how white women came to become increasingly segregated from black women.

One of the central consequences of the recognition that the Civil Rights Act and associated legal mandates applied to women was the creation of new segregated female managerial roles. These new women managers primarily managed other women. Thus, the matching of women managers to women workers created managerial opportunities that were primarily taken by white women. The racial authority hierarchy that had long existed between white men and black men was now mirrored in a new racial hierarchy among women. Elsewhere we have shown that this pattern of white women managing women of all races was one of the dominant patterns in post–Civil Rights Act corporate America (Stainback and Tomaskovic-Devey 2009). What is somewhat surprising in this analysis is that the pattern is so clear so early in the movement of corporations and regulators recognizing that equal employment opportunity was supposed to extend to women as well as black men.

Professional Jobs

Although managerial jobs continued to be dominated by white men, the trend in access to professional employment was quite different. One of the defining characteristics of professional occupations is that they require specific educational credentials. Engineers must have an engineering degree, accountants cannot be hired without an accounting degree, lawyers must have gone through law school and passed the bar. We believe that educational certification reduces the scope for race- and gender-based discrimination, and this is precisely why EEO progress is most visible in professional occupations. We evaluate this idea more formally in chapter 7, where we find that industries that selected more-educated workforces were more likely to hire African Americans and white women into good-quality jobs and desegregated roles.

What we find in this period of enforcement and gender-linked uncertainty is a very steep climb in white women's access to professional jobs in EEOC-reporting firms (see figure 4.8). White women's exclusion from professional jobs dropped a remarkable twenty points in only seven years. This was more than twice their rate of progress into managerial roles, and it was so great that it seems to have displaced some white men from these roles. White males' privileged control of professional jobs in the private

Figure 4.8   Regression-Adjusted Trends in Professional Representation, 1973 to 1980

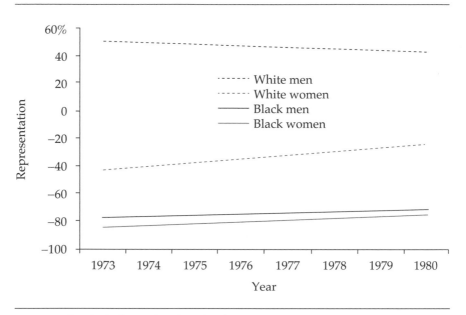

Source: Authors' calculations based on data from EEO-1 surveys (EEOC, various years).

sector dropped from 50 to 40 percent, a trend that, as we will see, continued and even accelerated across the remainder of the century.

Although they began the period from an initial position of near-exclusion, black men and black women also made strong gains in professional jobs. In only seven years, black men saw an improvement of 6 percent in their representation in professional occupations, while black women saw even more impressive gains of 9 percent. Hence, during the period of peak enforcement of equal employment opportunity law, we see that for one set of privileged occupations—the credentialed professions—black men, black women, and white women all made strong gains. Moreover, they did so to some extent at the expense of white men. In fact, even as there was an expansion of 250,000 new professional jobs in EEOC-reporting workplaces between 1973 and 1980, by 1980 white men filled 57,000 fewer professional jobs than they had in 1973. If white men had still held the 70.1 percent of professional jobs they populated in 1973, there would have been 234,000 more white male professionals in 1980—almost the entire quarter of a million new positions created by economic growth. Conversely, the sum of new professional jobs held by white women (220,025), black men

(13,936), and black women (21,538) nearly equaled both the new jobs created and the relative decline in white male professional positions.

Credential-based screening made professional jobs the easiest good jobs to integrate. One of the earliest foci of social closure theory was on the role of educational credentials (along with unionization and property rights) in group-based opportunity hoarding (Parkin 1979). Educational degrees are a mechanism for excluding competition from the noncredentialed and supporting claims for higher wages and workplace autonomy. Credentials help secure occupational rights to control the labor process, including hiring and firing, akin to the property rights that give capitalists control over workplaces. So, while educational credentials are historically mechanisms of exclusion, in the early post–Civil Rights Act period they combined with economic growth to become mechanisms of equal opportunity.

In these early post–Civil Rights Act years, there was a backlog of underemployed degree-holding white women, black women, and black men, mostly trained in segregated black or female colleges and universities, who were available to be hired into professional jobs. In 1972, Title IX amended the Civil Rights Act to require the withholding of federal payments, including tuition grants, from schools that discriminated on the basis of race and gender. Traditionally male and white colleges responded by changing their behavior very quickly (Jacobs 1995). In the short run, the availability of credentialed women and black men was important, but in the longer run it was the rapid adoption of equal opportunity practices and the resulting rapid desegregation of colleges and universities that was decisive in opening up the professions to groups other than white men.

Integration is not just a labor supply-side issue. Suitable white female, black male, and black female candidates must be matched with hiring agents who are willing to hire them. It is here that two additional mechanisms became crucial.

First, the classic social closure process around educational certification as a basis of exclusion began to work in favor of the previously barred candidates for professional jobs. Once women and minorities began to be considered for accounting jobs, for instance, the first hurdle was not one of race or gender, but of actually holding the degree. Discrimination on the basis of degree came to trump discrimination based on race or gender. Colleges and universities almost immediately changed their behavior after Title IX, which quickly integrated the supply of professionals available to be hired.

The second mechanism had to do with the hiring process. Unlike managers, who mostly learn on the job from other managers how to manage, or skilled crafts people, who are taught the tricks of the trade in apprenticeships to master craftsmen, professionals learn their entry-level skills outside the workplace. With the initial certification of professionals having been captured by colleges and universities, some of the discretion in the evaluation of candidate suitability was removed from the people currently doing the work. At the same time, human resource professionals were establishing a more race- and gender-conscious approach to the hiring process, instituting formal job descriptions, public posting of positions, and formal interviews as equal employment opportunity measures. Because of the centrality of educational credentials in the hiring of professionals, we think that new EEO human resource practices were likely to be the most effective in these occupations. After all, it is hard to hire a white male without a degree in favor of a black male with a degree for a professional job and not run afoul of the credential-based nature of professionalism and equal opportunity mandates linked to formal job descriptions. It simply became harder to discriminate in making professional appointments. That colleges and universities were simultaneously changing the supply of credentialed workers exacerbated and cemented this trend.

Craft Jobs

In the mid and late 1970s, access to skilled working-class jobs followed the same pattern as access to managerial jobs (see figure 4.9). White males showed continued gains, although those gains were not as rapid as in the earlier period. Between 1966 and 1971, white male overrepresentation in craft production jobs rose by 1.4 percent per year, dropping to a still remarkable one-third of a percent per year gain in what was the period of peak enforcement of equal opportunity law. During this same period, the absolute number of skilled working-class jobs actually fell by about 184,000. The continued monopolization of the best-quality working-class jobs by white men was largely accomplished through the nearly complete exclusion of women from these jobs.

This is not to say that other groups did not make gains in the declining craft production fields. Black males made strong gains of 1.4 percent per year. Although a considerable decline from the first period, when black male hiring into craft production jobs grew by more than 4 percent per year, this was still rapid improvement. By 1980, black men could be found in craft production jobs at almost the same rate as they were hired into the EEOC labor force overall. The continued very large gap with white men in these skilled jobs suggests that there was still a great deal of discrimination in access to training and hiring, but also that progress toward an equal opportunity future was rapid. In this case, one might say that black men were still the victims of racial discrimination but at the same time beneficiaries of gender discrimination—discrimination that all but banned

Figure 4.9 Regression-Adjusted Trends in Craft Occupation
Representation, 1973 to 1980

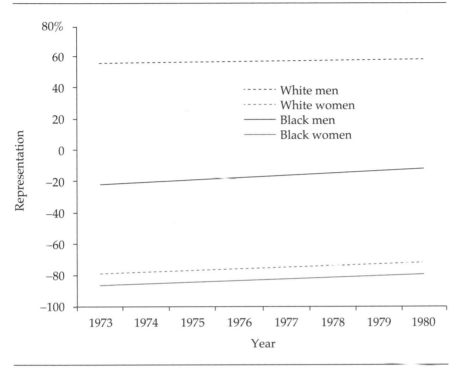

Source: Authors' calculations based on data from EEO-1 surveys (EEOC, various years).

women from skilled working-class jobs. Black women and white women made some initial gains in craft jobs during this period, but their total numbers were quite small: among the more than 3 million craft production jobs in the EEOC-reporting workplaces, fewer than 20,000 were additional female hires.

During the short period between 1973 and 1980—a time when corporate uncertainty shifted from demonstrating race- to gender-based equal opportunity and federal enforcement of equal opportunity law was at its peak—the basic patterns of desegregation and increased access to good jobs shifted fundamentally to favor white women. Net of shifts in the organization of the economy and in labor supply, white women made gains in craft, managerial, and especially professional jobs—after making no gains, or only weak gains, in the period immediately after the passage of the Civil Rights Act.

For black men, strong gains continued in all three occupations, but at lower rates than in the initial period of racial uncertainty. The contrast was most stark in craft production jobs, in which black male representation grew at 4 percent per year in the earlier period, but at only 1.4 percent a year after 1973. There was a similar, if not as extreme, slowdown in black male hiring into managerial jobs in the second period. Only in professional jobs, where access was first governed by field-specific college degrees, do we see black male gains in the enforcement period nearly keeping up with the burst of initial hiring seen after the Civil Rights Act.

Black women made limited gains in craft and managerial positions, but strong gains in professional positions. When it came to managerial jobs, black women did not seem to benefit from the new focus of corporate human resource managers on gender integration. On the other hand, access to professional positions accelerated. In fact, by 1980 there were more black women than black men in professional occupations in the EEOC workforce, a reversal of the 1973 and earlier pattern. Although white women would also eventually outnumber white men in professional jobs, they would not do so for another two decades. And while craft jobs remained male-dominated, between 1973 and 1980 black women filled an additional 10,474 jobs, 2,000 more than white women. It is not clear why black women had stronger gains in craft jobs than white women. On the one hand, we can speculate that this reflects the stronger association of black women with manual labor. On the other hand, it may simply represent white women's greater opportunities in the even more desirable high-status managerial and professional jobs.

The story for white men in this period is a lot like the earlier story. Their advantaged access to craft production and managerial roles grew, although at slower rates than had been the case in the immediate post–Civil Rights Act period. The key shift was in white men's control of professional positions, which had grown by 9 percent between 1966 and 1972. White men actually lost control of many professional jobs. Their overrepresentation dropped by 3 percent, and they experienced both absolute and relative jobs losses. The marriage of credential-based hiring to emerging equal opportunity practice seems to have produced the first post–Civil Rights Act evidence of a movement toward equal opportunity in access to good-quality jobs.

Did OFCCP Oversight Matter?

Although our narrative has stressed the uncertainty motivating corporate shifts in behavior, first around race and then gender, we have also pointed out that the period between 1973 and 1980 was the period of peak EEO enforcement by the federal government. It was during this period that the EEOC could become party to discrimination lawsuits and the OFCCP began to audit federal contractors and clarify what constituted progress toward equal opportunity. If there was a moment in history when the fear of federal intervention might motivate real equal opportunity changes, this was it. During this period, EEOC lawsuits targeted large firms, almost all of which were federal contractors. The OFCCP audited only federal contractors, using the threat of debarment from future federal contracts as the strongest regulatory threat in the federal arsenal. Thus, we might expect desegregation to have happened most rapidly during this period among federal contractors. Jonathan Leonard (1984a, 1984b) has documented gains, particularly for black men, during this period, but his analyses do not control for labor supply and shifts in the population of organizations as thoroughly as our approach does. We confirm these earlier findings, but not without a few surprises.

In the early 1970s, the regulatory context changed. Federal contractors were required by the Office of Federal Contract Compliance to maintain written affirmative action plans for all jobs in all workplaces, and large firms became the target of compliance audits around these plans. Congress gave the EEOC the right to sue companies for discriminatory behavior, and the EEOC also targeted the largest firms. At this time, the courts, the EEOC, and the OFCC all came to define nondiscrimination as conformity with best practices as defined initially in the Plans for Progress blueprint. The courts made the actual definition of best practices a moving target, and equal opportunity consultants and personnel managers became the corporate solution to managing uncertainty in compliance with equal opportunity pressures. As a result, the personnel function was expanded and strengthened, and new equal opportunity policies proliferated (Dobbin 2009).

The strengthened regulatory pressure from the government only enhanced uncertainty among regulated private-sector firms. Now firms knew that the Office of Federal Contract Compliance Programs (the name of the agency was changed in 1975) might actually monitor equal opportunity progress and that they could face embarrassing and potentially expensive lawsuits from the EEOC and private individuals. What they did not know was which personnel practices were discriminatory and which were signals of good-faith efforts. In addition, the case law changed rapidly, as did the best practices being endorsed by the courts as evidence of nondiscrimination. This uncertainty vastly strengthened the personnel function, particularly affirmative action compliance officers and new departments of equal opportunity. Unlike their predecessors, who were primarily tasked with preventing unionization or forestalling union goals and expansion as the goal of employee relations, these new equal opportunity personnel managers were in favor of equal opportunity.

It seems safe to assume that the new uncertainty over gender discrimination brought about by the women's movement and legislative affirmations of "sex" as a protected category would apply to all firms, but that federal contractors might have felt additional direct regulatory pressure to desegregate. If so, on what grounds would such pressure have been applied? We know that in the late 1960s the OFCCP was stressing racial discrimination as its target and downplaying the importance of gender equality. After 1972, it became clear that the U.S. Congress intended that the OFCCP would enforce gender equity as aggressively as racial progress, but we do not know if they did.

Federal Contractors and Black Men

Immediately after the enactment of the Civil Rights Act, black men made larger gains in managerial and professional jobs among federal contractors than they did in other firms. The trajectory of their equal-status job integration with white men among federal contractors was also steeper during this early period. Reflecting these gains in the immediate post–Civil Rights Act period, black men began the period with lower segrega-

Figure 4.10   Regression-Adjusted Comparison of Black Male Segregation from White Men and from White Women by Federal Regulatory Status, 1973 to 1980

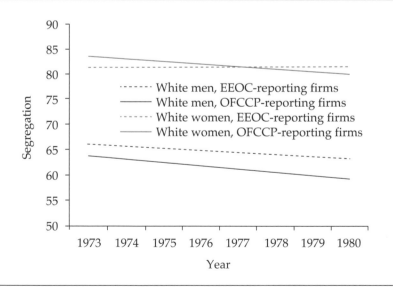

Source: Authors' calculations based on data from EEO-1 surveys (EEOC, various years).

Figure 4.11   Regression-Adjusted Black Male Occupational
Representation by Federal Reporting Status,
1973 to 1980

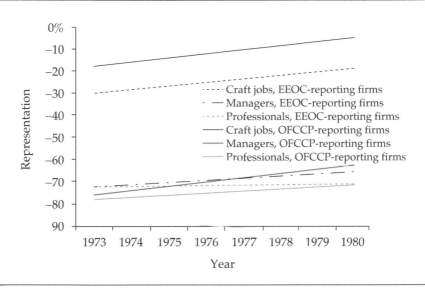

Craft jobs, EEOC-reporting firms
Managers, EEOC-reporting firms
Professionals, EEOC-reporting firms
Craft jobs, OFCCP-reporting firms
Managers, OFCCP-reporting firms
Professionals, OFCCP-reporting firms

Source: Authors' calculations based on data from EEO-1 surveys (EEOC, various years).

tion from white men in OFCCP-reporting firms and saw continued steeper
declines than in other firms during the enforcement period. In the earlier
period, black men saw no declines in segregation from white women
among federal contractors or noncontractors. For noncontractors, this pattern extended through 1980. For federal contractors, however, we see desegregation between black men and white women emerging (figure 4.10).

Black men also showed stronger patterns of incorporation into managerial, professional, and craft jobs in OFCCP-reporting firms than in noncontractor firms during this period. For managers, this difference in access
trajectories was quite dramatic: the growth in black men's access to managerial jobs among federal contractors was double that of noncontractors
(1.9 percent versus 0.96 percent per year). Black men saw no significant
gains in access to professional jobs among noncontractors, but gains among
contractors grew at a brisk 1 percent per year. Black men did not show
higher relative growth in access to craft jobs among contractors than among
firms not subject to OFCCP audits. Federal contractors' advantage over
noncontractors in the hiring and promotion of black men into managerial
and professional jobs actually doubled during this period (figure 4.11).

If we take the contrast between federal contractors and noncontractors as an indicator of the influence of regulatory enforcement, it appears that during the period of peak enforcement the advancement of black men into managerial and professional jobs became a signal to the OFCCP of equal opportunity progress.

Federal Contractors and White Women

As we have already seen, this period introduced profound uncertainty as to what constituted equal opportunity progress on the basis of gender. Our economy-wide analyses suggest that desegregation accelerated in particular for white women in this period. It remains to be seen whether gender equality had become incorporated into the regulatory call-and-response of the OFCCP and the firms that did business with the federal government and hoped to keep their lucrative federal contracts.

In 1973 white women who worked for federal contractors were considerably more segregated from both white men and black men than women employed elsewhere in the private sector. Because these estimates are adjusted for industrial composition, they do not reflect the type of work being done; they do, however, point to the lack of progress on gender segregation among federal contractors during the late 1960s, when the OFCCP made it quite clear that gender equity was not in its mandate (figure 4.12).

On the other hand, and in contrast with the earlier period, OFCCP-reporting firms showed much steeper declines in gender segregation than noncontractor firms. This was particularly true for segregation from white men, which declined about one point per year among federal contractors. Segregation from black men declined at about half that rate among contractors, but not at all among firms that were not accountable to the OFCCP.

When we examine access to the set of more desirable occupations, we find that OFCCP-reporting firms were no different from other firms in white women's access to managerial or craft jobs. The story is quite different, and dramatically so, for professional jobs. One of the most striking findings is that among noncontractors in 1973 white women's representation in professional jobs was almost at the same level as their representation in their local labor forces. On the other hand, and perhaps not surprisingly given their near-total exclusion from professional jobs among federal contractors, white women made very rapid gains after 1973 in professional jobs in OFCCP-regulated workplaces. Given women's lack of relative progress into managerial jobs, this movement is unlikely to represent a strong enforcement mandate on the part of the OFCCP. On the other hand, by comparison with noncontractors, one imagines that human re-

Figure 4.12   Regression-Adjusted Comparison of Segregation from White Women by Federal Reporting Status, 1973 to 1980

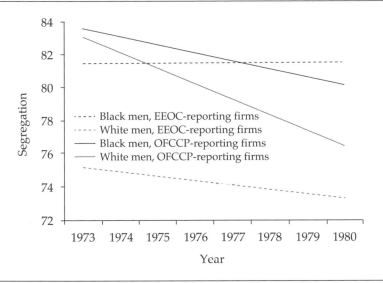

Source: Authors' calculations based on data from EEO-1 surveys (EEOC, various years).

source managers looking at their comparative statistics for the professional employment of women would have seen immediately that they had a problem. A comparison to managerial jobs at OFCCP-reporting firms would not have led to the same conclusion, since in 1973 white male overrepresentation and white female underrepresentation were higher in managerial jobs than in professional jobs.

There is good evidence here that after 1972 federal contractors began to take gender equity for white women more seriously, although this did not extend to the integration of managerial or craft jobs. Professional jobs, however, saw particularly rapid absorption of white women during this period. Despite these rapid gains, federal contractors ended the period well behind the rest of the private sector in the employment of white women in professional positions.

Federal Contractors and Black Women

Black women experienced weak declines in segregation from white men among both federal contractor firms and those firms not subject to affirmative action mandates. The desegregation trend was slightly steeper among federal contractors, although it started from a higher initial level in

Figure 4.13   Regression-Adjusted Trends in White Women's Access to Professional Occupations by Federal Regulatory Status, 1973 to 1980

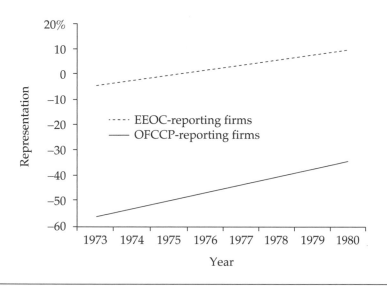

Source: Authors' calculations based on data from EEO-1 surveys (EEOC, various years).

1973. The interesting story is the workplace segregation of black women from white women (see figure 4.13). We have already seen that there was a small increase in race segregation among women in this period. It turns out that the increase was quite small, almost nonexistent, among firms not subject to OFCCP oversight. On the other hand, the trend toward the re-segregation of white women and black women was relatively steep among federal contractors, rising about 0.61 percent per year. This is two-thirds as large as the yearly desegregation trend among federal contractors in the immediate post–Civil Rights Act period. In 1966 race segregation of black and white women was seven points lower among federal contractors than it was among other firms. Presumably, this represented the earlier, pre-1966 integration of the work of some white women and black women employed by federal contractors. Amazingly, by 1980 this difference had shrunk to almost zero as federal contractors resegregated employment among black women and white women (figure 4.14).

When we examine the occupational representation of black women, we see that federal contractors were no different than other firms in opening access to professional and craft jobs. In the earlier period of racial uncer-

Figure 4.14   Regression-Adjusted Employment Race Segregation Among Black and White Women by Federal Regulatory Status, 1973 to 1980

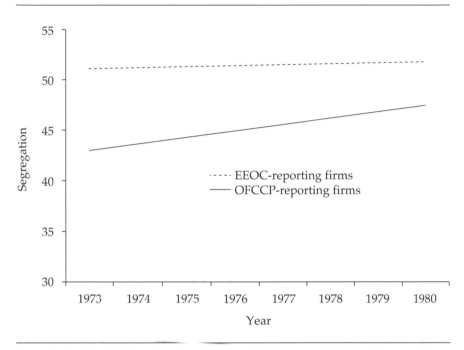

Source: Authors' calculations based on data from EEO-1 surveys (EEOC, various years).

tainty, federal contractors hired or promoted black women more quickly into professional and craft jobs than did other firms. In the earlier period, there was no difference between federal contractors and other firms in the rate of black female integration into managerial roles. In the 1970s regulatory period, OFCCP-monitored firms were actually somewhat less likely to move black women into managerial jobs. Thus, the quicker post-1972 desegregation of black women and white men that we see among federal contractors was a function of hiring black women and white men into the same lower-level jobs.

The resegregation of black women and white women among federal contractors was produced by the stronger gains that white women were making in traditionally male managerial and professional jobs. So, while OFCCP-reporting firms clearly changed their behavior toward white women after 1972, if anything they lost interest in promoting equal opportunity for black women. It would seem that any uncertainty around gender equity or either real or feared extension of regulatory oversight to monitor gender discrimination was not interpreted by federal contractors as extending to black women. If post-1972 was the beginning of uncertainty as to what constituted gender discrimination, the immediate response seems to have been to hire and promote white women into better jobs. Black women fared much better during the earlier period of racial uncertainty. Intersectional speculation aside, at least in the early post–Civil Rights Act period it turns out that black women, as potential employees, were seen more as *black* than as *women* in terms of the increased opportunities afforded by the prohibition of race and gender discrimination in employment. Even then, they tended (with the exception of professional jobs) to have fewer new opportunities compared to black men.

Federal Contractors and White Men

We have already seen that the desegregation of white men from black men, white women, and black women during this period was more pronounced among federal contractors than elsewhere in the private sector. White men in firms that held federal contracts also saw steeper declines (about one-half a percent per year) in social isolation (figure 4.15) than they did when they worked among noncontractors (one-third of a percent per year). This was not accomplished because white men had a particularly difficult time securing the good-quality jobs among federal contractors. On the contrary, they had a slightly higher rate of growth in access to managerial and craft jobs among federal contractors, and there was no difference from other EEOC-reporting firms in their declining control of professional jobs.

There is certainly evidence here that OFCCP oversight encouraged desegregation and, for white women and black men, opened more doors to managerial, professional, and craft production jobs. Paradoxically, the expansion of opportunities for white women led to increased employment segregation between them and black women.

What About Human Resource Practices?

It was during this period that prior research has documented the spread of human resource practices intended to signal compliance with emerging EEO law and regulatory practice (Dobbin 2009). Some have argued that this compliance was primarily symbolic—that it was targeted at averting lawsuits rather than actually fostering desegregation or equal opportunity. Although we think that this may often have been the corporate motive for instituting these human resource policies, it remains an empirically open issue as to whether these policies actually promoted equal

Figure 4.15   Regression-Adjusted Isolation Trends by Regulatory
Status, 1973 to 1980

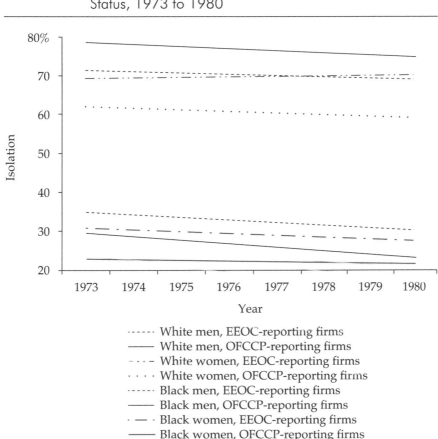

Source: Authors' calculations based on data from EEO-1 surveys (EEOC, various years).

opportunity or served as symbolic shields to merely prevent lawsuits or to legitimate current practices when lawsuits occurred.

The emerging equal opportunity experts founded corporate offices to track changes in the law and EEO best practices, proposed new managerial evaluation strategies to monitor the equal opportunity performance of managers, and set up grievance procedures to intercept complaints before they became lawsuits. While these three HR innovations were meant to signal to courts and regulators compliance with nondiscrimination mandates, personnel managers also proposed and implemented a series of formalized employment practices to fight bias. These included employment screening tests tailored to job performance, job descriptions that clearly defined qualifications, job posting to subvert network-based hiring, performance evaluation to eliminate subjective bias, and salary classification systems to combat segregation-linked wage disparities. All of these equal opportunity innovations were borrowed from earlier personnel practices and eventually confirmed by the courts as evidence of nondiscriminatory workplaces (Dobbin 2009). This is not to say that anyone was actually evaluating these practices to see whether they prevented discrimination or increased integration; but as best practices promulgated by an enthusiastic profession, they did become institutionally legitimized and eventually required even of the not-so-enthusiastic. Thus, as Dobbin and others have pointed out, their power may have been primarily symbolic.

On the other hand, some sociologists have argued that formalization of the human resource management function may promote equal opportunity precisely because it reduces the influence of the basic social psychological mechanisms that serve to reproduce status and power inequalities (Bielby 2000; Reskin 2000). Hence, while formalization may not eliminate workplace inequalities, it is expected to mitigate them (Anderson and Tomaskovic-Devey 1995; Reskin and McBrier 2000). Research has shown that formalization is associated with lower gender segregation (Tomaskovic-Devey 1993; Tomaskovic-Devey, Kalleberg, and Marsden 1996; Tomaskovic-Devey and Skaggs 1999b), smaller influences of gender segregation on the pay gap (Anderson and Tomaskovic-Devey 1995; Elvira and Graham 2002; Pfeffer and Cohen 1984), and increases in women's access to managerial and supervisory jobs (Reskin and McBrier 2000; Hultin and Szulkin 1999). In the absence of formal rules and procedures regarding the evaluation of applicants and employees, individuals are likely to base their decisions on stereotypical views and in-group preferences. When cognitive biases are countered by formal decision-making rules and accountability, they may, at least in some cases, be muted.

The EEOC data are not ideal for investigating managerial practices, because we do not have any information on workplace human resource practices. We can, however, identify whether the establishment was part of a large and presumably bureaucratized workplace. It is quite clear from prior research on the spread of formalization in human resource practices that larger firms led the way, as they solved the basic problem of coordination created by large-scale production. Research on the spread of human resource practices that might signal to regulators compliance with new equal opportunity law also suggests that it was in larger firms and among federal contractors that these practices spread first and most completely (Edelman 1990; Dobbin 2009).

We looked to see if large firm size (firms with more than 15,000 employ-

Table 4.4 Regression-Adjusted Segregation and Isolation Yearly Change by Contractor Types and Large Firm Size, 1973 to 1980

	Large EEOC-Reporting Firms	Other EEOC-Reporting Firms	Large OFCCP-Reporting Firms	Other OFCCP-Reporting Firms
Segregation from white men				
White women	0.046	–0.352	–1.112	–0.818
Black men	–0.018	–0.469	–0.638	–0.499
Black women	–0.158	–0.294	–0.871	–0.464
Segregation from white women				
Black men	0.412	–0.071	–0.626	–0.362
Black women	0.334	0.030	0.628	0.595
Isolation from contact with other groups				
White men	–0.512	–0.319	–0.653	–0.416
White women	0.095	0.044	–0.589	–0.226
Black men	–0.510	–0.680	–0.903	–0.852
Black women	0.198	–0.536	–0.172	0.198

Source: Authors' calculations based on data from EEO-1 surveys (EEOC, various years).

ees) as a proxy for formalization and regulatory visibility produced steeper rates of integration (table 4.4). In the last chapter, we found that prior to 1972 this was generally the case, but only for the federal contractors involved in the Plans for Progress self-regulation movement. Because the Plans for Progress initiative no longer existed as a collective effort of large federal contractors (Dobbin 2009), we are inclined to interpret any post-1972 large firm distinctions as the institutionalization, at least relative to other firms, of effective human resource capacity to foster EEO goals.

Among firms that reported to the EEOC but were not subject to OFCCP oversight and affirmative action guidelines, desegregation from white men was actually faster in small and medium-size firms than in the very large firms that employed 15,000 or more people, and black male and black female segregation from white women increased year over year in firms that reported only to the EEOC. The only exception to this pattern was that white male isolation from cross-group contact dropped marginally faster in large EEOC-reporting firms.

The pattern was reversed among federal contractors. Desegregation occurred at a considerably faster pace and social isolation dropped more steeply among the largest businesses subject to OFCCP oversight. Thus, it would appear that there is support for the notion that some combination of formalized human resource practices and the creation of affirmative action plans with goals and timetables, in conjunction with the regulatory threat associated with OFCCP audits of those plans, produced more rapid progress toward equal-status employment among the very largest federal contractors. Thus, the impact of regulation, whether through direct regulatory threats or the route of new human resource practices, appears to have been not merely symbolic but to have produced some real progress when accompanied by accountability to the OFCCP. In chapter 8, we review literatures on human resource practices, lawsuits, EEOC discrimination charges, and OFCCP audits. In all cases, either internal or external accountability is the key to equal employment opportunity progress.

The one glaring threat to this conclusion is that black women, while integrating relatively quickly with white men among large federal contractors, were also very quick to resegregate from white women in these same firms. It is difficult to believe that this was a direct response to regulatory mandates. Certainly, the historical record lacks such a directive, explicit or implied. Rather, it seems likely to us that the new human resource practices instituted to achieve compliance with equal opportunity expectations both within and outside the largest federal contractors also led to the unintended consequence of creating new managerial and professional jobs that were increasingly filled by white women.

One of the roles that white women came to dominate during this period was the job of human resource manager. By 1980, 35 percent of human resource managers were white women. White males plummeted from 70 percent of HR managers in 1968 to only 43 percent in 1980. Thus, the function entrusted with promoting racial and gender equal opportunity increasingly was organized by and perhaps from the point of view of white women. We will watch this process unfold further in the next chapter. In other work, we have documented that by 1980 the more general pattern of white women managing other women in gender-segregated task functions had become established in many workplaces (Stainback and Tomaskovic-Devey 2009).

Interestingly, when we look at access to managerial, professional, and craft production jobs, the pattern of large-firm OFCCP gains is present only for black men and black women. This makes sense if the gains were being driven by human resource routines rather than the new uncertainty produced by the women's movement. White women made very large gains only among the largest nonfederal contractors, and only in managerial and professional jobs. Because large noncontractor firms were now at risk for discrimination charges and even lawsuits from the EEOC, and many large retailers were also at risk of being faced with direct demands from the women's movement, they may have experienced sudden pressure to demonstrate compliance with equal opportunity expectations for women. They did not respond by desegregating their workforces generally, but by quickly expanding the number of women in their professional and managerial ranks.

Although our data are far from ideal for addressing the role of human resource practices, they do suggest that formalization, proxied by large size, was not enough to lead to desegregation. Given that desegregation did happen faster among very large federal contractors, we suspect that it was not merely the development of human resource practices intended to show compliance with equal opportunity mandates, but the historical context in which they developed. Confirming our interpretation, in a study looking at a sample of EEOC-reporting firms supplemented with a survey of firm human resource practices, Frank Dobbin, Daniel Schrage, and Alexandra Kalev (2010) find that formal personnel policies, in the absence of legal accountability, have no effects, or even negative effects, on managerial diversity. The same policies show some positive effects when the firm is under additional affirmative action oversight by the OFCCP. We discuss this literature in depth in chapter 8.

James Baron and his colleagues (2007) have argued that it is not merely the presence or absence of a policy or practice but the organizational logics, or values, undergirding rules that should affect ascription in organizations. Policies must be carried out, and there is always room for discretion and interpretation. Formalization promotes gender equity only if the underlying values that steer implementation are meritocratic. We think it likely that to rise above the merely symbolic, formalization targeted to promote merit-based equal employment opportunity must also be supported by workplace-level accountability in decision-making (Kalev, Dobbin, and Kelly 2006; Castilla 2008).

Gender Uncertainty and Regulatory Oversight, 1973 to 1980

Although the political retreat from the civil rights agenda was evident as early as the 1968 election, after 1972 it was a fixture of Republican electoral strategy and would remain so through the rest of the century. As white support for African American civil rights waned across the 1970s, so did the strength of the civil rights movement. From the point of view of private U.S. corporations, the threat of being accused of racial discrimination simply became less threatening, and the human resource practices that would be judged legitimate by courts and federal regulators became clearer. As uncertainty waned, so too did the rapid racial desegregation and progress into good jobs that had happened in the immediate aftermath of President Kennedy's executive order to federal contractors to take affirmative action and the landmark passage of the Civil Rights Act in 1964. Black progress continued, but at a slower rate. Among large federal contractors, black progress was the most pronounced in this period in which the racial rules of the EEO game became clarified. We think that this represents the institutionalization of relatively effective EEO human resource practices by federal contractors. Dobbin's (2009) explanation that it was these firms that earlier had responded most aggressively seems compelling to us. In the previous chapter, we saw that the original Plans for Progress firms showed initial advantages in black-white integration. We suspect that it was also in these firms in particular that HR managers proffering solutions to the problem of promoting equal opportunity became most influential.

The big gain across the 1970s, however, did not go to African Americans, the beneficiaries of regulatory oversight and HR planning, but to white women. White women made strong gains in jobs previously held only by men, typically by white men. They made rapid progress into managerial jobs; many of them newly segregated female managerial jobs as they replaced white men as the managers of choice for female-segregated production, sale, and service jobs. White women made extremely speedy progress into professional jobs, where their class-advantaged access to college degrees combined with the new formalization of hiring shifted these desirable opportunities increasingly from white men to white women. That white women's gains in good jobs were, if anything, slower among federal contractors and large firms signaled that it was general uncertainty over the new mandate to not discriminate on the basis of gender, rather than direct regulatory coercion, that drove EEO progress. Gender uncertainty was driven by a vigorous women's rights movement, continuous ERA politics across the decade, and the confirmation by the Supreme Court and the EEOC that gender was now a protected category when it came to employment law.

OFCCP regulation, especially of the largest contractor firms, is associated with more rapid overall gender desegregation during this period, but not with more rapid integration into good-quality jobs, suggesting that gender discrimination had not yet been effectively incorporated into their regulatory routines. In the next chapter, we see that after 1980 the political tide turned again: the Reagan administration repudiated affirmative action and equal opportunity as regulatory goals, and the OFCCP became largely ineffective at promoting further private-sector equal opportunity gains on the basis of race or gender.

Chapter 5 | Desegregation in the Neoliberal Era, 1980 to 2005

WHEN RONALD REAGAN became president, the regulatory environment changed again; the EEOC and OFCCP were instructed to back off their enforcement mission, and whatever proactive commitment to equal opportunity that had once emanated from the executive branch ceased. While Reagan was blocked by a Democratic Congress from completely gutting EEO enforcement, it was clear that the pressure was off. Across the 1980s, personnel managers rebranded themselves as human resource managers with a core goal of business efficiency. They also rebranded the formalization-linked EEO policies of the 1970s as simply efficient human resource management. Any race- or gender-targeted policy or practice was reframed as a productivity-enhancing diversity program. This professional flexibility ensured not only the survival of these policies as affirmative action mandates faded, but a strengthened connection to core business goals. This garnered increased support from CEOs newly committed to efficiency, especially as they became overtaken by the shareholder value movement in corporate governance.

THE POLITICS OF RACE

The election of 1980 was a defining moment in the rightward tilt of the Republican Party. Democratic incumbent Jimmy Carter's vague politics concerning civil rights, coupled with increasing white resistance to policies aimed at eradicating racial inequality, contributed to Ronald Reagan's victory in the 1980 presidential election. The Reagan-Bush campaign took an unambiguous position against affirmative action in employment, busing to achieve educational integration, and income transfers to the poor, while igniting whites' concerns over "reverse discrimination." The Reagan-Bush administration was able to fuel the racial fears of whites, particularly white men, and mobilize white voters to win the next three presidential elections.

In the 1988 presidential election, Vice President George H. W. Bush ran against Michael Dukakis, the Democratic governor from Massachusetts. Bush followed his predecessor's position on most issues and fueled white racial antagonisms with his blatant use of racist imagery in his political advertisements. Richard M. Nixon's 1968 campaign had connected crime and disorder to race in an effort to enrage whites and win elections, and the Bush campaign would employ a similar strategy to win the 1988 election. The Reagan administration had already primed American racist ideology, and Bush would capitalize on it.

Bush was falling far behind Dukakis in the polls when "Willie Horton" became the buzzword of political conversation. William J. Horton Jr. was an African American who was convicted of murder and serving his sentence in a Massachusetts prison. Horton was released for furlough, but did not return. He was later arrested in Maryland and charged with assault, kidnap, and rape of a white couple. The Bush campaign blamed Dukakis for the crime and made sure that the image of a black man walking through a revolving door out of prison was implanted in the minds of Americans.

According to historian Kenneth O'Reilly (1995), William Horton was never personally referred to as "Willie," but Lee Atwater, Bush's campaign strategist, decided to use the name because it would invoke a stronger race-linked reaction. The Bush campaign denied accusations of racism and claimed that the commercial was about Dukakis's record on crime and had nothing to do with race. Research on the advertisement itself suggests that it successfully invoked racial prejudice in viewers rather than fear of crime (Mendelberg 1997). The Bush campaign would later run a series of "weekend pass" television ads showing prison inmates moving in and out of prison through a revolving door and claiming that Dukakis was sending dangerous criminals back onto the streets to commit violent crimes. Dukakis fell in the polls, and Bush won the election (Jamieson 1992).

Compared to the 1988 election, the 1992 presidential election between George H. W. Bush, William J. Clinton, and Ross Perot was fairly quiet on both racial and gender politics. In 1993 President Clinton entered the presidential office with more supportive race and gender equality rhetoric than had been evident during the Reagan-Bush administrations. Shortly after taking office, he signed the Family Medical Leave Act, which required private-sector establishments with fifty or more employees to offer leave for childbirth, family medical issues, or personal health issues to employees who had worked more than twenty-five hours a week for the previous year. The act did not require that the employer pay the employee during a leave, but the employer had to continue to maintain health benefits as if the employee would be continuing to work. Employers were also required to provide the employee with a job that was the same or comparable when he or she returned to work. There was, however, a provision that employers were not required to provide the same or comparable employment to employees in high-level positions (salaried jobs with pay in the top 10 percent of all employees). Of course, these are also the employees who are most financially able to take time away from work without pay.

While Clinton's overall politics appeared supportive of equal opportunity for racial minorities and women, a counter political rhetoric in Congress opposing EEO/AA measures, especially in federal contracting, emerged during his first administration. During this period, Republican members of the House and Senate unsuccessfully introduced several bills seeking to end the use of affirmative action in various public and private spheres of work and federal contracting. In 1995 Sen. Jesse Helms (R-NC) unsuccessfully introduced the "Civil Rights Restoration Act of 1995." The act was intended to amend the Civil Rights Act of 1964 to make affirmative action an unfair labor practice and the use of affirmative action illegal in federal contracting as well as in public- and private-sector employment (see S. 26 and S. 318 and, for similar bills in the House, H.R. 1764 and H.R. 1840).

Clinton's support for affirmative action was ambivalent at best, and the enforcement agencies' budgets were not substantially increased during his presidency. While budgets were flat, OFCCP staffing, compliance reviews, and discrimination complaint resolutions all fell during the first term of the Clinton presidency (U.S. Commission on Civil Rights 1995). When affirmative action became the center of public discourse, Clinton responded with his 1996 "mend it don't end it" speech in which he claimed that the intended purpose of affirmative action mandates had not been achieved, but that the country should work to correct problems, oppose quotas, use strict evaluation in its implementation, and make sure that job candidates were qualified for positions. Who exactly was supposed to do this work was left unspecified.

REGULATORY RETREAT

The Reagan-Bush administration promulgated an openly hostile stance toward civil rights issues, especially those addressing issues of racial inequality, claiming that the federal government should shift greater responsibilities for governance to the states. In addition to the strong rhetorical stance against affirmative action, the Reagan-Bush administration also reduced funding and resources to civil rights enforcement agencies (Wood 1990). In her study of the OFCCP under the Reagan administration, Virginia duRivage (1992) finds that, owing to budgets cuts, OFCCP personnel were reduced by 52 percent between 1979 and 1985; compliance reviews

Figure 5.1   EEOC and OFCCP Funding and Staffing, 1981 to 1994

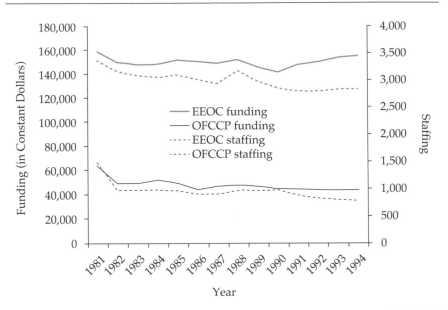

Source: Authors' compilation based on U.S. Commission on Civil Rights (1995).

fell by over 38 percent in 1982 alone; and back pay awards were reduced by 77 percent between 1980 and 1982. Cuts to the EEOC were similar (figure 5.1). These cuts occurred even as discrimination complaints to both agencies rose.

Reagan directed the new EEOC head, Clarence Thomas, to weaken consent decrees and cut funding and staff. At the OFCCP, staff was cut in half, compliance reviews and sanctions were weakened, and visible firms and industries were no longer targeted. Contractor debarments and findings of violations dropped, and the remaining, presumably more egregious violators were less likely to be required to do anything about their violations (Dobbin 2009, 136–37).

Despite the continued growth in discrimination complaints to the EEOC, the number of class-action lawsuits—traditionally the most effective way to change employers' actions—fell from 1,106 in 1975 to just 51 in 1989 (Donohue and Siegelman 1991). This rapid decline in class-action lawsuits was also a function of more conservative court rulings that increased the burden of proof for discrimination claims and increasingly favored individual rather than group claims. In addition, winning cases against employers became more difficult as the responsibility for proving discrimination shifted from defendant to plaintiff.

Major legislation aimed at eradicating racial inequality essentially stopped after 1972 and definitely did not pick up under the Reagan administration. A clear divergence around the politics of race and the politics of gender began to emerge in the late 1970s. Throughout the 1980s, despite President Reagan's opposition to the ERA, the women's movement made continued legislative gains. As a result of these gains, continued uncertainty was introduced into the regulatory and legal environments, especially from the increase in pregnancy discrimination and sexual harassment cases.

PREGNANCY DISCRIMINATION

Mark Edwards (1996, 247) finds that during the early 1990s women were successful in using EEO law to "shift the responsibility of pregnancy accommodation onto employers." He argues that this culminated with the passage of the Family Medical Leave Act. Prior to the 1970s, most companies fired women who became pregnant. This practice reflected the gender role assumption of the day—that mothers would not work—and an interpretation of employer insurance schemes as not covering pregnancy. Most firms allowed disability leaves for any disability except pregnancy. Dobbin (2009), in a careful analysis of the diffusion of maternity leave programs, shows that the notion that pregnancy was a disability and should be treated as such was first promulgated by the EEOC in its 1966 annual report, but at that time employers knew that the EEOC was not actively advocating for gender equality.

In 1972 the EEOC's new "Guidelines on Discrimination Because of Sex" declared that requiring pregnant women to resign and failing to offer pregnancy leaves was discrimination. By 1974, the EEOC had filed suit against eleven large companies, charging that pregnancy discrimination constituted gender discrimination. There was absolutely no case law supporting these charges until a district court upheld the EEOC's position in 1976. Immediately the EEOC filed 130 more pregnancy discrimination cases and warned an additional 250 companies that they were at risk of a suit. Eventually, in 1977, the Supreme Court ruled in the first of these cases, which was against General Electric. The Court ruled that pregnancy discrimination was *not* gender discrimination under Title VII of the Civil Rights Act, but at that point it was too late: personnel managers at companies across the country had already dropped pregnancy bans, established pregnancy leaves, and expanded insurance coverage to include pregnancy.

Thus, the EEOC was out ahead of the law, creating a regulatory threat that supported personnel managers' arguments to expand pregnancy protection. When Congress passed the Pregnancy Discrimination Act in 1978, it faced little corporate opposition because most large corporations had already changed their personnel practices. Similarly, when the Family Medical Leave Act of 1993 was passed, about 90 percent of firms already had maternity leave policies (Dobbin 2009).

Dobbin (2009) concludes that employers changed their policies around pregnancy because the pressure from the EEOC empowered an increasingly feminized personnel profession to push for expansive definitions of gender discrimination and larger realms of authority for themselves (figure 5.2). He points out that neither the market nor external social movements would have been contending causes because during this period unemployment was high and the women's movement was focused elsewhere. We are not so sure about his social movement analysis. It certainly was the case that major organizations like NOW were not focused on pregnancy discrimination or later on work-family balance, but they were visible in the press and in local communities. Thus, it is quite possible that, like the civil rights movement in the 1960s, the women's movement in the 1970s and 1980s played an indirect role by keeping gender equality both a visible and moving target—something for CEOs to take seriously because eventually the movement might get around to their companies or perhaps their wives and daughters.

The EEOC defined pregnancy discrimination as gender discrimination in the early 1970s and provided a credible legal threat to corporations in the mid-1970s. Corporate personnel managers took it from there, changing personnel rules before they were legally required to do so. In both cases, by the time Congress acted the policies were already widespread. Dobbin (2009, 192) describes this process as the women's movement acting within corporations through the feminization of the personnel profession:

> The EEOC continued to receive large numbers of race discrimination complaints, yet, in these years, much of the action in the workplace surrounded work-family and harassment issues. As the civil rights movement moved into the firm, then, the fact that it was now populated by white women shaped the issues the movement within-the-firm would take up.

Flexible work arrangements had been advocated by the personnel experts as part of the quality of work life movement in the 1960s and 1970s, and the federal government had experimented with similar programs in the 1970s. In the 1990s, human resource professionals rebranded flexible work options (flextime, the compressed workweek, job sharing, telecommuting) as family-friendly programs and added them to their arsenal

Figure 5.2 Human Resource Managerial Employment, 1968 to 2006

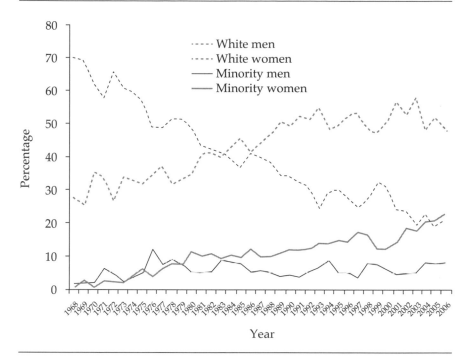

Source: Authors' compilation based on data from IPUMS-CPS (King et al. 2010).

of gender equalization schemes. This further expanded women's rights within many corporations (Dobbin 2009).

SEXUAL HARASSMENT

Unlike pregnancy discrimination, maternity leave, and work-family programs, sexual harassment was defined as gender discrimination by the women's movement in the late 1960s. But like those government-sponsored interventions, the interpretation of sexual harassment as discrimination did not become corporate policy until later, when it was adopted by personnel experts. These acts were confirmed by the courts as illegal only after corporations had already adopted sexual harassment policies and internal grievance procedures (Dobbin 2009).

In 1976 a lower court ruled for the first time that quid pro quo sexual harassment was a violation of Title VII (Williams v. Saxbe, 413 F. Supp.

Figure 5.3   Sexual Harassment Charges Filed with the EEOC,
              1980 to 2002

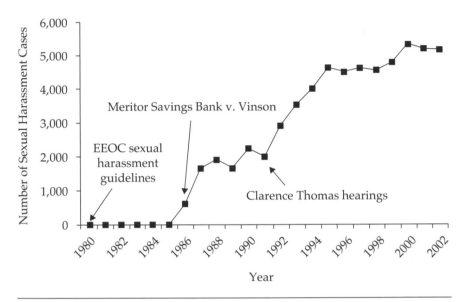

Source: Authors' calculations based on sexual harassment data from the Equal Employment
Opportunity Commission (EEOC 2012a).

654, 657 [D.C. Cir. 1976]). In 1980 the EEOC developed guidelines for sexual harassment (quid pro quo and hostile work environment) and considered it a form of gender discrimination. The Supreme Court did not rule
on a sexual harassment case until 1986, when, following the lower courts
and the EEOC's definition of the conditions under which sexual harassment violated Title VII, the Supreme Court ruled that sexual harassment
was a clear violation of Title VII regardless of whether an "economic" or
"tangible" loss was incurred (see *Meritor Savings Bank v. Vinson*, 477, U.S.
57, 1986).

Contemporaneously, sexual harassment became the centerpiece of
Clarence Thomas's 1991 Supreme Court nomination hearings. Thomas
was accused of sexually harassing Anita Hill when he was in charge of the
EEOC and she was an employee. The media coverage elevated public
awareness, which, coupled with the passage of the Civil Rights Act of
1991, led to a steep increase in the number of sexual harassment cases filed
with the EEOC. Figure 5.3 displays trends for the total number of sexual
harassment cases filed with the EEOC from the year the EEOC developed

guidelines in 1980 to 2002. Once sexual harassment became defined as a violation of Title VII by the courts its visibility as a problem increased.

There were few harassment complaints to the EEOC from 1980 until 1986, when the Supreme Court ruled that sexual harassment was a violation of Title VII in Meritor Savings Bank v. Vinson (1986). Sexual harassment complaints to the EEOC rose following the Meritor ruling and then leveled off through 1991. It is likely that the increasing rights granted to plaintiffs as a result of the Civil Rights Act of 1991, the visibility of sexual harassment in the widely publicized Clarence Thomas hearings, or some combination of the two factors was responsible for the rapid increase in sexual harassment cases after 1991. The trend of increased sexual harassment complaints then leveled off around 1995, before surging again in the late 1990s. Figure 5.3 suggests that periods of uncertainty varied over time and were likely to coincide with changes in workplace inequality.

THE SUPREME COURT MOVES TO THE RIGHT

Until 1988, Supreme Court decisions tended to expand the rights of plaintiffs in discrimination cases. But the composition of the Supreme Court became much more conservative across the 1980s (Nelson et al. 2008). Under Reagan, Associate Justice William Rehnquist, a Nixon nominee, was appointed Chief Justice. In addition, Reagan appointed Anthony Kennedy, Antonin Scalia, and Sandra Day O'Connor as new Supreme Court justices. George H. W. Bush appointed justices David Souter and Clarence Thomas to the high court. Now with a majority of Reagan-Bush appointees, the Supreme Court began to rule more conservatively on civil rights cases, particularly on employment cases. Starting in 1989 with two decisions, Price Waterhouse v. Hopkins and Wards Cove Packing Co. v. Antonio, the burden of proof in discrimination cases was shifted from employers defending against claims of discrimination to plaintiffs needing to claim harm and to prove both intent and the lack of business grounds as justification for discrimination.

In the 1970s, the EEOC encouraged, and the courts upheld, a broad "disparate impact" theory of discrimination—discrimination defined as intentional differences in treatment by the employer—thus reducing the need to prove intent and focusing instead on employment practices that harmed women or minorities (Goldman et al. 2006). By the late 1980s, the Supreme Court had undermined the disparate impact theory and moved the burden of proof to plaintiffs (Nelson et al. 2008).

As a result, contemporary legal theory is now tied to a motive-based notion of discrimination. This is at odds with the actual social science on discrimination, which has clearly shown that discrimination is often nonconscious, rooted in in-group preferences rather than out-group bias, and lodged in organizational routines rather than simply acts of conscious exclusion. Most social closure is accomplished by these routines or by unconscious bias rather than by outright prejudice. The recent work of Vincent Roscigno (2007) confirms this disjunction. His analyses of discrimination charges that were verified by the EEOC after the 1980s often contain evidence of explicit prejudiced statements, active race- or gender-linked harassment, and retaliation. For cases to satisfy the currently restrictive legal theory of what constitutes discrimination, discrimination must be explicit and egregious. This narrow legal definition of discrimination has made discrimination claims difficult to prove and rendered much of what social science has identified as biased employment practices difficult to admit as evidence of discrimination in court. During the 1980s, the balance of power in the legal arena decisively shifted to employers (table 5.1).

Although it occurred after the period under study in this book, the 2011 Supreme Court decision in Dukes v. Wal-Mart was particularly emblematic of the rightward tilt of Supreme Court employment discrimination decisions. In this case, the majority opinion ruled that because Wal-Mart had a nondiscrimination policy, the corporation was immunized against claims of company-wide discrimination. Since the literature clearly shows that companies often adopt policies for symbolic reasons, this ruling vastly strengthened the ability of companies to ignore discrimination and abandon equal opportunity goals.

The two exceptions to the increasingly conservative interpretation of discrimination law by the Supreme Court after 1988 had to do with sexual harassment and pregnancy discrimination. Here the Supreme Court expanded and clarified Title VII–based claims of "sex" discrimination to include sexual harassment and pregnancy. We believe that the message to private employers was that they would increasingly be supported by the courts in their defense of traditional hiring, firing, segregation, and pay disparity cases, but not for the more expansive gender-linked claims. Uncertainty around what was gender discrimination continued, even as racial discrimination became more difficult to prove.

The rightward drift of the Supreme Court did not go completely unchallenged. In 1990 Congress enacted the Civil Rights Act of 1990, seeking to override several Supreme Court decisions limiting discrimination law. President George H. W. Bush vetoed the act, calling it a quota bill, but Congress passed the legislation the following year as the Civil Rights Act of 1991. This act reinstated many of the rights of individuals claiming they had been discriminated against—rights that had been taken away by the courts in the late 1980s. The act also allowed for the first time that parties claiming gender discrimination could request jury trials and if success-

Table 5.1   Supreme Court Race/Gender Employment Discrimination
            Decisions, 1981 to 2011

Year	Case	Consequences
1981	County of Washington v. Gunther	Title VII pay discrimination claims can be broader than Equal Pay Act provisions.
1982	Connecticut v. Teal	Employer is liable for individual discrimination even when no group discrimination is observed.
1986	Meritor Savings Bank v. Vinson	Sexual harassment is discrimination under Title VII.
1987	Johnson v. Transportation Agency, Santa Clara County	The legal scope of affirmative action plans is narrowed to "conspicuous" underrepresentation and no harm to white men.
1988	Watson v. Fort Worth Bank & Trust	"Disparate impact" is broadened to include discretionary managerial decision-making.
1989	Price Waterhouse v. Hopkins	Employer defense against discrimination charges is broadened.
	Wards Cove Packing Co. v. Antonio	Disparate impact claims must show specific practices that cannot be justified on business grounds; the burden of proof shifts to employees.
	Lorance v. AT&T Technologies	A more expansive interpretation than the EEOC's of when discrimination claim begins is admitted.
1991	International Union, UAW, v. Johnson Controls	Definition of pregnancy discrimination is expanded.
	Gilmer v. Interstate/Johnson Lane	Title VII rights to sue are limited by a prior arbitration agreement.
1993	St. Mary's Honor Center v. Hicks	Even if plaintiff proves the employer defense is false, discrimination is not established.
	Harris v. Forklift Systems, Inc.	Proving sexual harassment does not require demonstrating psychological harm to the victim.
1998	Faragher v. City of Boca Raton and Burlington Industries, Inc., v. Ellerth	Definition of sexual harassment and content of an affirmative employer defense against harassment claims is clarified.
1998	Oncale v. Sundowner Offshore Services	Same-sex sexual harassment is prohibited under Title VII.
2000	Reeves v. Sanderson Plumbing Products, Inc.	If plaintiff proves employer defense is a lie, it is not necessary to demonstrate discrimination.
2011	Dukes v. Wal-Mart, Inc.	The presence of a nondiscrimination policy protects against class discrimination claims.

Source: Authors' compilation.

ful could recover compensatory and punitive damages in intentional employment discrimination cases. After 1991, class-action lawsuits became more numerous, especially lawsuits claiming gender discrimination.

EQUAL OPPORTUNITY BECOMES DIVERSITY MANAGEMENT

Regulatory threats to corporations faded in the 1980s, and personnel managers rebranded themselves and their mission as "diversity management" (Kelly and Dobbin 1999; Dobbin 2009). Although still formally required of federal contractors and embraced by some firms, affirmative action was no longer a legitimate rhetoric for promoting equal opportunity. The new argument was that diversity was good for companies, reflecting demographic shifts in both the labor force and customers in an increasingly globalized economy. "Equal opportunity" offices became "diversity" offices. During this period, EEO policies continued to spread, now driven by the professional projects of human resource managers. The proportion of firms with written EEO policies grew from 50 percent in 1980 to about 80 percent in 1990; almost all had such policies in place by 2000. Policies that specifically referenced diversity took off after 1985, growing to about 30 percent of workplaces by 2000. Similarly, diversity training, an attempt to sensitize employees to their cognitive biases, became widespread in the late 1980s and by the late 1990s was being used by almost half of all workplaces (Dobbin 2009). Although changes in human resource composition and practice are fairly well documented, we have poor evidence as to whether or not they actually promoted equal opportunity.

We think that Dobbin's contention that political and regulatory uncertainty in corporate environments strengthened the hands of human resource professionals is quite plausible. It seems likely, however, that the original social movement–based commitment to equal opportunity may also have faded from the professional project of successive generations of HR managers. "Personnel" managers, originally invested in equal opportunity projects, were reinvented in the 1980s as "human resource" managers who pressed the business advantages of diversity. We do know that environmental pressures for racial progress evaporated after 1980. There was a continued expansion of the terrain of gender discrimination, including issues related to sexual harassment, pregnancy protection, and work-family balance. It is difficult to guess where the center of gravity in this profession lies today, but we can be confident that it is no longer dominated by the civil rights equal opportunity agenda of the 1970s personnel profession.

Concurrently, the once-white male profession of personnel manager transitioned into a primarily white female occupation. Assuming a weakened commitment to generic equal opportunity progress and a small amount of in-group bias, we would not be surprised to see the suspension of progress for black males as a result of the lack of environmental pressures coupled with the absence of internal advocates. For women in general, and white women in particular, there were continued legal and political pressures to open new frontiers of equal opportunity, and the people in charge of routine human resource decisions within corporate America were increasingly white women.[1]

Continued progress for white women seems likely under this narrative. But how much progress? The equal opportunity political and regulatory expectations of the 1970s ended after Ronald Reagan was elected president. It remains to be seen how strong the residual pressures for equal opportunity were and if there was any continued variation with presidential administration. Although in theory the Clinton administration was more committed to equal employment opportunity for both blacks and women, we see little evidence in the historical record of either strong rhetorical or administrative commitment. Rather, the Clinton administration seems to have advanced the neoliberal project of regulatory retreat that was initiated in the late 1970s and concretized under the Reagan-Bush presidencies.

DESEGREGATION IN THE NEOLIBERAL ERA

Figure 5.4 reports segregation trends after 1980, adjusted as in earlier chapters for shifts in organizational composition, industrial structure, and labor supply. After African Americans' rapid gains in the 1960s and 1970s and white women's in the 1970s, the post-1980 period represented a clear deceleration in desegregation. Black employment integration with white men in the regulated private sector essentially came to a halt after 1980. Only white women showed clear continued gains relative to white men, and those gains were not particularly steep.

The increased segregation of black women from white women that began in the 1970s continued through 2000, when private-sector segregation between white women and black women stabilized at about 50 on the index of dissimilarity. Segregation between black men and white women also did not decline during the Reagan-Bush years, but there was some very slight progress during the Clinton and George H. W. Bush presidencies.

The clear pattern is that progress toward racial desegregation in the private sector that was produced by regulatory or political pressure rather than by changes in the industrial structure or labor supply came essentially to a halt after 1980. Although black male integration with white men and white women in the same jobs in the same workplace did increase marginally across all three presidential eras, the pace of change was gla-

Figure 5.4   Regression-Adjusted Segregation from White Men,
              1980 to 2005

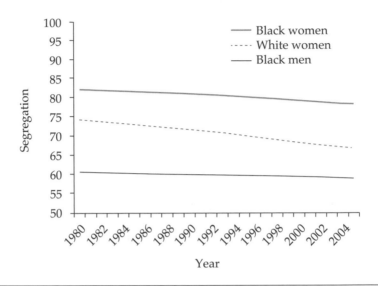

Source: Authors' calculations based on data from EEO-1 surveys (EEOC, various years).

cial compared to the pre-1980 era. In the quarter of a century after Ronald
Reagan became president, employment segregation between white men
and black men declined less than it did in two years in the 1960s.

Racial resegregation between black women and white women continued until 2000 (figure 5.5). After 2000, in contrast to the prior thirty years
of resegregation, there was essentially no change in employment segregation between white women and black women. This new stability was produced by the end of desegregation between white women and white men
in equal-status employment, and to a lesser extent between white women
and black men. When white women's increased access to male jobs
stopped after 2000, so did their increased segregation from black women.

After the federal government repudiated its role in regulating corporate behavior, it is clear that the large yearly equal employment opportunity gains of the 1970s were over (table 5.2). The continued uncertainty
around what constituted gender discrimination provided only a temporary basis for continued gender desegregation. The equal-status employment of both black women and white women with white men increased at
a creepingly slow pace after 1980—less than one-third the rate of progress
in the brief regulatory period in the 1970s. After 2000, even this residual

Figure 5.5   Regression-Adjusted Segregation from White Women, 1980 to 2005

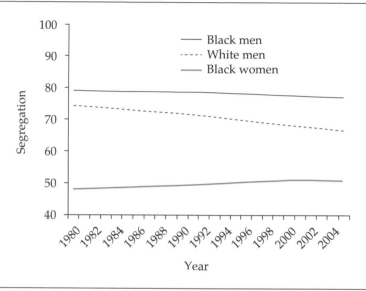

Source: Authors' calculations based on data from EEO-1 surveys (EEOC, various years).

progress in equal-status employment between white men and white women in the 1990s effectively came to a halt.

The Reagan-Bush administrations ushered in a clear political era distinction. The strong desegregation gains of the 1970s weakened or stopped after 1980. We do not see any striking political era distinctions between the most recent three political eras. Gender progress picked up somewhat during the Clinton era, and racial integration did so under the administration of George W. Bush in the 2000s. We cannot point to a clear political mechanism producing these steepening trajectories of desegregation. They may represent a stronger regulatory emphasis on gender during the Clinton administration and on race during the George W. Bush administration, but they are so weak that they very well may represent other factors we have not considered.

TRENDS IN ACCESS TO GOOD JOBS IN THE NEOLIBERAL ERA

When we examine access to good jobs, we see the same pattern of weak gains after 1980, but there was also a tendency for gains to be somewhat

Table 5.2 Regression Adjusted Yearly Desegregation Trajectories by Political Era

	Uncertainty: 1966 to 1972	Regulation: 1973 to 1980	Reagan/Bush: 1981 to 1992	Clinton: 1993 to 2000	G.W. Bush: 2001 to 2005
White men–black men	–0.890	–0.514	–0.056	–0.040	–0.128
White men–white women	–0.128	–0.733	–0.251	–0.374	–0.274
White men–black women	–0.331	–0.539	–0.113	–0.183	–0.209
White women–black men	–0.015	–0.343	–0.037	–0.113	–0.113
White women–black women	–0.848	+0.458	+0.132	+0.182	–0.029

Source: Authors' calculations based on data from EEO-1 surveys (EEOC, various years).

Figure 5.6   Regression-Adjusted Managerial Representation,
1980 to 2005

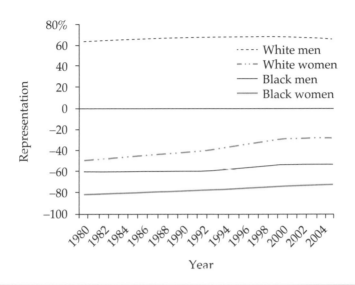

Source: Authors' calculations based on data from EEO-1 surveys (EEOC, various years).

stronger during the Clinton administration (figure 5.6). White women in particular showed relatively steep gains in access to managerial jobs during the Clinton presidency. After no gains at all during the 1980s, black men's access to managerial jobs also rose during this period. Both white women's and black men's increased access to managerial jobs essentially stopped after 2000. Black women made weak gains across the period, increasing slightly after 1992.

The patterns for access to professional jobs are similar, but here political era seems less clearly implicated (figure 5.7). White women made relatively strong gains through 2000, approaching labor market parity at the turn of the century, but made no gains, net of shifts in labor supply and industrial structure, thereafter. Black men and black women made weak gains in access to professional jobs throughout the period, with somewhat steeper trajectories during the Clinton administration.

The only notable shift in craft production representation after 1980 was an acceleration in white women's access to skilled working-class jobs during the Clinton administration (figure 5.8). If we were to interpret the differences in trajectories across political era, we might conclude that the Reagan administration weakened regulatory pressures for equal opportu-

Figure 5.7   Regression-Adjusted Professional Representation, 1980
             to 2005

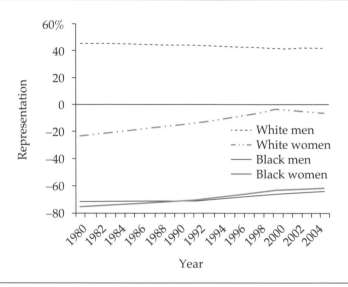

Source: Authors' calculations based on data from EEO-1 surveys (EEOC, various years).

nity for all groups. There is some evidence as well that under the Clinton administration white women became the focus of renewed, albeit weak, regulatory attention.

SOCIAL ISOLATION TRENDS

Not surprisingly, political and legal pressures produced little progress in terms of exposure to other groups after 1980 (figure 5.9). Black men and white men on average had decreased isolation scores of about four points over the last quarter of a century. For white women, that decrease was only three points. Black women saw the least progress, but of course they were the most exposed to other groups to begin with.

AFFIRMATIVE ACTION: MEND IT, DON'T END IT?

It seems likely that OFCCP oversight became less effective after the Reagan presidency. President Clinton famously came to the defense of affirmative action when he proclaimed that affirmative action should be fixed

Figure 5.8   Regression-Adjusted Craft Representation, 1980 to 2005

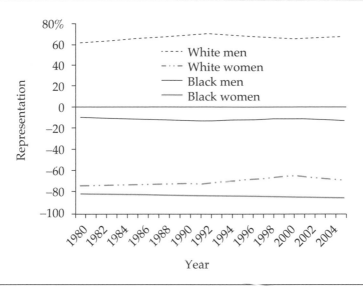

Source: Authors' calculations based on data from EEO-1 surveys (EEOC, various years).

rather than eliminated. It was never clear, however, what exactly he had in mind as being wrong, or what the proposed fix was to be. Because the attack on affirmative action was part of the more general racial backlash, there certainly was more political room to task the OFCCP to monitor gender progress more closely.

Comparing across political eras, we see that OFCCP regulation was associated with almost no new desegregation between white men and white women during the Clinton administration (figure 5.10). If anything, there is some evidence of weak regulatory pressure for women's integration with white men under the second Bush administration. In general after 1980, OFCCP oversight and the linked mandate that firms have affirmative action plans seem to have had very little influence on desegregating white male jobs. When we looked at the segregation of black men and black women from white women, OFCCP regulation of federal contractors produced no net integration (data not shown).

When we look at representation in managerial jobs, we see that OFCCP regulation during the Clinton administration was associated with increased white male and decreased white female, black male, and black female managerial representation relative to firms that were not federal contractors (figure 5.11). There was essentially no effect of OFCCP regula-

Figure 5.9   Adjusted Isolation Trends, 1980 to 2005

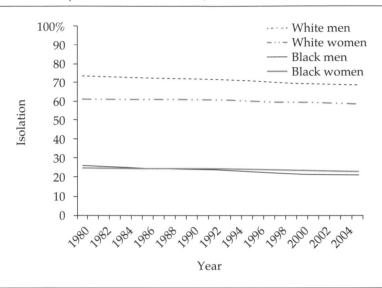

Source: Authors' calculations based on data from EEO-1 surveys (EEOC, various years).

Figure 5.10   Yearly Shifts in Segregation from White Men Associated with OFCCP Regulation, by Political Era

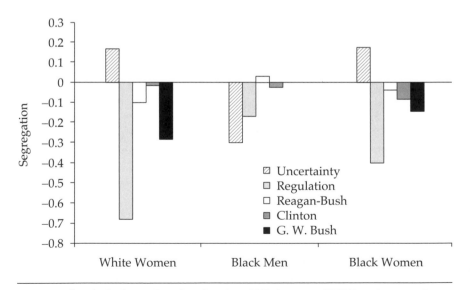

Source: Authors' calculations based on data from EEO-1 surveys (EEOC, various years).

Figure 5.11   Yearly Shifts in Managerial Representation Associated
with OFCCP Regulation, by Political Era

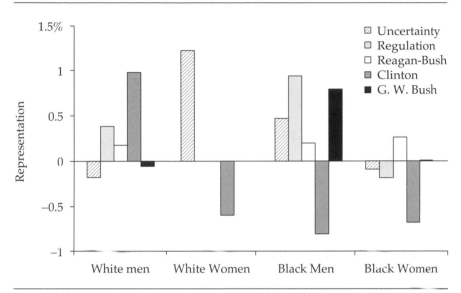

Source: Authors' calculations based on data from EEO-1 surveys (EEOC, various years).

tion under Republicans after 1980. This pattern reveals that Reagan's deregulation approach had already ended affirmative action in terms of access to managerial jobs. Moreover, the Clinton administration not only
failed to mend affirmative action but seems to have provided the political
cover that allowed federal contractors to increase the representation of
white men in managerial jobs. When we examined the influence of OF-
CCP regulation on access to professional jobs, we saw the same pattern.
After 1980, if there was any government-mandated affirmative action going on, it came to favor white men. For craft jobs, OFCCP regulation had
practically no effect on equal opportunity after 1980.

DESEGREGATION IN THE NEOLIBERAL ERA

The racial backlash that began in the late 1970s would prove central to the
political environment during the Reagan campaign and presidency. Affirmative action became suspect and suspicion of reverse discrimination
against white men widespread. The Reagan administration repudiated an
active role for the federal government in promoting equal employment
opportunity. At the same time, the courts became more conservative in
their interpretation of equal opportunity law, with the exception of pro-

tecting women from sexual harassment and pregnancy-related discrimination. Federal legislators reached across the aisle to promote family-friendly workplace laws as well. As the regulatory pressure on corporations to create equal opportunity workplaces eased up, legal and legislative pressure to protect women continued. The civil rights movement's struggle for racial equality waned even as the influence of the women's movement grew.

Corporate uncertainty as to what constituted defensible racial employment practices declined. The threat of federal contractor investigation evaporated, and no new race-linked rights or expectations developed. When the environmental pressure for racial progress stopped, so too did racial desegregation.

The political environment for gender integration, on the other hand, produced new uncertainties. Although women's integration into previously white male jobs, with the resultant equal-status contact with white men, was considerably weaker than during the brief regulatory era of the mid and late 1970s, it did continue. This was particularly true for white women, who were the only group whose integration with white men was sustained during the Clinton administration and whose access to craft, managerial, and professional jobs increased. Many of these gains seemed to flatten out or stop after 2000, suggesting that in the absence of new political pressures, white women's gains were stabilizing at a new status quo. It may be that racial equal employment opportunity progress started earlier and ended earlier than white women's progress, but that both will turn out to have been bounded by political pressures from social movements, the courts, new legislation, and federal regulators. It certainly was not the case that the HR profession was no longer a white women's profession after 2000. If anything, HR continued to become women's work, and diversity management, rather than equal opportunity, remained the rhetorical touchstone.

Today, in the absence of external political pressure, even the residual movement toward better employment opportunities for white women seems to have stalled. The civil rights movement undermined the cultural assumption that white men would control all high-skilled, autonomous, and authority-invested work in the U.S. economy. It set in motion political pressures both inside and outside of private-sector corporations to promote employment opportunities for other groups, initially African American men, then African American women, and eventually and most dramatically white women. Although the political backlash against the civil rights movement could be seen as early as 1968, it became institutionalized after 1980. The women's movement continued to be influential into the 1990s. By the late 1990s, equal employment opportunity no longer had strong political support in either social movements or the political projects of the major parties. Corporations had lost interest, and the HR profession had changed its agenda. Equal opportunity progress, which halted abruptly after 1980 for black Americans, sputtered to a halt even for white women at the turn of the century.

As national political pressures for further desegregation and equal opportunity advances waned, the important variation in equal opportunity trajectories came to operate in local labor markets, in specific industries, and in particular firms. The next three chapters examine the dynamics of desegregation at those levels of analysis.

PART II | Local Inequality Regimes

Chapter 6 | Local Labor Market Competition and New Status Hierarchies

WHILE EXAMINING THE influence of national politics on desegregation trends, we have observed that desegregation trajectories vary dramatically by both demographic status and historical period. In this chapter, we document regional convergences in the patterns of segregation and access to good-quality jobs. When the civil rights movement was at its peak, it represented in part a struggle between the South and the rest of the country. The pre–Civil War South was built on slave labor. The post–Civil War South reinstituted the subordination of black labor through state-sanctioned segregation and Jim Crow laws to limit black democratic participation. The civil rights movement struggled most bravely and was resisted most bloodily in the U.S. South.

Not surprisingly, after the Civil Rights Act of 1964 was passed, the attention of federal regulators was most intense in the South. The extension of civil and voting rights had its most far-reaching effects in the South as well. Remarkably, today the South differs little from the rest of the country in its levels of racial employment segregation, and black men have somewhat better access to skilled working-class jobs in the South than in the rest of the country. The one vestige of southern exceptionalism in racial segregation is a notably higher rate of segregation between black men and white women in the former Confederate states.

The demise of southern exceptionalism is perhaps one of the most fascinating, but by no means the only, geographic story present in the EEO data on private-sector employment. At the level of local labor markets, there is considerable variability in labor force composition and dynamics, both of which have important implications for local desegregation trajectories. In this chapter, we also explore the countervailing tendencies of changes in the composition of local labor queues. Increases in the labor

181

market representation of women and racialized minorities and the historical decrease in white male shares of the labor market created the demographic potential for increased equal-status employment integration. With fewer white males in the labor force, there would have been more room for the employment and advancement of others. No reduction in discrimination would have been necessary to produce these gains in view of the fact that there were simply fewer white men in the labor force overall. Conversely, the very same shifts might have produced a sense of competitive threat to white men. If that happened, we would expect increases in discrimination, in both its explicit and subtle forms.

Surprisingly, in the analyses that follow we find that competition processes predominate, particularly in the contemporary period. White men tended to gain even greater access to better-quality jobs as the size of competing demographic groups increased. This pattern suggests that the various interactional and organizational mechanisms producing white male advantage tend to strengthen in the face of labor market competition. The more racially and ethnically heterogeneous the labor market the higher the level of white males' privileged access to good jobs. Consistent with an increase in social closure with increased competitive threat, the reverse holds for white women, black men, and less dramatically black women.

This book started from the historical dynamics set in motion by the civil rights movement during a period when the United States was primarily a black and white country. Thus, our focus on the relative distance of white women, black men, and black women from white men fits the demographic trajectories set in motion in the 1960s. In the twenty-first century, this seems a bit dated. Hispanics are now a larger group than African Americans. Asian Americans have grown in size and cultural visibility. The immigration to the United States of people who are neither white nor black has soared. Indeed, current scholarship on race and ethnicity in the United States now focuses primarily on racism and ethnocentrism toward new immigrant communities, their implications for the fate of African Americans, and the very meaning of racial categories in a more diverse America.[1]

In this chapter, we also explore the relative standing of Hispanic and Asian employees as an addition to our core black-white focus. We use the concept of a labor queue to help organize these comparisons. So far, this book has been organized around the question: are we moving toward equal opportunity? The labor queue approach asks instead: what is the relative ranking of social groups? We ask this question about whites, blacks, Hispanics, and Asians, as well as the linked question: how does growth in the Hispanic and Asian populations affect the relative standing of white women, black men, and black women?

Relative to white men, we do not find an unambiguous labor queue for good jobs among white women, blacks, Hispanics, and Asians. Rather, everyone except white men is in a subordinate position in the labor queue for managerial and professional jobs. On average, across labor markets Hispanic and black men are equivalently placed behind white men in the queue for craft production jobs, and Asian men are closer to all women. Given our findings for segregation, this suggests that the real competition among groups other than white males is for the less desirable jobs in the economy. We do find that a growing Hispanic labor force increases segregation between whites and blacks in lower-ranked jobs.

The chapter closes with a listing of the best and worst labor markets in 2005 for representation in managerial jobs. We provide these lists as a crude indicator of where the EEOC, OFCCP, and private equal opportunity law firms might expect to find systemic discrimination. Although we document remarkable regional convergence in this chapter, we also find substantial local variation in labor market inequalities.

THE DEMISE OF SOUTHERN EXCEPTIONALISM

We focus first on regional distinctions in segregation and access to good jobs. It is possible, of course, that regional differences in segregation reflect differences in labor supply and industrial structure rather than, or in addition to, place-specific cultural-historical-political differences in race-ethnic and gender relations. Thus, when examining regional differences, we statistically control for labor supply, industry, and organizational characteristics, as we have been doing in the previous chapters.

Research has shown that prior to and just after passage of the Civil Rights Act the South was clearly more racially segregated than the rest of the United States (Abrahamson and Sigelman 1987; Fossett et al. 1986; King 1992). The heritage of slavery in the Jim Crow economy and polity, the lack of fair employment practice legislation prior to the Civil Rights Act, and perhaps the later economic transformation from an agricultural to an industrial base all caused the South to lag behind other regions in racial integration. We observed in chapter 3 that the relatively strong segregation decline in the U.S. South after the Civil Rights Act of 1964 reflected, at least in part, the earlier implementation of state-level FEP laws restricting racial employment discrimination in the non-South (see also Stainback et al. 2005). We have also already seen a fairly rapid convergence in segregation levels between the South and the rest of the country after 1966 (see figure 6.1).

Nevertheless, there remains a popular belief, at least outside the South,

Figure 6.1   Rapid Regional Convergence in Racial Segregation, 1966 to 2000

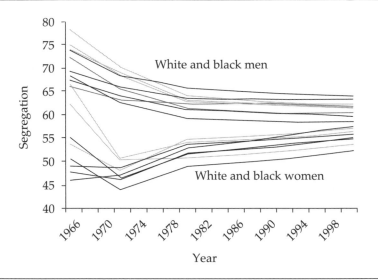

Source: Authors' calculations based on data from EEO-1 surveys (EEOC, various years).
Note: Southern regions in gray.

that the South lags behind other regions when it comes to the opportunities available to African Americans. We suspect that this belief is at least to some extent a function of our collective knowledge of state-sanctioned Jim Crow segregation and both personal and historical memories of the civil rights struggle. During and after the Civil Rights Act, employers in the South came under particularly strong pressure from government regulators and public opinion to racially desegregate. Indeed, the original Plans for Progress firms began their desegregation efforts in the South. The initial enforcement efforts of the EEOC were similarly targeted at the South. It seems to us that both the initial uncertainty about racial desegregation and later enforcement efforts were strongest in the South. Given this pattern, we would expect that racial desegregation in the South would have demonstrated the most progress. This was certainly true in the 1966 to 1972 analysis we presented in chapter 3.

When we extend the segregation time series through the turn of the century, the earlier findings hold. In 1966 racial segregation was higher in the South, particularly among women. Black-white segregation dropped most dramatically in the southern regions in the initial post–Civil Rights Act period. In all regions, black-white segregation among men dropped

Figure 6.2   Continued Regional Differences in Employment
Segregation Between White Women and Black Men

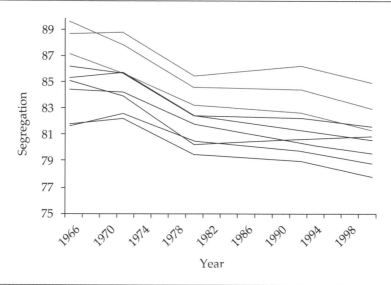

Source: Authors' calculations based on data from EEO-1 surveys (EEOC, various years).
Note: Southern regions in gray.

dramatically between 1966 and 1980, then hardly at all. Among women, black-white segregation dropped even more dramatically in the South between 1966 and 1972. In all regions, segregation between white women and black women rose across the remainder of the 1970s and continued to slowly increase after 1980. By the year 2000, racial segregation among women was almost as high as it was among men in all regions.

Some vestiges of southern exceptionalism remain visible in the employment patterns. For example, employment segregation between black men and white women was noticeably higher in the South than the non-South in 1966 and remained so by the turn of the century (figure 6.2). The general pattern across regions was of stagnation in employment segregation between black men and white women after 1980 and slow declines after 1992. The one exception was the West South Central region (Texas, Oklahoma, Arkansas, and Louisiana), where there is evidence of black male–white female resegregation beginning in the Reagan-Bush era of deregulation and racial backlash.

When we compare regional access to the best-quality jobs, there are no clear contemporary regional distinctions. We focus on the odds of being in managerial (figure 6.3), professional (not shown), and craft (figure 6.4)

Figure 6.3   Odds Relative to White Men of Employment in a
Managerial Job, 2000

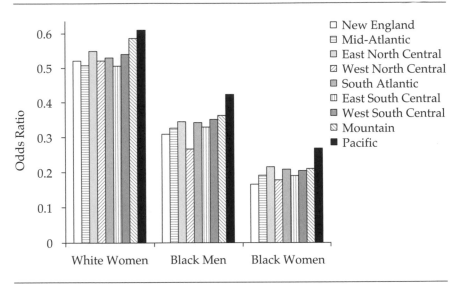

Source: Authors' calculations based on data from EEO-1 surveys (EEOC, various years).

jobs relative to white men in the year 2000. We report the odds of occupational representation relative to white men's representation to adjust for
regional differences in occupational structure. The South does not stand
out as particularly exclusionary in terms of access to managerial jobs.
Rather, the Pacific and New England regions seem to be exceptional. In
the case of the Pacific states, which include California, Washington, and
Oregon, we see the lowest levels of white males' privileged access to managerial jobs. New England shows the opposite pattern: relative to white
men, the odds of being in a managerial position were at or near their lowest for white women, black men, and black women. When we look at access to professional positions, the only regional distinction of note is that
for both black men and black women the Pacific region also stood out as
having the lowest level of exclusion from professional jobs.

Skilled working-class jobs also do not present many clear regional patterns. The one of note is that black men in the South had a higher relative
chance of securing craft jobs than in most other regions. Black male odds
were similarly high, however, in the Pacific and Mid-Atlantic states.

Regional convergence has been the dominant pattern in the half-
century since the Civil Rights Act was passed into law. There is little
contemporary evidence of any residual extra white advantage in the

Figure 6.4   Odds Relative to White Men of Being Employed in a
Skilled Craft Job, 2000

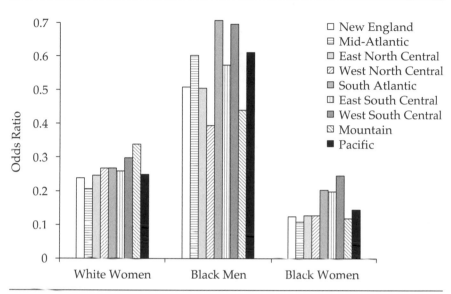

Source: Authors' calculations based on data from EEO-1 surveys (EEOC, various years).

private-sector South. Rather, there is some evidence that access to the best
working-class jobs for black men and black women has become somewhat
more open in the South than in most other regions. The one arena in which
we find a remaining southern exceptionalism is that segregation between
black men and white women, long the touchstone of cultural race fears in
the South, remains higher than elsewhere.

Other regional differences in segregation trajectories are minor. There is
some evidence that managerial opportunities for white women, black
men, and black women and professional and craft opportunities for black
men and black women are better in the Pacific region. Why this might be
the case is not evident to us. It could reflect a more egalitarian culture or
perhaps opportunities lodged in the relatively small size of the black population and the large immigrant population, particularly in California, the
dominant state.

Lisa Catanzarite (2000) points out that the uneven distribution of
minority groups across regions means that the likelihood of jobs developing into ethnic-typed employment is place-specific. She focused her research on Los Angeles, partly because it has the Hispanic concentration
necessary for the creation of "brown-collar" jobs. It seems plausible to us

that the growing concentrations of new immigrant populations might afford opportunities for African Americans and white women to secure increased access to more desirable jobs. We return to this idea later in the chapter.

If we were to look for a contemporary story of regional exceptionalism, we would not tell a story about the South. Rather, we might look to the Pacific states, a region where equal opportunity progress has been better than average, and New England, which has lagged behind the rest of the nation. We lack a systematic political or demographic explanation for these results. Did New England's status as the most progressive region in terms of segregation in 1966 (Tomaskovic-Devey et al. 2006) protect firms in that region from federal oversight in the 1960s and 1970s? Did the West Coast pattern result from the confluence of high Hispanic and Asian immigration and a relatively well-educated black and white workforce that pushed the latter up the labor queue and increased their access to good-quality jobs? We leave it up to future scholars to puzzle out the sources of these results.

LOCAL LABOR MARKET PROCESSES

In all of the previous analyses, we statistically controlled for local labor supply as an alternative explanation to the influence of uncertainty, regulatory environment, or region on desegregation trajectories. For our analyses of segregation and isolation, we did this statistically. For analyses of occupational representation, we standardized our measure of occupational representation by group employment in the local labor market. The logic of this approach is that over the past fifty years white men have been a declining proportion of the U.S. labor force; white women's labor force representation has risen; and other groups, particularly Hispanic and Asian labor, have become increasingly important, especially since 1980. Thus, we expect that some exposure, integration, and access to high-quality jobs simply results from the increasing scarcity of white men and the frequency of other groups in local labor markets.

The implicit expectation has been that when a group is a larger proportion of the local labor market, segregation declines and access to high-quality jobs improves. For example, we know that even during the Jim Crow period black males were more likely to be managers in the South than in other parts of the country simply because they were a much larger proportion of the labor force. Because white men are favored in the labor queue, their contraction as a proportion of the labor force potentially makes more positions available for other groups lower in the labor queue (Lieberson 1980; Reskin and Roos 1992; Stainback and Tomaskovic-Devey

2009). Thus, even with no change in discrimination pressures, representation in good jobs may increase and segregation may decrease simply as a function of changes in the supply of labor.

Contact theory (Allport 1955) hypothesizes that increased intergroup contact actually reduces prejudice and other forms of bias. There is substantial psychological evidence to support the contact hypothesis, but only in the fairly limited circumstances when contact is of equal status (for example, in integrated jobs) and in noncompetitive environments (Pettigrew and Tropp 2006). On the other hand, competition theory (Blalock 1967), which was developed during the civil rights struggle, posits that as the size of a minority group grows, that group represents an increased competitive threat to the majority group and the rate of discrimination is thus expected to increase as well. There is substantial evidence in favor of competition theory in previous research on labor markets, voting behavior, and racial violence (see the review in Cohen and Huffman 2007b).

Thus, if labor market competition is taking place and increasing the incidence of in-group bias and out-group closure, the impact of group size becomes ambiguous. Larger groups should foster integration by reducing stereotypes and taking up a large proportion of the labor queue, but that same process might lead to competitive threats that prompt exclusion, in-group preference, and segregation. Extreme forms of institutionalized discrimination, such as the pre–Civil Rights Act Jim Crow system in the U.S. South, racial apartheid in South Africa, religious apartheid in Northern Ireland, and Arab–Jewish segregation in contemporary Israel, all epitomize this inequality-generating process (Olzak 1994). Research on the United States since 1980 has found that white racism, black-white income inequality, and black-white differences in unemployment all are higher in communities with larger black populations (Quillian 1996; Cohen 1998; Barton et al. 1985).

Thus, there are actually two potentially contradictory mechanisms generated by shifts in labor supply (Cohen and Huffman 2007b). The first is an equality-generating effect from the growing representation of formally disadvantaged groups in the labor market. The second is an inequality-generating mechanism as dominant groups react to competitive pressures by increasing discriminatory practices such as social closure from desirable jobs. Thus, in the absence of discriminatory pressures emanating from competition, we expect positive effects of group size on integration and access. If both the equalizing influence of demographic opportunity and the inequality-generating process of discrimination based on competitive threat are operating in about equal measure, we would expect little or no influence of group composition, as the two contradictory mechanisms would cancel each other out. If the discrimination effect is stronger

Table 6.1   The Influence of a 10 Percent Increase in Group Size
             on Local Labor Market Segregation from White Men,
             1966 to 2005

	White Female	Black Male	Black Female
1966 to 1972	–0.56	1.46	0
1973 to 1980	–0.54	0	0
1981 to 1992	–1.04	–0.90	0
1993 to 2000	0	0	1.25
2000 to 2005	0.38	0.63	0.73

Source: Authors' calculations based on data from EEO-1 surveys (EEOC, various years).
Note: We report as zero estimates that are not statistically significant at or above a .01 probability.

than the egalitarian effect, we would expect that group size would be associated with higher segregation and lower access to good jobs for everyone except white men, who would benefit from increased discrimination
against nonwhites and women.

The civil rights and women's movements can be thought of as attempts
to delegitimate competition-based tendencies to install inequalities
through institutionalized discrimination. Thus, we would expect that the
inequality-enhancing influence of subordinate group composition, if it
was operating, to have been stronger earlier in time. On the other hand,
and as we have been arguing throughout this book, white males' monopoly on good-quality jobs in all labor markets was nearly absolute prior to
the Civil Rights Act. This would imply that there was little competition for
good jobs early in the period, but that it increased over time. Given what
we have seen in time trends, we would expect that for white women this
increased competition for good jobs happened continuously. For black
women and black men, it may have stabilized after 1980. But these earlier
results were for the entire country and purged of the influence of labor
supply, and so their implications for local labor supply processes are in no
way certain.

First, we explore the effect of group size on integration with white men
and white women (table 6.1). As before, these estimates are generated by
models that control for region, industry, and organizational characteristics.

From 1966 to 1992, the integration of white women and white men in
equal-status employment was enhanced by higher female labor force participation. This effect dropped to zero after 1993, just as white women's

labor force participation stabilized. It is also possible that the move to zero in the later period resulted from an increase in discrimination by white men threatened by white women's increased labor force participation. This interpretation seems to be confirmed by the positive effect of the percentage of white females in the labor force on white men's and white women's employment segregation after 2000.

On the other hand, in the immediate post–civil rights period black male integration with white men in equal-status work was clearly lower in labor markets where black men were a larger competitive threat. The competition effect seems to have dissipated over time and was overwhelmed by the egalitarian influence of group size between 1980 and 2000. After 2000, the competition effect became dominant again, and we see higher segregation of white and black men in labor markets with higher proportions of black men competing with white men for jobs. Black men's segregation from white women was consistently higher where black men presented a competitive threat. This was true in all periods, but weakened after 1992. It would seem that the larger and historically consistent competitive threat associated with black men happens in cross-gender equal-status contact.

In terms of integration with white men, black women showed no clear pattern before 1993, suggesting a rough balance in the egalitarian potential of group size and the competitive threat it engenders. After 1993, the estimate turned positive: increased black female labor force participation became associated with higher levels of segregation from white men.

If we look across groups and over time, it appears that local labor market competition strengthened for all comparisons. This suggests that segregation processes were increasingly local, fueled not by national institutional assumptions that race and gender employment segregation were right and proper, but by local race and gender dynamics. When the competitive threat associated with white women, black men, and black women was higher, so was segregation. Thus, the waning of national political and regulatory pressure for integration seems to have been replaced by local processes of labor market competition in which the social closure process that leads to white male employment monopolies grew with their level of labor market competition with other groups.

White women and black men have reduced access to managerial, professional, and craft jobs when they are a larger proportion of the labor force (table 6.2). This was true in all years and for all three kinds of desirable jobs. In addition, the magnitude of the effects did not shift much over time. If anything, moving away from the period of institutionalized white male advantage led to some strengthening of the size of the exclusionary tendency for black men. This is the opposite of the prediction of queuing

Table 6.2 The Influence of a 10 Percent Gain in Group Size in Local Labor Markets on Access to Managerial, Professional, and Craft Jobs, 1966 to 2005

	White Women			Black Men			Black Women		
	Manager	Professions	Craft	Manager	Professions	Craft	Manager	Professions	Craft
1966 to 1972	-0.12	-0.20	-0.06	-0.05	-0.04	-0.12	0	0	0
1973 to 1980	-0.13	-0.18	-0.05	-0.09	-0.09	-0.13	-0.06	-0.06	-0.05
1981 to 1992	-0.13	-0.19	-0.06	-0.16	-0.13	-0.23	-0.05	0	0
1993 to 2000	-0.17	-0.21	-0.09	-0.17	-0.13	-0.44	-0.05	0	0
2000 to 2005	-0.14	-0.18	-0.10	-0.19	-0.08	-0.48	-0.06	0	0

Source: Authors' calculations based on data from EEO-1 surveys (EEOC, various years).
Note: Access is standardized for group commuting zone population size. We report as zero estimates that are not statistically significant at or above an .01 probability.

or contact theories that, as groups grow in size, their access to jobs higher in the job queue will increase. On the contrary, competition processes seemed to predominate.

There is also evidence that an increase in the size of the black female labor force led to exclusionary backlashes, but that result is weaker and more sporadic. In the 1973 to 1980 period—the same period when the re-segregation of black and white women began—there is some evidence that black women's access to high-quality jobs was restricted when they comprised a higher proportion of the labor force. After 1970, there was a weak exclusionary tendency from managerial jobs associated with in-creased black female labor force participation.

There is clear evidence of a net competition process for black men and white women that is not era-dependent. As both became larger propor-tions of the local labor force, their access to good-quality jobs became re-stricted. For black women, access to good-quality jobs was weakly and sporadically governed by a labor market competition process. The clearest evidence is in their access to managerial jobs, which was restricted when black women were a larger proportion of the local labor force in all eras after 1973.

Black male access to good-quality jobs was consistently depressed in labor markets where black men were a larger proportion of the labor force. This result is not era-dependent. Early in the period, competitive threat effects also seemed to dominate the opportunity of black men to work in equal-status roles with white men. Regardless of period, competition ef-fects severely reduced the employment of black men and white women in the same jobs in the same workplaces.

White women's access to good-quality jobs was limited when they made up a higher proportion of the labor force. On the other hand, white women's integration into the same jobs in the same workplaces with white men was weakly facilitated across most of the period by higher labor force participation, although that weakened after 1993. A growing white female labor force led to the integration of lower-level jobs but increased white male status advantage in higher-level jobs.

Black women's access to high-quality jobs was not governed by com-petitive threat effects, with a weak exception in the short regulatory pe-riod of 1973 to 1981. Black women's integration with white women in lower-level jobs was strongly facilitated by demographic density early in the period, but this influence weakened over time.

As groups become a larger proportion of the local labor market, they generate both egalitarian tendencies powered by queuing processes and the potential for discriminatory backlashes. For black men and white women, these discriminatory backlashes were concentrated in their access to good-quality jobs. For black women, the initial post–Civil Rights Act period was one of strong integration into lower-level jobs based on their labor force participation.

WHAT ABOUT NEW IMMIGRANT POPULATIONS?

Sociologist Leslie McCall (2001) suggests that the intersection of multiple demographic groups in local labor markets can produce complex local configurations of race- and gender-based inequality. Queuing theory suggests that status groups tend to be ranked by employers in terms of their desirability as workers (Reskin and Roos 1992) and that these rankings can be dynamic (Lieberson 1980). Popular accounts of affirmative action have sometimes assumed that black women, because they have two protected statuses, might be higher in the preferred labor queue of employers that are actively attempting to desegregate their workplaces. If anything, the evidence suggests that the opposite is more typically the case (Browne 1999). Others have suggested that Asians are the new model minority and may be for all practical purposes honorary whites (Sakamoto et al. 2009).

Other research has speculated in particular on the influence of new immigrant groups on the employment opportunities of African Americans. Here the concern has been that competition from immigrant groups might reduce African American opportunity (Borjas, Grogger, and Hanson 2010). Consistent with this concern, in previous research on desegregation we observed that larger nonblack minority labor forces are associated with higher black-white segregation (McTague et al. 2009).

Queuing theory observes that individuals within local labor markets are simultaneously competing for jobs within a hierarchical set of employer preferences for specific status groups. A queuing approach to the question of multiple competing groups would look to see if opportunities for, say, black males are enhanced or hindered by the presence of competing Hispanic, Asian, or even white female labor forces. Under a queuing theory interpretation, we would expect that when a focal group is higher in the labor queue than growth in the size of other subordinate groups in the same labor market, then integration with dominants and better access to good jobs will transpire. Conversely, if the focal group is lower in the queue than the competitor group, then segregation will be higher and access to good jobs restricted for the lower-ranked group.

Table 6.3 reports the effects of other subordinate group representation in the local labor market on the degree of employment segregation between white men and white women. Prior to 1981, the presence of black women in local labor markets had no influence on gender segregation

Table 6.3   Queuing Processes and Segregation Between White Men
and White Women at a 10 Percent Increase in Group Size,
1966 to 2005

	Black Women	Black Men	Hispanic Women	Hispanic Men	Asian Women	Asian Men
1966 to 1972	0	1.48				
1973 to 1980	0	1.72				
1981 to 1992	−1.46	3.31	0	0.48	−5.00	−7.25
1993 to 2000	0	3.46	0.38	1.48	0	0
2000 to 2005	0	4.01	0	2.20	0	0

Source: Authors' calculations based on data from EEO-1 surveys (EEOC, various years).
Note: We report as zero estimates that are not statistically significant at or above an .01 probability.

among whites, suggesting that white women and black women were nearly equivalent in the labor queue for white male jobs. Between 1981 and 1992, this segregation-reducing effect strengthened, suggesting that white women made stronger gains into white male jobs where there were more black women to fill traditionally female jobs. There is no evidence that the presence of black women in the labor queue influenced white gender segregation after 1992. There is also slight evidence of any influence of Hispanic labor on white male–white female segregation, suggesting that white women do not typically compete with Hispanic women for the kinds of jobs typically filled by white men.

On the other hand, higher proportions of black males in the local labor market increased gender segregation among whites in all periods, and this effect strengthened over time. The pattern for Hispanic males was the same. Minority males were more likely to integrate white male jobs, thereby reducing the opportunity for white women to do so. Thus, African American men and Hispanic men tended to be competing with white women in the labor queue in terms of access to male jobs. This is an interesting finding in light of the results presented in the last chapter. White women made increased inroads into white male jobs after 1990, but these results suggest that progress was strongest in local labor markets with smaller black male and Hispanic male labor forces.

Asian labor market competition was associated with reduced white male–white female segregation, but only during the Reagan-Bush years. This suggests that for this short period white women were ahead of Asians of both genders in the labor queue for white male jobs, but that they were functionally equivalent thereafter.

In table 6.4, we look at the influence of the same processes on black male–white male employment segregation. The presence of black women

Table 6.4   Queuing Processes and Segregation Between White Men and
Black Men at a 10 Percent Increase in Group Size, 1966 to 2005

	White Women	Black Women	Hispanic Women	Hispanic Men	Asian Women	Asian Men
1966 to 1972	0	−1.83				
1973 to 1980	0.45	−1.44				
1981 to 1992	0	−0.57	1.89	0.76	−3.92	0
1993 to 2000	0.78	0	1.78	1.45	−5.74	8.85
2000 to 2005	0.63	0	1.45	1.21	0	0

Source: Authors' calculations based on data from EEO-1 surveys (EEOC, various years).
Note: We report as zero estimates that are not statistically significant at or above a .01 probability.

early on reduced segregation between black men and white men, but had lost any influence on black male and white male segregation by the late 1990s. Similarly, the presence of larger numbers of Asian women in a labor market tended to reduce segregation between white men and black men. On the other hand, there is also evidence that Hispanic immigration led to increased segregation between black men and white men. This was also a strong effect of the presence in a labor market of Asian men, but only briefly during the Clinton era. Why this might have been the case we do not know.

Larger white female labor forces were weakly associated with higher white male segregation from black men. This effect was not large, especially compared to the influence of black male labor on the employment of white women in white male jobs. Thus, black men seem to have been ahead of white women in the queue for the average male job. Gender segregation tendencies were stronger on average than pressures for racial segregation. This may reflect differences in social boundaries, but it is just as possible that it reflects differences in relative group size. In most labor markets, there have simply not been enough African American men to create a separate race-segregated labor market. In all communities, there have been sufficient women in general and white women in particular for employers to create gender-typed jobs and even whole occupations (such as secretarial work). As both racial and gender inequality became less institutionalized, we would expect that various local labor market queues would have emerged. If that is the case, we can expect that in some jobs and in some labor markets white women might actually have been ahead of black males in the queue for traditionally white male jobs. This seems most likely, given our earlier findings, for managerial and professional occupations.

Black women's access to equal-status employment with white women

Table 6.5   Queuing Processes and Segregation Between White
             Women and Black Women at a 10 Percent Increase in
             Group Size, 1966 to 2005

	Black Men	Hispanic Women	Hispanic Men	Asian Female	Asian Male
1966 to 1972	4.92				
1973 to 1980	1.61				
1981 to 1992	1.16	2.58	0	0	4.43
1993 to 2000	1.16	3.37	0	−4.95	8.44
2000 to 2005	1.72	2.99	0	0	0

Source: Authors' calculations based on data from EEO-1 surveys (EEOC, various years).
Note: We report as zero estimates that are not statistically significant at or above a .01 probability.

was weakened by the presence of African American men, Hispanic women, and Asian men in the local labor market (table 6.5). Thus, black women competed with all of these groups in terms of integration with white women. Hispanic men and, surprisingly, Asian women (except for the anomalous 1993 to 2000 estimate) were not normally competing for the same jobs in which black women and white women were being hired. White women were in an interesting place in most labor markets: they competed with men for male jobs and with women for female jobs.

We also look at labor queues for occupational representation. Because our measure of representation standardizes group occupational location by local labor market size, we can directly estimate the degree to which the presence of other groups in the local labor market increased or decreased access to good-quality jobs. We begin with white men, who, as we have seen, have had high and stable advantages in their access to managerial and craft jobs. Their access to professional jobs, though declining over time, has also been privileged. What we find is that almost without exception white male access to good-quality jobs increased as the size of minority groups in the local labor market grew. We focus here only on the 2000 to 2005 estimates. They are quite similar to the post-1990 estimates, and both are somewhat stronger than in earlier years.

An increase in the size of any subordinate group led to a higher representation of white men in managerial jobs. With two exceptions, most groups were roughly equivalent in their influence. A 10 percent increase in the local labor market representation of white women, black men, black women, Hispanic men, Hispanic women, and Asian men produced a 30 to 45 percent increase in white males' managerial representation. At first these may seem like large numbers, but it should be remembered that only

Figure 6.5   White Males' Increased Access to Managerial Jobs with a
              10 Percent Increase in Group Labor Market Presence,
              2001 to 2005

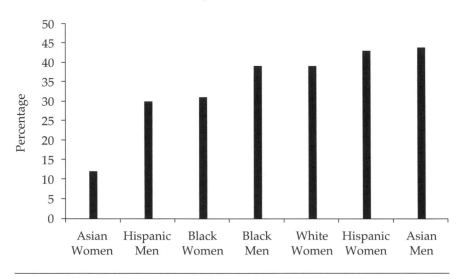

Source: Authors' calculations based on data from EEO-1 surveys (EEOC, various years).

about 15 percent of jobs were managerial and it was access to this small group of jobs that was enhanced by increased minority and female representation in mostly nonmanagerial positions. Asian women stand out for having had the least influence on white men's access to managerial jobs. The general pattern was the same in the preceding period, with most groups producing about a 30 percent increase in white male representation in managerial jobs when their presence in local labor markets shifted by 10 percent.

The pattern for white males' access to craft production jobs is similar (figure 6.6). The effect of most groups was of roughly similar size. When other groups shared a local labor market with white men, white males' privileged access to craft production jobs rose dramatically. Again, we see that the presense of increased numbers of Asian women in local labor markets produced a smaller bump in white male access to craft jobs, suggesting that Asian women and white men almost never competed for these jobs. Hispanic women in local labor markets also had relatively small effects on white males' priveleged access to skillled working-class jobs.

The labor queue propping up white male access to professional jobs follows a similar, if less dramatic, pattern (figure 6.7). In labor markets

Figure 6.6   White Males' Increased Craft Representation with a 10
Percent Increase in Other Groups in the Local Labor
Market, 2001 to 2005

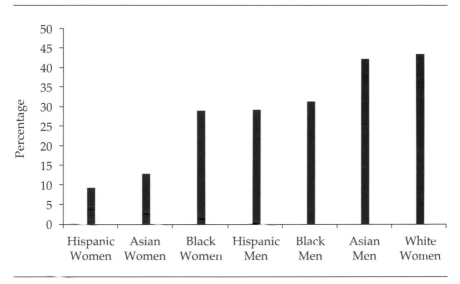

Source: Authors' calculations based on data from EEO-1 surveys (EEOC, various years).

with high or growing Asian female or Hispanic male labor forces, white
males reaped relatively small additional advantages in access to professional jobs. Except for the high estimate of Hispanic female influence,
there was a tendency for white males' professional access to be more
strongly influenced by minority male labor market composition. We suspect that this gender ordering reflects the still important gender segregation principle in many professions (for example, nursing versus engineering). On the other hand, these estimates are created with statistical controls
for detailed industry, which should capture much of this variation.

Every estimate suggests that white men's privileged access to good-
quality jobs has been enhanced in labor markets with large racial minority
and female presences. We do not take the rank ordering of the various
groups too seriously. When we look at estimates for the preceding period,
the basic ordering tends to be similar, but groups at the ends of the distribution do quite a bit of switching. It may be that the labor queues are dynamic. Certainly the Asian and Hispanic labor forces changed rapidly after 1980 both in terms of national and educational composition and in
terms of destination labor market. On the other hand, we would not be
surprised if the process here was much more complicated than our analy-

Figure 6.7   White Males' Increased Professional Representation with a
10 Percent Increase in Other Groups in the Local Labor
Market, 2001 to 2005

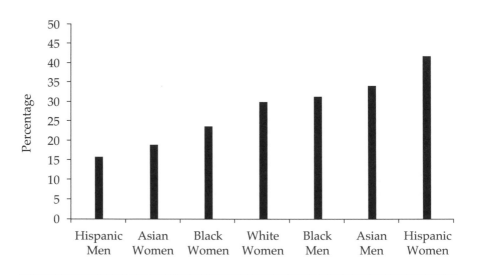

Source: Authors' calculations based on data from EEO-1 surveys (EEOC, various years).

ses suggest. The unambiguous conclusion is that white men's access to good jobs has been enhanced, not threatened, as they have declined as a proportion of local labor markets.

We explored these queuing processes further by looking at the influence of other groups on white female, black male, and black female access to good-quality jobs. We focused on the 1993 to 2000 and 2000 to 2005 periods, both of which showed stronger results than earlier periods. Our first observation is that all of our estimates of queuing effects were much smaller than they were for white men. Estimates of queuing effects for white male access to good-quality jobs were without exception statistically significant, positive, and large. When we looked at white female, black male, and black female access to managerial, professional, and craft jobs, many coefficients were not statistically significant and all were by comparison quite small. The dominant pattern is not that an institutionalized labor queue for good jobs exists among white women, blacks, Hispanics, and Asians, but that all nonwhite male labor forces are in roughly equivalent subordinate positions in the labor queue for these jobs. Given our findings for segregation, this suggests that the real competition among groups, other than white males, is for the less desirable jobs in the economy.

MANAGERIAL QUEUES IN LOCAL LABOR MARKETS?

The preceding estimates are national averages. We think that when race and gender status hierarchies are only weakly institutionalized at the national level we should observe local variation in the status hierarchies among groups. This variation may reflect local differences in human capital and class backgrounds, migration and immigration patterns, and differences in local levels of cultural bias and discrimination. We are not prepared to sort out these sources of variation, but we can use the EEOC data to describe differences in local labor market status hierarchies. We focus on the relative ranking of groups in access to managerial jobs, because managers are well represented in all labor markets. Table 6.6 reports the relative rankings of each status group's representation relative to their labor market presence in managerial jobs in the top twenty EEOC-reporting labor markets in the United States in 2005.

In every one of the top twenty labor markets, white males were the group most likely to be found in private-sector managerial jobs. In all of the top labor markets except Detroit, white women were the second most likely to get hired into managerial positions. In Detroit, Asian men were more likely than white women to be found in managerial jobs. In all of the other largest labor markets, Asian males trailed white women in their managerial representation. In Dallas, Houston, and San Francisco, Asian men also trailed black men in managerial representation. Black men were most often found in fourth position in access to managerial jobs, behind Asian men and ahead of Hispanic men. In New York, Boston, Detroit, Minneapolis, Hartford, and Cleveland, Hispanic men were more likely than black men to gain access to managerial jobs. Like black men, black women did particularly well in access to managerial jobs in Atlanta, Washington, and San Francisco. Black women and Asian women were more likely to be found in managerial jobs than Hispanic women, but less likely than all others. Asian men and Asian women were remarkably different. In most large cities, Asian men tended to be ranked behind only white men and white women in access to managerial jobs. Conversely, Asian women were the least likely to be in managerial roles in the largest U.S. labor markets.

We also looked at local labor markets with the largest proportions of African Americans, Hispanics (table 6.8), and Asians (table 6.9). Table 6.7 shows the rankings of groups in access to managerial positions in the ten largest labor markets in terms of African American employment.

All of these cities are in the "black belt" South. This is the coastal plain region of the South that was once dominated by plantation agriculture. These areas are now characterized by low-wage, low-skill manufacturing

Table 6.6   Relative Managerial Representation in the Top Twenty EEOC-Reporting Labor Markets, 2005

	White		Black		Hispanic		Asian	
	Male	Female	Male	Female	Male	Female	Male	Female
Los Angeles, Calif.	1	2	4	6	7	8	3	5
Chicago, Ill.	1	2	4	5	6	8	3	7
New York, N.Y.	1	2	5	7	4	8	3	7
Newark, N.J.	1	2	4	7	5	8	3	6
Philadelphia, Penn.	1	2	4	6	5	8	3	7
Boston, Mass.	1	2	5	7	4	8	3	6
Washington, D.C.	1	2	3	5	6	8	4	7
Atlanta, Ga.	1	2	3	5	6	7	4	8
Detroit, Mich.	1	3	5	6	4	8	2	7
Dallas, Tex.	1	2	4	6	5	8	3	7
Houston, Tex.	1	2	4	7	5	8	3	6
San Francisco, Calif.	1	2	3	5	6	8	4	7
Minneapolis, Minn.	1	2	5	8	4	6	3	7
Seattle, Wash.	1	2	4	7	5	6	3	8
Phoenix, Ariz.	1	2	4	6	5	8	3	7
Hartford, Conn.	1	2	5	7	4	8	3	6
Cleveland, Ohio	1	2	5	8	4	7	3	6
St. Louis, Mo.	1	2	5	8	4	7	3	6
Denver, Colo.	1	2	4	7	6	8	3	5
Tampa, Fla.	1	2	4	6	5	7	3	8
Range twenty largest labor markets	1	2–3	3–5	5–8	4–7	7–8	3–4	5–8
Mode twenty largest labor markets	1	2	4	7	4, 5	8	3	7

Source: Authors' calculations based on data from EEO-1 surveys (EEOC, various years).

branch plants and continued political dominance by largely white land-owners (Tomaskovic-Devey and Roscigno 1997). Although white men were the most likely to have priority access to managerial jobs in these black belt labor markets, Hispanic women (in Vicksburg, Mississippi) and Asian men (in Roanoke Rapids, North Carolina; Columbia, South Carolina; and Montgomery, Alabama) were occasionally more likely to be found in managerial roles than they were in the local labor market. From these data, we cannot tell exactly how this happened, but we suspect that it reflects the relative rarity of Hispanic women and Asian men in these jobs. The most likely explanation is that they were brought in as managers by national firms to cities where there were very few long-term Hispanic women or Asian men.

Table 6.7   Relative Managerial Representation in the Top Ten African American EEOC-Reporting Labor Markets, 2005

	White		Black		Hispanic		Asian	
	Male	Female	Male	Female	Male	Female	Male	Female
Vicksburg, Miss.	2	3	7	8	6	1	4	5
Roanoke Rapids, N.C.	2	3	5	7	6	8	1	4
Oxford, Miss.	1	5	6	8	3	2	4	7
Albany, Ga.	2	4	5	6	7	8	3	1
Columbia, S.C.	2	3	6	7	5	8	1	4
Starkville, Miss.	1	2	4	6	5	7	3	8
Jackson, Miss.	1	2	5	6	7	8	3	4
Montgomery, Ala.	2	3	5	6	7	8	1	4
Memphis, Tenn.	1	2	4	5	6	8	3	7
Rocky Mount, N.C.	1	3	5	6	7	8	2	4
Range	1–2	2–5	4–6	6–8	3–7	1–8	1–4	1–7
Mode	1, 2	3	5	6	7	8	3	4

Source: Authors' calculations based on data from EEO-1 surveys (EEOC, various years).

An important finding is that in high-proportion black local labor markets, Hispanic men and Hispanic women consistently ranked below black men and women in access to managerial jobs. Black men and women consistently ranked below whites and Asians in access to managerial jobs.

The pattern is quite a bit different in the top Hispanic labor markets. White men followed by white women were in the first and second rank when it came to managerial representation in most high-Hispanic localities. The exception was El Centro, California, where Asian males were the most likely to be found in managerial jobs, and El Paso, Texas, where they were the second most likely to fill these jobs. In most cities with a high Hispanic population, Asian males were ranked third and black men fourth in access to managerial jobs. Hispanic women were fairly consistently the least likely to be in managerial jobs in the largest Hispanic labor markets. Hispanic males were always unlikely to be in managerial roles, although their relative rank in the managerial labor queue varied from labor market to labor market.

Finally, we looked at managerial representation in the ten largest Asian population labor markets. In all of these labor markets, white men, followed by white women, were the most likely to be in managerial roles. In six of the ten cities, black males were ahead of Asian males in the managerial labor queue. In seven of ten cities, black women were ahead of Asian women. Although Hispanic women tended to be lowest in the managerial

Table 6.8   Relative Managerial Representation in the Top Ten Hispanic
EEOC-Reporting Labor Markets, 2005

	White		Black		Hispanic		Asian	
	Male	Female	Male	Female	Male	Female	Male	Female
McAllen, Tex.	1	2	5	8	4	6	3	7
El Paso, Tex.	1	3	4	7	6	8	2	5
El Centro, Calif.	2	3	4	5	7	8	1	6
Corpus Christi, Tex.	1	2	3	7	5	6	4	8
San Antonio, Tex.	1	2	4	7	5	8	3	6
Santa Fe, N.M.	1	2	5	7	4	8	3	6
Fresno, Calif.	1	2	5	6	4	8	3	7
Bakersfield, Calif.	1	2	4	5	6	8	3	7
Odessa, Tex.	1	2	4	8	6	7	5	3
Range	1–2	2–3	3–7	4–8	4–7	6–8	1–5	3–8
Mode	1	2	4	7	4, 5, 6	8	3	6, 7

Source: Authors' calculations based on data from EEO-1 surveys (EEOC, various years).

labor queue, in two cities (Seattle and Anchorage) they were more likely to be in managerial jobs than Asian women.

Our analysis of cities with large African American, Hispanic, and Asian labor forces suggests that for each group, when they are a large proportion of the local labor market, they are less likely to have access to managerial jobs. These patterns are most pronounced for large Asian and Hispanic population labor markets. In these places, African Americans have increased access to managerial jobs, presumably as managers of large immigrant labor forces.

WHITE MALE EXPOSURE TO INTERGROUP CONTACT

The general finding in this chapter that white men's access to good-quality jobs increases as competing groups in the local labor market grow in size may seem counterintuitive. After all, white men often experience racial and gender integration as a competitive threat, and the folk wisdom that affirmative action leads to the wholesale denial of white male opportunity is widespread. The problem here is that as individuals we can see integration, but segregation is by definition outside of our gaze. When we share a job in the same firm with someone of a different race or gender, we know it. When our boss comes from a different group, this is apparent as well. That the distribution of workers at our level or higher is created in

Table 6.9   Relative Managerial Representation in the Top Ten Asian EEOC-
            Reporting Labor Markets, 2005

	White		Black		Hispanic		Asian	
	Male	Female	Male	Female	Male	Female	Male	Female
San Jose, Calif.	1	2	3	5	6	8	4	7
San Francisco, Calif.	1	2	3	5	6	8	4	7
San Diego, Calif.	1	2	3	6	4	8	5	7
Los Angeles, Calif.	1	2	4	6	7	8	3	5
Sacramento, Calif.	1	2	3	5	6	8	4	7
Seattle, Wash.	1	2	4	7	5	6	3	8
Las Vegas, Nev.	1	2	3	5	7	8	4	6
Anchorage, Ark.	1	2	4	5	3	6	7	8
New York, N.Y.	1	2	5	7	4	8	3	6
Newark, N.Y.	1	2	4	7	5	8	3	6
Range	1	2	3–5	5–7	3–7	6–8	3–7	5–8
Mode	1	2	3	5	6	8	3	6–7

Source: Authors' calculations based on data from EEO-1 surveys (EEOC, various years).

part by the distribution of employees in lower-level jobs in our workplace
and by the sorting of people across workplaces is not apparent to most of
us when we go to work.

Figure 6.8 clearly shows that as other groups grew as a percentage of
local labor markets, white male exposure to other groups at work grew as
well. In all cases, the effects of a 10 percent rise in other groups was associated with less than a 10 percent rise in white male exposure. Thus,
the effect of group competition in the same labor market was not egalitarian, but at the same time it was integrative. Only for Asian males did
the effect even approach parity. White and black women had the smallest
effect on white male exposure to cross-group contact, presumably because of gender segregation across jobs and workplaces. Thus, as local
labor markets become more heterogeneous, white men will experience
their workplaces as more integrated even as some white men have enhanced access to the best jobs in the labor market. This is particularly true
when the labor market contains substantial percentages of Asian men
and black men.

The labor queues and competition processes that promote white male
access to good-quality jobs are not, however, visible. These take place elsewhere in the sorting of people into workplaces and jobs. Thus, we have
the perverse experience that even as their benefits from racial, ethnic, and
gender labor queues increase, white men in high-quality jobs experience
more integrated workplaces. The perception of competition and reverse

Figure 6.8   Increases in White Male Exposure to Intergroup Contact for a 10 Percent Increase in Group Labor Market Composition, 2001 to 2005

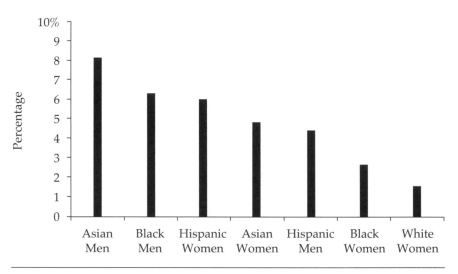

Source: Authors' calculations based on data from EEO-1 surveys (EEOC, various years).

discrimination is likely to be highest in labor markets where the benefits from social closure and discrimination are greatest.

THE VERY WORST LABOR MARKETS

After the Civil Rights Act of 1964, the EEOC and OFCCP were particularly aggressive in targeting southern employers, reasoning correctly that they had made the least progress and shown the most resistance to African Americans' struggles for civil and economic rights. Our analysis of regional convergence suggests that the South in general is no longer a reasonable regulatory target. On the other hand, our analyses at the labor market level show that there is significant local variation in segregation levels and access to good-quality jobs. Table 6.10 displays the local labor markets in which white men's advantaged access to managerial jobs is most extreme. In these twenty labor markets, white men were found in managerial roles at two to three times their representation in the local labor market more generally. The most striking result for white men is that sixteen of the top twenty labor markets were in the black belt South. These are the old plantation regions of the South. Previous research has identi-

Table 6.10 The Top Twenty Cities for White Male Overrepresentation and White Female, Black Male, and Black Female Underrepresentation in Managerial Jobs, 2005

White Male Overrepresentation		White Female Underrepresentation		Black Male Underrepresentation		Black Female Underrepresentation	
McAllen, Tex.	307.7%	Decorah, Iowa	51.0%	Bennettsville, S.C.	33.8%	Dyersburg, Tenn.	13.6%
Greenville, Miss.	280.4	McMinnville, Tenn.	54.5	Houma, La.	34.6	Bennettsville, S.C.	16.3
Americus, Ga.	271.7	Morganton, N.C.	57.9	Atmore, Ala.	35.7	Blytheville, Ark.	18.1
Henderson, N.C.	262.8	Columbus, Nev.	58.6	Milledgeville, Ga.	35.7	Americus, Ga.	19.3
McComb, Miss.	252.4	Glasgow, Ky.	59.7	Greenwood, Miss.	36.4	Spartanburg, S.C.	21.9
Laredo, Tex.	251.1	Greensburg, Ind.	59.7	Blytheville, Ark.	36.5	Paris, Tex.	22.1
Greenwood, Miss.	248.6	Spencer, Iowa	60.1	Tupelo, Miss.	37.2	Tupelo, Miss.	22.1
Milledgeville, Ga.	241.6	Rice Lake, Wis.	61.0	Meridian, Miss.	39.5	Jackson, Tenn.	22.8
Laurel, Miss.	235.6	Defiance, Ohio	61.1	Corsicana, Tex.	40.0	Dublin, Ga.	23.2
Clarksdale, Miss.	234.9	Hutchinson, Ind.	61.1	Alexandria, La.	40.7	Corinth, Miss.	23.2
Statesboro, Ga.	232.8	Brunswick, Ga.	61.1	Longview-Marshall, Tex.	40.7	Cambridge, Md.	23.3
Yuma, Ariz.	231.2	Searcy, Ark.	62.2	Dyersburg, Tenn.	42.4	Thomasville, Ga.	23.4
Goldsboro, N.C.	225.0	Sedalia, Mo.	62.8	Washington, N.C.	42.7	Toccoa, Ga.	24.7
Roanoke Rapids, N.C.	224.7	Owatonna, Minn.	63.6	South Boston, Va.	42.9	Corsicana, Tex.	25.6
Thomasville, Ga.	222.7	Keene, N.H.	63.7	Columbus, Miss.	43.3	El Dorado, Ark.	25.9
South Boston, Va.	221.6	Findlay, Ohio	63.8	Statesboro, Ga.	43.3	Gastonia, N.C.	27.2
El Paso, Tex.	217.7	Staunton, Va.	64.0	Chattanooga, Tenn.	43.6	Lufkin, Tex.	27.4
Vicksburg, Miss.	212.7	Henderson , Ky.	64.0	Dublin, Ga.	43.9	Ness City, Kans.	27.6
Nacogdoches, Tex.	205.9	Boone, N.C.	64.1	Martinsville, Va.	44.1	Charlottesville, Va.	27.9
Griffin, Ga.	205.2	Columbia, Tenn.	64.2	Jacksonville, N.C.	44.2	Longview-Marshall, Tex.	28.0
Rocky Mount, N.C.	201.1	Gillette, Wyo.	64.3	Spartanburg, S.C.	44.6	Laurel, Miss.	28.8

Source: Authors' calculations based on data from EEO-1 surveys (EEOC, various years).

Note: Limited to labor markets with more than thirty EEO-1 establishments; for black men and black women, limited to labor markets with at least 5 percent black employment.

fied these areas as having strong continued politics of race and racial inequality (Roscigno and Tomaskovic-Devey 1994; Tomaskovic-Devey and Roscigno 1996). The remaining four labor markets were all in the areas of the Southwest with high Hispanic immigrant populations. The labor markets in which black men and black women were least likely to be found in managerial jobs were also in the black belt region of the Old South. If the EEOC or OFCCP were to again target particular places, these labor markets might be the first places to look.

With the exception of Brunswick, Georgia, all of the labor markets where white women were the most severely underrepresented in managerial jobs were outside of the black belt South and Hispanic Southwest. White women were least likely to be found in managerial roles in the Midwest and Appalachian region of the eastern United States. Thus, a focus on the spatial underpinnings of systemic discrimination against white women would look to the middle of the country and particularly to locales with small minority populations.

IMPLICATIONS

Queuing processes strongly favor white male employment in the best-quality jobs. These results are generally consistent with Hubert Blalock's (1967) classic theory that competitive threats increase discrimination. The same results, however, could be produced by a constant rate of preference for white male labor in good-quality jobs and a simple shift in the labor supply queue. We suspect that this queuing process is dominant in the large cities described in table 6.6. Demographic diversity benefits white men by shifting the queue of job applicants. On the other hand, the placement of African Americans, Hispanics, and Asians lower in the managerial job queue in high-diversity labor markets (see tables 6.7 to 6.9) is probably more strongly governed by the principles of social closure and ethnic competition.

There is no strong evidence that Hispanic or Asian immigration has limited the employment of white women, black men, or black women in managerial or professional jobs. Not surprisingly, Hispanic men are preferred labor over white women and black women, but not over black men, in craft production jobs. Black-white segregation, on the other hand, rises with a growth in Hispanic and Asian labor forces. This pattern implies that the influence of immigrant competition is on access to lower-level jobs.

Economist George Borjas and various colleagues have examined the influence of immigration on the economic opportunities of white and black Americans. In their most comprehensive analysis (Borjas et al. 2010), they scrutinize the influence of immigrant-native labor market competition on black and white wages and employment. They find that both black and white employment and wages are reduced as the size of the immigrant population rises, but that these costs are almost entirely borne by low-education natives. A 10 percent increase in the size of the immigrant population is associated with about a 3 percent decrease in both black and white wages. A 10 percent rise in immigrant labor reduces black employment by 5.1 percent and white employment by only 1.6 percent. Almost all of both effects happen to workers with a high school education or less.

Our results, especially when combined with Borjas's work, suggest that there is competition between black and Hispanic labor in terms of access to low-wage jobs. Our statistical estimates suggest that there is not a similar systematic competition for higher-level jobs, but we think that much more research needs to be done to understand this process. Our estimates also suggest that growth in Hispanic and Asian labor in the EEOC-reporting labor force is associated with increased black-white segregation within workplaces. This might be produced simply by the larger advantage that white men and white women derive in access to good-quality jobs in more diverse labor markets. It may also be produced by decreased segregation between these two growing groups and African Americans.

Since the 1960s, the U.S. labor market has moved from one of institutionalized white male privilege and near-total employment segregation to a situation of local labor market variability. As a result, local labor market competition between groups for good jobs is an increasingly important process. The collective bias in favor of white men tends to increase with competitive threats from other groups. In the classic competition account, this is accomplished by increased discrimination at both the institutional level (for example, educational, residential, and employment segregation) and the interactional level (social closure and in-group bias in hiring, pay, and promotion decisions). We obviously cannot sort out these processes with the data we analyze here.

Sociologist Sheryl Skaggs (2008, 2010) finds that the trajectory of access to managerial jobs for women and African Americans is steeper in states where the population expresses more gender- and race-tolerant attitudes. Hence, variation in local culture may be important as well. Cultural change may produce changes in behavior. It seems equally likely to us that changes in competitive threats may influence cultural content (Quillian 1996). We cannot sort these explanations out here. We hope that future scholarship pays attention to local processes of competition, cultural, and relational dynamics. Now that race and gender status hierarchies are no longer strongly institutionalized nationally, we should expect increased local variation in discrimination, status hierarchies, and political and cultural pressures for equal opportunity.

The results reported in this chapter suggest strongly that efforts to promote equal opportunity should now concentrate on variation across labor markets in both institutional and direct discrimination. Because integration tends to rise with higher labor market participation, such efforts need to take into account that it is actually in those labor markets where white men are most likely to face equal-status contact with large minority and female labor forces that they are also likely to enjoy the greatest privileges in access to good-quality jobs. In contrast, white working-class men in these same localities face steeper competition for those jobs as racial minorities and women are excluded from managerial, professional, and skilled craft jobs and crowded into lower-level positions.

Chapter 7 | Sector and Industry Segregation Trajectories

WORKPLACES ARE NOT all alike. They produce different products and services, with distinct mixes of technology, divisions of labor, and market structure. In this chapter, we investigate the distribution of desegregation patterns across sectors of the economy and in different industries. Large-scale shifts in the nature of production are reflected in the sectors of the economy, while industries give us the local normative environments in which human resource practices develop. It is these normative environments that may nurture equal opportunity or tolerate discrimination.

In the late nineteenth and early twentieth centuries, technological revolutions dramatically altered the economic landscape. The period witnessed remarkable increases in agricultural productivity, which led to shifts in both capital investment and employment into the manufacturing sector. More recently, both productivity gains and the globalization of production have led to shifts in employment and investment into the service sector in the United States and other high-income countries. In the post-1964 period, the growth in U.S. employment has been heavily in services to households and businesses.

Changes in the structure of the economy have important implications for desegregation trajectories. We begin this chapter by documenting desegregation trajectories in the different sectors of the economy. The growing service sectors have been more receptive to the employment of women and minorities. Although all sectors desegregated before 1980, the older manufacturing, mining, construction, and extractive sectors have shown either little progress or resegregation since. These sectors also have had steep growth in white male managerial employment since 1966.

Another way to think about workplaces is in terms of the actual product or service produced—that is, in terms of industry. Industries tend to

211

share technologies, job structures, human resource practices, regulatory structures, and competition for both sales and employees. Across their careers, individuals often develop skills and social networks tied to particular kinds of work in particular industries. Organizational sociologists often think of industries as a normative environment that influences traditional divisions of labor into jobs, expectations for the kinds of people who fill those jobs, and human resource practices.

In this chapter, we chart desegregation trajectories for fifty-eight industries and find that segregation tends to rise when industry incomes rise, but falls when industries increase their reliance on educated labor. We interpret these trends in terms of increased motive for social closure in the case of wage barriers and increased meritocracy in hiring and promotion decisions around skill certification. We also identify those industries that presently display normative patterns of desegregation, resegregation, and inertia. Desegregation remains the dominant trend in terms of the relationship between white men and white women in most industries. Not surprisingly, given the results in the previous chapters, inertia has become the dominant industrial pattern for segregation between white men and black men. In the contemporary employment of white women and black women in the EEOC-reporting private sector, resegregation has become the most common industry pattern.

We end the chapter by singling out the ten best and ten worst industries in terms of managerial representation. If the EEOC was to pursue a systemic gender discrimination investigation targeting the most egregious industries in terms of managerial representation, good industries to start with might include construction, mining, petroleum and coal products, pipelines, railroads, and stone, clay and glass products. For race discrimination, good target industries would include agriculture, construction, furniture, and lumber and wood products. In contrast, if a policy lever of praise was to be invoked, apparel, banks, educational services, general merchandise stores, health services, hotels, insurance, legal services, membership organizations, and social services might be highlighted as industries with the best managerial opportunities for white and black women. Black men do best in auto repair, building material stores, food products, furniture, bus and railroad transport, tobacco manufacture, air transport, transportation equipment, and trucking and warehousing.

SECTOR TRAJECTORIES

In previous research, we have established that dramatic differences in desegregation levels and trajectories are associated with the sector of employment (Stainback and Tomaskovic-Devey 2009; Tomaskovic-Devey et al. 2006). Other researchers have shown variation in race and gender segregation at a more detailed industry level (Bridges 1982; Carrington and Troske 1998; Cartwright and Edwards 2002; Peterson and Morgan 1995). Together these studies highlight the potential importance of sectoral and industrial change as locations for status group changes in employment opportunities, but provide little explanation for these patterns.

It is clear that service-sector industries have higher proportions of female employees (Goldin 1990). Sociologists Maria Charles and David Grusky (2004) describe the rise of service industries as producing gender segregation through the cultural match between service provision and traditional female tasks (see also Hakim 2000). They argue that two fundamental tendencies exist in the creation of gender segregation. The first is a vertical dimension in which men tend to dominate the best jobs, a tendency we have documented repeatedly in this book. The second is the horizontal sorting of women into nonmanual and service-oriented positions. Charles and Grusky's argument is consistent with the higher representation of women in these industries. Similarly, Tiffany Taylor (2010) suggests that hiring women to perform services in the paid labor force is a simple extension of their traditional work in the domestic sphere and therefore is not culturally threatening to either employers or customers, not to mention male workers.

In the middle of the last century, African American employment outside of the South was disproportionately concentrated in the manufacturing sector. The decline of U.S. manufacturing as a source of employment has been repeatedly pointed to as producing unemployment and declining income opportunities for African Americans (Wilson 1979, 1997). Prior to the Civil Rights Act, African Americans in the South were heavily concentrated in agriculture and domestic service, two sectors with rapidly declining employment opportunities over the past fifty years (Branch 2011). Thus, the rise of service-sector employment has been an important source of employment for African Americans, although the explanations are structural rather than cultural. In addition, because the service sectors have been expanding, they may simply have had more room for new labor forces than manufacturing or extractive sectors.

We begin by reporting segregation levels and trends for eleven industrial sectors: extractive, mining, construction, nondurable manufacturing, durable manufacturing, transportation-communication-utilities, wholesale trade, retail trade, producer services, social services, and personal services. The extractive sector includes agriculture, fishing, and forestry activity.

In all sectors, there were strong declines in racial segregation among white and black men beginning in 1966 (figure 7.1). The uncertainty around racial segregation introduced by the Civil Rights Act and the development of regulatory pressure and human resource responses seem to have been fairly general. Even extractive firms, which began and ended the 1966 to 2005 observation period of this study with very high racial segregation among men, showed immediate declines after 1966. Durable manufacturing stands out as having the lowest observed average male racial segregation in 1966. This is the sector with the highest concentration of federal contractors, so it is not surprising that we find relative egalitarianism on this dimension so early.

Similar to national trends, in most sectors racial desegregation among men stalled in the 1980s. There were four exceptions worth noting. Durable manufacturing strongly *resegregated* after 1980. When the pressure on federal contractors evaporated, durable manufacturing firms began to sort white and black men into different jobs again. Although durable manufacturing was clearly the most equal sector in terms of the distribution of white men and black men in 1966, it relapsed to the middle of the distribution by 2005.

On the other hand, three sectors showed continued racial desegregation after 1980. Continued desegregation was most dramatic in business services, in which male racial segregation dropped sharply after 1990. Retail trade showed a similar, if less steep, desegregation trajectory after 1990. Continued post-1980 desegregation was least dramatic in social services, which despite continued small gains had the second-highest levels of racial segregation among men of any sector in 2005. Only agriculture, fishing, and forestry were worse.

The three service sectors ended the period with high (social services) and medium (personal and business services) levels of male employment segregation. Thus, the movement toward a service society had no necessary consequence for male racial segregation. Transportation, communication, and utilities stood out for the steepest initial declines in employment segregation and the lowest levels in the present period, and the steepest sustained desegregation between white men and black men occurred in business services. At the end of this chapter, we see that the transportation-related industries within this sector were among the most hospitable in extending black men's access to managerial jobs as well.

Turning to gender segregation between white men and white women (figure 7.2), each sector showed declines in employment segregation and most trajectories were roughly parallel. Retail and social services showed immediate declines after 1966, while none of the other sectors began to desegregate until the 1970s. For both the extractive and construction sectors, white male and white female desegregation stalled around 1990. After 1990, mining showed considerable gender resegregation among whites. Retail

Figure 7.1 Segregation Between White Men and Black Men by Sector, 1966 to 2005

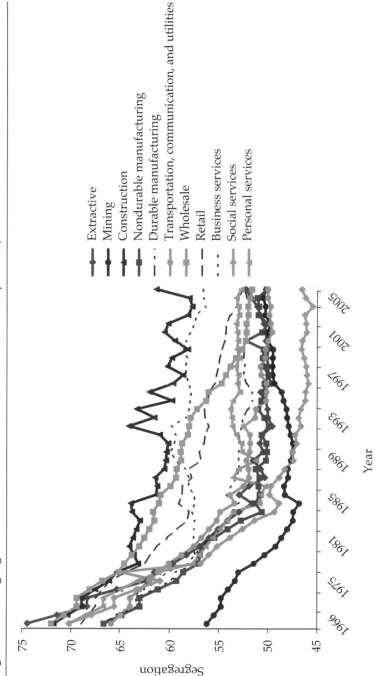

Figure 7.2 Segregation Between White Men and White Women by Sector, 1966 to 2005

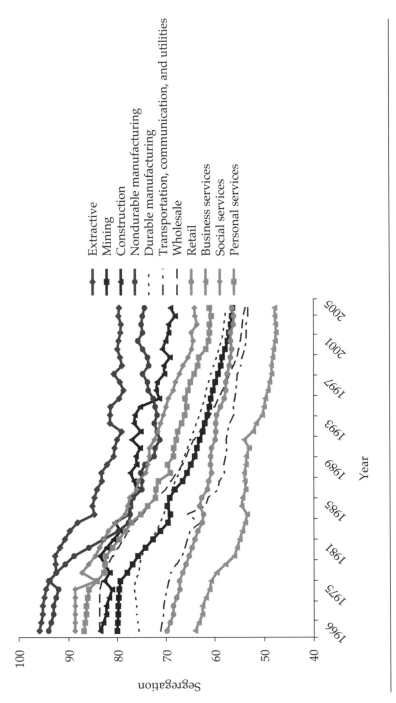

Source: Authors' calculations based on data from EEO-1 surveys (EEOC, various years).

trade, social services, and personal services had the lowest levels of gender segregation across the period. This latter pattern is consistent with the idea that the move toward a service society has propelled gender desegregation. These sectors, with the exception of business services, also stood out for having fairly low wage levels, an observation we return to shortly. Business services stood out for having the steepest and most sustained desegregation trajectory for white men and white women, as it did for white men and black men.

Racial segregation among women, as we have already seen, took a very different global trajectory (figure 7.3). Although there was a sharp drop in segregation between white women and black women after 1966, the economy-wide pattern beginning in the 1970s was one of resegregation as white women moved into male jobs and black women continued to be employed in more typically female and racialized positions. Of course, there were exceptions to this pattern. Retail trade, business services, social services, and personal services, the same sectors that showed the lowest levels of gender segregation among whites, did not display a pattern of resegregation between black women and white women after the 1970s. Thus, the dominant pattern of race resegregation among women happened not throughout the economy but in the more traditionally male sectors. It is these sectors that Charles and Grusky (2004) suggest may be the least hospitable to women. These results suggest that black women are particularly disadvantaged in these traditionally male sectors.

An examination of 2005 segregation levels across sectors (table 7.1) shows some consistent patterns. Gender segregation was consistently highest for all comparisons in the extractive, mining, and construction sectors. Both black women's and white women's segregation from white men was lowest in the social and personal service sectors, but white women and black men came into the most equal-status contact in business services, followed by durable manufacturing. Although there were some similarities in gender segregation across sectors, with the exception of the three most segregated sectors—extractive, mining, and construction— there was no simple pattern across all three comparisons. Personal services, perhaps, stood out for being consistently among the lowest in terms of gender segregation (and earnings, as we will see shortly).

By 2005, race segregation was even less clearly organized by sector. White men and black men were most likely to work in equal-status roles in the heterogeneous category of transportation, communication, and utilities. These industries are grouped together in official statistics not because they share similar technologies or products, as in other sectors, but because they all were regulated by the federal government under antitrust legislation at the beginning of the twentieth century. These are the indus-

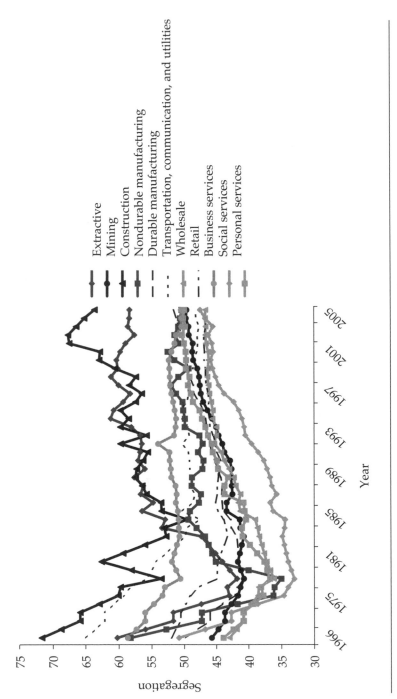

Figure 7.3 Segregation Between White Women and Black Women by Sector, 1966 to 2005

Extractive
Mining
Construction
Nondurable manufacturing
Durable manufacturing
Transportation, communication, and utilities
Wholesale
Retail
Business services
Social services
Personal services

Source: Authors' calculations based on data from EEO-1 surveys (EEOC, various years).

Table 7.1   Gender Segregation Levels by Sector, Ranked from Lowest to Highest, 2005

White Men–White Women		White Men–Black Women	
Social services	45	Social services	61
Personal services	51	Personal services	66
Business services	52	Durable manufacturing	69
Durable manufacturing	54	Retail	69
Retail	55	Business services	71
Nondurable manufacturing	56	Nondurable manufacturing	71
Wholesale	60	Transportation, communica-	
Transportation, communication,		tion, and utilities	74
and utilities	63	Wholesale	75
Extractive	68	Mining	82
Mining	74	Extractive	84
Construction	80	Construction	85

Source: Authors' calculations based on data from EEO-1 surveys (EEOC, various years).

tries with the longest history of federal regulation. This sector is also among the least race-segregated among women.

Compared to gender segregation, there was much less variability across sectors in the levels of race segregation (table 7.2). The top nine sectors were separated by only six points for men and five for women. The comparable spread for the three gender segregation comparisons in table 7.1 was four times larger at 20 percent.

In figure 7.4, we report sector trends in white male managerial representation. Although all sectors showed an increase in white males' access to managerial jobs after 1966, there was considerable variability in trajectories after the early 1970s. White males' overrepresentation was particularly high, and grew steeply, in mining and construction. Most other sectors produced slow growth in white male managerial representation. There were, however, a few exceptions. Transportation, communication, and utilities, as well as both producer and personal services, showed an essentially flat trajectory after 1972. Most strikingly, since 1966 social services have shown a strong downward trajectory for white male managers. In 1966 white men were employed as managers in social service firms at about their general labor market participation levels. After the initial bump produced by the post–Civil Rights Act inspired the hiring of minorities and women into lower-level jobs, white male representation in social service management declined steadily. By 2005, white men were 20 percent less likely to be managers in private social service firms than their general labor market participation level. In all other sectors, white men

Table 7.2   Race Segregation Levels by Sector, Ranked from Lowest to Highest, 2005

White Men–Black Men		White Women–Black Women	
Transportation, communication, and utilities	47	Retail	47
Personal services	50	Business services	47
Mining	50	Transportation, communication, and utilities	48
Durable manufacturing	50	Personal services	48
Business services	52	Durable manufacturing	50
Construction	52	Wholesale	50
Nondurable manufacturing	52	Mining	50
Retail	53	Social services	51
Wholesale	53	Nondurable manufacturing	52
Social services	57	Construction	59
Extractive	61	Extractive	64

Source: Authors' calculations based on data from EEO-1 surveys (EEOC, various years).

were overrepresented in managerial jobs, although there was considerable variation. Personal services showed the lowest level of white male overrepresentation in 2005, at 41 percent higher than their local labor force participation level. Construction was the highest in 2005, with white male managerial representation at 136 percent of their private-sector labor force participation in general.

One of the things that is most striking about figure 7.4 is that in 2005 white males' representation in management was lowest in retail trade and the three service sectors. These, of course, have been the high-growth employment sectors as the economy has moved away from manufacturing and toward a service economy. They also comprise relatively low-wage industries. If we look at the managerial representation of white women, black men, and black women in 2005, we find the reverse pattern. They were more likely to be employed as managers in these low-wage, high-growth sectors.

White women were employed as managers at about their local labor market representation in producer services, personal services, and retail firms, and they clearly dominated social service managerial jobs. For black men, the transportation, communication, and utilities sector—the three antitrust-regulated industries—was by far the most hospitable managerial location: their 2005 employment rates were nearly at their level of local labor market participation. In no sector did black women approach labor market parity. The social services sector provided black women with the greatest access to managerial roles, but they were still 26 percent less likely

Figure 7.4 White Male Managerial Representation by Sector, 1966 to 2005

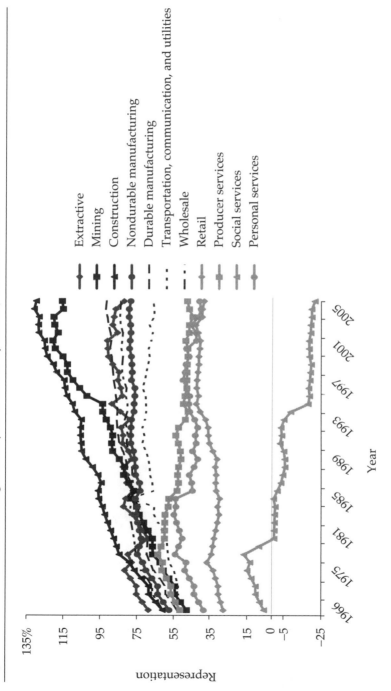

Source: Authors' calculations based on data from EEO-1 surveys (EEOC, various years).

Table 7.3   Managerial Representation Levels by Sector, Ranked from Highest to Lowest, 2005

White Men		White Women	
Construction	135	Social services	77
Mining	120	Producer services	6
Durable manufacturing	94	Personal services	2
Wholesale	86	Retail	–6
Extractive	84	Wholesale	–32
Nondurable manufacturing	80	Transportation, communication, and utilities	–34
Transportation, communication, and utilities	68	Nondurable manufacturing	–38
Producer services	49	Extractive	–51
Personal services	42	Durable manufacturing	–55
Retail	39	Construction	–67
Social services	–24	Mining	–71
Black Men		**Black Women**	
Transportation, communication, and utilities	–3	Social services	–26
Retail	–23	Transportation, communication, and utilities	–46
Personal services	–25	Personal services	–49
Nondurable manufacturing	–36	Retail	–53
Durable manufacturing	–44	Producer services	–54
Producer services	–46	Nondurable manufacturing	–75
Wholesale	–47	Wholesale	–81
Mining	–57	Durable manufacturing	–84
Social services	–64	Extractive	–91
Extractive	–70	Construction	–95
Construction	–76	Mining	–95

Source: Authors' calculations based on data from EEO-1 surveys (EEOC, various years).

to be managers than they were to be employed in the local private-sector economy.

In 2005, forty years after the Civil Rights Act outlawed discrimination and segregation, there were almost no black women in managerial roles in mining, construction, and the extractive sectors (table 7.3). Manufacturing and wholesale trade were little better. The worst sector for white male managerial representation, social services, was still better than any other sector for black women's access to managerial jobs. The best sector for white women's representation, social services, was still worse than the top six sectors for white male representation.

Extractive, mining, and construction all were high-segregation sectors in which white men dominated managerial jobs. For race segregation, durable manufacturing and transportation, communication, and utilities were initially the most responsive to desegregation pressures, but once those pressures eased, durable manufacturing resegregated, while transportation, communication, and utilities did not. In general, white women prospered where white men did not, and white men prospered where segregation remained high. Only in social services, where white women came to dominate managerial jobs, do we see both clear declines in white males' privileged access to management and low levels of gender segregation. This sector, however, has one of the highest levels of segregation between white men and black men.

INDUSTRIAL ENVIRONMENTS

Organizational theory points to industries as the proximate context in which normative expectations emerge concerning both the division of labor and the race and gender composition of typical jobs. In this framework, industry as an institutional field is a source of human resource practices and segregation expectations among employers (Beggs 1995; Milkman 1987; Stainback et al. 2010; Tomaskovic-Devey and Skaggs 1999b). Workplaces develop routines and divisions of labor that include notions about the typical race and gender composition of jobs. These expectations are reinforced by peer firms in the same industry. We have shown in earlier research that the largest firms in an industry are particularly influential in setting race and gender segregation norms (McTague et al. 2009).

Change in segregation can be expected to be constrained by industry norms. In the absence of pressure for increased equal opportunity, inertia is to be expected and new firms will tend to mimic industry practices. Because industries vary in their practices and typical segregation levels, we can also expect change to arise from the evolution of the industrial structure. If less-segregated industries grow faster than more-segregated ones, aggregate segregation will decline. It was this basic insight that motivated us to examine political and labor market dynamics in the last four chapters only after we had statistically controlled for changes in the industrial structure. In this chapter, rather than control industrial shifts away, we center our attention on that industry variability and its overall contribution to desegregation.

A series of potential mechanisms linked to industry may have an impact on segregation levels. The first is simple growth. It seems reasonable to expect that where jobs are growing and opportunities are more numerous, institutional expectations as to the proper race- or gender-based divisions of labor will be weaker, as will social closure pressures from current workforces to preserve their control of good jobs.

The social closure explanation in studies of segregation stresses the exclusion of women and minorities from desirable employment. Because service industries tend to pay lower wages, previous researchers have expected that social closure pressures might be lower in service industries, leading to both more racial minority and female representation and lower segregation within these industries. Sociologist Barbara Reskin (1988), among others, has suggested that racial minorities and women are more likely to find employment in the emerging service sector precisely because those jobs are less desirable to white men. Social closure approaches to race and gender segregation tend to predict that white males will attempt to monopolize good jobs; thus, the relative openness of the service sector or particular low-wage industries to racial minorities and women in managerial or professional jobs is predictable and may signal more limited progress than our previous analyses of access to good-quality jobs imply (see, for example, Taylor 2010). That is, racial minority and female access to managerial, professional, or craft jobs may be most rapid in low-wage industries.

On the other hand, we have discovered that relative to managerial or craft jobs, there are steeper and more consistent trajectories of access to professional jobs for black men, black women, and especially white women. That these gains have been accompanied by the erosion of white male dominance of professional occupations suggests an equal opportunity mechanism that is linked to professional jobs. We believe that the hiring prerequisite of a specific advanced educational degree has a meritocratic effect, reducing the influence of invidious race and gender distinctions while valorizing formal credentials in the selection process. We know that colleges and universities have been particularly responsive to calls for educational desegregation, and many professional degree programs desegregated quite rapidly after the 1972 passage of Title IX amendments to the Civil Rights Act. In this section, we find that industries that require a higher proportion of their employees to hold college degrees tend to exhibit lower levels of segregation and higher employment of white women, black women, and black men in good-quality jobs. White male representation actually tends to drop in industries with rising expectations for educational certification among their employees.

We focus on an intermediate level of industrial detail. The two-digit standard industrial classification (SIC) codes that we employ are meant to group firms that have similar production processes and products or services. Thus, to the extent that there are industry norms for race- and gender-based divisions of labor, these are probably fairly appropriate indicators of the normative organizational field that firms refer to when adopting internal divisions of labor and human resource practices.

Tables 7.4 and 7.5 display industries ranked by employment growth, income relative to the national average, and the proportion of employees

Table 7.4   Top Twenty Two-Digit Industries Ranked for Employment Growth, Relative Income, and Educational Requirements, 1973 to 1980

Employment Growth Rate	Income Percentage of Median	Percentage College Graduates
Pipelines, except natural gas	Petroleum and coal products	Educational services
Legal services	Pipelines, except natural gas	Engineering and management services
Engineering and management services	Security, commodity brokers, and investment	Security, commodity brokers, and investment
Transportation services	Transportation by air	Legal services
Miscellaneous repair services	Railroad transportation	Social services
Business services	Engineering and management services	Insurance
Health services	Chemicals and allied products	Petroleum and coal products
Auto repair, services, and parking	Mining	Business services
Eating and drinking places	Electric, gas, and sanitary services	Chemicals and allied products
Mining	Transportation equipment	Motion pictures
Banks	Communication	Membership organizations
Amusement and recreation services	Primary metal industries	Pipelines, except natural gas
Miscellaneous retail	Industrial machinery and equipment	Health services
Real estate	Water transportation	Banks
Instruments and related products	Paper and allied products	Transportation services
Transportation by air	Trucking and warehousing	Real estate
Industrial machinery and equipment	Wholesale trade	Transportation by air
Social services	Instruments and related products	Wholesale trade
Food stores	Fabricated metal products	Printing and publishing
Motion pictures	Rubber and miscellaneous plastics products	Instruments and related products

Source: Authors' calculations based on data from IPUMS-CPS (King et al. 2010).

with college degrees. Because the EEO-1 reports do not contain this information, we produced these calculations using the Current Population Survey (CPS). We see (1) employment growth, (2) income-based closure, and (3) meritocratic hiring rules as indicators of the three most promising mechanisms that might explain industry or firm variation in desegregation. Because we do not directly observe workplace dynamics, we are assuming that industrial context influences both the behaviors and resources available at the workplace level. We focus first on the 1973 to 1980 period, given that it was a period of strong desegregation for all groups.

During the 1970s, there was rapid employment growth among both

Table 7.5   Bottom Twenty Two-Digit Industries Ranked for Employment Growth, Relative Income, and Educational Requirements, 1973 to 1980

Employment Growth Rate	Income Percentage of Median	Percentage College Graduates
Furniture and home furnishings	Membership organizations	Local and interurban passenger transit
Paper and allied products	Furniture and fixtures	Miscellaneous manufacturing industries
Fabricated metal products	Motion pictures	
Agriculture, forestry, and fishery	Auto repair, services, and parking	Stone, clay, and glass products
Transportation equipment	Furniture and home furnishings	Hotels and other lodging places
Furniture and fixtures	Textile mill products	Railroad transportation
Lumber and wood products	Health services	Food and kindred products
Petroleum and coal products	Educational services	Construction
Stone, clay, and glass products	Miscellaneous retail	Automotive dealers and service stations
General merchandise stores	Social services	
Apparel and other textile products	Food stores	Miscellaneous repair services
Railroad transportation	Leather and leather products	Lumber and wood products
Automotive dealers and service stations	Apparel and other textile products	Trucking and warehousing
Food and kindred products	Amusement and recreation services	Agriculture, forestry, and fishery
Tobacco products	General merchandise stores	Textile mill products
Primary metal industries	Apparel and accessory stores	Eating and drinking places
Personal services	Hotels and other lodging places	Furniture and fixtures
Rubber and miscellaneous plastics products	Agriculture, forestry, and fishery	Food stores
Leather and leather products	Eating and drinking places	Apparel and other textile products
Textile mill products	Personal services	Auto repair, services, and parking
		Leather and leather products
		Personal services

Source: Authors' calculations based on data from IPUMS-CPS (King et al. 2010).

high- and low-earnings service industries. The high-earner service industries tend to be in the producer services sector and include various forms of financial, legal, engineering, and other business services. The highest-wage industries include these high-end producer services but also many manufacturing industries, trucking, and wholesalers. We again see producer services industries concentrated among those that require a high proportion of workers to have college degrees, but also included are social services, which, while on the list of high-growth industries, is not a high-wage industry. Social services are where white women have made the greatest gains in managerial employment and white men are now underrepresented.

If we concentrate on the least desirable set of industries from the point of view of the three mechanisms we have identified as potentially influencing the pace of desegregation, we see that the industries with slow employment growth, or even contraction, include many in the manufacturing and extractive sectors. Personal services and automotive dealers stand out for being the only industries in the service sectors that declined as a proportion of the labor force in the 1970s. The low-pay industries are concentrated, not surprisingly, in the service sector, but also include a few declining manufacturing industries such as textiles and leather. The low-education industries include a mix of service and manufacturing industries as well as agriculture, construction, and local and interurban transportation.

In Which Industries Did White Men Desegregate Most Rapidly During the Regulatory Period?

Because gender desegregation did not begin in earnest until after 1972, we focus on the 1973 to 1980 regulatory period to see which industries were moving most rapidly toward equal employment opportunity in their workforces (table 7.6). Almost all industries displayed some desegregation of white women, black men, and black women from white men during the short regulatory decade. The most rapid white male desegregation from both white females and black females largely happened in the same industries, almost all of which had very high levels of initial gender segregation. These were a mix of traditionally male industries, many of them relatively high-paying. For black men, we see the same pattern documented earlier: desegregation was steepest in the transportation, communication, and utility industries.

One of the most striking aspects of desegregation during the regulatory period (1973 to 1981) was the strong concentration of white male desegregation in high-income industries. For white women, half of the high-desegregation industries were in the top third of the industry earnings distribution. For segregation from black men, eight out of ten industries were among the top paying. For black women, it was four out of ten. Conversely, low-wage industries are barely visible in the table. Much of the most rapid desegregation in the regulatory period occurred in workplaces in high-wage industries. There was no particular tendency for these to also be credential-intensive or high-growth industries.

Table 7.6 Ten Steepest Yearly Desegregation Trajectories, 1973 to 1981

White Men–White Women		White Men–Black Men		White Men–Black Women	
Communication	-2.4	Miscellaneous repair services	-2.4	*Communication*	-1.7
Building materials and garden supplies	-2.2	*Railroad transportation*	-1.7	Building materials and garden supplies	-1.6
Petroleum and coal products	-1.9	*Pipelines, except natural gas*	-1.7	*Petroleum and coal products*	-1.5
Lumber and wood products	-1.6	*Petroleum and coal products*	-1.5	Tobacco products	-1.1
Chemicals and allied products	-1.4	Tobacco products	-1.5	Primary metal industries	-1.1
Pipelines, except natural gas	-1.4	*Electric, gas, and sanitary services*	-1.4	*Chemicals and allied products*	-1.1
Mining	-1.4	*Transportation by air*	-1.1	*Insurance*	-1.0
Business services	-1.4	*Trucking and warehousing*	-1.0	**General merchandise stores**	-0.9
Motion pictures	-1.3	**General merchandise stores**	-1.0	*Mining*	-0.8
Insurance	-1.3	*Chemicals and allied products*	-0.9	**Motion pictures**	-0.8

Source: Authors' calculations based on data from EEO-1 surveys (EEOC, various years).
Note: Italics indicates the industry is in the top third of the industry income distribution. **Bold** indicates the industry is in the bottom third of the industry income distribution.

In Which Industries Did White Men Become More Segregated During the Regulatory Period?

Even during the regulatory period, there were a few industries that were actually trending toward higher white male employment segregation (table 7.7). Segregation between white men and white women grew in nine industries. Black male segregation, on the other hand, was rising in only five industries, and black female segregation in only six. Most of these positive slopes were relatively weak. For all three groups in the few industries where segregation from white men was growing, wages tended to be among the lowest in the economy. The obvious exception was engineering and management services, which achieved a steep increase in racial segregation among men and a weak increase of white men and women during the period of peak regulation. We imagine that this industry was not on the regulatory radar screen, despite being one of the fastest-growing and highest-paying industries in the economy during this period.

Where Is White Male Desegregation and Resegregation Happening Now?

Although the pace of desegregation slowed considerably after 1980, desegregation trends continued after 2000 in numerous industries. Employment desegregation in private-sector EEOC-reporting firms remained the dominant trend for white men and white women. In forty-six of fifty-eight industries, the slope remained negative, although in many industries the gains were now slight. Gender desegregation among whites was still brisk in some industries, many of them the same ones that had shown steep desegregation trajectories in the 1970s. With a −0.8 percent improvement per year in this century, security, commodity brokers, and investments, which is by far the highest-paying industry in the economy, even makes the list. White men and black women were working in increased equal-status contact in some of the same industries as white women, but also in some low-wage industries such as food services, apparel, and personal services. The transportation industries, which showed particularly favorable trajectories for white male–black male segregation in the 1970s, now did as well for white and black women and men.

There is no strong pattern of high-wage industries being among the most rapidly desegregating in the latest period. For all three comparisons, the top-earning third of industries are underrepresented in table 7.8. Interestingly, these include two financial-sector industries (security, commodity brokers, and investment; banks) and two oil-related industries (petroleum and coal products; pipelines, except natural gas). These four

Table 7.7 Industries with Positive Segregation Trajectories, 1973 to 1981

White Men–White Women		White Men–Black Men		White Men–Black Women	
Miscellaneous repair services	0.6	*Engineering and management services*	8.2	**Membership organizations**	0.9
Educational services	0.4	**Membership organizations**	0.5	**Miscellaneous repair services**	0.6
Personal services	0.4	**Legal services**	0.4	**Personal services**	0.5
Food and kindred products	0.2	**Educational services**	0.2	**Auto repair, services, and parking**	0.4
Miscellaneous retail	0.2	**Leather and leather products**	0.1	**Real estate**	0.2
Apparel and other textile products	0.2			*Security, commodity brokers, and investment*	0.2
Local and interurban passenger transit	0.2				
Leather and leather products	0.2				
Engineering and management services	0.1				

Source: Authors' calculations based on data from EEO-1 surveys (EEOC, various years).

Note: Italics indicates the industry is in the top third of the industry income distribution. **Bold** indicates the industry is in the bottom third of the industry income distribution.

Table 7.8   Ten Steepest Yearly Desegregation Trajectories, 2001 to 2005

White Men–White Women		White Men–Black Men		White Men–Black Women	
Building materials and garden supplies	-2.0	**Personal services**	-1.8	**Personal services**	-1.6
Trucking and warehousing	-1.5	Real estate	-0.7	Building materials and garden supplies	-1.4
Personal services	-1.4	**General merchandise stores**	-0.6	Fabricated metal products	-0.7
Apparel and other textile products	-1.4	**Apparel and other textile products**	-0.6	**Apparel and other textile products**	-0.6
Miscellaneous manufacturing industries	-1.1	Building materials and garden supplies	-0.5	**Miscellaneous repair services**	-0.6
Miscellaneous repair services	-0.9	*Instruments and related products*	-0.5	*Pipelines, except natural gas*	-0.6
Water transportation	-0.9	*Petroleum and coal products*	-0.5	*Banks*	-0.5
Transportation services	-0.8	**Agriculture, forestry, and fishery**	-0.5	Water transportation	-0.5
Fabricated metal products	-0.8	Miscellaneous manufacturing industries	-0.5	**Trucking and warehousing**	-0.5
Security, commodity brokers, and investment	-0.8	*Banks*	-0.5	**Food stores**	-0.4

Source: Authors' calculations based on data from EEO-1 surveys (EEOC, various years).

Note: Italics indicates the industry is in the top third of the industry income distribution. **Bold** indicates the industry is in the bottom third of the industry income distribution.

industries consistently pay much higher wages than the rest of the economy. In addition, the two finance-sector industries have particularly high incidences of college-educated employees. If anything, the more prominent pattern after 2000, at least among women, was a shift toward faster desegregation with white men in low-wage industries.

The most striking aspect of table 7.9 is the widespread resegregation of white men and black men. Nineteen of fifty-eight industries—nearly one-third of all industries—showed a trend toward racial resegregation among white men and black men in this century. Most of these were in the middle of the industry income distribution. The resegregation of white men and white women was less common, occurring in only seven industries, every one of which was either a high- or low-earning industry. Most, however, were high-earning industries and two (pipelines and mining) were among the industries with the most rapid *desegregation* during the short regulatory decade of the 1970s.

Black women increasingly became employed in different jobs from white men in eleven industries, four of which were among the lowest-wage industries and two of which were among the highest. There is almost no overlap with the 1973 to 1981 lists, except that mining was on the most rapid desegregation list in the regulatory period and also among those industries that resegregated more recently. For black women, like black men, most resegregation happened in the middle of the industry wage distribution.

What About Segregation Trajectories Between White Women and Black Women?

In both the regulatory and contemporary periods, the dominant industry trajectory between white women and black women was toward increased segregation (table 7.10). During the short regulatory decade, 70 percent of industries showed increased employment segregation between white women and black women. Including 60 percent of industries, resegregation was slightly less common in this century, but still the dominant pattern. The pace of employment resegregation between black women and white women is less steep today than it was in the 1970s. For the last half-century in most industries, white women and black women have become less likely to work together in the same job in the same workplace. This is a striking and disturbing pattern.

Because segregation was the norm across industries, we focus here on the top twenty industries in terms of increased employment segregation between white women and black women. There is a remarkable degree of overlap in the lists from the two time periods. Six of the top twenty indus-

Table 7.9 Industries with Positive Segregation Trajectories, 2001 to 2005

White Men–White Women		White Men–Black Men		White Men–Black Women	
Pipelines, except natural gas	0.5	Transportation services	1.2	Lumber and wood products	0.5
Transportation by air	0.5	Lumber and wood products	0.7	Transportation by air	0.4
Railroad transportation	0.4	Leather and leather products	0.6	**Leather and leather products**	0.2
Local and interurban passenger transit	0.3	Motion pictures	0.6	*Mining*	0.2
General merchandise stores	0.2	Transportation by air	0.5	*Railroad transportation*	0.2
Instruments and related products	0.1	Amusement and recreation services	0.5	**Automotive dealers and service stations**	0.2
Mining	0.1	Pipelines, except natural gas	0.4	**Textile mill products**	0.2
		Stone, clay, and glass products	0.3	**Social services**	0.1
		Primary metal industries	0.3	Stone, clay, and glass products	0.1
		Rubber and miscellaneous plastics products	0.3	Transportation services	0.1
		Industrial machinery and equipment	0.3	Lumber and wood products	0.5
		Construction	0.3		
		Social services	0.2		
		Textile mill products	0.2		
		Apparel and accessory stores	0.2		
		Educational services	0.2		
		Wholesale trade	0.1		
		Security, commodity brokers, and investment	0.1		

Source: Authors' calculations based on data from EEO-1 surveys (EEOC, various years).

Note: Italics indicates the industry is in the top third of the industry income distribution. **Bold** indicates the industry is in the bottom third of the industry income distribution.

Table 7.10   Top Twenty Industries with Increasing White Female–Black Female Segregation Trajectories, 1973 to 1980 and 2001 to 2005

Regulatory Period, 1973 to 1980		Contemporary Period, 2001 to 2005	
Pipelines, except natural gas	3.6	**Miscellaneous repair services**	2.6
Petroleum and coal products	2.6	*Railroad transportation*	0.8
Construction	2.2	*Transportation equipment*	0.6
Mining	2.0	Transportation services	0.5
Insurance	1.9	Paper and allied products	0.5
Automotive dealers and service stations	1.6	Stone, clay, and glass products	0.5
		Furniture and fixtures	0.5
Engineering and management services	1.4	**Apparel and accessory stores**	0.5
Wholesale trade	1.4	**Textile mill products**	0.4
Primary metal industries	1.4	Printing and publishing	0.4
Chemicals and allied products	1.4	*Mining*	0.3
Stone, clay, and glass products	1.4	Trucking and warehousing	0.3
Security, commodity brokers, and investment	1.4	*Legal services*	0.3
Electric, gas, and sanitary services	1.3	*Electric, gas, and sanitary services*	0.3
Fabricated metal products	1.0	Food and kindred products	0.3
Building materials and garden supplies	0.9	*Security, commodity brokers, and investment*	0.3
Real estate	0.9	*Electronic and other electric equipment*	0.3
Legal services	0.8	*Chemicals and allied products*	0.2
Local and interurban passenger transit	0.7	**Amusement and recreation services**	0.2
Paper and allied products	0.6	**Auto repair, services, and parking**	0.2
Communication	0.6		

Source: Authors' calculations based on data from EEO-1 surveys (EEOC, various years).
Note: Italics indicates the industry is in the top third of the industry income distribution. **Bold** indicates the industry is in the bottom third of the industry income distribution.

tries in terms of increased employment segregation between black women and white women are on both lists. These include automotive dealers and service stations; chemicals and allied products; electric, gas, and sanitary services; legal services; mining; and security, commodity brokers, and investment firms. During the regulatory period, the pattern was overwhelmingly one in which increased segregation between black women and white women happened most dramatically in high-wage industries.

It is notable that no low-wage industries were among the top resegregation contexts in the regulatory period. In contrast, in this century six low-wage industries have been resegregating—about what we would expect in a sample of twenty. Thus, during the initial period of employment resegregation between black women and white women, racial distinctions in occupational assignments grew fastest where the opportunities for high earnings were the greatest. These are the same types of industries in which white women made the most rapid employment gains into previously white male firms and jobs. In the current period, racial resegregation among women, although disturbingly widespread, does not seem to be strongly associated with industry earnings potential. Later in this chapter, we reexamine this observation more formally.

Again, the prominent exception is the security, commodity brokers, and investment industry. This industry, infamous for its role in selling mortgage-backed securities that precipitated the 2008 financial crisis, had a pattern of racial resegregation for both men and women after 2000. At the same time, it had one of the steepest desegregation trajectories between white women and white men in this century. Since 1980, this industry has also made by far the greatest relative income gains of any industry in the U.S. economy. From the point of view of earnings growth, this was the best place in the economy to be employed, and it was white women who gained access to the high-wage jobs, even as black men and black women became more socially distant from whites over time. This does not mean that within this industry gender distinctions were muted; on the contrary, gender earnings inequalities grew substantially (Tomaskovic-Devey and Lin 2011). But even being relatively low paid in an investment bank or hedge fund was a higher wage than in the rest of the economy.

INDUSTRY GROWTH, RELATIVE INCOME, AND EDUCATIONAL SCREENING

The preceding analyses have largely been descriptive. We have paid particular attention to the earnings potential associated with industries, because we began the chapter with a strong suspicion that equal opportunity progress has been most apparent in low-wage industries. For segregation, the story is clearly not that simple, although for access to good-quality jobs it does seem to generally be the case.

Nevertheless, earnings are clearly not the only potential factor influencing the trajectories of desegregation. One explanation for the importance of the service economy for the incorporation of new labor forces is simply that the increased employment opportunities available in growing industries make desegregation easier. Incumbents certainly have the advantage in attempting to monopolize positions, but monopolies may be less necessary when opportunity is abundant. It may simply be that there is less resistance and more opportunity to create newly integrated jobs and work-places when the current workforce need not directly compete for the same job with new status groups.

Social closure theory predicts that the more desirable the job, the more actors will attempt to hoard opportunities on the basis of status character-istics. Although we have been addressing the quality of employment by focusing on managerial, professional, and craft occupations, we should note that the quality of a managerial job is not the same in, say, an invest-ment bank and a flower shop. There are very large wage differences be-tween industries, even among otherwise good jobs. We gauge desirability as a function of the relative wage in the industry. Thus, the higher the wage in an industry the more we expect exclusionary behavior.

Finally, in industries that display higher levels of educated workers we suspect that education becomes a favored screening mechanism for all jobs, but particularly for managerial and professional jobs. Because an educational credential is a clear alternative to race and gender as a selec-tion mechanism, we expect lower levels of segregation and higher levels of opportunity for racial minorities and women in industries with higher concentrations of educated employees.

Because we have three mechanisms that are somewhat correlated with each other, we examine these three processes simultaneously. Our ap-proach is to estimate statistical models that predict change in group em-ployment, segregation, and occupational representation within industries as a function of employment growth, industry relative income, and cre-dential-based employment screening.[1] Because the models control for un-measured but stable industry characteristics, the fixed-effects models we employ are useful for inferring a causal process, as we are attempting to do here. We estimate these models at the industry level, not because we think that these mechanisms are unique to industries, but because the EEO-1 reports do not contain information on income or credential screen-ing at the workplace or firm levels. We can, however, get this information from the monthly Current Population Surveys, as we do here. These CPS data can be matched to industry but not to specific workplaces. This is not to say that industries are merely convenient units of observation in the absence of better data. Institutional theory is quite clear that firms often derive their expectations for divisions of labor and managerial practices and policies from their industrial environment (Stainback et al. 2010).

We estimate these models across the entire 1966 to 2005 period, but also estimate a series of models of change before and after 1981 to see whether results are dependent on when they occurred in the history of desegrega-tion politics. The basic results for labor force composition and segregation are summarized in table 7.11. There is a weak pattern of industry employ-

Table 7.11   Changes in Industry Employment and Segregation as a
Function of Growth, Closure, and Credentialing
Mechanisms, 1966 to 2005

	Employment Growth Rate	Relative Income	College Degrees
Percent Employment			
White men	0.001	0.002	−0.73
White women	0	−0.0009	0
Black men	0.0003	0	0
Black women	0	−0.0023	0.11
Segregation			
White men–white women	0	9.7	−0.14
White men–black men	0	7.1	−0.92
White men–black women	0	13.8	−1.07

Source: Authors' calculations based on data from EEO-1 surveys (EEOC, various years).
Note: Fixed-effects estimates, balanced industry-period data, N = 280 (58 industries, 5 periods). Reported coefficients significant at or above a probability level of .05. Zero (0) indicates nonsignificant effect.

ment growth facilitating the growth of black male and white male employment. But even the most extreme observed industry growth rates (78 percent for oil pipelines in the 2001 to 2005 period) suggest a predicted increase in white male employment of only 8 percent. One standard deviation in employment growth rates, a more reasonable metric, is only 7 percent and would therefore produce a predicted increase in white male employment of only 0.7 percent. The shift for black men is only one-third as large. Employment growth is not consistently associated with shifts in the race and gender composition of employment, nor, as we will see, is it typically associated with segregation or occupational representation.[2]

On the other hand, in industries with growing levels of income, white male employment increases and both black women's employment and white women's employment decline. These effects are also quite small. There is no association between industry relative income and black male employment shifts. The big exception to this string of small or no effects is associated with college degrees. Industries with higher proportions of employees with college degrees have substantially lower white male employment. Here a 1 percent increase in college degrees among the workforce leads to a 0.75 percent drop in white males in the industry. There is also a weak tendency for industries that hire more college graduates to see a growth in black women among their workers, but we find that this result is limited to the post-1980 period.

Employment growth is also not associated with change in segregation for any comparisons. Income and college degree variation are, however, influential. White men's segregation from all three groups—white women, black men, and black women—tends to increase with rising industry earnings. On the other hand, industries that are becoming more knowledge-intensive, presumably because they are also becoming more meritocratic, display declining levels of white male employment segregation from white women, black men, and black women. Although present across the entire post-1966 period, for black men the egalitarian influence of credential-based hiring was stronger before 1980, when pressures for black male inclusion were also greater. For white women and black women, the influence of credential-based screening on egalitarian employment with white men was stronger after 1980, when progress for both groups was less rapid but both groups actually had much higher rates of college completion than they did prior to 1980. Workplace segregation between white men and white women, black men, and black women rises when wages are growing and declines when industries become increasingly reliant on credentials for selecting employees. These are fairly striking results, supporting both the social closure and meritocracy hypotheses about the sources of employment segregation and desegregation.

The general pattern of white male advantage rising in high-income industries and dropping as credentials become a more prominent selection mechanism extends to representation in higher-quality occupations. Again, simple employment growth is not a source of integration into desirable occupations. Higher-income industries produce fewer managerial jobs for all groups, but the negative effect for black men is about one-third higher than it is for white men and white women. For black women, the negative influence of industry income is twice the size of its effect on white men and white women. Black men and black women are less likely than white men and white women to become managers in high-wage industries.

The same general pattern also holds for access to professional jobs. As wages go up, black representation in the professions goes down. Craft jobs display a slight variation on this theme: when wages in an industry rise, white male employment in skilled working-class jobs rises as well. White women's and black men's representation in skilled working-class jobs declines when industry wages are rising. There is a clear pattern that rising earnings potentials are associated with the exclusion of black men and black women from desirable occupations. White women do not face the same blanket exclusion, except in craft production jobs. As we have seen, employment segregation from white men tends to increase—or to decrease more slowly—in industries with rising relative wages.

That segregation and exclusion would rise with higher income oppor-

Table 7.12   Changes in Managerial, Professional, and Craft
Representation as a Function of Growth, Closure, and
Credentialing Mechanisms, 1966 to 2005

	Employment Growth Rate	Relative Income	College Degrees
Managerial representation			
White men	0	−0.17	0.95
White women	0	−0.16	2.19
Black men	0	−0.21	1.29
Black women	0	−0.33	1.99
Professional representation			
White men	0	0	−0.48
White women	0	0	2.93
Black men	0	−0.13	1.18
Black women	0	−0.13	1.40
Craft representation			
White men	0	0.37	0
White women	0	−0.48	1.32
Black men	0	−0.59	1.46
Black women	0	0	0.47

Source: Authors' calculations based on data from EEO-1 surveys (EEOC, various years).
Note: Fixed-effects estimates, balanced industry-period data, N = 280 (58 industries, 5 periods). Reported coefficients are significant at or below .05 probability. Zero (0) indicates effects that were not statistically different from zero.

tunities is expected if social closure is a mechanism generating segregation and producing inequality. One might speculate that it is not the exclusion of white women, black men, and black women from high-paying jobs, but the selection of more productive white men into these jobs. This is the standard human capital explanation of group income differences. Because the models include educational screening as an alternative mechanism, this interpretation seems extremely unlikely. The interpretation that white men are more productive than all others is particularly implausible given that the stable result is that industries with rising demand for educated employees hire fewer white men.

Credentialing, on the other hand, promotes racial and gender desegregation. Firms in industries with rising educational levels increasingly hire and promote white women, black men, and black women into their best-quality jobs. While high-education industries create more managerial jobs for all groups, the process is considerably weaker for white men. For white women, black men, and black women, a rise in industry reliance on educated labor increases access to good-quality jobs dramatically.

A 1 percent increase in college degrees in an industry leads to just under a 1 percent increase in white male managerial representation, but for white women the impact is a 2.2 percent surge in access to management jobs. For black women, the benefit is almost as high, at 2 percent. With increased educational screening, black men's managerial access rises less strongly (1.3 percent), but this is still a 37 percent stronger effect than is found among white men.

For the professions, the jobs most closely tied to a credentialing process, white men encounter a 0.5 percent decline in representation following a one-year rise in industry average education. White women's representation in professional jobs also stands out for being particularly strong in education-intensive industries, with a nearly 3 percent surge. For black men, the benefit is 1.2 percent. Black women's managerial access jumps 1.4 percent.

Craft jobs typically do not require college degrees, so that the same pattern holds for selection into these jobs is strong confirmation that the effects we are observing are tapping some underlying selection process that favors credentials over race or gender in the screening process. In more meritocratic industries, white male representation in skilled working-class jobs drops and white women and black male employment grows.

Although not reported in table 7.12, in parallel analyses we find that the credentialing effect for white women's access to managerial jobs strengthened in the post-1981 era. Prior to 1981, when the political pressures for racial equal opportunity were still present, the credentialing effect was substantially stronger for black men and black women in all three occupational destinations. This suggests to us that as the pressure for equal opportunity moved into the feminizing human resource function within firms it was white women, at least in managerial jobs, who benefited the most. Conversely, the influence of credential-based screening on white women's access to skilled craft jobs was weaker after 1981.

INDUSTRY NORMS AND ORGANIZATIONAL SEGREGATION TRAJECTORIES

Earlier in the chapter, we looked at which industries had the best and worst contemporary EEO trajectories. These analyses did not distinguish between change that happened within firms and the birth and death of new workplaces. Nor did we distinguish between change that was strong and systematic and trajectories that were nearly flat. In this section, we identify the industries in which workplaces had the steepest and most systematic *within-organization* segregation trajectories. Workplace-level change is typically the goal of equal opportunity initiatives, whether they arise in the regulatory environment, from lawsuits, or from internal constituencies.

We know that firms often develop their own internal practices by copying the behavior of other firms in their industry. In the next chapter, we will see that regulatory pressures are typically most successful when they change industry norms. Human resource professionals look to others in their industry as sources of best practice. Even in class-action lawsuits, statistical analyses of the composition of employment often use industry comparisons as the baseline for legitimate levels of segregation or occupational representation. In this sense the industry is a normative field providing models and legitimacy for organizational employment patterns and practices.

We wanted to classify industries in terms of their segregation norms in the current postregulatory period. To do this we drew a panel sample of workplaces from 1990 to 2005 that is representative of the entire EEOC-reporting population of private-sector firms. We link workplaces together over time and then observe the within-workplace segregation trajectories for each industry. This is simply the time trend in segregation across workplaces within each industry. The more workplaces within an industry share a common trajectory, the stronger the norm within that industry. Since the political pressure on firms to develop equal opportunity plans and monitor progress has waned, most contemporary change must come from the normative practices that firms currently have or can copy from other firms in their field of reference.

What we are interested in discovering is whether there are normative patterns of desegregation, resegregation, or inertia within specific industries. If an industry displays a statistically significant downward slope in segregation, we treat this as evidence of a normative tendency in that industry to desegregate. A trend that is statistically significant but positive indicates that the workplaces in that industry tend to share norms consistent with increased segregation. This might be generated by active resistance to equal opportunity agendas that diffuse across the industry, but we suspect that the more likely source is an attitude of neglect. If managers in an industry begin to assume that diversity is no longer a goal worth having, perhaps because that industry never institutionalized the required human resource practices, they might cease to actively manage workplace diversity. This would allow social closure pressures and bias processes to reassert themselves, leading to industry-wide resegregation. A nonsignificant time trend suggests that the industry has reached a new equilibrium, with no systematic equal opportunity progress, but also no regression to some earlier, more discriminatory baseline. This result could also be produced by a lack of normative consensus across firms within an industry as to best practices.

White Male–White Female Industry Segregation

Seventy-eight percent of the industries we examine had statistically significant within-firm declines in employment segregation between white men and white women after 1990 (see the list in table 7.13). In contrast, five industries had systematically *rising* employment segregation between white men and white women. These are listed in table 7.14 and include tobacco product manufacturers; apparel stores; stone, clay, and glass manufacturers; repair businesses; and restaurants and bars. Fifteen percent of industries seem to have reached a new equilibrium of stable gender segregation among whites.

The many industries with steep gender desegregation among whites are found in all sectors of the economy. There are only a handful of industries with sustained resegregation between white men and white women, and they are scattered across the manufacturing, retail, and personal services sectors. Any resegregation is shocking, and industry-wide resegregation is disappointing to discover given that it most likely signals a failure to manage diversity, at the level not simply of individual firms but of entire industries. It would certainly be preferable to discover only instances of inertia and desegregation. If backsliding away from post–Civil Rights Act desegregation happens in five industries, obviously it could spread to others over time.

White Male–Black Male Industry Segregation Trends

After 1990, twenty-four industries continued to systematically exhibit employment desegregation between white and black men. This movement toward equal opportunity in employment was most rapid in miscellaneous services, motion picture production, and real estate. Among these desegregating industries, the declines were as fast as the industry desegregation trajectories of white men and white women. Encouragingly, these strong gains in internal workplace practices also occurred in all sectors of the economy.

Less encouragingly, desegregation trends were statistically significant in only 42 percent of industries. In almost as many industries (41 percent), there was no evidence of within-workplace employment desegregation between white men and black men, suggesting that they had moved to a

Table 7.13 Ten Steepest Within-Workplace Industry Desegregation Trajectories, 1990 to 2005

White Men–White Women		White Men–Black Men		White Women–Black Women	
Services, NEC	-2.2	Services, NEC	-2.7	Railroad transportation	-1.5
Water transportation	-1.9	Motion pictures	-2.1	Educational services	-1.3
Pipelines	-1.7	Real estate	-1.9	Social services	-0.5
Miscellaneous manufacturing	-1.1	Miscellaneous manufacturing	-1.2	Construction	-0.5
Legal services	-1.0	Amusement and recreation		Banks	-0.3
Membership organizations	-0.9	services	-1.2	Printing and publishing	-0.2
Building and garden supplies	-0.9	Tobacco	-1.1	Business services	-0.2
Railroads	-0.9	Railroad transportation	-1.0	Health services	-0.1
Banks	-0.9	Membership organizations	-0.9		
Social services	-0.8	Instruments and related	-0.8		
		Security, commodity/brokers, and investment	-0.7		

Source: Authors' calculations based on data from EEO-1 surveys (EEOC, various years).

Table 7.14 Within-Workplace Industry Resegregation Trajectories, 1990 to 2005

White Men–White Women		White Men–Black Men		White Women–Black Women	
Tobacco products	1.4	Leather products	0.9	Services, NEC	3.6
Apparel stores	0.8	Mining	0.6	Leather products	2.1
Stone, clay, and glass	0.3	Health services	0.5	Miscellaneous repair	1.2
Miscellaneous repair	0.3	Textile mill products	0.4	Mining	1.2
Eating and drinking	0.2	Transportation services	0.3	Instruments	0.9
		Air transportation	0.3	Apparel stores	0.9
		Rubber, plastics	0.3	Electric, gas, sanitary	0.8
		Industrial machinery	0.2	Food products	0.7
		Trucking and warehousing	0.2	Personal services	0.6
				Hotels	0.5
				Electronic equipment	0.5
				Transportation equipment	0.4
				Textile mill products	0.4
				Paper products	0.4
				Automotive dealers and stations	0.4
				Engineering and management services	0.4
				Apparel and textile products	0.4
				Wholesale trade	0.3
				Air transportation	0.3
				Industrial machinery	0.3
				Insurance	0.3
				Auto repair and parking	0.2
				Food stores	0.2
				Eating and drinking places	0.2

Source: Authors' calculations based on data from EEO-1 surveys (EEOC, various years).

new equilibrium. In these stable industries, human resource practices reproduce the current level of integration but do not promote future gains. Together, continued desegregation and inertia are the dominant pattern, occurring in 84 percent of industries; in nine industries (16 percent), there has been significant growth in male racial employment segregation within workplaces since 1990 (see table 7.14). Leather manufacturing, mining, and health services are the worst offenders, all displaying resegregation trajectories between a half-point and one point a year.

White Female–Black Female Industry Segregation

Not surprisingly given our earlier findings, segregation between white women and black women shows the most disturbing industry-specific trends. We found only eight industries in which the average workplace was systematically hiring or promoting white women and black women into equal-status employment. These were the exceptions, the most promising of which included railroads, educational services, social services, construction, and banks. On the other hand, the long list of industries in table 7.14 in which the average workplace was hiring or promoting white women and black women into increasingly segregated roles is a bleak testament to the widespread reversal of racial desegregation among women. Miscellaneous services, leather products, repair industries, mining, and instruments had the strongest tendency toward increased segregation between white women and black women.

Forty-one percent of industries displayed no trend at all. Together, inertia and desegregation characterized only 57 percent of industries. In fully 43 percent of industries in the U.S. private sector, the new institutional pattern was toward increased race segregation among women. It seems clear to us that in many industries equal opportunity between white women and black women is not being actively managed. Given the time trends for resegregation documented in earlier chapters, we suspect that this has been the case since the 1960s. We also note that industries that are resegregating in one comparison are often resegregating in another. Industries with systematic workplace resegregation for two or more comparisons in table 7.14 include apparel, miscellaneous repair, eating and drinking places, leather manufacturing, mining, textile manufacturing, air transportation, and industrial machinery and equipment manufacturing. The coincidence of resegregation patterns across dimensions is consistent with emerging industry-wide norms of failure to manage diversity at all or perhaps even the positive sanctioning of renewed discrimination. We can imagine industry norms diffusing from leader firms in the industry or perhaps within industry-specific communities of human resource professionals.

By the same logic, we might suspect that the industries that appear multiple times in table 7.13 developed sustained equal opportunity norms that have become more effectively managed and more widely diffused over time. These include miscellaneous manufacturing, membership organizations, banks, social services, railroads, and miscellaneous services. Clearly there may be other explanations, but it is possible that at least some of these industries have established equal opportunity progress as normative industry practices.

Where Are We Now?

We end this chapter with an accounting of the best and worst industries in terms of access to managerial jobs (table 7.15). Only managers are found in every industry, and so this comparison makes the most sense for industries, as it did in the previous chapter for labor markets. Although the lists are far from mirror opposites, there is a clear pattern. In industries where white men are most likely to be managers, women are least likely to find managerial employment. The pattern is even clearer in industries with low white male managerial representation. In the industries where white men are least likely to be employed as managers, black women and white women encounter their best managerial opportunities. There is a clear pattern of industry gender segregation in access to managerial jobs. This is reflected in the similarity of the top ten lists for black women and white women. Because almost all managerial jobs in 1966 were held by white men (93 percent), the desegregation of managerial work has really meant a resegregation into male and female enclaves, a pattern we discuss in the next chapter.

Managerial opportunities for black men and white men, on the other hand, are not at all similar, nor are they mirror images of each other. Rather, black men have their best access to managerial jobs in a different set of industries than white men. The exceptions are health services and insurance and legal services, which are among the lowest managerial opportunity industries for both black men and white men and the highest for black women and white women. Railroad transportation stands out as the industry with high managerial opportunities for both black men and white men. There are no cross-gender cases of industry convergence on these top-ten and bottom-ten lists.

When we look across all industries, we see that in 2005, as white male managerial, professional, and craft representation rose, white female and black female representation in those occupations declined dramatically.[3]

Table 7.15 Ten Best and Worst Industries for Managerial Employment

Ten Best		Ten Worst	
White Men	White Women	Black Men	Black Women
Automotive dealers and service stations	*Construction*	Agriculture, forestry, and fishery	Agriculture, forestry, and fishery
Construction	Fabricated Metal Products	*Construction*	*Construction*
Electric, gas, and sanitary services	*Mining*	Furniture and fixtures	Fabricated metal products
Mining	Paper and allied products	Health services	Furniture and fixtures
Miscellaneous repair services	*Petroleum and coal products*	Insurance	Lumber and wood products
Paper and allied products	*Pipelines, except natural gas*	Legal services	*Mining*
Petroleum and coal products	*Primary metal industries*	Lumber and wood products	*Petroleum and coal products*
Pipelines, except natural gas	*Railroad transportation*	Printing and publishing	*Pipelines, except natural gas*
Railroad transportation	Stone, clay, and glass products	Security, commodity brokers, and investment	Primary metal industries
Stone, clay, and glass products	Transportation equipment	Water transportation	*Stone, clay, and glass products*

Table 7.15 (Continued)

White Men	White Women	Black Men	Black Women
Ten Best		Ten Worst	
Apparel and accessory stores	*Apparel and accessory stores*	Auto repair, services, and parking	*Apparel and accessory stores*
Banks	*Banks*	Building materials and garden supplies	*Banks*
Educational services	*Educational services*	Food and kindred products	Communication
General merchandise stores	*General merchandise stores*	Furniture and home furnishings stores	*Educational services*
Health services	*Health services*	Local and interurban passenger transit	*General merchandise stores*
Hotels and other lodging places	*Insurance*	Railroad transportation	*Health services*
Insurance	*Legal services*	Tobacco products	*Hotels and other lodging places*
Legal services	*Membership organizations*	Transportation by air	*Insurance*
Membership organizations	*Real estate*	Transportation equipment	Local and interurban passenger transit
Social services	*Social services*	Trucking and warehousing	*Social services*

Source: Authors' calculations based on data from EEO-1 surveys (EEOC, various years).
Note: Italics indicates industries that are the best for white men and the worst for the other groups or vice versa.

In contrast, black male and white male representation in desirable jobs showed no one-to-one trade-off, and no complementarities either.

IMPLICATIONS

This chapter has demonstrated that there is a great deal of industry-linked variation in desegregation trajectories. One important implication has to do with the enforcement of equal opportunity laws and the creation of new uncertainties. One of the most obvious results that this chapter shares with previous ones is that aggregate progress for African Americans ground to a near-halt after 1980. Although the EEOC and others charged with the enforcement of equal opportunity law have no power over the political pressures that produce uncertainty and movements toward more equal opportunity employment practices, they might identify where employers are doing better and worse.

We find clear evidence that social closure around desirable high-income employment is a widespread mechanism that promotes the segregation of white men from other groups and their access to the best-quality jobs. Conversely, meritocratic selection mechanisms, here indexed by hiring credentialed labor forces, promote desegregation and equal opportunity for white women, black men, and black women. This result is all the more powerful because human capital explanations tend to rely on assumptions of white male superiority in productive capacity. When industries have rising educational expectations of their labor forces, they hire *fewer* white men and *more* white women, black men, and black women. Importantly, simple employment growth or contraction does not drive desegregation or resegregation trajectories.

This chapter also suggests to us that one way to select enforcement targets might be to identify the industries with the worst or deteriorating track records. These might be industries with recent histories of resegregation or very high levels of white male representation in good jobs (or low representation among other groups). Targeting the worst performers in the worst-performing industries might have the salutary effect of bringing up the bottom. Certainly a yearly list of the best- and worst-performing industries from an equal employment opportunity point of view might be useful information for job-seekers trying to decide where to make a career. Such a list might also be of interest to class-action lawyers trying to determine which firms in which industries should be targeted for discrimination lawsuits. Because firms tend to mimic the behavior of leader firms in their industry, targeting the largest or most profitable firms in the worst-performing industries might be particularly effective.

Chapter 8 | Contemporary Workplace Dynamics

WE HAVE BEEN focusing on the influence of political, industry, and spatial environments on workplace equal employment opportunity trajectories. In most approaches to organizational dynamics, it is such environmental factors that motivate firms to adjust their behavior. Capitalism, for example, is a dynamic economic system. That dynamism is thought to arise primarily from competition in markets that threaten the survival of stagnant firms. Market competition is the environmental pressure that forces innovation in production technologies and the invention of new products and services. In contrast, organizations in stable environments have a tendency toward inertia. Monopolists become lazy.

Similarly, in the absence of new environmental pressures for equal opportunity, existing divisions of labor and recruitment and selection processes, along with bureaucratic rules, will tend to preserve and reproduce existing hiring and promotion patterns and the inequalities linked to them. If in the 1960s employers had to speculate about how much they had to do to prove nondiscrimination, in the absence of sustained environmental pressures today they may no longer be asking the question at all. Or they may be asking a less fundamental question, such as: What are the minimum opportunities or respect that must be extended to racial minority and female workers in order to avoid lawsuits?

We are now in a period when it is likely that organizational inertia is settling in, if at a more integrated status quo than in 1964. Inertia in organizational racial and gender inequalities is reinforced by the legitimacy and taken-for-grantedness of current employment patterns. In the absence of external actors questioning the legitimacy of current practices, such as social movements or federal regulators, we are left with internal constituencies pressuring for change. It is also possible that there will be internal constituencies within firms motivated to roll back equal opportunity advances. In this chapter, we encounter evidence of both tendencies.

We begin our investigation of organizational variation in EEO trajectories by distinguishing between contemporary change produced by changes in hiring and promotion practices within workplaces and those produced by the birth and death of workplaces. Firms and workplaces are constantly being founded, even as others go out of business. If the new firms are less segregated than the ones they replace, then we have good evidence that something in the institutional or political environment may still be producing pressures toward more equal employment opportunity. For example, if younger people have more diverse networks or lower levels of cognitive bias, the workplaces they found might be more diverse and less segregated than those they replace. What we find is that new firms tend to be slightly *more* race-segregated but also slightly less gender-segregated than the firms they replace.

In our analyses, we identify the context in which contemporary workplace segregation is produced. We reconfirm that at this point in history there is very little temporal variation in segregation levels. We also show that both industry and firm context are in the present period relatively weak influences on race and gender staffing patterns. What we do find is that most variation happens at the workplace level and that workplace segregation is now fairly stable over time.

We also examine the contemporary relevance of the affirmative action requirements targeted at federal contractors and the impact of lawsuits and EEOC compliance reviews on equal opportunity progress. Although local and national politics around equal opportunity have weakened substantially and so removed the more general uncertainty that propelled the rapid desegregation of the 1960s and 1970s, the regulatory and legal apparatus remains, and when they are activated there is some contemporary evidence of both backlash and EEO progress. Regulation and legal pressure to promote further equal opportunity progress are now effective only if situated in supportive normative environments or when there is substantial managerial accountability. Even under these restrictive conditions, only white women consistently benefit from contemporary environmental pressures.

We go on to examine the impact of internal organizational practices. We focus on the long-term impact of hiring more diverse workforces and the integration of managerial jobs on future progress toward desegregated workplaces and increased diversity in good-quality jobs. Here the most important and consistent finding is that management accountability, rather than symbolic compliance or diversity training, fosters contemporary equal opportunity progress.

We also review the literature on the human resource practices that seem to promote more meritocratic workplaces and those that do not. We find that the status characteristics of current managers are very consequential for future managerial hiring and even have some weak influence over hiring in the nonmanagerial workforce. This seems to reflect both a process of homosocial reproduction in which people tend to hire similar others and the matching of managers to workers on the basis of both race and gender. At the same time, white men still are much more likely to manage employees in other status groups. Increasingly, white women manage all women. Black men and black women rarely manage whites.

As in the previous chapters, we produce original estimates of organizational change using EEO-1 reports. In this chapter, we focus on the process of organizational change since 1990 and use a panel sample from the EEO-1 reports. This sample is created by taking a 1 percent sample of firms in every year since 1990 and then assembling all workplace reports for those firms from 1990 to 2005. This allows us to produce estimates of dynamic models of workplace change for a representative sample of workplaces across the period.

In addition, much of this chapter reports the very new and important research being done by other scholars who are also using EEOC data. We began this book by pointing out that while the EEOC has been collecting data on the diversity of workplaces since 1966, very little research has been done with these data to document the progress we have made, or failed to make, since the Civil Rights Act. Now that social scientists are gaining access to these data, there has been an explosion of high-quality research that answers questions about the sources of organizational change, the human resource practices that reduce inequality and those that do not, and the efficacy of regulatory and legal pressures.

ORGANIZATIONAL BIRTHS AND DEATHS

Until now, we have not distinguished between equal opportunity changes that were produced by changes in workplace hiring and promotion behavior and those resulting from the founding of new firms and the death of others. Because organizations tend toward inertia, they are strongly influenced by the legitimate and normative practices that were in place when they were founded (Stinchcombe 1965). Thus, change produced by the birth of new workplaces is a leading indicator of the likely future diversity profile. We are also interested in examining the contribution of

Figure 8.1   Contributions to Segregation Change from Shifts in
Workplace Practices and the Founding of New
Workplaces, 1990 to 2005

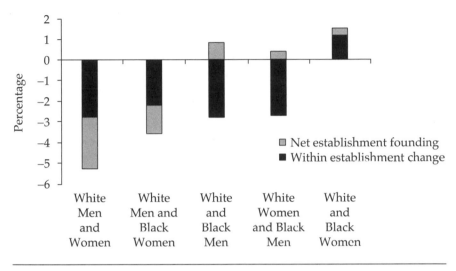

Source: Authors' calculations based on data from EEO-1 surveys (EEOC, various years).

contemporary changes in workplace staffing patterns to segregation trajectories. It is this change within workplaces that most contemporary human resource EEO policies and external regulatory and legal pressures on firms intend to influence.

Figure 8.1 shows the total change in segregation from 1990 to 2005, separately for within-workplace change and change in the population of workplaces. Employment segregation between white men and white women dropped by six points over this fifteen-year period. Just over half of that decline was produced by the internal desegregation of workplaces, while slightly less than half was produced by older, more segregated workplaces being closed and new, less segregated workplaces being founded. A similar pattern holds for segregation between white men and black women. Gender desegregation is being produced about equally by both continued EEO progress within workplaces and the birth of new workplaces that are less segregated than the ones they replace. Although it is clear that the pace of change has been very slow, after 1990 the average workplace was still moving toward more gender equality. Importantly, new workplaces contribute to that shift by being more gender-integrated than the ones they replace.

Black men's segregation from white men and white women shows within-workplace declines of about the same magnitude as the decline in employment segregation between white men and white women. At only three points in fifteen years, this is far from an impressive rate of change. But it suggests that on average there has been a continued, if slow, movement toward equal opportunity within workplaces.

One striking finding is that the net effect of firm births and deaths is a slight increase in race segregation between whites of both genders and black men and between white women and black women. New establishments are slightly *more* race-segregated than the workplaces they replace. The magnitude of this effect is very small, with contributions to increased race segregation of less than 1 percent over the fifteen-year period.

The general pattern is a weak tendency for new workplaces to be more racially segregated but less gender-segregated than the establishments they replace. This suggests that there remains a weak tendency toward gender desegregation, but that if anything the tendency is for new firms to be less concerned with equal opportunity for African Americans than the ones they replace. New firms are far from egalitarian. Even for gender segregation, they are only marginally less segregated than the average older workplace, which still had a segregation index of over 50 in 2005.

This also suggests that the norms for new divisions of labor weakly favor men and women working in the same jobs. That this has been happening both within firms and in new firms since 1990 suggests that progress, however weak, may continue, at least into the near future. While the countertendency of new firms to be more racially segregated than older firms is weak, it indicates that new firms are not particularly concerned about racial diversity when they hire their complement of employees. These new workplaces actually tend toward more racial distinctions in the hiring of their workforces than existing firms. We see this finding as strong and unsettling evidence that we have entered a period in which, barring new political pressure, expectations for further progress in racial desegregation should be very low.

That there continues to be some progress toward racial desegregation within workplaces suggests to us that it is now constituencies internal to firms, rather than environmental pressures, that are the primary force driving what little progress toward white-black equal opportunity is being made. The lack of evidence, on average, of a wholesale retreat from the equal opportunity progress of the past suggests a new inertia rather than a widespread racial or gender backlash and concomitant backslide toward the segregated past. As we have seen in the last chapter, however, there is evidence in many industries of such a retreat.

ENVIRONMENTAL CONTEXTS AND
ORGANIZATIONAL VARIATION

Firms are typically the source of both human resource policies and organizational leadership. Class-action discrimination lawsuits, although few in number, tend to be filed against firms that have a demonstrated, company-wide pattern and practice of discrimination. In these workplaces, the existing policies, as practiced, do not prevent discrimination outcomes and in some cases may actually encourage them.

Industries are the source of normative understandings about how work should be organized and so, as we saw in the last chapter, can provide models for how work, including racial and gender divisions of labor, might be organized. Because most organizations copy the divisions of labor, personnel policies, and hiring practices of other organizations in their environment, it would not be surprising to find industry to be an important context for changes in the levels of workplace segregation and occupational advancement.

Figure 8.2 reports the share of post-1990 workplace variation in employment segregation associated with time, industry, firm, and the workplace itself. If there was a strong societal tendency toward desegregation, we would see a large variance component associated with time. Firms tend to establish employment policies for their various workplaces, with some firms tolerating discrimination and others preventing it. To the extent that this is a powerful social force, we would see a large firm component. Similarly, if most of the differences across workplaces reflected the institutional culture of their industry, then industry would predominate.

Figure 8.2 confirms right away that there was very little temporal variability in segregation after 1990. In addition, we see that for all segregation comparisons the majority of variability in employment segregation was a stable establishment trait. Inertia was the most important source of between-workplace differences in segregation levels. Only a fraction of this inertia was associated with the industry and firm within which the establishment was located. In all cases, the industry and firm components were of roughly similar magnitude, and for most comparisons firm and industry were associated with only about 10 percent of the total workplace variation in contemporary segregation. The exception was employment segregation between white men and white women: here the influence of firm and industry were about twice as high.[1]

Stable establishment differences in segregation account for the majority of the workplace variation in segregation in all comparisons. Segregation between white men and white women was the most stable. Approxi-

Figure 8.2 Total Variance in Segregation Associated with Time, Industry, Firm, and Establishment, 1990 to 2005

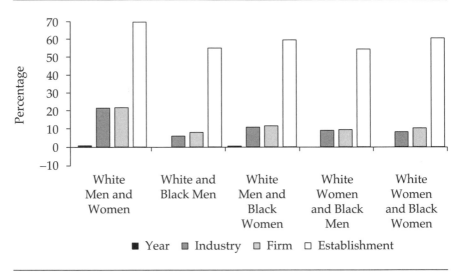

Source: Authors' calculations based on data from EEO-1 surveys (EEOC, various years).

mately 71 percent of the variation in white male–white female segregation was a stable trait of workplaces across the fifteen-year comparison. At 55 percent of total variation between 1990 and 2005, segregation between white men and black men, white women, and black women also displayed substantial inertia.

The remaining change was produced by the birth and death of workplaces and the within-workplace change in segregation levels we examined previously. Although inertia was clearly large, there was also change going on. That this change is not particularly associated with time means that segregation was both rising and falling within workplaces but societal progress was nearly absent.

Although we are primarily interested in segregation dynamics, the strong inertia component emphatically suggests that absent a change in the external environment, there has been essentially no tendency toward societal change, either desegregation or resegregation, in the workplace positions of white men and white women. There has been more fluctuation in cross-race segregation, especially between whites and black men, suggesting workplace change. Because net change has been very small, change in some workplaces in some years was progressive and in others regressive.

It is well known in the technical literature that there is a random component to segregation change that results from the sorting of people across positions. This random component is small when firms are large and status groups are of roughly similar proportions (for example, men and women), but large when firms and status groups are small (Tomaskovic-Devey and Skaggs 1999b). Because black men and black women make up a small proportion of employment in most workplaces, the loss or gain of a few workers can produce a relatively large year-to-year fluctuation in segregation. Thus, it is quite possible that the lower stable establishment variability in segregation in cross-race comparisons in figure 8.2 simply reflects higher random fluctuations rather than lower inertia in workplace practices.

EEOC ENFORCEMENT

Despite the fact that we have been examining data collected by the EEOC, we have been virtually silent on the effectiveness of the EEOC as a regulatory agency. We saw in the first chapter that there has been a long-term tendency for white men to find an increasing share of their employment in the nonregulated small-firm private sector. We know of no research that has looked into this shift, but it is certainly consistent with either a perception or reality that equal opportunity law limits white males' opportunities in larger workplaces that report to the EEOC. Certainly, our account of the history of legal uncertainty and regulatory pressures suggests that EEOC enforcement was once an important force driving workplace desegregation. Although our data do not allow us to examine this directly, there have been some excellent studies documenting the past and contemporary patterns and consequences of EEOC enforcement. We begin with some description of the enforcement process and then move on to highlight the studies that evaluate the consequences of EEOC enforcement.

Despite having access to the same data we have been examining in this book, the EEOC does not search out companies with bad records. Rather, it responds to discrimination complaints. The EEOC receives discrimination complaints around race, gender, national origin, religion, disability, and age discrimination. In 2009, 36 percent of all complaints included allegations of racial discrimination. This was down slightly from 41 percent in 1992. But as is evident from figure 8.3, the total number of discrimination complaints to the EEOC has been rising over time. The EEOC received 93,277 complaints in 2009, up nearly 30 percent from 1992. Complaints of racial discrimination also rose from 29,548 in 1992 to 33,579 in 2009. Gender discrimination complaints to the EEOC stayed fairly level at around 30 percent of the caseload from 1992 to 2009. Age and disability claims are also substantial portions of the EEOC caseload. Religion and

Figure 8.3   Trends in EEOC Complaints by Type of Discrimination, 1992 to 2009

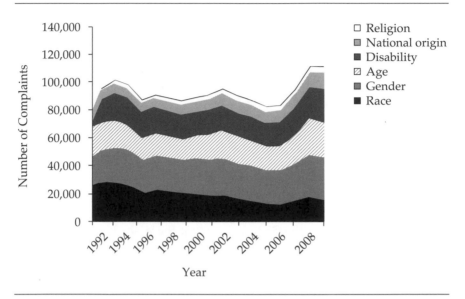

Source: Authors' compilation based on data from Equal Employment Opportunity Commission charge statistics (EEOC 2012b).

national-origin complaints are a much smaller proportion, although both have shown some growth over time as a proportion of all discrimination complaints.

If we take into account relative population size, race discrimination complaints to the EEOC are considerably higher than gender discrimination complaints. This difference peaked at about five times higher in the mid-1970s, during the period of highest enforcement, and fell closer to three times higher after 1990. Both race and gender discrimination complaints tend to rise when legal structures facilitate claims and also when unemployment rises, reducing the attraction of simply leaving for a new job (Wakefield and Uggen 2004).

The best research on the distribution and efficacy of EEOC enforcement has been done by Elizabeth Hirsh. She provides a thorough description of the process through which the EEOC processes complaints. Before employees who suspect discrimination can sue their employer, they must first submit a charge of discrimination to the EEOC. The EEOC ranks cases from A (strong evidence of discrimination) to C (evidence is weak or absent). About 19 percent of cases are classified as A. These are the cases that the EEOC puts much of its investigatory efforts into, but in only 5 to 10 percent of cases does the EEOC eventually find "reasonable cause" of discrimination. A reasonable cause finding typically leads to some administrative settlement rather than a lawsuit. Of the 100,000 or so discrimination complaints it receives each year, only a few hundred are litigated by the EEOC. As a result, the EEOC complaint process, as Elizabeth Hirsh (2008) describes it, is primarily an administrative, rather than legal, intervention. Although the EEOC files few lawsuits, it does issue "right to sue" documents in the vast majority of cases that it fails to investigate. Of these, Hirsh estimates that about 10,000 enter the courts in some form.

Hirsh combined the same EEO-1 reports we have been analyzing in this book with the EEOC's records of discrimination complaints and case outcomes for a sample of workplaces between 1990 and 2002. In a study published in 2009, Hirsh gauges the influence of EEOC discrimination charges on subsequent racial and gender employment segregation. Given that the EEOC process is largely administrative, any change in employers' behavior would probably be precipitated by having their attention drawn to normatively unacceptable discrimination. Hirsh reasons that because most contemporary forms of discrimination are subtle, embedded in cognitive biases and organizational practices, making discrimination visible to employers might be sufficient to motivate better managerial practices and oversight.

There might also be the stronger motive of financial loss: the EEOC can negotiate financial settlements as part of the administrative process and for the few cases that go to court advocate for large punitive as well as direct damages. This is particularly likely for class-action lawsuits in which an entire class of employees in a firm, such as all women or all African Americans, alleges to have suffered from widespread discriminatory practices. Hirsh's (2009) core finding is that only 14 percent of race charges and 19 percent of gender charges result in a settlement favorable to the complainant. In these cases, about two-thirds result in a monetary settlement, which averages only about $19,000. Thus, for most companies the direct financial threat of an EEOC discrimination charge is not very large.

Hirsh's (2009) most striking finding is that EEOC charges and settlements generally do not directly reduce race or gender employment segregation. In fact, the evidence is that among firms charged with discrimination by the EEOC, both race and gender segregation tend to rise modestly in the year following the resolution of the charge. It seems likely that discrimination charges lead to some form of managerial retaliation, antagonism, or avoidance. When we review the evidence on lawsuits later in this chapter, we will see that such backlashes are not uncommon.

Hirsh (2009) also found, however, that higher incidences of charges of gender discrimination in an industry actually reduce the level of employment segregation among organizations that have been charged directly. Thus, while being formally charged with discrimination produces a backlash, being formally charged in an industry with a high density of lawsuits leads to changes in employers' behavior. Hirsh also found that in industries with more settlements favorable to plaintiffs claiming gender discrimination, even those firms that had not been charged showed gender desegregation trajectories. Thus, the primary effect of EEOC charges for gender is diffuse. Organizational behavior changes in line with the threat of EEOC regulation at the industry level, while direct legal action generates backlash against racial minorities and women.

There was no similarly diffuse industry influence of EEOC charges on racial segregation. Consistent with the findings for OFCCP enforcement discussed later in the chapter, racial discrimination enforcement in the post-1980 political era seems to have been largely ineffective in promoting further desegregation. This does not mean that it has been totally ineffective. We cannot rule out the possibility that in the absence of even weak enforcement the routine pressures for white advantage might lead to rising levels of racial segregation and the exclusion of African Americans from even more good-quality jobs. We can certainly see multiple industries in which this is now taking place. Thus, weak enforcement may be required to prevent further erosions of African Americans' position in the private-sector workplace.

Employers, especially large firms and firms that have had experience with prior discrimination charges, tend to be advantaged in the discrimination complaint process vis-à-vis aggrieved parties. This is not something unique to EEO law, but general to encounters with the law. Although both parties to a dispute are formally equivalent before the law, typically parties are not evenly matched in terms of resources and experience. Employers usually have access to greater financial and legal resources than their employees claiming discrimination. Well-resourced firms have the ability to manage the process and hire expertise as needed. They also control the employment records and the testimony of management needed to prosecute a discrimination claim. In addition, large employers can successfully defend against discrimination complaints simply by demonstrating that they have symbolically complied with the intent of the law (Edelman 1990; Dobbin 2009).

In another study, Hirsh (2008) again used EEO-1 reports and EEOC charge records to assess the impact of these organizational advantages. She finds that larger organizations, federal contractors, and workplaces that have been faced with previous EEOC charges of race or gender discrimination are more likely to successfully defend themselves against new charges. Firm resources and legal experience lead to increased organizational capacity to defend against discrimination charges. She interprets the success of federal contractors in defending against discrimination complaints as likely to reflect their higher use of human resource practices that are taken by the EEOC and the courts as symbolic signals of compliance. Ironically, the organizations most likely to face charges of discrimination become the most legally adept at defending themselves. On the other hand, when the EEOC has multiple plaintiffs from a single workplace or firm and bundles the charges into a class action, the balance of power shifts and plaintiffs' odds of a favorable outcome increase dramatically.

One of the most surprising results of Hirsh's research is that the actual degree of race or gender segregation in a workplace has no influence on case outcomes. Rather, what appears to be crucial is the amount of legal resources that can be deployed in defending or prosecuting a case. Because the EEOC is so important as the venue in which discrimination complaints must first be made, the fact that the resources of the EEOC have never been sufficient and have only shrunk over time makes the legal route to promoting workplace equal opportunity and challenging both explicit and more subtle discrimination an increasingly weak tool.

The Residue of OFCCP Regulation

We have already seen that the big impacts of OFCCP regulation happened prior to 1980. In the 1960s, the largest federal contractors, identified with the group Plans for Progress, generated particularly dramatic declines in black male segregation from white men. Also in the 1960s and early 1970s, OFCCP oversight produced large gains in employment for black men, black women, and even white women, but no striking integration of managerial and professional occupations. There was, however, substantial integration into equal-status work for white men and black men in lower-level jobs in the 1960s. Federal contractors also saw steeper desegregation trajectories between white men and white women in the 1970s.

After 1980, both OFCCP oversight and corporate uncertainty dissipated. Our analyses show almost no influence of OFCCP regulation on segregation trajectories after 1980. With respect to affirmative action, President Clinton famously suggested, "Mend it, don't end it," but our analyses suggest that it was already fairly ineffective when he deployed that slogan, even as the regulatory structure continued to exist. It may also be the case, however, that the convergence in the 1980s of segregation trajectories between federal contractors and other EEOC-reporting firms was produced by continued desegregation among older contractors and the founding of new firms that were either unaware of or unconcerned with earlier enforcement practices.

It is important to remember that even in the absence of political or regulatory pressures, federal contractors are still required to have affirmative action plans and to keep records on their hiring and promotion outcomes. Thus, even in quiet political moments the threat of the federal government taking renewed interest in race and gender workplace equity never dies. It seems reasonable to suspect that this threat may have been used at least in some workplaces by human resource professionals to prevent resegregation and to foster internal equal opportunity agendas.

It is not clear to us that the OFCCP was ever particularly effective in making direct regulatory threats to employers. In a finding consistent with Hirsh's research on EEOC charges, we have shown elsewhere that the strong influence of OFCCP regulation on racial desegregation was largely produced indirectly, through the diffusion of equal opportunity norms in industries with a high concentration of federal contractors (McTague et al. 2009). Erin Kelly, Alexandra Kalev, and Frank Dobbin (2010) also find that it is the industry density of OFCCP compliance reviews that has led to changes in both managerial and craft representation for white women, black men, black women, and Hispanic men.

After 1990, we strongly suspect, any potential OFCCP effect on organizational behavior, if it existed at all, was not the result of direct regulatory threat but of more normative expectations from the industrial environment or perhaps the more effective internal mobilization of firm resources by human resource professionals attempting to advance an equal employment opportunity agenda.

To explore these expectations we examine the influence of both direct OFCCP regulation and the density of federal contractors in the industrial environment on workplace segregation and desegregation trajectories using the workplace panel data set described earlier in this chapter. We use workplace fixed-effects panel models. These models eliminate the influence of establishment births and deaths and limit the influence of OFCCP regulation and normative environments to internal changes in workplace employment patterns. Table 8.1 reports the average yearly change in segregation associated with being a federal contractor (OFCCP) and with being in an industry populated by many defense contractors (industry OFCCP density). We produce these estimates for the entire 1990 to 2005 period and also for the three presidential administrations. Given our earlier findings on the ineffectiveness of the OFCCP after 1980, we expect little or no influence.

Focusing on the entire sixteen-year period (1990 to 2005), we find that

Table 8.1   Direct OFCCP Regulation and OFCCP Industry Density
Effects on Changes in Segregation, 1990 to 2005

	White Men– White Women	White Men– Black Men	White Men– Black Women	White Women– Black Women
Direct OFCCP regulation	0.23	0.28	0.23	0.25
Industry OFCCP density	−1.31	0	−0.64	0.56

Source: Authors' calculations based on data from EEO-1 surveys (EEOC, various years).
Note: Fixed-effects estimates, reported coefficients are statistically significant at or below .05
probability. Zero (0) indicates effects that were not statistically different from zero.
N = 392,231.

direct OFCCP regulation was associated with *increased* employment segregation between white men and white women, white men and black men, white men and black women, and white women and black women. There was no statistically significant influence of OFCCP regulation on segregation between white women and black men. Overall, the evidence suggests that federal contractors have become more segregated since 1990—increasing segregation by about 0.25 percent per year.

On the other hand, industries with high densities of federal contractors displayed declines in gender segregation from white men. These declines were particularly strong for white women's access to equal-status employment with white men. The likely mechanism for this change was the strengthening of an increasingly female human resource managerial staff in industries with a high density of federal contractors.

None of these effects are strong in a statistical sense. That is, while statistically significant, they show high variance across workplaces. When we estimate the influence of the OFCCP within presidential administrations (results not shown), most effects become statistically insignificant. There are a few exceptions. The administrations of both Bushes are notable for increased white male segregation from white women among federal contractors and compensating declines in high-contractor-density industries. There is also some evidence that during the Clinton administration direct OFCCP regulation again became a weak force for desegregation, at least for the movement of white women into equal employment roles with both black men and white men.

In table 8.2, we see that both white women and black women continued to make managerial gains among federal contractors after 1990. This effect was much stronger for white women and was particularly pronounced

Table 8.2   The Impact of OFCCP Regulation and OFCCP Industry
Environment on Percentage Changes in Managerial
Representation, 1990 to 2005

	White Men	White Women	Black Men	Black Women
Direct OFCCP regulation	0	3.0	–1.6	1.5
Industry OFCCP density	1.8	4.3	0	0

Source: Authors' calculations based on data from EEO-1 surveys (EEOC, various years).
Note: Fixed-effects estimates, reported coefficients are statistically significant at or below .05 probability. Zero (0) indicates effects that were not statistically different from zero.

during the Clinton administration. Black men showed relative losses in access to managerial jobs, a pattern that was confined to the George W. Bush administration, during which they fared particularly poorly.

Normatively, contractor density is associated with white men and white women having increased access to managerial jobs, but not at the expense of black men and black women. These are not zero-sum games, and the great growth in Hispanic and Asian employment is probably responsible for these shifts in opportunity. Recall that in chapter 6 we saw that white men's access to managerial jobs is enhanced by the growth of all other status groups.

OFCCP Compliance Reviews

The Office of Federal Contract Compliance Programs has the power to review any federal contractor for compliance with the record-keeping and affirmative action plans required of federal contractors under the executive orders of President Kennedy and President Johnson. Jonathan Leonard (1984b, 1990) found that compliance reviews increased African American employment in the 1970s, but not after the Reagan-era retreat from an equal opportunity regulatory agenda began in 1980. During the same period, compliance reviews were also associated with black male progress into better-quality jobs. White women, however, did not benefit from compliance reviews. Although the OFCCP has claimed that it targets firms with poor EEO records for compliance reviews, based on a review of the same EEO-1 data we have been examining, Leonard (1984b) concludes that this was probably not the case.

Although the vast majority of OFCCP action is passive and of declining importance, the OFCCP can and still does review firms for compliance with the mandate to have an affirmative action plan and to self-monitor progress. Here the evidence for effectiveness is somewhat better. Kalev and her colleagues (2006) matched a sample of EEO-1 workplaces to survey data on workplace practices and history. One of their findings was that having ever had an OFCCP compliance review reduced the odds of white men being in management positions by about 8 percent, while boosting the odds for black men and white women by about the same amount. There was no effect for black women, consistent with our findings throughout this book that the OFCCP never had black women on its enforcement agenda. Compliance reviews in their sample had happened to only about 15 percent of firms over the thirty years they observed. The one study that distinguishes between the direct effects of a compliance review on a workplace and the density of compliance reviews in an industry suggests that most of this effect of OFCCP enforcement is likely to happen indirectly through changes in industry norms around equal opportunity (Hirsh 2009).

In the most careful study to date, Alexandra Kalev and Frank Dobbin (2006) find that compliance reviews initiated in the 1970s increased white female and African American access to managerial jobs. But as we have seen, the political era mattered a great deal. Compliance reviews in the 1980s had a weaker influence than earlier reviews, and none at all for black women. By the 1990s, compliance reviews by the OFCCP had no influence on managerial diversity.

Hirsh (2008) points out that the reason why OFCCP regulation has so little effect on desegregation or managerial advancement may lie in the limited nature of those policies, which typically focus on increasing the hiring of minorities and women rather than on the jobs into which they are hired or promoted. Devah Pager and Hana Shepherd (2008) suggest that hiring discrimination is the least visible form of racial employment discrimination but may be the most common; as such, the mismatch between the legal and regulatory apparatus and actual problems is particularly severe.

Lawsuits

The actual rate at which people take legal action in the face of discrimination is very low. Laura Beth Neilsen and Robert Nelson (2005), using the best data available, estimated for 2001 that of the 3.4 million African Americans who probably faced some sort of employment discrimination that year, fewer than 1 percent filed claims with the EEOC. Of these, only about 7,500 led to the filing of a lawsuit, and only 289 ever got to trial. For most people, the psychological, social, and financial costs of a discrimination claim far outweigh any potential benefit. Even though lawyers will only accept employment discrimination lawsuits with strong evidence, the vast majority of discrimination suits are won by the corporation charged with discrimination.

Jonathan Leonard (1984a) found that between 1966 and 1978 class-action lawsuits were associated with increased black—but not white female—total employment and movement into managerial jobs. John Donohue and Peter Siegelman (1991) argued that lawsuits were more effective in the 1960s and 1970s because they directly changed firm behavior while simultaneously serving as a general threat to other firms. They argue that as the most egregious discrimination was eliminated both directly and through the diffusion of human resource practices to firms attempting to avoid lawsuits, lawsuits themselves became less effective in changing workplace staffing patterns. In contrast, Frank Dobbin (2009) concludes, based on a thorough review of human resource practices, that in fact corporations strategically deployed the presence of these human resource practices as a legal defense, thus deflecting the courts from investigating discrimination or promoting equal opportunity outcomes.

Alexandra Kalev and her colleagues (2006) looked at the influence of past discrimination lawsuits—most of which were individual rather than class-action lawsuits—on managerial representation. The estimates from their thirty-year panel study of EEO-1 workplaces indicate that a past lawsuit reduced the odds of a white man being a manager by about 11 percent, while raising the odds for white women by 14 percent. Black women made a smaller but significant gain of 4 percent, and the gain for black men was smaller still, but still statistically significant, at 3 percent. At least one discrimination lawsuit had been brought against about one-third of the firms in their sample.

In another study using the same data, Kalev and Dobbin (2006) point out that OFCCP compliance reviews and lawsuits, while both exerting environmental pressures on firms to promote equal opportunity, are different in their mechanisms. Compliance reviews attempt to change human resource practices, while lawsuits attempt to discourage discrimination by imposing monetary and reputational costs on firms. Compliance reviews target inertia, and lawsuits target reputation. This is the only study that directly compares the efficacy of compliance reviews and lawsuits (of all types) in changing organizational behavior. The findings show that lawsuits are a much weaker source of EEO progress than OFCCP compliance reviews, but that the efficacy of both was specific to political eras. In this study, lawsuits had no direct effect on managerial diversity in the 1970s, but in the 1980s lawsuits were associated with a decline in white male managerial representation and a rise in white female managers. African American representation was not responsive to discrimination lawsuits. By the 1990s, there was no effect of new lawsuits on managerial diversity, although firms that had been sued in the 1980s continued to show improved white female access to managerial jobs at the expense of white males. Unfortunately, these same firms saw a *decrease* in the access of black men and black women to managerial jobs as a result of earlier lawsuits. In some ways this is not surprising. Lawsuits are typically about race or gender, and almost never about both. Thus, if most successful suits are about gender, then the remedy will also target gender, leading to increased hiring and promotion of women into management. We cannot rule out the possibility, however, that post-lawsuit retaliation and backlash against African American employees is more common as well.

The result that *white* women, rather than *all* women, benefit from lawsuits is harder to explain. Kimberle Crenshaw (1989) reviews a series of court cases in which judges ruled that black women could not represent white women in class-action gender discrimination cases, nor could they represent black men in race discrimination cases. Crenshaw's conclusion is that courts cannot deal with the intersection of protected statuses and prefer to keep discrimination claims narrow. Thus, from the courts' point of view, black women can be women or black, but not both. This conclusion also means that the kinds of complex inequalities we have found continually in this study are incommensurable with the legal framework around discrimination law. If one thing is clear from the findings in this book it is that black women's progress is not simply the average between black men and white women, but rather that they have had uniquely negative trajectories in terms of equal-status employment in the U.S. private sector, particularly since the 1970s.

In a well-designed set of studies, Sheryl Skaggs (2008, 2009, 2010) focused on the effect of class-action lawsuits on changes in the access of women and African Americans to managerial positions in the supermarket industry. Class-action discrimination lawsuits bundle multiple discrimination claims against a company into a larger lawsuit alleging not simply that an individual was discriminated against but that a whole class of people were subject to a pattern and practice of discrimination. These cases are always much larger and more visible than individual cases, require greater investments in defense by the firm accused, and can take a long time to work their way through the courts. Hirsh (2008) found that plaintiffs were more likely to prevail in class-action lawsuits, presumably because plaintiffs have much more support from the EEOC and from private law firms interested in litigating potentially high-damage cases.

Skaggs focused on the supermarket industry for two reasons. First, it was the target of over twenty class-action lawsuits alleging race or gender discrimination between 1985 and the late 1990s. Thus, it seemed reasonable to expect that these suits would change not only the behavior of the workplaces within the firm that was sued but the entire organizational field. The second reason had to do with how supermarkets organize their labor markets. They tend to hire entry-level, uncredentialed workers and promote from within the organization. Supermarket managers tend to start at the bottom and work their way up, and the few managerial positions in each store tend to be paid very high wages. Thus, this industry was close to a natural experiment for exploring the influence of lawsuits on managerial integration.

Skaggs's basic results suggest that class-action lawsuits in the supermarket industry did help to integrate managerial jobs, but that the process was different for African Americans and women. The core finding was that after a lawsuit women's managerial representation jumped by 20 percent and the long-term consequence of a class-action lawsuit was about a 50 percent increase in managerial representation. Such large gains were possible partly because of the very low level of representation of women in management in the industry. In the average workplace, women were 38 percent as likely as men to be in managerial jobs. Thus, the lawsuit moved them toward being only 57 percent less likely to be in a management job. This was still far from equal opportunity, but it was also a pretty substantial gain.

Skaggs also showed that, after a lawsuit, African American managerial representation jumped immediately by about 20 percent but one year later dropped by about 10 percent. Thus, the long-term gain was quite modest. Prior to the lawsuit, whites' advantaged access to managerial jobs was about 62 percent higher than African Americans' employment in these top-paying jobs. Interestingly, firms that experienced a lawsuit were 10 percent below the industry norm in their employment of black managers. The effect of lawsuits was to bring the firms that had been sued up to the industry average, rather than to move the industry in a more equal opportunity direction. These results echo Hirsh's (2008) finding that the EEOC is more likely to recognize gender than racial employment discrimination, and of course they are also entirely consistent with our findings in this book—after 1980 black-white desegregation stalled in the United States. Providing further evidence of the importance of industry normative transmission of equal opportunity expectations, Skaggs (2008) finds that firms with no class-action lawsuit but located in the same region as ones with pending litigation experienced faster managerial integration.

Lynn Wooten and Erika James (2004) point out that a firm can respond to lawsuits in either a *reactive* or *reflective* manner. Reactive firms embrace defensive damage control and sometimes retaliate, but they do not attempt to change their human resource practices. The adversarial nature of lawsuits encourages such reactions. Where the reactive impulse dominates, we expect little effect of lawsuits on diversity and in fact might not be surprised to see backlash and retaliation. Skaggs's finding that after lawsuits African American managerial representation rose quickly but then dropped back to the industry average suggests exactly such a response. To show good faith during the lawsuit, firms immediately promoted African Americans into managerial jobs, but about half of those gains disappeared almost immediately.

Because the firms were now at the industry average, they had a statistical defense against future lawsuits. A common practice in discrimination lawsuits is to compare the demographic distribution of the company that is being sued to that of other companies in its industry. Companies at or above the industry average in terms of workplace demography will claim that there is no shortfall and that what appears to be low racial minority or female employment rates simply mirrors labor supply. The supermarket chains that had been sued could claim, after the lawsuit, that their black managerial labor force, although still few in number, simply reflected the supply of talented blacks in their industry.

A more *reflective* response to lawsuits might incorporate the lessons from the suit to change human resource practices or managerial evaluations. Not surprisingly, research shows that when managers are held accountable for EEO progress, there is greater EEO progress (Kalev et al. 2006). Successful discrimination lawsuits often require companies to change their policies to monitor progress or to institute managerial accountability. Again referring to Skaggs's findings, this time for women's access to management, there is evidence of long-term gains after class-action lawsuits, suggesting that the typical firm responded, in part at least, in a reflective manner. From Skaggs's research we cannot tell whether this was a function of the terms of settlements or managers were in some way better able to be reflective when the charge was gender, rather than race, discrimination. We believe that the latter speculation is consistent with the strong evidence in our study as well as in the literature on enforcement showing that, at least since 1980, white women in particular have made more sustained and widespread gains than black men or black women.

In another innovative attempt to ferret out the influence of lawsuits on corporate EEO behavior, Elizabeth Hirsh and Youngjoo Cha (2010) looked at the influence of 175 high-profile lawsuits on managerial representation in publicly traded U.S. firms. They reason that the stock market's reaction to discrimination lawsuits could be a critical context motivating employers to react to lawsuits as intended—by increasing the diversity of their workforce. This idea is strongly supported, but again, only for white women. If stock prices fall more than 5 percent after the lawsuit is reported in the press, firms increase the representation of white women in management. This lesson is evidently a powerful one, given that the effect of a loss in stock value actually strengthens over time. For firms with stock declines, white women's hiring or promotion into managerial jobs rose more steeply three years later than it did in the first year of the suit.

For firms that have not experienced a stock market shock, the corporate reactions to a lawsuit look a great deal like Sheryl Skaggs's findings for African American managerial representation. There is an initial strong increase in white women's managerial representation, followed by a continued small increase in year two, but by year three backlash has set in and most of the gains have been erased. Thus, the firms that look to be *reflective* in their reaction to lawsuits were probably reacting to the much larger threat of declining stock prices.

Reactive legal defenses, coupled with retaliation, seem to be much more common. In the research of Hirsh and Cha (2010), not only did white women fail to gain from lawsuits in the absence of a stock price shock, but black men and black women both lost access to managerial jobs as a result of large visible lawsuits. This backlash reaction to a lawsuit was strengthened when there were large monetary damages or the discrimination case was followed in the *New York Times* (Hirsh and Cha 2010). We suspect that the dominance of reactive, punitive responses to lawsuits is connected to their isolation from corporate accountability mechanisms. CEOs are evaluated for performance, either on their balance sheets or in the stock market, not for EEO progress. In this sense, lawsuits are an annoyance rather than an opportunity to increase the effectiveness of human resource practices.

The Hirsh and Cha study does find evidence that when the lawsuit settlement includes requirements for increased EEO managerial accountability, the access of white women, black men, and black women to managerial jobs is increased. We will see later in this chapter that managerial accountability, whether imposed externally or internally, is central to producing workplace equal opportunity progress, at least in the current environment where firms do not face political or regulatory uncertainty.

More evidence of the reactive nature of employers to lawsuits can be found in the rising level of retaliation toward employees who file discrimination suits (figure 8.4). In 1992 about one in seven EEOC complaints included a charge of retaliation. By 2009 that number had risen to more than one in three. Although people who file discrimination claims are legally protected from retaliation, employer retaliation is common. The doubling of retaliation charges in just fifteen years suggests some institutional change. If this had been a change in how the EEOC recorded complaints,

Figure 8.4   Discrimination Charges Filed with the EEOC That
             Reported Employer Retaliation, 1992 to 2009

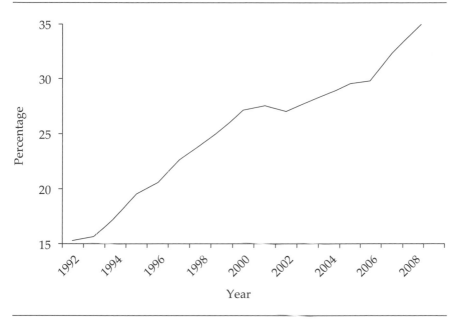

Source: Authors' compilation based on data from Equal Employment Opportunity Commission charge statistics (EEOC 2012b).

we would expect a sudden jump in retaliation charges as the EEOC initiated a new protocol. However, the steady increase over fifteen years suggests a more gradual process. This might represent increased hostility from employers who feel confident that the consequences of breaking the law will be mild at best. It might also reflect a conscious strategy by legal counsel to intimidate employees so that they withdraw their complaints and to warn others not to file. It does not seem to be a strategy promoted by plaintiffs' lawyers, since retaliation charges do not seem to increase the chances of a favorable outcome for the plaintiff.[2]

James and Wooten (2006) provide some insight into why lawsuits might have a weaker, often negative influence on African American access to good jobs. They look at how forty-nine firms managed seventy-six class-action discrimination lawsuits, most of which were about race- or gender-based discrimination. Focusing on what the companies said about the lawsuits in public settings, they found that race and gender cases tended to be managed quite differently. While in all cases the firms initially denied that any discrimination had taken place, by the time the class was certified by the courts, different corporate strategies had emerged. Allegations of gender employment discrimination moved to settlement fairly quickly and with no retaliation by the firm. For race cases, initial denials tended to be reinforced with further denials, attempts to stall the legal process, retaliation toward those who had filed the discrimination claim, and eventual mobilization by African American political and religious leaders before the company would agree to a settlement. These settlements often included some public promise to change managerial practice.

Although the reasons for these differences are obscured by James and Wooten's (2006) lack of access to internal corporate discussions for most of the cases they studied, we might surmise that it was easier for firm leaders to admit discrimination on the basis of gender than race and that race cases as a result turned out to be far more dramatic and confrontational. That race cases generate fewer real gains for claimants may very well be because of a greater failure of corporate managers to learn from these cases, perhaps augmented by a refusal to admit bias and the ensuing conflict.

The Skaggs and Hirsh studies suggest that lawsuits have increased managerial diversity in some firms. Kalev and Dobbin (2006), however, find no such effect after the 1980s. Their study differed from Skaggs's and Hirsh's in two ways, either of which might have produced this contrast in results. Skaggs and Hirsh focused on highly visible class-action lawsuits, but Kalev and Dobbin's survey data included reports by the firm of any lawsuit. Given that the vast majority of lawsuits are filed by individuals and very few are successful for the plaintiff, it is not surprising that there were no effects on corporate behavior. This should especially be the case as the political environment became hostile to equal opportunity claims. Class-action lawsuits, in contrast, are by their very nature attempts to define discrimination as a collective organizational process, and they demand collective managerial responses. Given this reasoning, we might conclude that individual lawsuits are unlikely to change organizational behavior, but at least under some circumstances class-action lawsuits might.

The second difference is that both Skaggs and Hirsh looked for specific institutional contexts in which the impact of lawsuits might be strengthened. In the case of the supermarket industry, an important circumstance was the large number of high-profile class-action lawsuits in this organizational field. Supermarket companies were probably well aware of the need to treat these lawsuits as serious threats to business as usual. Similarly in the Hirsh study, we might expect that the threat of a fall in stock prices would keep corporate leaders' attention focused on EEO progress.

Federal Circuit Courts

Because discrimination is illegal under federal law, most discrimination lawsuits are filed in federal district courts. Rulings at the district level can be appealed to the circuit court level. In her supermarket studies, Skaggs also looks at the influence of circuit courts on the outcomes of class-action lawsuits. In one paper, she focuses on the differences in women's managerial advancement as a function of the political composition of the sitting circuit court judges. These judges are appointed by the president but must also be approved by the sitting senators in the circuit district and so tend to share the political orientation of the appointing president and senators. She finds that discrimination lawsuits filed in the Second Circuit Court were much more likely to lead to increased managerial representation for women. The Second Circuit includes the states of Vermont, New York, and Connecticut, and a majority of the sitting judges across the entire study period were appointed prior to or after the Reagan-Bush administrations. In contrast, lawsuits filed in the Sixth Circuit Court (Ohio, Kentucky, Tennessee, and Michigan) were associated with immediate declines in women's access to managerial jobs. This court was dominated by Reagan-Bush appointees. Where firms believed that the courts would side with them, lawsuits were less of a threat and more of a motive for retaliation.

In a second paper, Skaggs (2009) explores the influence of the demographic composition of circuit court judges. Following an impressive set of prior studies on the influence of demographic background on judicial decision-making, she reasons that judges who are minorities or women might be more sympathetic, or perceived by corporate lawyers as more sympathetic, to discrimination complaints. In this article, she also measures the political ideology of judges based on a set of policy preference indicators for the appointing president and sitting senators. She finds that it is not the political ideology under which the judges were appointed that seems to matter, but the simple demographic composition of courts. Class-action lawsuits in courts with a higher percentage of women and minority judges are associated with more rapid gains in black managerial employment. She reasons that it is not demography per se that produces this result, but that women and minority judges, even when appointed by conservative presidents, are more likely to see discrimination as a problem for the courts to take seriously.

INTERNAL CONSTITUENCIES

Most contemporary organizational theory focuses on the role of environmental pressures, whether coercive pressures like lawsuits and EEOC charges or normative models as in standard industry practices. But organizations also have an internal political order. The authority associated with ownership and managerial roles is the most obvious. Certain groups of workers, perhaps because they are organized along craft or professional lines, may be particularly powerful relative to their own labor process. Other groups of workers may be influential because they are organized through unions. Equal opportunity training often targets managers because they have decision-making power.

Many have argued that integration of the managerial ranks is particularly important because it will produce an internal constituency with decision-making power to advocate for equal opportunity policy and diversity in hiring and promotion decisions (Cohen and Huffman 2007a; Hultin and Szulkin 1999). We focus here on both managers and nonmanagerial employees as potential internal constituencies in unique social and political locations to promote or resist equal opportunity practices.

Managerial Diversity

An emerging theme in our study is the rise of human resource managers as advocates for equal opportunity policies and practices. Dobbin (2009) persuasively argues that uncertainty in the corporate environment around what constitutes compliance with EEO law strengthened the hand of human resource managers in their dealings with corporate management. Cockburn (1991) suggests that human resource professionals charged with equal opportunity goals often have a short-term practical agenda and a series of more ambitious initiatives that cannot be enacted without support from corporate leaders.

Recently Erin Kelly and her colleagues (2010) have shown that while corporate maternity policies preceded the enactment of the Family Medical Leave Act in 1993, those policies did not actually help women advance until after 1993. The implication is that although human resource professionals created the policies, they did not create the environment that would allow women to take advantage of the policies. Only when political pressure from outside the firm created a clear sense that these were employment rights did the policies have positive outcomes in women's careers. It may also be the case that as the human resource profession has moved from an almost entirely white male field to an increasingly white female one, these managers may have become more effective advocates for the careers of women in general and white women in particular.

One argument for increasing racial minority and female access to managerial roles is that it can produce a spillover effect, decreasing bias and increasing opportunity for women and minorities elsewhere in the firm.

Kanter (1977) characterized the reproduction of white male managerial staffs as homosocial reproduction in which the quest for comfort and trust in social similarity led to exclusion and stereotyping of women and minorities. As we have seen, there has been considerable desegregation of managerial jobs since the early 1970s, when Kanter did her research. Presumably this emerging diversity has muted those tendencies and produced new internal leadership cadres to advocate for desegregation and equal opportunity.

Racial minority and women managers may act as mentors to minority and female employees in the lower ranks of a firm's hierarchy, actively training them in firm-specific job skills as well as the social skills necessary to succeed at the firm (Athey, Avery, and Zemsky 2000). Because the performance of racial minorities and female employees is sometimes less favorably evaluated by white male supervisors (Tsui and O'Reilly 1989; Giuliano, Leonard, and Levine 2006), managerial diversity may also reduce bias in performance evaluation. There is also good evidence that white women managers tend to advance the adoption of corporate equal opportunity programs while white male managers attempt to block such programs (Dobbin, Koo, and Kalev 2011).

Looking at California banks, Lisa Cohen, Joseph Broschak, and Heather Haveman (1998) found increased external recruitment of female managers when there were more female managers already in the workplace. In addition to recruiting qualified females directly to the managerial positions of the firm, women managers may increase the recruitment of women to lower-level positions, thereby creating a larger pool of nonmanagerial female employees (Carrington and Troske 1995, 1998). Women managers can also have the effect of facilitating growth in female managerial representation through improved retention of both female nonmanagers and managers. For example, Laura Giuliano, Jonathan Leonard, and David Levine (2006) find that female employees demonstrate lower quit rates working under female supervisors than under male supervisors.

Managerial diversity may also *indirectly* improve diversity in the firm by challenging stereotypes and suggesting that the firm is a low-discrimination workplace. For example, women who have attained visibility in top positions of the corporate hierarchy weaken traditional stereotypes that women are less capable than men (Blau, Ferber, and Winkler 2006). Exposure to successful women or minorities in managerial roles can be expected to reduce bias in future candidate selection (Ely 1994; Heilmann and Martell 1986). It also is possible that minority and female managers act as role models for employees at lower levels of the firm hierarchy even without actually mentoring them. The presence of a large share of minority or female managers might serve as a signal to lower-level employees that rising through the firm's ranks is feasible and hence motivate them to persevere. The presence of a large share of minority and female minority managers may also serve as an external signal in the labor market that the firm provides a hospitable environment, and this may attract highly qualified applicants to both managerial and nonmanagerial jobs.

There have been some studies examining the relationship between the share of women in management and internal promotions of women employees within firms. Richard Chused (1988) found that women law professors are more likely to be granted tenure in faculties with a higher proportion of tenured women. Cohen, Broschak, and Haveman (1998) found that women are more likely to be promoted into a managerial job in banks where women are already well represented among managers. A Swedish study found that when there are more men in managerial roles, women's wages are lower (Hultin and Szulkin 1999). This result is particularly large when wage setting is decentralized below the level of top management. Consistently, Mia Hultin and Ryszard Szulkin (2003) showed in a subsequent article that it is likely to be the gender composition of supervisors rather than top managers that generates workplace gender wage gaps. On the other hand, other research suggests that women in leadership roles have no influence on wage inequality (Penner and Torro-Tulla 2010; Penner et al. 2010).

Recently, there have been studies using EEO-1 reports to gauge the influence of managerial composition on desegregation. Kalev and her colleagues (2006) find that having more minorities in top management positions is associated with growth in minorities in lower-level management positions. Presumably because they are a small proportion of managers in most workplaces, there is no significant reduction of white men's or women's access to managerial jobs in workplaces where minority top managers facilitate the hiring of lower-level managers. These researchers had similar results for women. When women are in top management positions, however, there are significant declines in white and black men in management jobs. Presumably this reflects the larger population of women in most workplaces: because women represent a large enough group, their successes might displace some opportunity for men.

Matt Huffman and his colleagues (2010) find that having more women in management positions is linked to declining gender segregation among nonmanagers. In this study utilizing EEOC data, the positive influence of women managers on gender desegregation is fairly robust, with consistent findings across different industries and firms of different sizes. Women managers are particularly associated with stronger desegregation in larger and growing establishments. Huffman and his colleagues interpret these results as a reflection of increased formalization of human resource practices in large workplaces and increased opportunity to hire and promote new classes of workers when opportunities are growing. Their research also finds the same period effects, consistent with the finding in our analyses and in the literature. The influence of women in management on desegregation was strongest during the 1970s and weakened over time. By 2005, there was no influence at all.

In another study, Hirsh (2009) looks at the influence of racial minorities and women minorities in management on both race and gender desegregation. Like Huffman and his colleagues, she also finds that the presence of more women in management is associated with declining gender segregation. Importantly, she finds that minority managerial representation is associated with race desegregation as well, particularly in firms that have been investigated by the EEOC for race discrimination. The influence of women managers on future gender desegregation is also substantially stronger at firms that have received an EEOC discrimination charge. In both cases, the administrative intrusion by the EEOC seems to strengthen the capacity of women and minority managers to promote equal employment opportunity. Consistent with Dobbin's (2009) discussion of lawsuits strengthening the influence of human resource professionals with an equal opportunity agenda, EEOC investigations may do this for managers with equal opportunity agendas. Indeed, Hirsh also shows that larger firms, presumably with more elaborate human resource capacity, are more likely to take gender desegregation further in response to the density of EEOC settlements in favor of plaintiffs in their industry.

Kurtulus and Tomaskovic-Devey (2012), also using EEO-1 reports for the post-1983 period, find that growth in the proportion of women in headquarters management is associated with further growth in women's managerial representation in branch plants, but that the effect drops rapidly over time. Most of the influence of new women in management on future managerial diversity is short-term. Importantly, and consistent with many of the findings in this book, white female managers are much more effective at promoting the future employment of white female managers than were minority women managers.

Workforce Diversity and Bottom-Up Ascription

There are good reasons to suspect that as nonmanagerial workforces become more diverse, they will become an internal constituency for further desegregation and the expansion of equal opportunity in their workplaces. Sociologists James Elliott and Ryan Smith (2001; Smith and Elliott 2002, 2004) suggest that subordinate group incursions into dominant group managerial monopolies is most likely to occur when managers supervise minority or female employees. This pattern of managerial incorporation, which they refer to as "bottom-up ascription," is interpreted as a reaction to demands for inclusion by minority and female workforces. This is why minorities or women who gain access to supervisory or managerial positions often do so in the segregated sphere of supervising others within the same status group (see, for example, Cohen and Huffman 2007b; Elliott and Smith 2001; Stainback and Tomaskovic-Devey 2009).

We have shown elsewhere that such patterns of bottom-up ascription are widespread (Stainback and Tomaskovic-Devey 2009). White men are most likely to be managers when nonmanagers are white men. The same is true for white women, black men, and black women, all of whom are most likely to be managers when they match the workforce they manage (see also Kalev 2009). Importantly, this pattern established itself in the U.S. private sector around 1980 and has been fairly stable ever since. Before then, almost all managers were white men, and the general pattern was that white men managed everyone. White men are still more likely to manage other groups than other groups are to manage white men.

Assessing the Impact of Internal Constituencies

We estimate the influence of changes in managerial and nonmanagerial workforce composition in the previous year on shifts in current-year managerial representation. There is certainly enough prior research and theorizing to lead us to suspect that homosocial reproduction is widespread. Similarly, the bottom-up ascription model predicts that the nonmanagerial workforce will be a source of recruitment and demographic matching in the managerial workforce.

Figure 8.5 makes clear that both managerial reproduction and bottom-up ascription was operating for all four groups. Also for all four groups, past managerial composition was a much stronger influence on future managerial composition than the demographic background of other employees. Additionally, the effect of managerial reproduction was about 10 percent stronger for white men and white women than it was for black men and black women. The dynamic race-gender matching of managers to workers was strongest for white men and weakest for black women. On the other hand, the magnitude and pattern of these effects was fairly similar across groups.

Although a statistical advantage to white men is evident in these estimates, we suspect that in actual workplaces these small status differences in the rate of homosocial reproduction would be indistinguishable. Thus, on the shop floor it might look like each group tends to favor and manage others of the same race and gender. However, the actual mechanisms pro-

Figure 8.5   Influence of a 1 Percent Change in Managerial and Nonmanagerial Group Size on Workforce and Managerial
Composition, Lagged Panel Models, 1990 to 2005

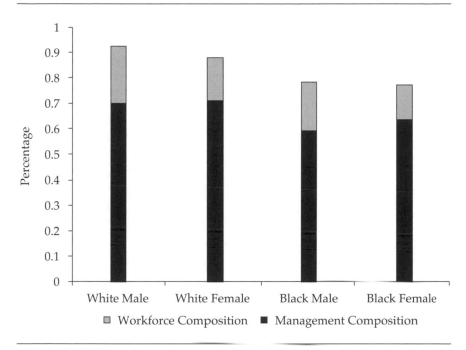

Source: Authors' calculations based on data from EEO-1 surveys (EEOC, various years).

ducing these demographic matching outcomes, such as equal opportunity preferences, in-group bias, social demands for representation, network-based recruitment, or human resource practices, are unlikely to be clearly visible.

We also developed a fixed-effects model equivalent to the results displayed in figure 8.5. These models, presented in figure 8.6, additionally control for any stable unobserved attributes of workplaces, including most routine behaviors and human resource personnel practices. The model statistically controls for organizational inertia, leaving only organizational change to be explained. A surprisingly high proportion of the variance associated with top-down and bottom-up ascription remains. Based on those models, figure 8.6 allows us to see both the inertia-linked and more instantaneous effects of composition on managerial representation.

The inertia components tend to account for slightly more than half of the influence of both current workforces and current management on fu-

Figure 8.6   Inertial and Dynamic Influences of a 1 Percent Change in
Managerial and Nonmanagerial Group Size on
Managerial Composition, 1990 to 2005

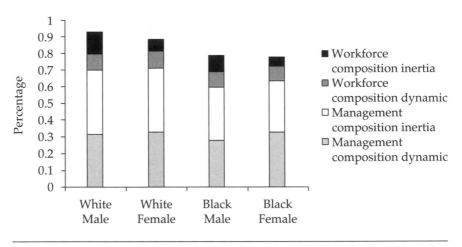

Source: Authors' calculations based on data from EEO-1 surveys (EEOC, various years).

ture managerial hires. The exception is among black women: there was very little stable matching of black women workers to black women managers.

Curious as to whether managerial demographic composition influences hiring elsewhere in the workplace, we also looked at the entire workforce, as well as at professional and craft production jobs. The first bars in figure 8.7 reproduce the influence of changes in managerial composition on future changes in managerial composition from figure 8.6. The results are striking. Increasing the diversity of managerial jobs tended to produce increased diversity in managerial jobs in the future. Increasing the proportion of white males did the same. Increased managerial diversity also led to increased diversity in hiring overall in the workplace and in skilled working-class jobs, but the effects were relatively small. For black men and black women managers, there was also a small increased hiring of black men and black women in professional jobs.

Thus, there is evidence at least after 1990, when this panel data set begins, that the demographic composition of managers influences the future diversity trajectory of the workplace. But that influence is most pronounced in the future hiring of managers and has only a marginal effect on changes in hiring patterns more generally. Again, we have statistically controlled for inertia, so it is possible that the really important effects of

Figure 8.7   Influence of a 1 Percent Growth in Group Managerial
Composition on Change in Managerial, Establishment,
Craft, and Professional Workforce Composition,
Establishment Fixed-Effects Panel Estimates, 1990
to 2005

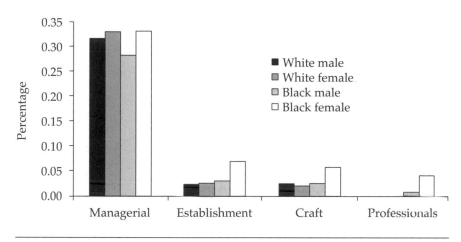

Source: Authors' calculations based on data from EEO-1 surveys (EEOC, various years).

managerial diversity are in sustaining whatever equal opportunity progress has already been accomplished.

Manager-Worker Status Matching

When the equal opportunity goal was merely diversity, we measured
progress as the increasing representation of previously excluded groups.
This seems to us to be the right metric for 1975 or even 1980, when the big
innovation in corporate thinking and behavior was the hiring and promotion of women and minorities. By 1977, as Rosabeth Moss Kanter pointed
out, many workplaces had hired token women and minorities into managerial roles, but equal-status representation was still to be accomplished.
Earlier in this study, we showed that by the late 1970s the representation
of white women, black men, and black women in other than the best-
quality jobs had made rapid strides in EEOC-regulated workplaces. But a
truly equal opportunity workplace would not be one in which black
women primarily worked in low-paid jobs or perhaps could only aspire to
manage other black women, but one in which black women were equally
likely to manage all demographic groups.

Figure 8.8   Relative Declines in Managerial Representation with the
               Growth of Nonmanagerial Workforces, Dynamic Fixed-
               Effects Panel Estimates, 1990 to 2005

Source: Authors' calculations based on data from EEO-1 surveys (EEOC, various years).

Following a method we devised in an earlier study (Stainback and
Tomaskovic-Devey 2009), we estimated the influence of changes in workforce composition on access to management jobs for each of our groups.
We display these results in figure 8.8. The shorter the bar, the smaller the
social distance between managers and various workforces. The taller the
bars the lower the odds that the target group of managers is matched to
the employee group.

Focusing first on white men, we see that growth in the employment of most workforces was consistent with growth in white male managerial representation. The exceptions are growth in employment of black women and Hispanic women workers, who were least likely to be matched to white male managers. All other groups were more likely to be matched to white male managers than they were to any other managerial demographic (except perhaps their own group in the process of bottom-up ascription described earlier). There was essentially no contemporary social distance to impede white men from managing Asian men and very little relative to Hispanic men, black men, white women, and Asian women.

White women managers were more socially distant than white men from all workforces other than Asian women. White women were as likely to become managers in workplaces employing more Asian women as they were to fill management jobs in workplaces that hired more white women. Although compared to white men the social distance was quite large, after 1990 white women were most likely to move into management in firms where male workforces were growing.

White women, like white men, were least likely to move into management when the black female and Hispanic female workforces were growing. This is further evidence that white women were increasingly moving into contact—in this case as their superiors—with male workers. The more common pattern, of course, was white women moving into jobs managing white women and Asian women.

Suggesting a greater social distance, the bars are all much higher for black women's and black men's movement into managerial jobs. Black women primarily became managers in workplaces with growing nonmanagerial workforces made up of black women. Black male managers were similarly matched to growing black male workforces. For both black women and black men, the group they were next most likely to manage was also black but of the opposite gender. They were least likely to move into managerial roles in establishments with growing white workforces. African Americans managing whites was the least likely trajectory for contemporary workplaces. Black men were similarly unlikely to manage Asian women, and black women were unlikely to manage Asian males. Because there were no social distinctions between white women and Asian women and between white men and Asian men, we conclude that, at least in the status hierarchy of different groups managing different workforces, white and Asian workforces were functionally equivalent in both their social closeness to each other and their social distance from African American managers. This finding provides some support for the claim by Art Sakamoto and his colleagues (2009) that Asians are the new model minority and may be for all practical purposes honorary whites.

HUMAN RESOURCE POLICIES AND PRACTICES

One of the key innovations in personnel practice after the Civil Rights Act was to formalize employee selection and promotion in order to achieve equal opportunity or at least signal good-faith efforts at compliance with emerging EEO law (Dobbin 2009). The logic of these innovations was that discrimination, segregation, and limited access to good jobs all share a common set of proximate mechanisms: prejudice, social network–based exclusion, in-group preferences in selection and mentoring, and cognitive bias in assessing the quality and skills of applicants. Formalization of the application and candidate review process, including written job descriptions, public postings of job openings, and panel reviews of candidates, as well as various due process procedures such as formal yearly evaluations, were all thought to reduce the causal influence of these various bias mechanisms (Bielby 2000; Reskin 2000).

Hirsh and Kmec (2009) point out that in addition to holding decision-makers accountable and raising awareness of discrimination, formalization may also give employees a higher set of expectations for due process and a higher awareness of their employment rights. Evidence supports this reasoning. Firms with EEO officers actually generate more discrimination complaints to the EEOC and internal grievances as well (Edelman, Uggen, and Erlanger 1999). Hirsh and Kmec, using the EEO-1 reports and a survey of human resource practices in a sample of hospitals, found more discrimination charges to the EEOC when the hospital had an EEO manager or office and when they provided training to employees as to their rights under discrimination law.

There is also support for the idea that formalization increases equal opportunity. Studies have found that segregation is lower, wage gaps are smaller, and female and nonwhite access to managerial roles is increased in workplaces with more formalized personnel systems (Anderson and Tomaskovic-Devey 1995; Elvira and Graham 2002; Konrad and Linnehan 1995; Reskin and McBrier 2000; Tomaskovic-Devey 1993). Formalized screening procedures for hiring and promotion have also been associated with lower reports of discrimination by employees (Hirsh and Lyons 2010). Although based on single-firm case studies, some research has shown that, in formalized workplaces with strong equal opportunity agendas, women's rates of promotion surpass those of men (Spilerman and Petersen 1999; Petersen and Saporta 2004; Dencker 2008).

In our previous research, we have shown that both occupational and managerial desegregation is more pronounced in larger organizations (Tomaskovic-Devey et al. 2006; McTague et al. 2009; Stainback and Tomaskovic-Devey 2009), which presumably are more formalized in their EEO practices. Lauren Edelman (1992) as well as Frank Dobbin and John Sutton (1998) have expressed considerable skepticism that these formal human resource practices reduce bias, reasoning that most firms adopted them to signal compliance with the law but in the absence of any firm or court evaluation of whether they actually worked. That is, in this argument, formal human resource practices were adopted for symbolic, not managerial, reasons, and in the absence of evidence of their effectiveness, they may have had no real influence on equal opportunity outcomes.

James Baron and his colleagues (2007) show that workplaces vary in their underlying cultural logics. They define a bureaucratic culture as one that selects workers primarily based on skills and uses formal rules to coordinate production. Looking at engineering firms, they find that bureaucratic workplaces, defined culturally, tend to hire more women engineers than workplaces with higher levels of peer or direct production control or workplaces that select workers based on "fit" or star potential. This result is very similar to our finding in the last chapter that industries with education-linked selection mechanisms have made more EEO progress.

Studies have also shown that not all formalization leads to reduced racial and gender inequality. Internal labor markets have been found to heighten both gender and ethnic inequality (DiPrete 1989; Huffman 1995; Baldi and McBrier 1997). Because internal labor markets allow the current labor force to make promotion decisions, this is not surprising. In some ways, internal labor markets, like long periods of on-the-job training (Tomaskovic-Devey and Skaggs 2002), are ideal organizational practices for instituting social closure by existing work groups. Departmentalization has also been linked to higher gender segregation (Tomaskovic-Devey and Skaggs 1999b), presumably because it facilitates both the creation of gender-typical jobs and gender-segregated managerial hierarchies.

Emilio Castilla (2008), in a case study of a firm that employed very structured meritocratic performance reviews, found no race or gender bias in performance evaluations, consistent with the notion that formal meritocratic procedures dampen bias. The same study, however, showed that at the next stage, when performance evaluations were tied to salary raises, bias crept back into the system and racial minorities and women received lower raises for equivalent performance evaluations. Castilla's study suggests that formalization is far from a panacea even in the most well-intentioned firm.

Following this line of reasoning, Julie Kmec (2005) examined the effect of various organizational staffing procedures on the likelihood that an organization would hire a male or female into a gender-neutral job or into a traditionally male- or female-dominated job. Her findings were quite mixed, leading her to suggest that

> bureaucratization or formalization of an organization's hiring process does not automatically eliminate gender-based hiring decisions; instead, they may institutionalize women's and men's different employment options in formal job descriptions and requirements. (Kmec 2005, 343)

The most damning evidence against the universal efficacy of formalization in preventing discrimination comes from the study of discrimination complaints by Vincent Roscigno (2007). He found that many discrimination complaints reported that employers vigorously enforced formal employment rules for female and especially minority employees, but not for white men. In this case, formalization was the mechanism through which discrimination operated. When confronted with a discrimination complaint, such employers would vigorously document violations of formal firm policy by the employee who had lodged the complaint precisely in order to discredit him or her. Even in the face of egregious, verified discrimination, most employers respond to discrimination charges with defenses that stress meritocratic human resource practices (Light, Roscigno, and Kalev 2011). It is exactly these types of formal practices that employers have been able to use to convince the courts that they are nondiscriminatory equal opportunity employers (Dobbin 2009).

Another way to think about formalization is to focus not on the presence or absence of bureaucratic rules, but on the underlying logic that is promoting bureaucratization. Bureaucratization is essentially a system of control and coordination. But control and coordination toward what goals? In most workplaces, the core goals of bureaucratization in general are to enhance the efficiency of the organization or perhaps the power of organizational leaders, but certainly not race or gender equality. These are secondary goals stemming from the efforts of some constituency—leaders, workers, regulators—who cared enough and was influential enough to motivate the policies and practices that promote equal opportunity.

In contrast, Trond Petersen and his colleagues have argued that because discrimination is now illegal and corporate human resource managers are aware and monitor the problem, employment discrimination is unlikely. They provide good case study evidence to support this argument in three firms with active equal opportunity policies (Spilerman and Petersen 1999; Petersen and Saporta 2004; Dencker 2008). Further, the Castilla (2008) article suggests that even in such firms, subtle discrimination can still exist. But firms clearly vary in their commitment to equal opportunity outcomes. The evidence of increased segregation in entire industries in the last chapter certainly supports this conclusion.

Alexandra Kalev (2010), in a study that looks at the effect of downsizing on racial minorities and women, shows that what matters is how firms downsize. When firms target specific occupations and low-tenure employees, minorities and women lose disproportionally. When downsizing involves decision-maker accountability, is reviewed by corporate lawyers, and is based on performance evaluations, white men are more likely to lose their jobs than white women, black men, and black women. Kalev summarized this as "how you downsize is who you downsize." Similarly, Stainback and Kwon (2012) find that organizations that have experienced an employment loss of 10 percent or more tend to be less gender-segregated than workplaces that have not experienced downsizing. This finding is consistent with Kalev's findings and with recent research that suggests that downsizing may lead to the elimination of feminized departments and jobs (Haveman, Broschak, and Cohen 2009).

Soohan Koo (2010) shows that a firm that has had a prior discrimination lawsuit or a long history of EEO accountability is less likely to use temporary labor as an alternative to permanent employees. Because both lawyers and economists have recommended using temporary labor to avoid discrimination lawsuits around promotions and firing, Koo reasons that this represents an emerging cultural orientation in the firm toward equal opportunity.

The best study to date on the actual diversity policies that have been adopted by workplaces is by Alexandra Kalev, Frank Dobbin, and Erin Kelly (2006). They combined EEO-1 reports from 1971 to 2002 with survey data on human resource policies and practices at various points in time. This allowed them to estimate the causal influence of the adoption of specific practices on diversity in managerial employment. Their research generated some interesting and potentially controversial findings. Until their article, there had been no direct evidence that EEO-inspired changes in human resource practices actually lead to equal opportunity outcomes. The studies of formalization reviewed earlier more often focus on the incidence of policies associated with due process and meritocracy rather than the motivation of EEO concerns. That is, they could not distinguish between, on the one hand, formalization as a concern with efficiency or even the preservation of a leader's power and, on the other, the kinds of human resource practices that had been invented precisely to promote equal opportunity and fight discrimination.

Kalev, Dobbin, and Kelly (2006) distinguish between policies that attempt to eradicate psychological biases, such as diversity training, networking programs designed to integrate racial minorities and women into the workplace culture and influence structures, and the creation of practices that assign and monitor responsibility for equal opportunity progress. The human resource practices that decreased white males' advantaged access to managerial jobs were ones that created responsibility structures, such as a full-time diversity manager or office, oversight or advocacy committees, and to a lesser extent, affirmative action plans.

Workplaces that created formal structures responsible for monitoring equal opportunity progress, such as full-time diversity managers or standing diversity committees, had more white women, black men, and black women move into managerial roles. Both diversity managers and diversity committees were particularly effective in firms that were *not* also government contractors. In these firms, the presence of an affirmative action plan was associated with a decrease in white managerial representation and an increase in managerial access for white women and black men. Because being a government contractor requires an affirmative action plan, we might imagine that the presence of an affirmative action plan was a proxy for OFCCP regulation. This was not the case. Seven percent of government contractors never reported having an affirmative action plan, and 20 percent of noncontractors had such a plan, despite the lack of any legal requirement. It was *voluntary* affirmative action plans, not ones adopted to fulfill government reporting requirements, that led to more white women getting access to managerial jobs and reduced white men's employment in these same jobs. Consistent with our earlier results on the OFCCP, only black men benefited from affirmative action plans among government contractors, and never at the expense of white male managerial employment.

The evaluation of managers for equal opportunity progress, a policy that would seem to mirror the creation of accountability positions and structures, facilitated the managerial advancement of white women but harmed that of black men and black women. It seems likely that managers responded to these evaluations by hiring and promoting white women into managerial positions, at least partly at the expense of African Americans. This interpretation is supported by the finding that evaluating managers in terms of their progress on meeting diversity goals did not lead to any reduction in white male movement into managerial jobs.

Networking and mentoring programs, which are intended to reduce social isolation and promote both learning and visibility for minorities and women, delivered mixed results. Network programs bring together minority or female employees in support networks to share information and advocate for their group. Mentoring programs team senior employees with minority and women employees, providing the kinds of network help that whites and men are reputed to get naturally (McDonald 2010;

McDonald et al. 2009; Royster 2003). Kalev and her colleagues (2006) find that for white women networking programs are associated with increased managerial representation, but not among government contractors. Instituting networking programs actually was associated with declining access to managerial jobs for black men, perhaps because they were ineffective or perhaps because they worked so much better for white women, who got the jobs instead of black men. Mentoring programs, on the other hand, helped only black women gain access to managerial jobs, and then only in the presence of policies that held managers accountable for equal opportunity progress.

Surprisingly, Kalev and her colleagues (2006) found that on average diversity training, which is intended to make decision-makers aware of cognitive bias processes, had no impact across their sample in access to managerial jobs. Among firms that were not government contractors, white women and black women actually *lost access* to managerial jobs after diversity training was instituted as a human resource practice. In contrast, among government contractors diversity training increased white women's, black men's, and black women's access to managerial jobs, and at the expense of white men. Hirsh and Kmec (2009), in their study of hospitals, found that managerial diversity training did reduce sexual harassment charges filed with the EEOC. In another study of firms that had defended themselves against high-visibility lawsuits, Hirsh and Cha (2010) found that when diversity training was mandated in the settlement, it enhanced white women's access to managerial jobs but seemed to produce on average a backlash against black men and women.

The evidence on diversity training is mixed at best. Dobbin and Kalev (2008) look more closely at the actual content of diversity training in their panel survey of private-sector workplaces. Most diversity training includes discussions on the legal prohibitions against discrimination and the threats posed to the company by lawsuits, as well as training on cultural sensitivity and psychological self-reflection. Dobbin and Kalev find that training that contains *any* information about the legal threat associated with discrimination is associated with *increased* hiring of white men into managerial jobs and *decreases* in the representation of minorities and women. Diversity training that focuses only on the cultural and psychological bias processes, in contrast, leads to increased movement of white women and black men into management and fewer white men. Given that 76 percent of training includes at least some legal content, they conclude that the vast majority of diversity training does more harm than good. They also find that mandatory diversity training is associated with decreased equal opportunity progress into managerial jobs.

In another study, Dobbin, Schrage, and Kalev (2010) find that corporate guidelines and rules are ineffective in promoting diversity unless programs are directly tied to specific goals. They also look at human resource practices that are not tied to diversity goals but often are pushed by human resource professionals and accepted by the courts as signals of corporate good-faith efforts to extend equal opportunity and prevent discrimination, such as job posting, job descriptions, internal promotion systems, and employment tests. On average, none produce equal opportunity progress. On the other hand, Dobbin and Kalev find that when there is regulatory oversight, these programs work as advertised. In the absence of some external accountability, these programs actually favor white men's career advancement over other groups.

Looking across all of this research, we have reached the following conclusions. Although closure, bias, and network processes may be powerful in creating workplace inequalities, the literature points to one remedy: simple managerial accountability. People do not need to be taught to be unbiased. In fact, this approach may produce as much backlash as progress, if not more. Social networks do not need to be created where none exist. Rather, the personnel practices that increase managerial diversity are quite conventional: setting goals and assigning responsibility. This is, of course, how most workplaces foster productivity or marketing gains, so it is not surprising that these practices work for employment diversity as well. Hirsh and Cha's (2010) finding that after class-action lawsuits' settlements that mandate new or expanded accountability structures actually increase managerial diversity supports this result, even in the antagonistic, reactive context of lawsuits.

Organizational scholars have long recognized that rules and practices are not the same thing. Often, rules are decoupled from goals or evaluation and may be ignored or used symbolically or both (Meyer and Rowan 1977). Institutional sociologists have long suspected that most equal opportunity innovations primarily signal symbolic compliance with the law. The practices that seem to work as advertised are accompanied by managerial accountability and so are not decoupled from goals and evaluation. That the courts have taken the mere presence of these practices in the absence of accountability as evidence of equal opportunity compliance and the absence of discrimination is clearly a legal error of gigantic proportions.

While most studies focus on formal rules, human resource practices, and managerial behavior, it is not inconceivable that work cultures are also important. Laurel Smith-Doerr (2004), following women scientists' careers in academia, the pharmaceutical industry, and biotech firms, finds greater career mobility for women in biotech firms. She attributes this to the cooperative, rather than competitive, basis of work organization and reward in these firms. Kalev (2009), examining how the formal organization of work affects access to managerial jobs for women and blacks, finds greater managerial attainment for previously disadvantaged groups in firms where work is organized using teams with less rigid hierarchical job distinctions. She suggests that these newer forms of work organization are efficacious for improving equal opportunity because they increase intergroup contact and possibilities for networking, all of which serve to reduce stereotypes and increase minority and female access to managerial positions. These results are consistent with social psychological predictions that increased intergroup contact in cooperative (rather than competitive) settings will reduce stereotype and attribution bias (Pettigrew and Tropp 2006). Because the basic social closure mechanism for preserving group advantage is segregation, reducing the social distance between jobs is likely to also reduce the motive for social closure between jobs (Tomaskovic-Devey 1993).

IMPLICATIONS

Hiring more white men into management jobs is likely to reduce equal opportunity progress, both because white men tend to hire other white men and because they tend to oppose the development of equal opportunity human resource practices. Increasing managerial diversity seems to hold some promise for creating future desegregation trajectories. It does so both through hiring and promotion mechanisms and by creating influential internal constituencies who advocate to preserve whatever diversity exists and in strategic moments extend opportunities to new groups. Most importantly, systems of accountability increase the influence of internal constituencies with EEO agendas.

The race and gender matching of managers to workers tends to produce a new form of segregation. This is certainly progress relative to the 1960s, when almost all managers were white men. Black men, black women, and especially white women have now gained access to managerial jobs, but most often managing workers from their own demographic groups. Black men and black women are almost never hired or promoted into managerial positions in workplaces to manage white employees. On the other hand, white women are moving into managerial positions in workplaces with growing male workforces.

In the current period, EEOC charges, OFCCP compliance reviews, and lawsuits seem to produce as much, or more, backlash as further equal opportunity progress. The exceptions can be found when there is some additional external or internal pressure to adopt equal opportunity practices. Systems of accountability counteract backlash and produce EEO gains in the presence of external regulatory or legal pressure. Formalization with accountability may reduce bias in hierarchical settings, but hierarchy may not be the only solution. There is also intriguing evidence that equal-status contact and cooperation may be essential to reducing bias in nonhierarchical workplace settings. Of course, the goal of desegregation is precisely that, equal-status contact. Social closure theory reminds us, however, that desegregation is difficult to achieve when inequalities in power and rewards are high.

Chapter 9 | National to Local Segregation Trajectories

HISTORY UNFOLDS AS a series of local events and cultural accounts. Local action produces local stories and understandings that over time accumulate into behaviors, trajectories of social change, or periods of equilibrium. These narratives are both material, embodied in practices, relationships, organizations, and the like, and cultural, retold as stories of what is natural, normal, right, and proper. People negotiate their social order and the boundaries of their practical and material constraints and their neighbors' cultural understandings of what is possible and reasonable. The civil rights movement, the Civil Rights Act, and the women's movement punctuated the monolithic mid-twentieth-century status hierarchy of white over black and male over female and set in motion trajectories of change. These political interventions changed the standard practices and organizational rules in employment, while also weakening the cultural biases and stereotypes that supported black and female subordination.

These political and social movements led to changes in human resource practices, law, regulation, and employment segregation. While they destabilized white male monopolies over good jobs, they did not dislodge them, and they did not extinguish cultural stereotypes or past organizational practices. Rather, they changed the relative power of actors and moved implicit status hierarchies into the realm of locally contested status orders. Samuel Lucas (2008) describes this shift as a movement from an era of "condoned exploitation" to one of "contested prejudice." This movement implies a shift from a deeply institutionalized cultural and interactional assumption of white male advantage to locally negotiated status orders. A static equilibrium with little local variation was transformed into multiple local trajectories of segregation and integration.

Richard Alba (2009) refers to this same transition as one from "bright"

293

to "blurred" boundaries between groups. When status boundaries were bright, segregation was total. Now they are blurred, and segregation remains common, often expected, but far from total. Encountering a white woman in a CEO position is remarkable but not shocking. To see whites working under a black manager is momentarily surprising but not unthinkable. Both situations, however, are noteworthy, precisely because nearly fifty years after the Civil Rights Act we still expect to find the best jobs populated by white men.

NATIONAL POLITICS AND NATIONAL TRAJECTORIES

Employment desegregation was propelled by multiple mechanisms. Initially the inertia of past practice, long supported by the taken-for-granted cultural hegemony of racial and gender stratification, was challenged by the social movement struggle for African Americans' civil and economic rights. The political will to challenge white privilege grew as the civil rights movement strengthened and gained allies among some whites who were concerned about social justice and others who were worried about the reputation of the United States in the postcolonial cold war world. These political pressures led to consequential political interventions into private-sector workplaces, most notably President John F. Kennedy's 1961 order to federal contractors to take affirmative action in the hiring of black labor and the 1964 Civil Rights Act, which outlawed employment discrimination and segregation on the basis of race and gender more generally.

These were not the first political interventions, but they were probably the first that instigated widespread change in corporate behavior. They differed from earlier political interventions, particularly earlier presidential executive orders and state-level fair employment practice laws, in that both Presidents Kennedy and Johnson clearly signaled their seriousness and the civil rights movement clearly signaled its commitment. Both conventional and social movement political pressure led to the crumbling of the cultural and legal hegemony of racial apartheid in the United States. As this happened, some private-sector workplaces, especially federal government contractors, began to experiment with integrating African American men into traditionally white male jobs and African American women into traditionally white female jobs.

The political pressure on most of these firms was not typically direct. President Kennedy no doubt did lean on some CEOs, either directly or through agents. The NAACP certainly did the same. The strong social force generated by these political interventions, at least at first, was not direct and coercive, but rather, the changing political environment generated uncertainty. In a very short period of time, the forty months between Kennedy's

1961 executive order and the 1964 signing of the Civil Rights Act, CEOs and personnel managers became aware that the cultural domination of white racial privilege had crumbled and that they would eventually be held responsible for creating a new, nonracialized workplace. The magnitude of this challenge is now hard to comprehend. CEOs and personnel managers had to imagine a world in which they had never lived. They had to create a world they could barely imagine. They no doubt worried that, when the social movements or the emerging federal government regulatory apparatus came to ask for an accounting of their progress, the evidence they presented would not be deemed acceptable. This was the uncertainty they faced: a changing world where they could not predict what the rules of the game would be. They did not know what evidence of "nondiscrimination" or "affirmative action" might actually look like. Hence, political pressure created uncertainty, and uncertainty was a motive for action.

Prior to the social and political changes in the early 1960s, workplaces had firmly established routines for hiring and promoting employees— routines that had been invented with the expectation of stable racialized and gendered hierarchies. Firms had predictable divisions of labor; jobs were arrayed in skill and authority hierarchies with both technical and cognitive expectations as to the typical incumbent. Race and gender segregation within workplaces was nearly absolute. White men worked in jobs with other white men. White women worked with other white women. Many workplaces employed no black men or black women at all, but when they did they tended to sort black men and women into segregated, low-skill, low-wage jobs with no authority. At the level of interaction, white and male privilege was nearly universal and, if not universally embraced as legitimate, nearly universally practiced.

While in the early 1960s political uncertainty produced a mounting pressure for racial equality in large private-sector workplaces, an equally large set of counterpressures arose in routine practices, segregated divisions of labor, and interactional customs within workplaces. And to make change even more difficult, equal opportunity was not the core goal of private-sector workplaces. The production of goods and services was the core goal. Disruptions of everyday production routines were no doubt experienced as threatening the firm's ability to get products and services to market, in addition to the obvious threats to established racial and gender status hierarchies.

Not surprisingly, employers' initial reaction to the political and legal changes was to hire black men and black women into low-level jobs. Personnel managers retasked earlier repertoires developed for unionized employees to create avenues for hiring and training black workers. Next, black men also began to be hired into skilled blue-collar jobs and black women into clerical jobs. Federal contractors moved first, although they did so without exposing white men, especially white managers, to increased equal-status contact with black men.

In the late 1960s, private-sector firms began to hire white women, black men, and especially black women in much larger numbers. As they did, white men were pushed up in the occupational division of labor. White men's representation in managerial, professional, and skilled blue-collar jobs surged as white women, black men, and black women began to populate the lower rungs of the blue- and white-collar occupational hierarchy. Race segregation declined sharply, particularly in the South, where racial segregation had been extreme. Black men and black women increasingly found themselves working side by side with whites in gender-segregated roles. Black men made rapid progress into skilled blue-collar jobs, but weaker progress into managerial and professional roles.

With few exceptions, gender segregation and male privilege were left untouched by the politics of the 1960s. Although the law had changed and gender-based discrimination in employment was formally illegal, the nascent regulators at the Equal Employment Opportunity Commission and the Office of Federal Contract Compliance reassured employers that the regulatory intent was to foster racial, but not gender, equal opportunity. But by the late 1960s, the National Organization for Women and other women's movement organizations had formed and were gaining influence. After 1972, the political and legislative momentum shifted from race to gender equality, and firms responded. Although still rare, during the 1970s white women and black women began to be employed in the same jobs in the same workplaces with white men. Desegregation relative to white men was rapid for all three groups, but particularly for white women. Black men and white women made impressive progress among large federal contractors, presumably because these firms had instituted human resource practices that fostered equal opportunity in response to vague affirmative action mandates emanating from the OFCC.

While some black women gained access to white male jobs across the short regulatory decade between 1972 and 1980, they became increasingly segregated from white women. Strikingly, racial segregation among women rose dramatically among the largest federal contractors. White women's progress into what had traditionally been white male jobs left black women behind in typically female and increasingly minority positions. The strong regulatory pressure and the corporate adoption of human resource practices did not ensure that black women and white women would make comparable gains. Some of the differences no doubt reflected the average educational advantages of white women, but we suspect that they also benefited from the privilege of being white.

By the end of the 1970s, the Republican Party had adopted a racially divisive electoral strategy to court white votes, particularly in the South.

Democrats responded by becoming increasingly race-neutral in their political messages and legislative agendas. Civil rights movement organizations became less active. After Ronald Reagan was elected in 1980, the
federal government withdrew from activist equal opportunity enforcement, cutting budgets and squashing the activist core of both the EEOC
and OFCCP. The national racial desegregation trajectory stalled, and aggregate racial progress stopped. By the late 1980s, when Supreme Court
decisions began to unravel earlier decisions supporting discrimination
claims in lawsuits, the organizational pressures for inertia and racial bias
had become on average about as strong as any residual human resource
or employee pressures for equal opportunity. After the Reagan election,
political uncertainty and regulatory pressures disappeared. Importantly,
the abrupt stop in African American progress after 1980 is not consistent
with the conventional explanation that black employment lagged because
of lower education than whites. In 1980 the educational convergence between the black and white labor forces was very steep, and that convergence continued to be rapid through the 1990s. The real discontinuity was
in federal policy and social movement pressure.

At the same time, the legal and corporate interpretation of what constituted gender discrimination expanded, including first sexual harassment,
then pregnancy, and eventually family-friendliness and even sexual orientation. Even as racial progress stalled, segregation between white men and
both white women and black women continued to decline. White women
made dramatic gains in professional and managerial occupations, even
after accounting for the rise of women-friendly, low-wage service-sector
positions. But even for white women, most of the aggregate gains stopped
after 2000 as the organizational pressures for inertia and gender bias finally overcame the uncertainty, regulatory, and human resource pressures
for change that had been unleashed in the early 1970s.

Black men, black women, and white women had different trajectories
of integration into white male jobs. Black men integrated earlier and most
rapidly, but by 1980 they were making no further aggregate progress.
White women made little progress before the early 1970s, and none after
accounting for changes in the industrial structure, but then made rapid
progress through the 1980s. White women's progress decelerated in the
1990s and stalled around the turn of the millennium. Black women experienced the least amount of progress of the groups examined. They made
no gains until the early 1970s and very little after 1980. These general patterns map quite well onto the patterns of national political pressure we
discussed in part I of the book. When the civil rights movement was strong
and supported at the executive, legislative, and judicial levels, black men
made sustained and rapid progress. When the pressure for racial equal
opportunity evaporated, so too did further gains. When the women's

Figure 9.1   Employment Segregation from White Men in EEOC-
             Reporting Private-Sector Workplaces, 1966 to 2005

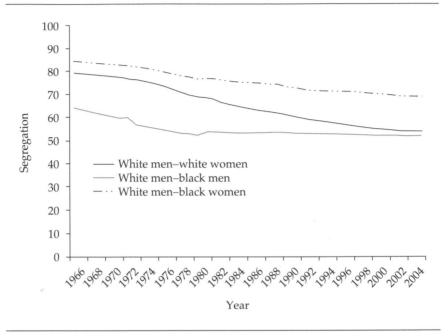

Source: Authors' calculations based on data from EEO-1 surveys (EEOC, various years).

movement was strong and the courts and legislature expanded the bases
on which gender discrimination claims could be made, white women integrated into white male jobs. There never was a political rejection of
gender-based equal opportunity in the way there was for race under the
Reagan administration and across the 1990s. Even though new political
pressure was weak, gains continued to be made. We suspect that this reflected the rise of white women as internal constituencies inside private-
sector corporations, particularly as human resource managers—a job title
that became increasingly held by white women. By 2000, the workplace
equal rights pressures unleashed by the Civil Rights Act had run their
course and further progress, even for white women, stalled.

Although the 1964 Civil Rights Act outlawed segregation and discrimination and mandated that the EEOC chart progress toward equal opportunity, it is clear that segregation levels are still very high. Because we do
not observe job title distinctions, our estimates underestimate segregation;
however, it was still the case that in 2005 black men, white women, and
especially black women rarely worked in the same occupation in the same
workplace as white men. To produce completely integrated private-sector

workplaces today would require that more than half of all workers switch jobs. Only white women have made appreciable progress since 1980, and even that progress has now stalled.

LOCAL INEQUALITY REGIMES

In 1966 the privileged employment position of white men was deeply institutionalized. Racial and gender subordination was taken for granted and enacted continuously in the vast majority of workplaces. Segregation levels were essentially total, but have since dropped dramatically. Although progress has stalled, there is now substantial room for variation across workplaces. In 1966 all workplaces were almost totally segregated. Today some have low levels of segregation, although many highly segregated workplaces remain. Increasingly, the important question is not, *is* there white male privilege, but rather, *where* is there white male privilege?

We think that it is now time to stop asking what the average national segregation trajectories are and instead to focus on the shape of the distribution. In 1966 the most common organizational segregation level of black men, black women, and white women from white men was 100—complete segregation—and almost all organizations had segregation values above 80 for all three comparisons. Complete segregation was the norm. By 2005 the distributions had all moved to the left. The average organization today has segregation levels that are quite a bit lower than in 1966, but quite a bit higher than one could imagine. Notably, many organizations still display total segregation of white men from others, and except for white women and black women, almost no organizations have very low segregation levels. The national political pressure to disrupt institutionalized racism and sexism has shifted organizational processes from simply enacting institutionalized discrimination to negotiating local versions of racial and gender integration.

The first half of this book was about national politics and the separate politically mediated desegregation trajectories of status groups, and the second half was about the creation of local inequality regimes. These local inequalities are the product of interactions in specific workplaces influenced by their local cultural context, competition among groups (including new immigrants in local labor markets), industrial expectations, and workplace managerial practices.

In the absence of renewed national politics to create new uncertainties or new regulatory pressures, we suspect that future progress toward equal opportunity will arise because of pressures on workplaces from internal workplace constituencies, as well as environmental pressures originating from firm, industry, and community contexts. The reverse holds as well: future pressure for increased segregation and white male privileges will

Figure 9.2   Density Plots of Organizational Variation in Segregation,
1966 to 2005

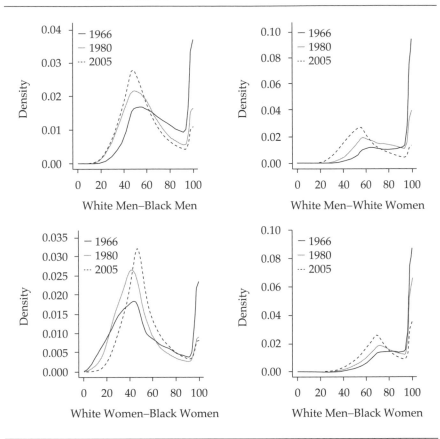

Source: Authors' calculations based on data from EEO-1 surveys (EEOC, various years).

be rooted in local interactions and their environmental context. In the last
three chapters, we encountered many instances of resegregation and competitive pressures that increased white males' preferred access to good-
quality jobs. If prior to the Civil Rights Act white males' racial and gender
status privilege was nearly uncontested, today we see multiple local con-
tests for equal opportunity and group advantage. We think that it is very
important for social scientists in particular to recognize workplace variation in segregation and discrimination and to develop systematic research
programs to explain their sources and consequences.

Figure 9.2 displays such variation and leads to a new set of research
questions. Why are some firms still totally segregated? Under what cir-

cumstances does a workplace move from totally segregated to only some-what segregated? Under what circumstances do workplaces become more segregated? How important are human resource practices? Are the key human resource practices about promoting equal opportunity or about installing meritocratic procedures? Can corporate leadership effectively promote segregation or desegregation? If so, by what mechanisms? Are there firms that still respond proactively to the threat of OFCCP oversight? Why and under what circumstances? Can the threat of lawsuits motivate equal opportunity progress, or do legally oriented defenses against dis-crimination actually undermine diversity goals? Under what circum-stances do employees encourage equal opportunity, and when can they hoard opportunities only for people who look like themselves?

CURRENT ORGANIZATIONAL VARIATION

Figures 9.1 and 9.2 highlight the shift from nationally institutionalized segregation to variation based in increasingly local dynamics. Although we have outlined various factors that contribute to current variation in EEO patterns for white men, white women, black men, and black women throughout the previous chapters, here we emphasize (1) processes of so-cial closure and meritocracy, (2) compliance and accountability, and (3) the changing race and ethnic landscape of the U.S. labor force. Each of these factors generates multiple localized race, ethnic, and gender queues that result from particular configurations of social groups and their relational dynamics within both communities and workplaces.

Social Closure and Meritocracy

The contemporary reality of status segregation in American workplaces operates at the levels of industries, communities, and concrete work set-tings. Industry is now an important context for understanding change and stability in status-linked inequalities. Many have remarked that the rise of the service sector has produced new employment opportunities for racial minorities and women. Some have attributed this to the low wages in these industries, which make the jobs less desirable to white men, and some point to the increase in merit-based screening in workplaces in the post–civil rights area. Others have surmised that it was simple employ-ment growth that produced opportunities for new labor market entrants.

We focused in chapter 7 on these three explanations for why contempo-rary status inequalities may vary across industries—growth in employ-ment, social closure from desirable jobs, and meritocracy in hiring and promotion. Although many scholars have assumed that expanding indus-tries provide the structural opportunity to "make room" for previously excluded groups, our results provide little or no evidence that simple employment growth produces EEO progress. Rather, what we do find is that segregation tends to be most associated with social closure and credentialing mechanisms. Segregation tends to increase with increases in relative industry wages and declines in industries that are more reliant on workers with a college degree. In industries where relative wages are high, organizational decision-makers and workers have a vested interest in monopolizing desirable job opportunities. Segregation drops, however, in industries that recruit educated labor. A complementary interpretation is that credentialing as a basis for employment screening tends to crowd out considerations of race or gender in the hiring decision. In view of the increase in opportunities for nonwhites and women to achieve college degrees in the United States, both groups benefit strongly from education-based screening for jobs.

Industries vary tremendously in the kind and quality of work available and the status groups normatively deemed appropriate for specific jobs. Because industries generate different products and services, they tend to operate in environments that also differ with regard to technology and the organization of the labor process, as well as competition and market structure. Industry also functions as a normative field for the diffusion of human resource policies and practices. One of the key findings in chapter 8 is that the influence of OFCCP audits, EEOC complaints, and class-action lawsuits tends to diffuse across workplaces that share an industrial context.

The principle of equality of opportunity is arguably one of the most strongly held American values. Despite the fact that the principle is widely accepted, the extent to which it is put into practice for all Americans is much more inconsistent and contested. Interestingly, although academics, policymakers, and the general public may have varied views of how much EEO progress we have made in the employment sector, few would argue that progress is absent altogether. Our examination of patterns of race and gender integration across industries identifies various EEO trajectories. Segregation between white men and white women is the only comparison in which we find continued progress in almost all industries. Enhanced employment equality between white men and black men appears to have stalled thirty years ago, and perhaps most disturbingly, white women and black women are becoming *increasingly* segregated in most U.S. industries.

We are convinced that meritocratic selection and social closure are the primary mechanisms encouraging future desegregation and resegregation in U.S. employment, respectively. The evidence we provide and review in chapters 7 and 8 leads us to believe that meritocratic selection is supported when there is diversity in the managerial ranks, when educational and other formal screening is used to allocate organizational resources, and when managers are held accountable to work toward meritocratic goals. Meritocratic equal opportunity outcomes are far from automatic. At the same time, pressures for exclusion and opportunity hoarding of the best jobs for their incumbents rise when wages increase, when informal selection criteria are used, and when managerial oversight is absent.

David Cotter, Joan Hermsen, and Reeve Vanneman (2004) show that much gender occupational desegregation has happened in middle-class jobs but that little has changed in working-class jobs. This outcome was probably produced by the same merit-linked and closure-based processes. In other words, reliance on educational screening generates increased integration. High-wage jobs with weak credential requirements, on the other hand, are resistant to integration, presumably because social closure processes are stronger. Paula England (2010) speculates that this class-linked shift in segregation results from gendered mobility strategies among women. Middle-class women invested in advanced education and moved into male jobs, while ambitious working-class women moved into female-typed clerical and sales jobs. These working-class women had options for upward mobility without transgressing gender boundaries. By contrast, middle-class women had to enter male jobs if they wished to be mobile. Men rarely move into typically female jobs. England's account, an interpretation of what might have happened, seems reasonable. On the other hand, it ignores the role of powerful decision-makers already in and around male jobs—the men and managers making the selection and training decisions about skilled working-class jobs. It is our position that the gender boundary is enforced by both men and women.

Regulatory Compliance and Accountability

The adoption of organizational equal opportunity policies and practices animated a body of organizational research in the 1990s. Most notably, the work of Lauren Edelman and of Frank Dobbin and John Sutton sheds light on the establishment and elaboration of human resource practices in response to federal laws and regulatory mandates for equal opportunity. Much of this work argues that the adoption of organizational structures, policies, and practices was generally an effort at symbolic compliance to deflect regulatory or legal threats. From this perspective, innovations in human resource practices resulted from responses to the uncertainty associated with ambiguous laws and regulatory mandates. Interestingly, new practices, policies, and structures were adopted, not to reach equal opportunity goals, but rather to signal symbolic compliance. As organizations tried to contain uncertainty, they began to adopt structures and policies that demonstrated legal compliance (for example, by establishing formal EEO/AA offices). This literature generally posits that these practices were only loosely coupled with actual hiring, promotion, and termination decisions. Hence, although this research demonstrates the diffusion of these organizational structures and policies, their mere presence does not guarantee equal employment opportunity.

Much of what we find in the early chapters of this book is that progress did transpire. However, it was uneven across time and federal contractor status. Progress also differed for each race-gender group and by outcome examined. We documented not only stalled progress but in some cases even resegregation. Progress was taking place when political pressure was high and corporations were uncertain as to what compliance would look like. This was particularly the case among federal contractors. Progress for African American men in particular preceded the adoption of equal opportunity human resource practices or the regulatory clarification of what evidence might protect firms from oversight or lawsuits. We think uncertainty in the corporate regulatory and legal environments was fundamental to equal employment opportunity progress in private-sector firms. The waning of political pressure for EEO progress from jurists, legislators, regulators, and social movements is certainly consistent with CEOs in many firms, and even across whole industries, turning their attention to other goals.

Recent organizational research suggests that contemporary workplace inequalities are not likely to be influenced by the mere presence of symbolic organizational policies, but rather require accountability structures that hold decision-makers responsible for the staffing choices they make. Although we cannot observe the effects of accountability structures directly in our analysis of EEO-1 reports, the literature reviewed in chapter 8 strongly indicates that in the absence of uncertainty, accountability is central to challenging race and gender inequality in contemporary U.S. workplaces. It is human resource practices that build managerial accountability into personnel decision-making that are most consistently linked to EEO progress. Diversity training and social networking practices have no effects, weak effects, or in some cases even negative effects on diversity. Even when uncertainty is high, as when a firm is audited by the OFCCP, sanctioned by the EEOC, or faced with a class-action lawsuit, we do not see EEO progress unless it is supported by normative encouragement at the industry level or when it occurs in progressive court districts where the fear of losing the case and facing stiff fines or public embarrassment is high. Accordingly, although accountability can be internal or external, it seems to be central to producing contemporary organizational progress toward more equal opportunity workplaces.

Environmental uncertainty, regulatory oversight that requires more than simply symbolic compliance, and coercive and normative pressures in the environment all play a role in motivating equal opportunity progress. In the contemporary period, legal threats alone, whether delivered through regulatory agencies, civil lawsuits, or diversity training, appear to produce at least as much backlash as forward progress. The literature identifies symbolic compliance as the core corporate response to equal opportunity mandates. Our reading of our own research and that of others is that this is an accurate assessment when equal opportunity goals have been recast as legal rather than moral or business problems. The one exception may be in federal district courts where the sitting judges support equal opportunity goals. Appointments of female and minority judges who place civil rights above the perquisites of corporate autonomy may also make a difference in how firms react to lawsuits.

Ethnic Complexity

The majority of this book focuses on segregation and access to quality jobs for white and black men and women. A reasonable criticism of our work is that by starting with the implications of the Civil Rights Act for black and white men and women, we have neglected the increasing importance of new immigrant groups, especially the influence and fates of Hispanic and Asian Americans in U.S. labor markets. Because the Civil Rights Act was primarily aimed at reducing ascriptive inequality for African Americans—and for black men in particular—we chose to center our attention on the legal and political shifts that affected black and white Americans' life chances. Moreover, other racial and ethnic groups comprised a very small proportion of private-sector employment in the early years following the passage of the Civil Rights Act. The increasing complexity of ethnic employment patterns demands much more attention than we have been able to provide in this book.

Douglas Massey (2007) suggests that discrimination against Hispanics has increased since the mid-1980s as national politics has increasingly targeted Latino immigrants as a threat to native workers. In work reported elsewhere, we find that among men Hispanic-white private-sector segregation was high and flat in the 1960s, dropped in the 1970s, and plateaued after 1980 (Tomaskovic-Devey and Stainback 2007). White female–Hispanic female segregation rose across the entire post–Civil Rights Act period. The general trajectories for Hispanic-white segregation are, if anything, worse than for black-white segregation. Of course, during the same period there has been a surge in both documented and undocumented immigration from Latin America, much of it by people with low levels of education and limited English-language skills. Some of the stalled or worsening segregation trajectories will be produced by the growing immigration-linked human capital disparity between white and Hispanic labor forces.

Our analyses also suggest slow declines in Asian-white employment segregation for men and slow increases among women. Because Asian Americans, both native-born and immigrant, tend to have higher education than native whites, some of this segregation probably results from Asians' superior access to professional occupations. The latest research suggests that no wage penalties are associated with U.S.-born Asian status once educational credentials have been taken into account (Kim and Sakamoto 2010). Our analyses of the matching of managers to employees in chapter 8 certainly suggest that the least social distance in private-sector workplaces is that between Asians and whites.

In chapter 6, we turned our attention to the spatial dynamics influencing racial and gender inequality in U.S. labor markets, and it was here that we examined the implications for black and white segregation trajectories of the presence of new minority groups. The Civil Rights Act of 1964 was partially designed to attack racial discrimination in the South, and we show regional convergence during the period that followed. However, a more focused look at the changes in group size of various racial and ethnic groups within local labor markets reveals that local labor queues influence both segregation and access to managerial jobs.

Because the U.S. labor force has become increasingly diverse, and because these composition dynamics vary across place, contemporary variation in equal employment opportunity results in part from these local configurations of relative power and social group dynamics. Our analyses suggest the increasing importance of local competition processes in particular in shaping equal opportunity trajectories.

The demographic composition of labor markets can be expected to influence employment opportunities by affecting the relative power of social groups within labor markets. For example, as the percentage of African Americans or women in a labor market increases, we might expect them to have greater relative power vis-à-vis men and whites. Such changes in the balance of power may reduce men's and whites' ability to monopolize valued jobs in local economies. In contrast, increases in female and nonwhite populations may also set in motion competition and threat dynamics, which may in turn lead men and whites to engage in more exclusionary practices.

In the 1960s and 1970s, segregation declined and access to good jobs increased when white women, black men, and black women were growing proportions of the labor market. When political pressures were strong, empowerment processes dominated. After 1980, the local labor market patterns reversed and converged toward a pattern of increased segregation and exclusion when these groups were larger. Today local competitive threat processes dominate.

A consistent finding is that white men benefit from diversity in local labor markets. The practical consequence of labor market competition with other demographic groups is that white men's access to the best white- and blue-collar jobs increases. As the labor queue becomes more diverse, a larger proportion of white men, who still stand at the front of the line for jobs, get access to the best jobs in local labor markets (figure 9.3).

Richard Alba (2009) points out that the decreasing size of the white population and increasing ethnic diversity in the U.S. labor force may present opportunities for increased access to good jobs for African Americans. Our analyses suggest that he is correct. With fewer whites—especially fewer white men—to compete with, African Americans should experience both increased integration and decreased segregation. Our analyses of ethnic queuing processes suggest that, in the absence of new uncertainties promoting increased access for other groups, the same trends should increase white men's access to good-quality jobs. The result will be more integrated workplaces, increased advantages for white men, and an opening of opportunities for minorities into some good-quality jobs. Our analyses further suggest that these opportunities are most likely to be found in more meritocratic workplaces and in lower-wage workplaces. White working-class men and women will be the most integrated in their workplaces and will face the stiffest wage competition as the labor force becomes more international and less white.

The fact that Hispanic and Asian immigrants are growing proportions of the labor force suggests some additional opportunities for African Americans in high-immigrant-destination cities. In most large cities, African American men rank above Hispanic men but below Asian men in access to managerial jobs. The exceptions are Washington, D.C., and Atlanta, Georgia, two cities with significant black political and economic power. African Americans in these cities also rank above Asians in access to managerial jobs. In the cities with the largest Hispanic and Asian populations, African American men tend to be more highly ranked than Hispanic men and Asian men, respectively, in the managerial labor queue as well. Thus, the growth of an immigrant population may provide particular opportunities for good-quality jobs in locales where African Americans are more influential and immigrant density is high. Presumably

Figure 9.3   U.S. Labor Force Composition in 2005 and Projected
             in 2050

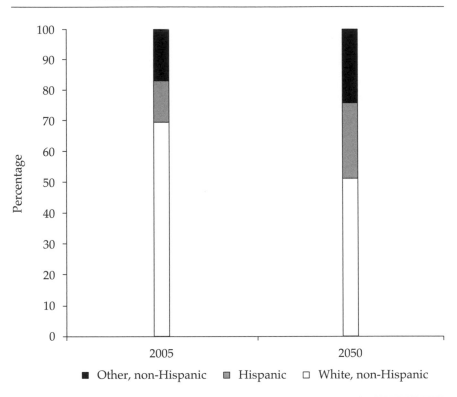

Source: Authors' calculations based on data from Lee, Mather, and Ron (2008).

these are labor markets where low-skill immigrant populations cluster
and African Americans benefit from their superior education and English-
language skills.

THE IMPLICATION OF LOCAL VARIATION

The insight developed in this book that equal opportunity progress and
regress are increasingly localized—taking place within industries, communities, and workplaces—holds crucial implications for a range of future activities, ranging from human resource management to regulatory
enforcement to future social science research. We discuss these factors in
turn.

Human Resource Managers

In 1964, when segregation was total and there were bright boundaries between jobs and people, it may have appeared as if there was a single national system of racial and gender apartheid in U.S. firms. In a cultural sense this was the case: racial and gender hierarchies were so strongly institutionalized that they appeared permanent and outside of the control of any particular firm or personnel department. But of course, this was not the case. The taken-for-granted nature of racial and gender hierarchies was shattered by the civil rights and women's movements, and the insulation of corporate personnel practices was stripped away by the uncertainty that ensued. Personnel managers mobilized to institute human resource practices that opened up opportunities first to African Americans and later to white women and other minorities. That many of these practices were justified to defend companies from regulatory or legal threats is clear; that few were formally evaluated is clear as well. Most importantly, however, change did happen, and in the 1960s and 1970s it happened fairly rapidly. When political pressure and environmental uncertainty receded, so too did equal opportunity progress.

Under what conditions might we expect human resource managers to once again adopt proactive equal opportunity agendas? Under what conditions might they be successful in implementing them? If we look to the historical record, we see that legal and social uncertainty over proper human resource practices in the corporate environment can be a source of power for human resource managers with an equal opportunity agenda. The flowering of such an agenda today would probably require a strong link to basic problems of production. At a time when diversity managers claim to increase productivity and reduce costly employee turnover, EEO uncertainty would be most likely to reappear as a way to provide solutions to problems of productivity or labor costs. Clearly, the biggest opportunity here is the continued decline of white men as a source of labor in the United States. The looming human resource problem will be the increasing proportion of nonwhites in the pool of job applicants for all positions. Because the racial and immigrant composition of the labor force varies tremendously across localities, HR offices may be forced to embrace local diversity strategies that reflect local labor forces. Such a development would be in contrast to the initial rise of equal opportunity policies, which were national in scope and a reaction to the national political and regulatory pressure to increase opportunities for African Americans. In that instance, as Frank Dobbin (2009) has so ably documented, personnel managers were crucial in defining the policies and practices that would later be certified by the courts and regulators as evidence of good-faith efforts toward equal opportunity. In the absence of a concerted professional project and a unifying politics, a likely outcome might simply be a series of local solutions that fall back on current practice, stereotypes, and cultural pressures. This would produce multiple local trajectories, with inertia and various new patterns of segregation and opportunity hoarding being likely outcomes as well.

This is not to say that HR managers are powerless in the absence of new uncertainties and political pressures. They still have their jobs to do, and those jobs still include preventing or at least discouraging discrimination and segregation. Here they have potential allies among their minority and female workforces and within corporate leadership. Increased demographic diversity among corporate leaders is one potential resource to strengthen the equal opportunity hand of HR managers. Our research and that of others suggest that managerial diversity reduces pay inequality, increases job integration, and promotes further managerial diversity. We presume that these widespread effects reflect the strengthening of meritocratic principles in the hiring and promotion of employees.

Corporations often defend themselves from discrimination lawsuits by pointing to the presence of nondiscrimination policies or requirements for routine personnel evaluations (Dobbin 2009). But it is not the presence of an official policy that makes the difference, but what actually happens in routine organizational practice. Antidiscrimination policies without accountability are equivalent to no policy at all. A personnel evaluation procedure that is only implemented sporadically or to justify exclusionary decisions can be a tool for discrimination rather than a safeguard against it (Roscigno 2007). Asserting a strong equal opportunity commitment with no oversight can lead managers to assume that actually promoting fairness in employment decisions happens elsewhere in the company, and so no one takes responsibility for ensuring that this is the case (Castilla and Benard 2010).

Bureaucratic rules are always at risk of being decoupled from everyday practice. Worse, they can create unreasonable requirements that reduce the commitment of all concerned to equal opportunity goals. Many companies continue to advertise in expensive print media for all jobs because those who crafted the EEOC guidelines in the 1970s thought that this was a good mechanism to provide information on job openings to minority populations. This practice might have made sense at the time, and it still might for some jobs, but in fields where all job search now occurs via the Internet, such requirements are obviously decoupled from the original goals and may reduce faith in the sincerity of HR departments or legal compliance officers about promoting diversity.

Some might worry that meritocratic goals are synonymous with bureaucracy, but this equivalence seems wrongheaded to us. Accountability, rather than bureaucracy, seems to be the best tool for the design of equal opportunity programs. How do private-sector firms achieve process or product innovations? They do not make a rule that innovation shall happen. They typically set goals and evaluate managers for meeting those goals. They let managers and local work teams discover innovations that work. Similarly, the best research on equal opportunity policies also points to managerial accountability as the most effective way to promote employment diversity (Kalev, Dobbin, and Kelly 2006). But only about 17 percent of the workplaces that Kalev and her colleagues studied had such oversight, so the practice is far from widespread. Of course, goals and targets, the consistent recipe for effective decentralized management, was the original language of affirmative action. As part of the backlash against racial progress, that language was attacked as leading to hiring quotas and likely to promote reverse discrimination. It is ironic that one of the key tools that managers rely upon to get past organizational inertia in production—centralized goals and decentralized implementation—has been most effectively resisted when applied to generating equal employment opportunity (Bergmann 1996). A cynical view might be that opposition was strongest because giving managers goals and making them accountable is the strategy most likely to succeed. It seems just as likely that this opposition was the result of misplaced fears of reverse discrimination, endorsed by a Supreme Court too removed from the everyday reality of managerial practice to understand its absurdity.

Figure 9.4 charts the density of EEOC-reporting workplaces by the representation of black women in managerial jobs from 1966 to the present. All values below zero represent underrepresentation relative to the local labor market. Over time the underrepresentation of black women in managerial jobs receded weakly, but at no time, not in 1966, not in 1980, and not today, have more than a handful of workplaces had black women *overrepresented* in managerial jobs. Even today, black women are severely underrepresented in managerial jobs relative to their availability in the vast majority of workplaces. In the only high-quality study of reverse discrimination, Fred Pincus (2003) finds that race discrimination complaints to the EEOC by whites and gender discrimination complaints by men are rare. Reverse discrimination court cases are even rarer. His conclusion is that reverse discrimination is mostly a myth—an apocryphal story told and retold as part of the backlash against affirmative action and equal opportunity politics.

There is not now and has never been a widespread pattern of reverse discrimination. Rather, we have demonstrated that white men's advantaged access to good jobs, with the exception of the credentialed profes-

Figure 9.4   Distributions of Black Women in Management Relative
to Their Representation in Local Labor Markets in EEOC-
Reporting Private-Sector Workplaces, 1966, 1980, and
2005

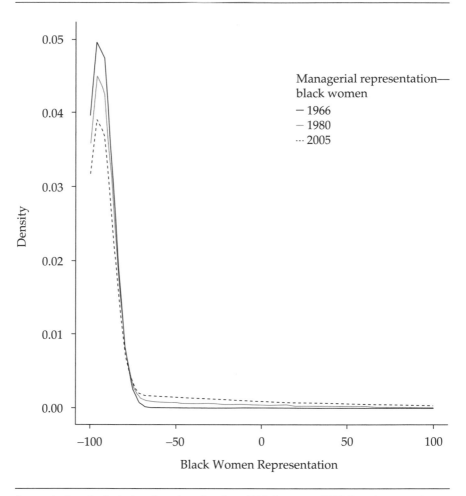

Source: Authors' calculations based on data from EEO-1 surveys (EEOC, various years).

sions, has been enhanced rather than reduced across the post–Civil Rights
Act era. White men's advantages also grow in more diverse firms and labor markets. The EEOC has had these data all along, but lacked the organizational capacity to examine the absurd fears associated with claims of
reverse discrimination. That a whole branch of case law was allowed to

develop around a false problem was in some ways the result of the absence of sound social science analysis of what was really happening.

The vast majority of firms have the HR practices associated with symbolic compliance, such as nondiscrimination statements, job posting requirements, and affirmative action training, but most firms do very little to monitor employment diversity. Among federal contractors, the most common practice is a workplace-specific inventory on the race-by-gender diversity in job assignments. HR departments could decide to not merely create these tables, decoupled from managerial evaluation, but to publish workplace statistics for the firm once a year, monitor trends, and reward and sanction managers for their performance. One of the most disturbing findings in this volume is that racial resegregation is widespread in the U.S. private sector. Many firms are actually getting worse over time. Unless they pay very close attention, HR directors are unlikely to even recognize such trends. Because we received the EEOC data only on condition of promising confidentiality, we cannot reveal which firms are getting worse, but the firms themselves could, even if only to themselves.

Corporate CEOs often endorse equal opportunity and diversity as both personal and corporate values. CEOs also value efficiency, quality, and profit. A big difference in these two commitments is that CEOs monitor trends in efficiency, quality, and profit, rewarding and punishing managers as appropriate. True corporate equal opportunity leadership would convert the value placed on meritocratic evaluation and employee diversity into behaviors monitored in the firm's normal accounting and reward systems. This type of shift might also move the center of power over corporate equal opportunity policy from lawyers defending against discrimination complaints to human resource managers endeavoring to create welcoming, fair, dynamic workplaces.

THE FUTURE OF FEDERAL REGULATION AND ENFORCEMENT

Current equal opportunity enforcement is mostly administrative. If the EEOC receives a discrimination complaint, the complaint is investigated on a case-by-case basis. If the complaint appears serious and staff resources are available, a more thorough investigation may take place. Most complaints are not investigated because resources are insufficient. When complaints are investigated and judged to be serious, administrative negotiations tend to be the remedy. Only in rare cases are fines levied. In very rare cases the EEOC may join a class-action lawsuit, typically initiated by private lawyers. It is also the case that the EEOC commissioners, who are bipartisan presidential appointees, have the authority to initiate an investigation in the absence of a specific discrimination complaint.

Because case law developed around the practice of comparing company staffing patterns to industry and labor market peers, the EEOC and the courts use industry and local labor market benchmarks when evaluating discrimination complaints. It is clear from our work that both local labor markets and industries vary widely in their segregation levels and trajectories. Because current enforcement practice typically ignores these sources of systemic discrimination, a fundamental disconnect arises between the big-picture view of EEO progress and the routine processing of discrimination complaints. This is to some extent a problem reinforced by the low level of analytic staffing and funding at the EEOC. The EEOC is a legally oriented administrative unit with underdeveloped analytic capacity. Neither the EEOC nor any other federal agency has ever had the funding to develop sustained analytic capacity.

The EEOC recognized this problem in 2006 when then-commissioner Leslie Silverman issued a report highlighting this disconnect and pointing out that a consequence was the inability to investigate systemic employment bias. By "systemic" the report was referring to widespread problems of exclusion and discrimination, not only in particular firms, as in class-action lawsuits, but also in entire industries and labor markets (Silverman 2006). If the EEOC had the capacity to generate analyses similar to the ones in this book that identify the firms, industries, and localities that are the likeliest sites of systemic discrimination, commissioner charges could be employed as the mechanism to convert that knowledge into investigations.

The same EEOC report also criticized the difficulty of using EEOC employment and complaint data to support the investigation of discrimination complaints. Because the EEOC lacks the resources to investigate the vast majority of discrimination complaints, investigators might be better able to choose which cases to devote their energies to if they could quickly identify whether a workplace had a particularly egregious record compared to other similarly situated employers. The EEOC has since developed EEO1-Analytics, a software product that allows field investigators to make within-industry and labor market comparisons when they receive discrimination complaints against particular employers. The EEOC has also begun to staff field offices with social science–trained staff who can use the EEO-1 reports to do more sophisticated, company-wide investigations rather than workplace-specific investigations only. These are clear advances in the analytic capacity of investigators, but they do not advance the EEOC's own goal of identifying and responding to systemic discrimination.

The OFCCP exists to enforce affirmative action requirements for federal contractors. It occasionally responds to discrimination complaints from multiple workers, but more often this agency conducts random compliance reviews of companies to see whether firms have an adequate affirmative action plan on file and whether that plan is being carried out. If a company is audited and the affirmative action plan does not exist or is not being followed, the OFCCP negotiates an acceptable plan to create and enact one. In rare cases the OFCCP requires back pay or hiring remedies. Only very rarely do corporations become debarred from further federal contracts. Almost all of the evidence in this book suggests that the OFCCP is no longer effectively encouraging desegregation trajectories or increasing female or minority employment opportunities. Making the OFCCP more effective in the short run might be as simple as increasing the rate of fines and debarments. This would inject a rapid dose of uncertainty among federal contractors, old affirmative action plans would be dusted off and reexamined, and HR offices across the country might regain their focus on EEO goals.

Today both the EEOC and OFCCP are much less prominent than they were during the initial two decades following the Civil Rights Act, although there was an uptick in both funding and staffing after President Obama was elected (figure 9.5). As activist organizations creating regulations and legal expectations, these agencies were key sources of uncertainty in the corporate environment after the Civil Rights Act. Importantly, their responsibilities have expanded over time even as their resources and political support have contracted. The definition of protected classes has expanded to include age, disability, veteran status, and, perhaps in the near future, sexual orientation.

The OFCCP and EEOC remain important actors. The threat of OFCCP audits, EEOC-sanctioned discrimination complaints, and even just the record-keeping and reporting requirements have maintained equal opportunity visibility inside corporations as the political uncertainty and regulatory threat have receded. Human resource managers with equal opportunity commitments can point to both agencies as reasons for managers to support those agendas. Defense lawyers charged with inoculating firms against discrimination charges can do the same. Although we can fault the regulatory agencies for being too timid, and Congress for not providing sufficient funding, their absence might leave HR managers with no leverage at all in corporations that have lost interest in equal opportunity goals. If a more aggressive attack on employment discrimination were to arise, these agencies stand ready to be retooled, retasked, and reinvigorated.

The Civil Rights Act authorized the EEOC to collect data on private-sector firms' employment distributions in order to monitor progress toward a more equal opportunity society. The EEOC was never, however,

Figure 9.5   EEOC and OFCCP Staffing, 1994 to 2010

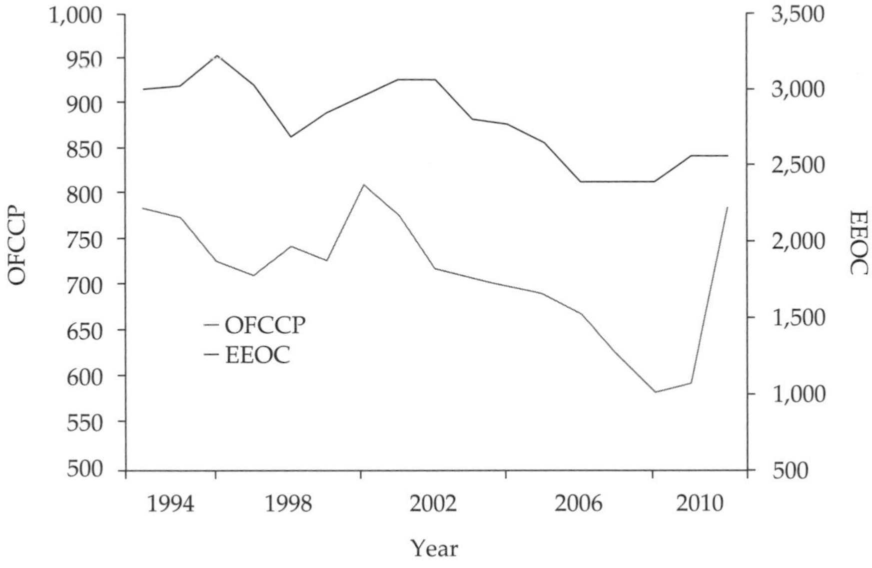

Source: Authors' compilation based on U.S. Commission on Civil Rights (1995).

given funding to actually accomplish that task. Rather, insufficient resources have gone to the enforcement task of evaluating and certifying
employment discrimination claims. Even here, for the vast majority of
claims of discrimination the EEOC, lacking the resources to investigate,
simply issues an authorization to the claimant to pursue a civil action if he
or she has the individual resources and can find a lawyer to take the case.

The EEOC sometimes uses EEO-1 reports to examine employment distributions in firms that have been the target of multiple accusations of
discrimination. These same reports could be used in a proactive manner to
identify firms where minority or female representation is worse than in
comparable firms. These analyses could then be shared with the OFCCP
and become the basis for proactive compliance reviews.[1] Of course, this
would require an increased capacity at the OFCCP to carry out such reviews. Even in the absence of increased capacity, reviews targeting firms
with egregious employment records would be likely to create new uncertainties for firms and encourage them to pay more attention to what is
happening on the equal opportunity front. Firms would become interested in comparing their employment of minorities and women to the employment practices of their industry and labor market peers. One might

imagine the EEOC providing a new fee-based service in which it provided external benchmark data so that firms could see how well they were doing relative to their competitors. Mary Graham and Julie Hotchkiss (2009) outline what they call a Systemic Gender EEO Scorecard, which might be used to identify outlier firms and industries. Their argument is similar to what we have been proposing here, but they also connect systemic investigations to good management practice. They point out that even as management has become increasingly data-driven in strengthening efficiency and performance, regulators still rely on reactive approaches to discrimination complaints. The data are available to be systematic and more effective in identifying and targeting firms with high levels of disparity.

The EEOC also collects data on public-sector employment, which it also lacks the organizational capacity to analyze. The same type of automated benchmarking studies of cities and states could be done and then passed along to the Department of Justice to pursue discrimination inquiries, consent decrees, or even litigation against public employers. For public employers and for EEOC-reporting private firms that are not federal contractors, current practice would probably limit enforcement until after a discrimination complaint had been filed, but analyses that benchmark employers to themselves and to their competitors could be routinely used in self-assessment, regulation, and perhaps even in litigation in the meantime. We suspect that non-adversarial self-assessment and regulatory negotiation would produce less backlash than litigation. High-profile lawsuits, however, may be influential in injecting uncertainty and so destabilizing the emerging inertia and resegregation that are so widespread in contemporary private-sector firms.

A more fundamental break with the past would be to combine praise and shaming tools. The EEOC could use methods similar to those developed in this book to list the best- and worst-performing industries and communities. Cities could be ranked in terms of their relative opportunities for minorities and women. Descriptions in terms of industry and region of the types of firms that have the worst EEO records could be released yearly. Such descriptions would put all firms in those organizational fields on notice and perhaps produce the kind of industry field effects that we have seen in this book for EEOC investigations, OFCCP regulation, and class-action lawsuits.

Public praise and shaming could even be done for specific firms. Many magazines release annual rankings of top ten and top one hundred firms. Using actual firm employment data, the EEOC could release the names of the top one hundred firms in terms of desegregation and managerial representation as role models for other firms to emulate. The most segregated firms or the firms with the highest concentrations of white males could be identified as well. These types of data are already released by the Securities and Exchange Commission (SEC) on corporate financial performance and by the Environmental Protection Agency (EPA) on pollution releases. It seems absurd that in a democratic society we provide confidentiality to companies with lousy records of providing equal employment opportunities while exposing polluters and prosecuting insider trading.

In 2007 the EEOC began collecting data on its EEO-1 forms that differentiated middle managers from executives. These data have not yet been used for enforcement or social science purposes. There has been some discussion of adding information on race- and gender-specific earnings levels within the current EEO-1 gender-by-race-by-occupation matrix. Similar data have long been collected on public-sector EEO surveys. The 1963 Equal Pay Act made it illegal to pay men and women in the same job different wages based on gender alone. Collecting, analyzing, and incorporating such data into their regulatory program would open up an entire new arena of potential EEOC and OFCCP enforcement, with relatively clear legislative guidelines and the potential to foster substantial compliance uncertainty.

A more active and creative EEO agenda out of the EEOC, OFCCP, and Department of Justice might create the type of uncertainty necessary to reinvigorate equal opportunity progress in the United States. Certainly, past history suggests that this is most likely to happen when there is political pressure from the executive, legislative, and judicial branches of government. The government is more attentive when politicians are competing for votes or government is facing disruption in the streets. On the other hand, the civil rights agenda has enforcement arms—the EEOC, OFCCP, and Department of Justice Civil Rights Division—and perhaps something less than a mass movement could wake them up and stimulate innovation.

We think that the analyses in this book demonstrate that with modest additional resources the EEOC could vastly strengthen its analytic capacity and in so doing strengthen its regulatory mission as well. As the Silverman (2006) report points out, changing the culture of the EEOC from a largely administrative and reactive legal orientation to a more analytic, proactive, systemic, and uncertainty-generating mission will take executive leadership.

MORAL LEADERSHIP

The civil rights and women's movements played powerful moral and political roles in delegitimizing the white male apartheid system in U.S. firms. These movements pushed society and its leaders to adopt legal and cultural prohibitions against discrimination. When that political and cultural pressure was at its height, political and corporate leaders stepped forward and spoke out for equality and against discrimination. Their voices strengthened the movements and nurtured a professional commitment to equal opportunity among personnel managers in many private-sector firms.

In the absence of social movement pressure, leadership is more difficult. The Republican Party has for the last forty years used racial fears as an electoral strategy. Democrats, fearing the loss of even more white votes, have hung back. New social movements supporting the employment rights of gays, the disabled, and the elderly have generated the political courage of some elected leaders and HR managers, but the equal opportunity employment agenda is far from central to contemporary politics or corporate concerns.

This is not to say that there is no role for moral leadership today, but rather that leaders will need to be braver without a social movement backing them up. Facilitating such bravery will be the normative shift in the society: at least in principle, most people are now in favor of equal opportunity in employment. Although done quietly, the Obama administration has proposed increased funding for the EEOC and OFCCP, which would partially reverse a thirty-year decline in the fortunes of both regulatory organizations. These organizations certainly have the capacity to insert new uncertainties into private-sector employment practices. If the EEOC successfully introduces a systemic enforcement capacity, it could put on notice large swaths of the private sector that symbolic compliance will not be enough to remain shielded from embarrassing public scrutiny. If the EEOC and Department of Justice collaborate, the same could happen for public-sector employers. Recent research by George Wilson and Vincent Roscigno (2011) suggests that the initially higher equal opportunity commitments of public-sector employers have eroded in recent years.

There is a role for congressional leadership as well. Fifty years after Kennedy's executive order, the federal government still lacks the organizational capacity to develop measurement tools to identify organizational variation in discrimination or equal opportunity. Funding for the EEOC or the Department of Labor to develop that capacity is clearly required. This might mean strengthening funding for internal research capacity, creating external capacity, or both. It is simply amazing that in the fifty years since the Civil Rights Act, no consistent social science has been funded by the federal government to investigate discrimination or equal opportunity. This is in contrast with the considerable research resources dedicated to health, technological innovation, employment and unemployment, crime, environmental protection, and economic growth and competitiveness.

Congressional mandates that the Department of Justice, the EEOC, and the OFCCP collaborate in enforcement and utilize the data that they have available seem crucial as well. Although one might argue that equal opportunity enforcement was weak by design, we no longer live in an era when corporations and congressmen actively oppose equal opportunity or protect their freedom to discriminate. One can imagine more aggressive congressional leadership in the form of hearings and legislation as well. Authorizing the EEOC to make EEO-1 and discrimination complaint data publicly available would be an important contribution, allowing private organizations with an equal opportunity agenda to further publicize good and bad corporate behavior. A similar sunshine proposal would be appropriate for OFCCP audit results.

From our point of view, the most effective form of leadership may be moral. We certainly need leaders who raise the issues, define discrimination as a problem, and pursue equal opportunity *progress* as a national goal.

FUTURE TRAJECTORIES: INERTIA, DESEGREGATION, OR RESEGREGATION?

At this point in the history of private-sector equal opportunity, the dominant pattern is inertia. Little or no national aggregate progress is being made in terms of either desegregation or access to good jobs. Nationally, progress toward workplace equal opportunity has stalled. Moreover, it is disturbing to note that in many workplaces, communities, and industries segregation is increasing—particularly segregation between white women and black women, but also segregation between white men and white women and white men and black men in some firms, industries, and local labor markets.

If there are no new pressures for equal opportunity, it is likely that over time we will see more workplaces showing increased segregation and decreased access of groups other than white men and perhaps their near-neighbors—white women and Asian men—to good jobs. If other workplaces have hit an equilibrium position with no net progress or regress, then in the future we will see increased segregation and reduced opportunity for women and minorities in national statistics. In the absence of some normative or coercive pressure, there is no reason to expect racial or gender status distinctions to become smaller over time. Despite the absence of progress over the last thirty years, there is evidence that white racial resentment is building and that whites often see antiracism as a zero-sum game that they will lose (Norton and Sommers 2011). Many whites believe that there have been steady declines in antiblack racism since the 1950s, although all the evidence indicates that this has not been the case over the last thirty years. In addition, as we have discovered in this book, black advancement, at least in employment, does not take place in a zero-sum context, because whites, especially white males, are a declining proportion of the labor force. On the contrary, many white male employment advantages have been stable and substantial.

Not only have employment segregation trajectories hit a plateau, but as we saw in chapter 1, so has the general normative endorsement of racial and gender stereotypes. Thus, it is general inertia in organizational practices and perhaps in equal opportunity–producing human resource practices and internal coalitions within workplaces that promotes the current stagnant levels of segregation and inequality. The potential for normative backlash among whites is also clearly present. Absent any environmental pressure to sustain equal opportunity practices, they may simply wither. Since 1990, 43 percent of industries have had significant increases in employment segregation between white women and black women. Racial segregation among men is growing in one in six industries. Even gender segregation among whites is growing in a handful of industries. Although movement back to the near-complete institutionalization of racial and gender distinctions at work is clearly unlikely, local backsliding and backlash can be expected.

From a policy point of view, we are facing the potential for resegregation in many private-sector workplaces. We believe that there is a general moral consensus in the United States that the racial and gender apartheid of the pre–civil rights era is not acceptable. In some senses we have won the moral war against institutionalized white and male privilege but have not yet figured out the practical mechanisms that will produce equal opportunity. This has resulted in part from a misplaced faith in legal changes and formal organizational policies. Legal change cannot produce behavioral change until it becomes practice. Political pressure from both within and without moves firms to adopt equal opportunity goals and practices. We suspect that both will be important if we are to prevent the resegregation of American workplaces.

When we look forward, we should be looking for opportunities for social change, not assuming that past practices must reproduce current inequalities. Just as there were multiple potential trajectories in 1964, there will also be multiple paths into the future of U.S. equal opportunity in employment. Whether the dominant trajectories are resegregation, inertia, or further desegregation, whether they are national or local, will be a function of the political pressures and organizational practices we create and nurture.

Methodological Appendix

THIS APPENDIX PROVIDES a deeper introduction to the EEO-1 data that support this book and to the analytic choices we have made. The most complete description of the data can be found in Robinson et al. (2005). The first few sections of this appendix draw heavily on that article.

EEO-1 reports are a partial antidote to the near-absence of available time-series workplace data. Because there are now millions of observations, these data allow for disaggregation of segregation trends to the community and industry level as well. In addition, these data have the potential to follow segregation trends in specific workplaces over time, nested in their corporate, industrial, and community contexts. We use the data in this way in chapters 6, 7, and 8.

THE EEO-1 DATA

Title VII of the Civil Rights Act of 1964 and its amendments mandate that both public and private employers submit annual reports on the race-ethnic and gender makeup of their employees to the Equal Employment Opportunity Commission. These reports include private-sector Employer Information Reports (EEO-1), Apprenticeship Information Reports (EEO-2 and 2E), Local Union Reports (EEO-3), State and Local Government Information Reports (EEO-4), Elementary-Secondary Staff Information Reports (EEO-5), and Higher Education Staff Information Reports (EEO-6) (Equal Employment Opportunity Commission 1981). In the past, these data have rarely been available to the scientific community. We focus in this book only on EEO-1 reports of private-sector firms. The EEOC publishes aggregate statistics based on these data and also uses them for regulatory purposes.

Workplace reports are treated by the EEOC as confidential. Access to confidential EEO-1 reports was gained through the use of an Intergovernmental Personnel Act agreement under which Tomaskovic-Devey became an unpaid employee of the EEOC for the purposes of conducting this research. As part of that agreement, we are prohibited from identifying individual workplaces or firms.

EEO-1 reports contain establishment employment counts of gender by five race-ethnic (white, black, Hispanic, Asian/Pacific Islander, American Indian/Alaskan Native) groups for nine occupational categories—officials and managers, professionals, technicians, sales workers, office and clerical workers, craft workers, operatives, laborers, and service workers. In 2007 distinctions between top and other managers were introduced to the EEO-1 survey form. Firms determine the methods used to tally and classify employees within occupations. The preferred method before 2007 was a "visual inspection." Currently the preferred method is self-identification by the employee. EEO-1 reports also include information on the establishment's parent company, industry, and geographic location. Finally, each record states whether or not the firm is a federal contractor. There is no information on other characteristics of employees, such as education and tenure, or of jobs, such as training or earnings.

Coverage is limited to all private firms with fifty or more employees if federal contractors and one hundred or more employers if noncontractors. Prior to 1983, separate reports were required for contractor firms with twenty-five or more employees and noncontractor firms with fifty or more employees. Firms are instructed that employees do not include temporary or casual employees, but do include leased employees as well as both part-time and full-time employees.

In accordance with guidelines established in Title VII of the Civil Rights Act of 1964, employers use various forms of EEOC reporting. Reporting is contingent on the layout and structure of the firm. A single-establishment firm with one hundred or more employees (or fifty or more employees and a federal contract) files a single-establishment report. In the year 2000, there were 14,065 single-establishment reports. A multi-establishment firm with one hundred or more employees (or fifty or more employees and a federal contract) is required to file a company-wide consolidated report, a headquarters unit report, and individual establishment reports for each establishment with fifty or more employees. It is the case, however, that many firms file establishment reports for workplaces with fewer than fifty employees, and these observations appear among establishment reports. There were 25,410 such firm reports in the year 2000, with individual establishment reports for 158,250 unique workplaces. For the year 2000, there were 224,471 unique establishment reports.

Headquarter and individual establishment reports contain geographic, industry, and employment information for each unit with one hundred or more employees or fifty or more employees and a federal contract in the firm. There is also a category referred to as "special reports" in the EEO-1 files. Special reports include the employment counts for multiple small establishments (fewer than fifty employees) that are part of a larger firm. There were 1,059 special reports filed in the year 2000. We do not analyze special reports, as they are not workplaces and their geography and industry are not defined.

COVERAGE RATES

The EEOC estimated in 1966 that 75 percent of all employers with one hundred or more employees who were required to file EEO-1 reports actually did so (Equal Employment Opportunity Commission 1967). We have no idea how that response rate was calculated, and no one at the EEOC remembers, fifty years on, who was responsible. Later EEOC reports do not include response rate estimates. Across all sectors, total private-sector employment coverage dropped from over 50 percent in 1966 to just over 40 percent in 1999. All of the drop in coverage took place between 1982 and 1985 and was a function of changes in EEO firm size reporting requirements in 1983. With the exception of the dip in 1983, EEO employment coverage has remained relatively stable over time. Although a smaller proportion of all private-sector establishments were captured after 1983, coverage rates gradually increased for most industries. In 2007 the EEOC increased coverage by using other Dunn and Bradstreet data to identify eligible firms that were not reporting. In the single year between 2006 and 2007, the EEOC added almost 30,000 new workplaces, covering a half-million additional employees, to the EEO-1 database.

EEO-1 coverage is higher in sectors with larger firms. Manufacturing has the highest coverage rates (65 to 75 percent over time) and construction the lowest (10 to 20 percent over time). EEO coverage in services is roughly one-third of that reported by the Bureau of Labor Statistics. Industries characterized by small firms and small workplaces (such as construction, retail trade, services, and agriculture) are not well represented. It is also worth reiterating that the EEOC's definition of "employee" excludes temporary and casual workers "hired for a specified period of time or for the duration of a specified job"; this exclusion may further explain coverage issues for certain industries (Equal Employment Opportunity Commission 1981, vii).

DATA QUALITY

EEO-1 data for the years 1966 through 2005 contain little missing data or out-of-range values across more than 5 million workplace records examined. The original reliability of firm reports is unknown. There is likely to be measurement error associated with the method and quality of reporting used by firms (Becker 1980; Smith and Welch 1984). The EEO-1 survey instrument collects information on the methods used by firms to assess employment composition (that is, visual inspection versus payroll records). However, this variable is not in the current data files.[1] The EEOC does not perform external validity checks on reporting. The only suggestion we can find in the literature of systematic misreporting is provided by Smith and Welch (1984). They indirectly infer from aggregate comparisons with Current Population Survey data that, in the early years of EEO-1 reports, some firms may have reclassified professionals to managers in order to appear more integrated in their managerial ranks by race, ethnicity, and gender. This analysis was not conclusive. It focused on aggregate CPS and EEO-1 data comparisons and ignored alternative explanations such as possible changes in occupational composition resulting from secular shifts in industrial structure or firm composition over time.

We found a few issues with the EEO-1 data worth noting for researchers. In a very few cases (fewer than 0.1 percent), establishments lacked an assigned standard industrial classification (SIC) code. By comparison, 3.6 percent of CPS cases have insufficient industry and occupation data (Robinson et al. 2005). A few establishments reported suspiciously high levels of employment, although these cases were so rare as to be inconsequential in aggregate analyses. We investigated some of these cases by comparing the name and location of firms to corporate website information on employment. We concluded that, occasionally, consolidated firm reports were miscoded as headquarter or individual establishment reports. This type of miscoding, while rare, might be consequential for more focused studies of specific industries or communities. We ignore this potential small source of error in our analyses.

EEOC data are relatively easy to use and have improved over time. Despite changes in computing technology and political support, EEO-1 reports contain almost no missing data and contain few cases with extreme or unusual values. Data quality seems to be as high as or higher than academic and government surveys of individuals or firms. Response rates are probably comparable or superior to surveys of individuals or organizations, although this conclusion is based on the 1966 reported response rate and the relative stability of employment coverage over time.

MEASURING RACE

The categories used by the EEOC do not distinguish between race and ethnicity. The data collection instrument instructs respondents to report all Hispanics, regardless of race, as Hispanic. Thus, it is not possible to treat race and ethnicity as conceptually distinct or to examine variation associated with how individuals self-categorize. This reporting convention may be a source of measurement error, at least under some conceptualizations of race and ethnicity. On the other hand, reported ethnic distinctions are from the point of view of the firm and probably match the socially constructed conceptions of race-ethnicity in these workplaces. In any case, researchers have no choice but to proceed under the assumption that these race-ethnic categories are mutually exclusive and socially meaningful.

Prior to 1990, EEO-1 survey forms did not contain separate counts for white employment. For these years, data analysts must estimate the white counts by totaling the number of nonwhites in each occupation (Asian-American/Pacific Islanders, African Americans, American Indians/Alaskan Natives, and Hispanics) and then subtracting this number from the grand totals in each occupational category. Prior to 1990, a small proportion (fewer than 0.1 percent) of individual establishments contained erroneous grand totals. This could have been a result of reporting errors or errors in the data entry process. After 1993, the data were virtually free of this problem. This suggests that EEOC data-cleaning procedures improved in the early 1990s. In our analyses, we constrain any negative counts to zero. Beginning in 2007, further distinctions between Hawaiian/Pacific Islanders and other Asians were introduced. Our analyses end in 2005. We also limit our analysis to the continental United States because of the use of different race-ethnic classifications in Hawaii and a lack of meaningful labor market boundaries for Alaska.

INDUSTRY CODES

Standard industrial classification (SIC) codes have evolved over time. SIC codes changed in the years 1959, 1972, 1977, and 1987. The North American industrial classification system (NAICS) has now replaced the SIC system. This is reflected in the EEO-1 data. Although firms are responsible for specifically describing their "major activity," the EEOC assigns the SIC codes in the data. This suggests that in most cases firms provide enough information for the EEOC to assign industry codes.

Prior to 1974, the EEO-1 reports contained the 1957 SIC scheme. Between 1974 and 1991, the 1972 SIC scheme was used. After 1991, the 1987 SIC scheme was used.[2] In the late 1990s, the NAICS scheme was also present in the data files. We have created a conversion convention for our own work that identifies changes in SIC codes and standardizes to the 1987 coding scheme. The vast majority of codes did not change between the 1957 and 1987 SIC schemes. Four types of code changes occurred:

1. New codes were created for new industries (for example, 484 cable TV).

2. New codes were created when new industries split out of old ones (for example, 124 coal mining services split out of both 111 anthracite mining and 121 bituminous mining).

3. Old codes were discontinued and merged into new, more global codes.

4. Old codes were discontinued and broken up into two new, more specific codes.

We treat newly created industries as simple changes in the economy and make no adjustments in industry codes for them. It is likely, however, that when 484 cable TV was created as a new code, some establishments were reclassified from television to cable television. When a code change was not the creation of a new industry, we use the transformation matrix in table A.1, always standardizing to the more recent coding scheme.

OBSERVING LOCAL LABOR MARKETS

The most common way to observe spatial variation in labor market outcomes in the United States is to look at regions, states, and metropolitan areas. For some analyses, we concentrate on regions and states. For most analyses, we are interested in controlling for local labor supply, and in chapter 6 we examine directly labor market differences in segregation levels and trends. We do not use metropolitan areas for this purpose. The argument for metropolitan areas is that they are by far the most familiar. We see two large shortcomings, however, in these indicators. First, they exclude rural areas. Second, while metropolitan areas are meant to capture local economies by combining contiguous counties around one or more central cities, their composition is strongly influenced by political lobbying to include multiple cities and counties in order to increase population size.

Since we are interested in labor markets, we prefer commuting zones, a measure of local economies based on the actual commuting patterns in an area. Commuting zones are aggregations of counties, not confined to state boundaries, and are calculated based on decennial Census surveys documenting the density of individuals' commutes to work from where they live (Tolbert and Sizer 1996). Therefore, commuting zones describe local labor markets. We impose 1990 commuting zone boundaries on all years of data in these analyses for consistency purposes. The use of stable geography allows us to compare localities over time.

Table A.1   SIC Standardization Rules

1957 Code	1987 Code	1957 Industry Name	1987 Industry Name
012	017	Fruit, tree nut, and vegetable farms	Same
014	019	General farms	Same
073	078	Horticultural services	Landscape counseling and planning
151	152	General building contractors	Residential building contractors
151	153		(non-residential building)
398	399	Miscellaneous manufacturing	Manufacturing, NEC
402	401	Railroad sleeping and passenger	} Railroad
404	401	Railway express agency, inc	
522	507	Heating and plumbing equipment	Same
532	596	Mail-order houses	}
534	596	Merchandise vending machines	} Nonstore retailers
535	596	Direct selling organizations	}
595	594	Sporting goods stores	Miscellaneous shopping
597	594	Jewelry stores	goods stores
604	609	Trust companies, no deposits	Functions related to deposit banking
612	603	Savings and loans	Savings institutions
613	615	Agricultural credit institutions	Business credit institutions
656	153	Operative builders, real estate	Operative builders, construction
739	738	Business services, NEC	Miscellaneous business services

1972 Code	1987 Code	1972 Industry Name	1987 Industry Name
082	083	Forest nurseries and tree seeds	Forest nurseries and gathering
084	083	Gathering of food products	of food
111	123	Anthracite mining	Same
121	122	Bituminous mining	Same
None	124	(Was included in 111 and 121)	Coal mining services
264	267	Converted paper and paperboard	} Converted paper and paperboard
266	267	Building paper and paperboard	}
303	306	Reclaimed rubber	Fabricated rubber, NEC
304	305	Rubber and plastic hose and belting	Gaskets, packing and sealing devices, and rubber
307	308	Miscellaneous plastic products	Plastic products, NEC
383	382	Optical instruments and lenses	Laboratory apparatus and analytical, optical
445	448	Local water transport	Water transport of passengers
446	449	Services incidental to water transport	Same
471	473	Freight forwarding	Arrangement of transportation of freight and cargo

Source: Authors' compilation.

MEASURING OCCUPATIONS

The EEOC provides the following occupational definitions for employers filling out the EEO-1 surveys. They also provide detailed census-based coding, but since these are not widely used by employers, they probably play a smaller role than these descriptions in helping employers fill out the surveys. Beginning in 2006, further distinctions between executives and lower-level managers were introduced. Our analyses end in 2005.

EEO-1 Occupational Definitions

Managers: Individuals who plan, direct, and formulate policies, set strategy, and provide the overall direction of enterprises/organizations for the development and delivery of products or services. Individuals who oversee and direct the delivery of products, services, or functions at group, regional, or divisional levels of organizations. Individuals who serve at functional, line of business segment, or branch levels and are responsible for directing and executing the day-to-day operational objectives of enterprises/organizations, conveying the directions of higher-level officials and managers to subordinate personnel and, in some instances, directly supervising the activities of exempt and non-exempt personnel. This category includes all managers from first-line managers to chief executives. It does not include supervisors who lack the responsibilities detailed above. Supervisors are to be counted with the occupation they supervise.

Professionals: Most jobs in this category require bachelor and graduate degrees and/or professional certification. In some instances, comparable experience may establish a person's qualifications. Examples of these kinds of positions include: accountants and auditors; airplane pilots and flight engineers; architects; artists; chemists; computer programmers; designers; dietitians; editors; engineers; lawyers; librarians; mathematical scientists; natural scientists; registered nurses; physical scientists; physicians and surgeons; social scientists; teachers; and surveyors.

Technicians: Jobs in this category include activities that require applied scientific skills, usually obtained by postsecondary education of varying lengths, depending on the particular occupation, recognizing that in some instances additional training, certification, or comparable experience is required. Examples of these types of positions include: drafters; emergency medical technicians; chemical technicians; and broadcast and sound engineering technicians.

Sales workers: These jobs include nonmanagerial activities that wholly and primarily involve direct sales. Examples of these types of positions include: advertising sales agents; insurance sales agents; real estate brokers and sales agents; wholesale sales representatives; securities, commodities, and financial services sales agents; telemarketers; demonstrators; retail salespersons; counter and rental clerks; and cashiers.

Clerical, administrative support workers: These jobs involve nonmanagerial tasks providing administrative and support assistance, primarily in office settings. Examples of these types of positions include: office and administrative support workers; bookkeeping; accounting and auditing clerks; cargo and freight agents; dispatchers; couriers; data entry keyers; computer operators; shipping, receiving, and traffic clerks; word processors and typists; proofreaders; desktop publishers; and general office clerks.

Craft workers: Most jobs in this category includes higher-skilled occupations in construction (building trades craft workers and their formal apprentices) and natural resource extraction workers. Examples of these types of positions include: boilermakers; brick and stone masons; carpenters; electricians; painters (both construction and maintenance); glaziers; pipe layers, plumbers, pipefitters, and steamfitters; plasterers; roofers; elevator installers; earth drillers; derrick operators; oil and gas rotary drill operators; and blasters and explosive workers. This category also includes occupations related to the installation, maintenance, and part replacement of equipment, machines, and tools, such as: automotive mechanics; aircraft mechanics; and electrical and electronic equipment repairers. This category also includes some production occupations that are distinguished by the high degree of skill and precision required to perform them, based on clearly defined task specifications, such as: millwrights; etchers and engravers; tool and die makers; and pattern makers.

Operatives: Most jobs in this category include intermediate-skilled occupations and include workers who operate machines or factory-related processing equipment. Most of these occupations do not usually require more than several months of training. Examples include: textile machine workers; laundry and dry cleaning workers; photographic process workers; weaving machine operators; electrical and electronic equipment assemblers; semiconductor processors; testers, graders, and sorters; bakers; and butchers and other meat, poultry, and fish processing workers. This category also includes occupations of generally intermediate-skill levels that are concerned with operating and controlling equipment to facilitate the movement of people or materials, such as: bridge and lock tenders; truck, bus, or taxi drivers; industrial truck and tractor (forklift) operators; parking lot attendants; sailors; conveyor operators; and hand packers and packagers.

Laborers and helpers: Jobs in this category include workers with more limited skills who require only brief training to perform tasks that require little or no independent judgment. Examples include: production and construction worker helpers; vehicle and equipment cleaners; laborers; freight, stock, and material movers; service station attendants; construction laborers; refuse and recyclable materials collectors; septic tank servicers; and sewer pipe cleaners.

Service workers: Jobs in this category include food service, cleaning service, personal service, and protective service activities. Skill may be acquired through formal training, job-related training, or direct experience. Examples of food service positions include: cooks; bartenders; and other food service workers. Examples of personal service positions include: medical assistants and other health care support positions; hairdressers; ushers; and transportation attendants. Examples of cleaning service positions include: cleaners; janitors; and porters. Examples of protective service positions include: transit and railroad police and firefighters; guards; private detectives and investigators.

A clear limitation of these data is that gender and race distributions are aggregated into occupational groups, not the actual jobs used to organize work and its rewards. There is a large substantive difference between a plant manager and a retail assistant manager. Not surprisingly, comparisons to available jobs within firm data show that when using EEO-1 estimates we underestimate segregation relative to its true level (Robinson et al. 2005). These analyses show that these underestimates are not systematically related to the true score, nor do they distort associations with important covariates like firm size or status composition. On the other hand, we see large residual variation across industries in estimates of segregation based on job-title versus occupational aggregations within establishments, reflecting variations in industry-based divisions of labor. This suggests that these data are more powerful for segregation-trend than segregation-level comparisons across industries and for segregation-level comparisons within industries.

ADJUSTING SEGREGATION MEASURES FOR OCCUPATIONAL-JOB MISMATCH

Following our prior work (Tomaskovic-Devey et al. 2006), we correct for occupational-job mismatch in three ways. First, since job titles proliferate with organizational size, all analyses of segregation control for the log of employment size. Second, since the source of measurement error is a mismatch between actual job distinctions and occupational distinctions, we make use of information on occupational heterogeneity—the dispersion of cases across the nine occupational categories—to adjust segregation measures upward (Gibbs and Martin 1962).[3]

When employees are found in fewer occupations, we reason that this represents a larger mismatch between job titles and occupational titles. Establishments with low occupational heterogeneity will also have low segregation because of an increased disjunction between the EEOC occupational categories and actual divisions of labor. An occupationally heterogeneous workplace might have substantial employment in all nine occupational categories. As such, it has an increased chance of displaying high levels of segregation because there are more positions to distribute people across. A firm with all employment in only one occupational category will have no observed segregation in the EEO-1 data. In the real world, however, this firm might make numerous job distinctions within that one occupational category and so have high segregation in practice. We directly adjust our measures of segregation to account for this source of measurement error.

We estimated group-specific (for example, white male–white female) regressions of segregation on the Gibbs-Martin index of occupational heterogeneity and find, as expected, that more occupationally heterogeneous workplaces have higher measured segregation. Since the maximum value on the Gibbs-Martin index is 89, we took the difference between the observed workplace level and 89 and multiplied by the estimated regression coefficient to adjust segregation measures upward to what they would have been if we had observed maximum heterogeneity. This still produces estimates of segregation that are lower than those observed with job title data. On the other hand, it reduces measurement error and makes between-industry comparisons more reasonable.

Our third approach to measurement error resulting from the use of occupational data is to remember that we are still underestimating actual job-level workplace segregation with these data. Thus, for analyses of specific management, professional, and craft occupations, we are missing some distinctions (for example, plant manager versus foreman) that may

be sources of gender- or race-based distinction. So here again, our occupational analyses understate real inequality.

STATISTICAL MODELING FOR
CHAPTERS 3 TO 6

The first section of the book analyzes trends in segregation and access to
desirable jobs in the context of national politics and regulatory structures
(chapters 3 to 5). To support these interpretations of trends, we estimate
statistical models to absorb the influence of other factors that may also be
changing over time and producing desegregation or even increased segregation in their own right.

In chapters 3 to 5, we focus on the national time trends in measures of
segregation and access to desirable occupations. In these chapters, we are
primarily interested in the influence of historical time on outcome measures, net of other sources of change. Prior research suggests that the two
most important other sources of compositional change in the economy
have to do with labor supply and industrial structure.

Women's, especially white women's, labor force participation expanded rapidly between 1966 and 1990. After 1980, new labor forces, especially Asian and Hispanic ones, expanded as well. The African American labor force did not change very much as a proportion of the labor
force, although, like Hispanics and Asian Americans, African Americans
are unevenly distributed across local labor markets. We control for both
shifts in labor supply and the uneven spatial distribution of various
groups by including in our model variables that measure labor force composition in local labor markets. These composition variables are computed
directly from the EEO-1 reports and are most literally the labor force of
EEOC-reporting private-sector firms.

We use commuting zones as our proxy for local labor markets. Commuting zones are aggregations of counties, not confined to state boundaries, and are calculated based on decennial Census surveys documenting
the distance that individuals travel to work from where they live (Tolbert
and Sizer 1996). Therefore, they describe local labor markets. We impose
1990 commuting zone boundaries on all years of data in these analyses for
consistency purposes. The use of stable geography allows us to compare
localities over time. Commuting zone composition does not change radically over time.

The industrial structure of the United States has changed dramatically
since the 1960s, with rapid rises in service-oriented businesses and a clear
decline in most manufacturing industries. Industries vary in a number of

ways that are likely to be consequential for segregation. Because industries vary in their average wage rates, some offer more desirable places of employment than others, and so the incentives for the current labor force to resist integration are increased. Variations in skill requirements makes some industries easier to integrate with new labor forces than others. Industries vary in their growth rates. We control for shifts in industry composition by including fixed effects for detailed, harmonized three-digit SIC codes in our models for estimating national and regional trends in chapters 3 to 6.

In the immediate aftermath of the Civil Rights Act, many employers thought that the primary purpose of the act was to improve the employment prospects of black men in the South. Outside the South, some states had enacted fair employment practice laws to limit racial discrimination prior to the Civil Rights Act. Thus, our models also control for region and FEP laws enacted prior to 1964.

Finally, there are some changes in the organizational composition of the sample that may influence segregation trends in their own right. The most important of these is the 1983 change in reporting requirements, which reduced the incidence of small workplaces mandated to report to the EEOC. Other changes in organizational composition include: changes in the relative incidence of firms that are covered by the OFCCP and so mandated to have affirmative action plans; changes in the incidence of very large firms that may be particularly visible to regulators and at risk for large class-action lawsuits; and changes in the structural nature of the workplace (for example, single-establishment firm, branch establishment, headquarters).

Thus, our baseline model for chapters 3 to 6 looks like this:

$Y_{et} = \beta_{0et} + \beta_1 Year + \beta_{2-10czt}$ Labor Force Composition (percentage of commuting zone white female, black male, black female, Hispanic female, Hispanic male, Asian female, Asian male, Native American female, Native American male) + β_{11et1} Logged Workplace Employment Size + β_{12-21e} Eight Census Regions (Middle Atlantic, South Atlantic, East South, West South, East North Central, West North Central, Pacific, Mountain, [New England reference]) + β_{22-23s} FEP(fair employment practice law before 1950, FEP law 1951 to 1963, [no law reference]) + β_{24ft} OFCCP + β_{25ft} Large Firm (more than 15,000 employees) + $\beta_{26-27ft}$ Organizational Type (headquarters, single establishment, [branch plant reference]) + α_{et} Detailed Industry (435 SIC codes) Fixed Effect + u_{et}

Where the βs are estimated in ordinary least squares (OLS), the fixed effect α is absorbed but not estimated, and the subscripts t, e, cz, s, f refer to time, establishment, commuting zone, state, and firm levels of measurement, respectively. These models are estimated within distinct historical eras to capture the changing institutional and political environments in which firms develop their human resource policies and practices. This basic estimation method was developed in two prior papers (Tomaskovic-Devey et al. 2006; Stainback and Tomaskovic-Devey 2009).

When we present simple national trends, we are presenting predicted values based on β_1, which is the estimate of the influence of time (Year) controlling for labor force, industry, and organizational composition of the economy. When we display trends for specific contexts (for example, region, OFCCP reporting, Plans for Progress firms, FEP states), we add year*context interactions to the basic model. In chapter 6, the estimates for labor market composition effects come from the baseline model. As such, they are estimates of the levels of segregation or occupational representation within each political era rather than time trends.

STATISTICAL MODELING FOR CHAPTER 7

Chapter 7 is concerned with three issues. The first is documenting industry-specific trends in desegregation. These estimates are simple descriptions with no statistical adjustments. We present these trends first by broad sector. We then report the within-era segregation and representation trends by two-digit industry (N = 58). We do not control for organizational characteristics because we conceptualize them as largely a function of industry. Thus, controlling for organizational characteristics might absorb some real industry effects. This model—also estimated within political eras—is:

$Y_{et} = \beta_{0et} + \beta_1$ Year $+ \beta_{2-10czt}$ Labor Force Composition (percentage of commuting zone white female, black male, black female, Hispanic female, Hispanic male, Asian female, Asian male, Native American female, Native American male) $+ \beta_{11-20e}$ Nine Census Regions (Middle Atlantic, South Atlantic, East South, West South, East North Central, West North Central, Pacific, Mountain, [New England reference]) $+ \beta_{11-63et}$ 52 Industries $+ \beta_{64-115et}$ Year*52 Industries $+ u_{et}$

We then focus our attention on the industry-specific slopes, documenting in particular their association within each political era with CPS-based estimates of average relative industry earnings, industry average educational levels, and era-specific employment growth rates. Thus, we focus on three potential mechanisms: social closure measured as access to high-wage industries, meritocracy as indexed by the density of employees with advanced educational certification, and the simple opportunity to diversify employment composition. These analyses utilize an industry-by-era panel data set. We use five eras to match the political eras in the rest of the book: 1966 to 1972, 1973 to 1980, 1981 to 1992, 1993 to 2000, and 2001 to 2005. By using eras, we were also able to use multiple CPS years to estimate industry measures or relative income, percentage of college degrees, and employment growth. Within each year, individual yearly income for full-time employees was measured as a ratio of average income for all individuals. Aggregate industry files were then produced, yielding the income in the industry relative to all incomes in the economy. The models were simple:

$$Y_{ie} = \beta_{0ie} + \beta_{1i} \text{ Relative Income} + \beta_{2ie} \text{ Percent Employees with College Degrees} + \beta3_{ie} \text{ Total Employment} + \alpha_i \text{ Industry Fixed Effect} + u_{ie},$$

where i represents industry and e represents era.

STATISTICAL MODELING FOR CHAPTER 8

In chapter 8, we focus on contemporary organizational change processes. We created a panel data set by taking a 1 percent sample of firms weighted by total employment size for every year between 1990 and 2005, collecting all firm IDs over this period and then selecting all establishments whose firm had been selected in any of the previous years. This produced a panel of 73,987 unique establishments and 477,840 establishment-year observations. The average establishment is in the panel for 6.5 years.

We conceptualize change as arising out of both the environment and internal organizational dynamics. In some models, we are interested in total change and use a one-year lag model. In others, we want to estimate only within workplace change and use a workplace fixed-effect model. This controls for stable characteristics of workplaces, including industry, region, organizational structure, and commuting zone.

Models look like:

$$Y_{et} = \beta_{0et} + \beta_{1et} \text{ Year} + \beta_{2et-1} \text{ Management Percent White Male} + \beta_{3-11et-1} \text{ Establishment Nonmanagerial Labor Force}$$

Composition (percentage of employees white male, white female, black male, black female, Hispanic female, Hispanic male, Asian female, Asian male, Native American female, Native American male [reference category is white male; for representation model it is the focal group]) + β_{12et-1} Establishment Size + β_{13ft-1} Headquarters Percent White Male + β_{14ft-1} Firm Complexity (scale of number of establishments, total firm size) + β_{15ft-1} OFCCP + β_{16ft-1} Large Firm (more than 15,000 employees) + α_e Establishment Fixed Effect + u_{et}

where e represents establishment and t represents year.

Estimated coefficients β indicate the influence of their associated measures with change in segregation or representation net of other variables in the model and any stable organizational characteristics. Since we do not measure actual human resource practices or the relative power of various work groups directly, the interpretation of effects needs to include the possibility that an estimated effect is mediated by changes in human resource practices and the relative power of status groups.

Notes

INTRODUCTION

1. This is not to say that white women, black men, and black women were equivalent in their cultural position in the early 1960s. White women received racial benefits in household and educational resources. As we document in this book, these benefits, as well as the benefit of whiteness, became increasingly important for white women in private-sector employment as the society retreated from institutionalized white male advantages in employment.

CHAPTER 1

1. It is important to recognize that this is a study of EEO change in the United States. The U.S. state has rarely attempted to change corporate behavior through administrative fiat and typically has preferred symbolic regulation. The strength of mimetic isomorphism in U.S. EEO diffusion may simply reflect the weakness of U.S. federal coercive mechanisms.
2. We identify whites by subtraction before 1980. See the methodological appendix for more detail.
3. Of course, some whites and blacks counted in the EEO-1 forms are immigrants, but they are a much smaller proportion, and so we use the designations "African American" and "European American."
4. The EEOC reporting forms collect occupational distributions (for example, managers, professionals, technical, sales, clerical, craft, operatives, laborer, and service) and so ignore within-occupation, job-title segregation. We treat this as a form of measurement error and adjust reported segregation measures upward to take into account observed occupational heterogeneity at the workplace level. The technical discussion behind this adjustment can be found in Tomaskovic-Devey et al. (2006) and in the methodological appendix. The index of dissimilarity is computed across occupations within establishments as follows:

$$D = \frac{1}{2} \sum_{oe=1 \text{ to } 9}^{N_{oe}} |P_{oex} - P_{oey}|$$

where P_{oex} and P_{oey} are the proportions of group x and y, respectively, within an occupation in an establishment.

5. The isolation index is computed across occupations within establishments as follows:

$$\sum_{i=1 \text{ to } 9}^{N} \left(\left(\frac{x_i}{X} \right) \times \left(\frac{x_i}{t_i} \right) \right)$$

where x is the number of the group in occupation i, X is the total number of group x in the workplace, and t_i is the number of workers in occupation i.

6. For example, we calculate craft representation as:

Craft Representation (CR) = $(((Xc_{it}/Tc_{it})/\Sigma (X_{ijt}/\Sigma T_{ijt})) - 1) \times 100$

where Xc_{it} is the number of status group members (for example, white males) in the craft occupational category within an establishment in a given year; Tc_{it} is the total number of individuals in the craft occupational category c within establishment i in a given year t; Σ ($Xijt$) is the total number of status group X members in commuting zone j in a given year t; and Σ (T_{ijt}) is the sum of employment across all establishments in commuting zone j for a specific year t.

7. Commuting zones are aggregations of counties; not confined to state boundaries, they are calculated based on decennial Census surveys that document the distance that individuals travel to work from where they live (Tolbert and Sizer 1996). Therefore, they describe local labor markets. We impose 1990 commuting zone boundaries on all years of data in these analyses for consistency purposes. The use of stable geography allows us to compare localities over time. Further discussion is in methodological appendix.

8. We do this by statistically controlling for a fixed effect for detailed three-digit industry in statistical models to estimate time trends net of shifts in industrial structure. Technical examples of this approach can be found in Tomaskovic-Devey et al. (2006) and Stainback and Tomaskovic-Devey (2009). Formal models are presented in the methodological appendix.

9. All groups dropped between 1980 and 1985, when reporting requirements by small firms were eased by the EEOC.

10. In the sharecropping system, tenants had long-term, sometimes intergenerational ties to specific land, which was typically owned by the same large

landholding family that had once controlled the slave-based plantation on the same land. Although formally free to leave the land, sharecropping was a system of debt peonage in which the sharecropper would get loans of money or materials from the landowner in order to produce a crop. The landowner, in return, would receive a share of the agricultural production, and it was not unusual that at the end of the season the tenant owed the landlord everything he had earned, or even more—and so indebted, he was not free to leave.

CHAPTER 2

1. In an earlier study, we showed that our estimates using the EEO-1 reports just for California for 1971 are quite comparable to Baron and Bielby's (1986) estimates using seven occupational groups within workplaces (see Robinson et al. 2005). This suggests that their sample of 290 establishments was fairly representative of the California economy. Of course, when segregation is nearly total across an entire economy, any sample will be reasonably accurate.
2. Kim Blankenship (1993) estimated that the law applied to two-thirds of white women and fewer than one-third of black women, but she wildly underestimated the degree of workplace sex segregation. We doubt that across the whole economy more than 5 percent of women worked in the same job with men in 1963.
3. Of course, because we do not actually observe change, these results may merely reflect some other geographic differences, perhaps in industrial composition.
4. We also looked at whether the largest federal contractors were distinguished in some way in terms of the other possible segregation comparisons. Black male–white female segregation was the only noteworthy comparison in that it was four points lower than other federal contractors among the PFP firms.

CHAPTER 3

1. Unfortunately, the EEOC no longer has the data available for 1967 to 1970. We use 1966, 1971, and 1972 data and interpolate the missing years.
2. Alfred Blumrosen (1970) provides a fascinating account of the first year of the EEOC as it struggled to translate a vague statutory mandate into the agenda of an activist organization. In his account, there was a certain amount of what he calls "administrative creativity" to expand the reach of the organization and to generate increased uncertainty for corporations as to what compliance would turn out to be.
3. This is not to say that Republicans were consistently liberal on racial issues. On the contrary, there was a consistent resistance to regulation of private

business of any kind, and both fair employment practice laws at the state level and the Civil Rights Act were opposed, sometimes actively and sometimes passively, by many Republican legislators, if not most of them. The Republican argument might be summarized as in favor of equal opportunity, against racism, but even more opposed to business regulation (see Chen 2009).

4. We do this in a modeling framework in which we statistically control for establishment size, detailed industry, and local labor market composition in a fixed-effects framework. We then use 1966 intercepts to anchor our trends and model coefficients for time and other variables (for example, OFCCP, large federal contractor) to produce trend lines. We do not estimate these models as within-firm or -workplace change, but rather as aggregate demographic change. This allows us to observe both within-workplace change and the desegregation associated with the birth of new workplaces and the death of old workplaces. Technical applications of this method can be found in Tomaskovic-Devey et al. (2006) and Stainback and Tomaskovic-Devey (2009).

5. We do not display the trends for white women and black women in skilled working-class jobs because they were only trivially represented across the entire period and show no significant trend.

CHAPTER 5

1. It is possible of course, perhaps even probable, that human resource management shifted from being the preserve of white men to one for white women because this was an increasingly marginalized job within the corporate management function. Both the decline of unionization and of social movement pressure for equal opportunity and affirmative action plausibly contributed to such a decline.

CHAPTER 6

1. This literature is much too large to examine here in any detail. To summarize all too briefly, there is evidence that discrimination against Hispanics is rising and that it is being produced directly by political leaders reacting to the perceived threat of immigration to native workers (Massey 2007). There is debate as to whether Hispanics will become a minority group equivalent to African Americans or bifurcate into assimilated light-skinned and discriminated-against dark-skinned groups. We think that the evidence points toward the latter outcome (see, for example, Frank, Akresh, and Lu 2010), but we also are aware that the future is not predictable with any certainty based simply on current tendencies. Asian immigration is also heterogeneous, with variations in both skin tone and class resources, although here the literature tends to

predict assimilation, with Asians, like the Irish, Jewish, and Polish before them, becoming socially "white" in the United States (Sakamoto et al. 2009).

CHAPTER 7

1. We estimate industry fixed-effects panel models across the whole period. The model controls for the stable aspects of the industry, focusing on how changes in employment opportunities, relative income, and credentialing are associated with changes in segregation and representation. We also estimated models separately for each period using both ordinary least squares and seemingly unrelated regression and found the same basic patterns.
2. We experimented with total industry employment as an alternative measure to growth rates, with the same null results.
3. The correlations ranged from a low of –0.64 for the representation of white men and black women in craft jobs to a high of –0.92 for the representation of white men and white women in both managerial and professional occupations.

CHAPTER 8

1. These estimates are produced through separate fixed-effects regression models for each trait. There is substantial overlap in industry and firm. Most firms operate in only one industry, so the empirical distinction between these two environmental contexts is much weaker than the theoretical distinction.
2. Charges of retaliation are equally common in EEOC complaints that are verified and those that are not (estimates provided by Professor Vincent Roscigno, The Ohio State University, personal communication, November 4, 2010).

CHAPTER 9

1. Amazingly, the OFCCP and EEOC have a long history of not cooperating with each other in fostering equal opportunity.

APPENDIX

1. Based on our discussions with EEOC representatives, no one recalls ever using this item; therefore, analysis files were standardized such that this item was deleted from all years of data.
2. In some years the EEO-1 files contain multiple codes. Later in the appendix we identify the variables in each EEO-1 reporting year file that correspond to these basic codes.

3. We use the Gibbs-Martin index of heterogeneity:

$$H = 100*[1 - ((\Sigma X_{O1-9}^2)/(\Sigma X_{O1-9})^2)]$$

where (ΣX_{O1-9}^2) is establishment employment in each occupation squared and then summed across all nine occupations and $(\Sigma X_{O1-9})^2$ is total establishment employment squared.

References

Abbott, Andrew. 1992. "What Do Cases Do? Some Notes on Activity in Sociological Analysis." In *What Is a Case: Exploring the Foundations of Social Inquiry*, edited by Charles C. Ragin and Howard S. Becker. New York: Cambridge University Press.

Abrahamson, Mark, and Lee Sigelman. 1987. "Occupational Sex Segregation in Metropolitan Areas." *American Sociological Review* 52(October): 588–97.

Alba, Richard. 2009. *Blurring the Color Line: The New Chance for a More Integrated America*. Cambridge, Mass.: Harvard University Press.

Allport, Gordon. 1955. *The Nature of Prejudice*. New York: Doubleday.

Anderson, Cynthia, and Donald Tomaskovic-Devey. 1995. "Patriarchal Pressures: An Exploration of Organizational Processes That Exacerbate and Erode Sex Earnings Inequality." *Work and Occupations* 22: 328–56.

Athey, Susan, Christopher Avery, and Peter Zemsky. 2000. "Mentoring and Diversity." *American Economic Review* 90(4, September): 765–86.

Avent-Holt, Dustin, and Donald Tomaskovic-Devey. 2010. "The Relational Basis of Inequality: Generic and Contingent Wage Distribution Processes." *Work and Occupations* 37: 162–93.

Baldi, Stephane, and Debra Branch McBrier. 1997. "Do the Determinants of Promotion Differ for Blacks and Whites? Evidence from the U.S. Labor Market." *Work and Occupations* 24: 478–97.

Baron, James N. 1991. "Organizational Evidence of Ascription in Labor Markets." In *New Approaches to Economic and Social Analyses of Discrimination*, edited by Richard Cornwall and Phanindra Wunnava. New York: Praeger.

Baron, James N., and William T. Bielby. 1980. "Bringing the Firms Back in: Stratification, Segmentation, and the Organization of Work." *American Sociological Review* 45: 737–65.

———. 1986. "The Proliferation of Job Titles in Organizations." *Administrative Science Quarterly* 31: 561–86.

Baron, James N., Michael T. Hannan, Greta Hsu, and Özgecan Koçak. 2007. "In the

345

Company of Women: Gender Inequality and the Logic of Bureaucracy in Start-Up Firms." *Work and Occupations* 34: 35–66.

Baron, James N., Brian S. Mittman, and Andrew E. Newman. 1991. "Targets of Opportunity: Organizational and Environmental Determinants of Gender Integration Within the California Civil Service, 1979–1985." *American Journal of Sociology* 96: 1362–1401.

Becker, Gary S. 1971. *The Economics of Discrimination*, 2nd ed. Chicago: University of Chicago Press. (Originally published in 1957.)

Becker, Henry Jay. 1980. "Racial Segregation Among Places of Employment." *Social Forces* 58: 761–76.

Beggs, John J. 1995. "The Institutional Environment: Implications for Race and Gender Inequality in the U.S. Labor Market." *American Sociological Review* 60: 612–33.

Beller, Andrea H. 1982. "Occupational Segregation by Sex: Determinants and Changes." *Journal of Human Resources* 17: 371–92.

Bergmann, Barbara. 1996. *In Defense of Affirmative Action*. New York: Basic Books.

Bielby, William T. 2000. "How to Minimize Workplace Gender and Racial Bias." *Contemporary Sociology* 29: 190–209.

Bielby, William T., and James N. Baron. 1986. "Men and Women at Work: Sex Segregation and Statistical Discrimination." *American Journal of Sociology* 91: 759–99.

Blalock, Hubert. 1967. *Toward a Theory of Minority Group Relations*. New York: Wiley.

Blankenship, Kim M. 1993. "Bringing Gender and Race in: U.S. Employment Discrimination Policy." *Gender and Society* 7(2): 204–26.

Blau, Francine D., Marianne Ferber, and Anne Winkler. 2006. *The Economics of Women, Men, and Work*. 5th ed. Englewood Cliffs, N.J.: Prentice-Hall.

Bloom, Jack M. 1987. *Class, Race, and the Civil Rights Movement: The Changing Political Economy of Southern Racism*. Bloomington: Indiana University Press.

Blumrosen, Alfred W. 1970. "Administrative Creativity: The First Year of the Equal Employment Opportunity Commission." *George Washington Law Review* 38: 694–751.

———. 1993. *Modern Law: The Law Transmission System and Equal Opportunity*. Madison: University of Wisconsin Press.

Bonilla-Silva, Eduardo. 1997. "Rethinking Racism: Toward a Structural Interpretation." *American Sociological Review* 62: 465–80.

Boris, Eileen, and Michael Honey. 1988. "Gender, Race, and the Policies of the Labor Department." *Monthly Labor Review* 111: 26–36.

Borjas, George J., Jeffrey Grogger, and Gordon H. Hanson. 2010. "Immigration and the Economic Status of African-American Men." *Economica* 77: 255–82.

Braestrup, Peter. 1961. "12 Concerns Sign Anti-Bias Vows: More Defense Contractors Act in White House Rite." *New York Times*, November 25, p. 20.

Branch, Enobong Hannah. 2011. *Opportunity Denied: Limiting Black Women to Devalued Work*. New Brunswick, N.J.: Rutgers University Press.

Brauer, Carl M. 1983. "Women Activists, Southern Conservatives, and the Prohibition of Sex Discrimination in Title VII of the 1964 Civil Rights Act." *Journal of Southern History* 49(1, February): 37–56.

Bridges, William P. 1982. "The Sexual Segregation of Occupations: Theories of Labor Stratification in Industry." *American Journal of Sociology* 88: 270–95.

Browne, Irene, ed. 1999. *Latinas and African American Women at Work: Race, Gender, and Economic Inequality*. New York: Russell Sage Foundation.

Browne, Irene, and Ivy Kennelly. 1999. "Stereotypes and Realities: Black Women in the Labor Market." In *Latinas and African American Women at Work: Race, Gender, and Economic Inequality*, edited by Irene Browne. New York: Russell Sage Foundation.

Bryner, Gary. 1981. "Congress, Courts, and Agencies: Equal Employment and the Limits of Policy Implementation." *Political Science Quarterly* 96: 411–30.

Burk, Robert F. 1984. "Dwight D. Eisenhower and Civil Rights Conservatism." Proceedings of the third annual presidential conference, "Dwight D. Eisenhower: Soldier, President, Statesman." Hofstra University, Hempstead, N.Y. (March 29–31).

Burstein, Paul. 1979. "Equal Employment Opportunity Legislation and the Incomes of Women and Nonwhites." *American Sociological Review* 44: 367–91.

———. 1985. *Discrimination, Jobs, and Politics: The Struggle for Equal Employment Opportunity in the U.S. Since the New Deal*. Chicago: University of Chicago Press.

———. 1998. *Discrimination, Jobs, and Politics: The Struggle for Equal Employment Opportunity in the United States Since the New Deal*. With a new introduction. Chicago: University of Chicago Press. (Originally published in 1985.)

Cardoso, Ana Rute, and Rudolf Winter-Ebmer. 2010. "Female-Led Firms and Gender Wage Policies." *Industrial and Labor Relations Review* 64(1): 143–63.

Carmines, Edward G., and Edward A. Stimson. 1989. *Issue Evolution: Race and the Transformation of American Politics*. Princeton, N.J.: Princeton University Press.

Carrington, William J., and Kenneth R. Troske. 1995. "Gender Segregation in Small Firms." *Journal of Human Resources* 30(3): 505–33.

———. 1998. "Sex Segregation in U.S. Manufacturing." *Industrial and Labor Relations Review* 51: 445–64.

Cartwright, Bliss, and Patrick Ronald Edwards. 2002. "Sex Segregation Measured by Job Groups and Industry." Paper presented to the annual meeting of the American Sociological Association. Chicago (August).

Castilla, Emilio. 2008. "Gender, Race, and Meritocracy in Organizational Careers." *American Journal of Sociology* 113: 1479–1526.

Castilla, Emilio, and Steve Benard. 2010. "The Paradox of Meritocracy in Organizations." *Administrative Science Quarterly* 55(4): 543–76.

Catanzarite, Lisa. 2000. "Brown-Collar Jobs: Occupational Segregation and Earnings of Recent-Immigrant Latinos." *Sociological Perspectives* 43(1): 45–75.

Charles, Maria, and David B. Grusky. 2004. *Occupational Ghettos: The Worldwide Segregation of Women from Men.* Stanford, Calif.: Stanford University Press.

Chay, Kenneth Y. 1998. "The Impact of Federal Civil Rights Policy on Black Economic Progress: Evidence from the Equal Employment Opportunity Act of 1972." *ILR Review* 51: 608–32.

Chen, Anthony S. 2009. *The Fifth Freedom: Jobs, Politics, and Civil Rights in the United States, 1941–1971.* Princeton, N.J.: Princeton University Press.

Chused, Richard H. 1988. "The Hiring and Retention of Minorities and Women on American Law School Faculties." *University of Pennsylvania Law Review* 137(2, December): 537–69.

Cockburn, Cynthia. 1991. *In the Way of Women: Men's Resistance to Sex Equality in Organizations.* Ithaca, N.Y.: ILR Press.

Cohen, Lisa E., Joseph P. Broschak, and Heather Haveman. 1998. "And Then There Were More? The Effect of Organizational Sex Composition on the Hiring and Promotion of Managers." *American Sociological Review* 63: 711–27.

Cohen, Philip N. 1998. "Black Concentration Effects on Black-White and Gender Inequality: Multilevel Analysis for U.S. Metropolitan Areas." *Social Forces* 77: 207–29.

Cohen, Philip N., and Matt L. Huffman. 2003. "Occupational Segregation and the Devaluation of Women's Work Across U.S. Labor Markets." *Social Forces* 81(2): 881–907.

———. 2007a. "Working for the Woman? Female Managers and the Gender Wage Gap." *American Sociological Review* 72(2): 681–704.

———. 2007b. "Black Underrepresentation in Management Across U.S. Labor Markets." *Annals of the American Association of Political and Social Sciences* 609: 181–99.

Collins, Sharon M. 1997. *Black Corporate Executives: The Making and Breaking of a Black Middle Class.* Philadelphia: Temple University Press.

Collins, William. 2000. "African-American Economic Mobility in the 1940s: A Portrait from the Palmer Survey." *Journal of Economic History* 60: 756–81.

———. 2001. "Race, Roosevelt, and Wartime Production: Fair Employment in World War II Labor Markets." *American Economic Review* 91(1, March): 272–86.

Correll, Shelley J., Stephen Benard, and In Paik. 2007. "Getting a Job: Is There a Motherhood Penalty?" *American Journal of Sociology* 112: 1297–1338.

Cotter, David A., Joan Hermsen, and Reeve Vanneman. 2004. *Gender Inequality at Work.* New York: Russell Sage Foundation.

Crenshaw, Kimberle. 1989. "Demarginalizing the Intersection of Race and Sex: A Black Feminist Critique of Antidiscrimination Doctrine, Feminist Theory, and Antiracist Politics." *University of Chicago Legal Forum* 1989: 139–67.

Cunningham, William A., John B. Nezlek, and Mahzarin R. Banaji. 2004. "Implicit and Explicit Ethnocentrism: Revisiting Ideologies of Prejudice." *Personality and Social Psychology Bulletin* 30: 1332–46.

Dahl, Robert A. 1967. *Pluralist Democracy in the United States: Conflict and Consent.* Chicago: Rand McNally.

Davis, Kingsley and Wilbert E. Moore. 1945. "Some Principle of Stratification." *American Sociological Review* 10: 242–49.

Deitch, Cynthia. 1993. "Gender, Race, and Class Politics and the Inclusion of Women in Title VII of the 1964 Civil Rights Act." *Gender and Society* 7: 183–203.

Dencker, John. 2008. "Corporate Restructuring and Sex Differences in Managerial Promotion." *American Sociological Review* 73: 455–76.

DiMaggio, Paul J., and Walter W. Powell. 1983. "The Iron Cage Revisited: Institutional Isomorphism and Collective Rationality in Organizational Fields." *American Sociological Review* 48: 147–60.

DiPrete, Thomas A. 1989. *The Bureaucratic Labor Market: The Case of the Federal Civil Service.* New York: Plenum Press.

DiTomaso, Nancy, Corinne Post, and Rochelle Parks-Yancy. 2007. "Workforce Diversity and Inequality: Power, Status, and Numbers." *Annual Review of Sociology* 33: 473–501.

Dobbin, Frank. 2009. *Inventing Equal Opportunity.* Princeton, N.J.: Princeton University Press.

Dobbin, Frank, and Alexandra Kalev. 2008. "'You Can't Make Me': Resistance to Corporate Diversity Training." Working paper. Cambridge, Mass.: Harvard University, Department of Sociology.

Dobbin, Frank, Soohan Koo, and Alexandra Kalev. 2011. "'You Can't Always Get What You Need': Organizational Determinants of Diversity Programs." *American Sociological Review* 76: 386–411.

Dobbin, Frank, Daniel Schrage, and Alexandra Kalev. 2010. "'Someone to Watch over Me': Coupling, Decoupling, and Unintended Consequences in Corporate Equal Opportunity." Working paper, Harvard University.

Dobbin, Frank, and John R. Sutton. 1998. "The Strength of a Weak State: The Rights Revolution and the Rise of Human Resources Management Division." *American Journal of Sociology* 104: 441–76.

Dobbin, Frank, John R. Sutton, John W. Meyer, and Richard Scott. 1993. "Equal Opportunity Law and the Construction of Internal Labor Markets." *American Journal of Sociology* 99: 396–427.

Donohue, John J., and James Heckman. 1991. "Continuous Versus Episodic Change: The Impact of Civil Rights Policy on the Economic Status of Blacks." *Journal of Economic Literature* 29(4): 1603–43.

Donohue, John J., and Peter Siegelman. 1991. "The Changing Nature of Employment Discrimination Litigation." *Stanford Law Review* 43: 983–1033.

Dulebohn, James H., Gerald R. Ferris, and James T. Stodd. 1995. "The History and

Evolution of Human Resource Management." In *Handbook of Human Resource Management*, edited by Gerald R. Ferris, Sherman D. Rosen, and Darold T. Barnum. Cambridge, Mass.: Blackwell.

duRivage, Virginia, ed. 1992. *New Policies for the Part-time and Contingent Workforce.* Armonk, N.Y.: M. E. Sharpe.

Edelman, Lauren B. 1990. "Legal Environments and Organizational Governance: The Expansion of Due Process in the American Workplace." *American Journal of Sociology* 95(6): 1401–40.

———. 1992. "Legal Ambiguity and Symbolic Structures: Organizational Mediation of Civil Rights Law." *American Journal of Sociology* 97: 1531–76.

Edelman, Lauren B., Christopher Uggen, and Howard S. Erlanger. 1999. "The Endogeneity of Legal Regulations: Grievance Procedures as Rational Myth." *American Journal of Sociology* 105: 406–54.

Edwards, Mark E.1996. "Pregnancy Discrimination Litigation: Legal Erosion of Capitalist Ideology Under Equal Employment Opportunity Law." *Social Forces* 75: 247–68.

Edwards, Richard C. 1979. *Contested Terrain: The Transformation of the Workplace in the Twentieth Century.* New York: Basic Books.

Eisenberg, Susan. 1999. *We'll Call You If We Need You: Experiences of Women Working Construction.* Ithaca, N.Y.: Cornell University Press.

Eisenhower, Dwight D. 1957. "Radio and Television Address to the American People on the Situation in Little Rock" as reprinted in Steven F. Lawson and Charles Payne, *Debating the Civil Rights Movement, 1945–1968.* Lanham, Md.: Rowan & Littlefield Publishers, Inc., 1998, 60–64.

Elliott, James R., and Ryan A. Smith. 2001. "Ethnic Matching of Supervisors to Subordinate Work Groups: Findings on 'Bottom-Up' Ascription and Social Closure." *Social Problems* 48: 258–76.

———. 2004. "Race, Gender, and Workplace Power." *American Sociological Review* 69: 365–86.

Elvira, Marta M., and Mary E. Graham. 2002. "Not Just a Formality: Pay Systems and Sex-Related Earnings Effects." *Organization Science* 13: 601–17.

Ely, Robin J. 1994. "The Effects of Organizational Demographics and Social Identity on Relationships Among Professional Women." *Administrative Science Quarterly* 39: 203–38.

England, Paula. 2010. "The Gender Revolution: Uneven and Stalled." *Gender and Society* 24: 149–66.

Equal Employment Opportunity Commission. 1967. *Job Patterns for Minorities and Women in Private Industry, 1966.* Washington: U.S. Government Printing Office.

———. 1981. *Job Patterns for Minorities and Women in Private Industry, 1980.* Washington: U.S. Government Printing Office.

———. 2012a. "Sexual Harassment Statistics." Available at: http://www.eeoc.gov/eeoc/statistics/enforcement/sexual_harassment.cfm (accessed April 1, 2012).

———. 2012b. "Charge Statistics." Available at: http://www.eeoc.gov/eeoc/sta tistics/enforcement/charges.cfm (accessed April 1, 2012).

———. Various years. *EEO-1 Survey Reports* [Machine Readable Dataset]. Washington, D.C.: EEOC.

Ferree, Myra Marx, and Beth Hess. 1985. *Controversy and Coalition: The New Feminist Movement.* New York: Routledge.

Fossett, Mark A., Omer R. Galle, and William R. Kelly. 1986. "Racial Occupational Inequality, 1940–1980: National and Regional Trends." *American Sociological Review* 51: 421–429.

Frank, Reanne, Ilana Redstone Akresh, and Bo Lu. 2010. "Latino Immigrants and the U.S. Racial Order: How and Where Do They Fit In?" *American Sociological Review* 75: 378–401.

Garfinkel, Herbert. 1969. *When Negroes March: The March on Washington Movement in the Organizational Politics for FEPC.* New York: Atheneum.

Gibbs, Jack P., and William T. Martin. 1962. "Urbanization, Technology, and the Division of Labor." *American Sociology Review* 27: 667–77.

Giuliano, Laura, Jonathan Leonard, and David I. Levine. 2006. "Do Race, Gender, and Age Differences Affect Manager-Employee Relations? An Analysis of Quits, Dismissals, and Promotions at a Large Retail Firm." Working paper. Berkeley, Calif.: Institute for Research on Labor and Employment.

Goldin, Claudia. 1990. *Understanding the Gender Gap: An Economic History of American Women.* Oxford: Oxford University Press.

Goldman, Barry M., Barbara A. Gutek, Jordan H. Stein, and Kyle Lewis. 2006. "Employment Discrimination in Organizations: Antecedents and Consequences." *Journal of Management* 32: 786–830.

Gorman, Elizabeth H. 2005. "Gender Stereotypes, Same-Gender Preferences, and Organizational Variation in the Hiring of Women: Evidence from Law Firms." *American Sociological Review* 70(4): 702–28.

Graham, Mary E., and Julie L. Hotchkiss. 2009. "A More Proactive Approach to Addressing Gender-Related Employment Disparities in the United States." *Gender in Management* 24: 577–95.

Guthrie, Douglas A., and Lois M. Roth. 1999. "The State, Courts, and Equal Opportunities for Female CEOs in U.S. Organizations: Specifying Institutional Mechanisms." *Social Forces* 78: 511–42.

Hakim, Catherine. 2000. *Work-Lifestyle Choices in the Twenty-First Century: Preference Theory.* Oxford: Oxford University Press.

Harrison, Cynthia. 1988. *On Account of Sex: The Politics of Women's Issues 1945–1968.* Berkeley: University of California Press.

Harvey, David. 2005. *A Brief History of Neoliberalism.* New York: Oxford University Press.

Haveman, Heather A., Joseph P. Broschak, and Lisa E. Cohen. 2009. "Good Times, Bad Times: The Effects of Organizational Dynamics on the Careers of Male and

Female Managers." In *Research in the Sociology of Work*, edited by Nina Bandelj. Bingley, U.K.: Emerald Publishing Group.

Heckman, James J. 1976. "Simultaneous Equation Models with Continuous and Discrete Endogenous Variables and Structural Shifts." In *Studies in Non-Linear Estimation*, edited by Stephen M. Goldfeld and Richard E. Quandt. Cambridge, Mass.: Ballinger.

Heilmann, Madeline E., and Richard F. Martell. 1986. "Exposure to Successful Women: Antidote to Sex Discrimination in Applicant Screening Decisions?" *Organizational Behavior and Human Decision Processes* 37: 376–90.

Hirsh, Elizabeth. 2008. "Settling for Less? The Organizational Determinants of Discrimination-Charge Outcomes." *Law and Society Review* 42: 239–74.

Hirsh, C. Elizabeth. 2009. "The Strength of Weak Enforcement: The Impact of Discrimination Charges on Sex and Race Segregation in the Workplace." *American Sociological Review* 74(2): 245–71.

Hirsh, C. Elizabeth, and Youngjoo Cha. 2010. "For Law or Markets? Discrimination Lawsuits, Market Performance, and Managerial Diversity." Working paper. Vancouver: University of British Columbia, Department of Sociology.

Hirsh, C. Elizabeth, and Julie A. Kmec. 2009. "Human Resource Structures: Reducing Discrimination or Raising Rights Awareness?" *Industrial Relations* 48: 512–32.

Hirsh, C. Elizabeth, and Christopher J. Lyons. 2010. "Perceiving Discrimination on the Job: Legal Consciousness, Workplace Context, and the Construction of Race Discrimination." *Law and Society Review* 44: 269–98.

Holzer, Harry. 1996. *What Employers Want: Job Prospects for Less-Educated Workers.* New York: Russell Sage Foundation.

Huffman, Matt. 1995. "Organizations, Internal Labor Market Policies, and Gender Inequality in Workplace Supervisory Authority." *Sociological Perspectives* 38: 381–97.

Huffman, Matt L., and Philip N. Cohen, 2004. "Occupational Segregation and the Gender Gap in Workplace Authority: National Versus Local Labor Markets." *Sociological Forum* 19: 121–47.

Huffman, Matt L., Philip N. Cohen, and Jessica Pearlman. 2010. "Engendering Change: Organizational Dynamics and Workplace Gender Segregation, 1975–2005." *Administrative Science Quarterly* 55(2): 255–77.

Hultin, Mia, and Ryszard Szulkin. 1999. "Wages and Unequal Access to Organizational Power." *Administrative Science Quarterly* 44(3): 453–72.

———. 2003. "Mechanisms of Inequality: Unequal Access to Organizational Power and the Gender Wage Gap." *European Sociological Review* 19(2): 143–59.

IPUMS-CPS. Various years. Integrated Public Use Microdata Series, Current Population Survey. [Machine-readable database]. University of Minnesota.

Jackson, Robert M. 1998. *Destined for Equality: The Inevitable Rise of Women's Status.* Cambridge, Mass.: Harvard University Press.

Jacobs, Jerry. 1995. "Gender and Academic Specialties: Trends Among Recipients of College Degrees in the 1980s." *Sociology of Education* 68: 81–98.

James, Erika Hayes, and Lynn Perry Wooten. 2006. "Diversity Crises: How Firms Manage Discrimination Lawsuits." *Academy of Management Journal* 49(6): 1103–18.

Jamieson, Kathleen Hall. 1992. *Dirty Politics: Deception, Distraction, and Democracy.* New York: Oxford University Press.

Jenkins, J. Craig, David Jacobs, and Jon Agnone. 2003. "Political Opportunities and African-American Protest, 1948–1997." *American Journal of Sociology* 109: 277–303.

Kalev, Alexandra. 2009. "Cracking the Glass Cages? Restructuring and Ascriptive Inequality at Work." *American Journal of Sociology* 114: 1591–1643.

———. 2010. "How You Downsize Is Who You Downsize." Working paper. Tel Aviv: Tel Aviv University.

Kalev, Alexandra, and Frank Dobbin. 2006. "Enforcement of Civil Rights Law in Private Workplaces: The Effects of Compliance Reviews and Lawsuits over Time." *Law and Social Inquiry* 31: 855–903.

Kalev, Alexandra, Frank Dobbin, and Erin Kelly. 2006. "Best Practices or Best Guesses? Assessing the Efficacy of Corporate Affirmative Action and Diversity Policies." *American Sociological Review* 71: 589–617.

Kanter, Rosabeth Moss. 1977. *Men and Women of the Corporation.* New York: Basic Books.

Kaufman, Bruce E. 2008. *Managing the Human Factor: The Early Years of Human Resource Management in American Industry.* Ithaca, N.Y.: ILR Press.

Kelly, Erin L., and Frank Dobbin. 1999. "Civil Rights Law at Work: Sex Discrimination and the Rise of Maternity Leave Policies." *American Journal of Sociology* 105: 455–92.

Kelly, Erin L., Alexandra Kalev, and Frank Dobbin. 2010. "Corporate Family Leave Policies, the Family and Medical Leave Act, and Women's Occupational Standing in U.S. Firms." Working paper. Minneapolis: University of Minnesota, Department of Sociology.

Kesselman, Louis C. 1948. *The Social Politics of FEPC: A Study in Reform Pressure Movements.* Chapel Hill, N.C.: University of North Carolina Press.

Kessler, Ronald C., K. D. Mickelson, and David R. Williams. 1999. "The Prevalence, Distribution, and Mental Health Correlates of Perceived Discrimination in the United States." *Journal of Health and Social Behavior* 40: 208–30.

Kim, ChangHwan, and Arthur Sakamoto. 2010. "Have Asian American Men Achieved Labor Market Parity with White Men?" *American Sociological Review* 75: 934–57.

King, Mary C. 1992. "Occupational Segregation by Race and Sex: 1940–1988." *Monthly Labor Review* 115(4): 30–37.

King, Miriam, Steven Ruggles, J. Trent Alexander, Sarah Flood, Katie Genadek,

Matthew B. Schroeder, Brandon Trampe, and Rebecca Vick. 2010. *Integrated Public Use Microdata Series, Current Population Survey*: Version 3.0. [Machine-readable database]. Minneapolis: University of Minnesota.

Kirschenman, Joleen, and Kathryn M. Neckerman. 1991. "We'd Love to Hire Them, But . . . ': The Meaning of Race for Employers." In *The Urban Underclass*, edited by Christopher Jencks and Paul E. Peterson. Washington, D.C.: Brookings Institution.

Kmec, Julie A. 2001. "Minority Job Concentration and Wages." *Social Problems* 50: 38–59.

———. 2005. "Setting Occupational Sex Segregation in Motion: Demand-Side Explanations of Sex Traditional Employment." *Work and Occupations* 32: 322–54.

Konrad, Alison M., and Frank Linnehan. 1995. "Formalized HRM Structure: Coordinating Equal Employment Opportunity or Concealing Organizational Practice?" *Academy of Management Journal* 38: 787–820.

Koo, Soohan. 2010. "Do Employment Protections Diffuse Temporary Hires? Evidence from the Adoption of Temporary Help Agencies in U.S. Organizations, 1971–2000." Working paper. Cambridge, Mass.: Harvard University, Department of Sociology.

Kurtulus, Fidan, and Donald Tomaskovic-Devey. 2012. "Do Women Top Managers Help Women Advance? A Panel Study Using EEO-1 Records." *Annals of the American Academy of Political and Social Science* 639: 173–97.

Landes, William M. 1968. "The Economics of Fair Employment Laws." *Journal of Political Economy* 76: 507–52.

Lee, Marlene A., Mark Mathar, and Hira Ron. 2008. "U.S. Labor Force Trends." *Population Bulletin* 63: 3–16.

Leonard, Jonathan S. 1984a. "Employment and Occupational Advance Under Affirmative Action." *Review of Economics and Statistics* 66: 377–85.

———. 1984b. "Anti-discrimination or Reverse Discrimination: The Impact of Changing Demographics, Title VII, and Affirmative Action on Productivity." *Journal of Human Resources* 19(Spring): 145–74.

———. 1989. "Women and Affirmative-Action." *Journal of Economic Perspectives* 3: 61–75.

———. 1990. "The Impact of Affirmative Action Regulation and Equal Employment Opportunity Law on Black Employment." *Journal of Economic Perspectives* 4: 47–63.

Lieberson, Stanley. 1980. *A Piece of the Pie: Black and White Immigrants Since 1880*. Berkeley: University of California Press.

Light, Ryan, Vincent J. Roscigno, and Alexandra Kalev. 2011. "Discrimination and Interpretation at Work." *Annals of the American Academy of Political and Social Sciences* 634(1): 39–59.

Lucas, Samuel Roundfield. 2008. *Theorizing Discrimination in an Era of Contested*

Prejudice: Discrimination in the United States. Philadelphia: Temple University Press.

Lydon, Christopher. 1976a. "Carter Defends All White Areas; Says Government Shouldn't Try to End 'Ethnic Purity' of Some Neighborhoods." *New York Times*, April 7, p. 85.

———. 1976b. "Carter Issues an Apology on 'Ethnic Purity' Phrase; But He Says He Would Not 'Use Federal Force' to Change a Neighborhood; Some See Setback to Campaign; Carter Issues an Apology for 'Ethnic Purity' Term." *New York Times*, April 9, p. 1.

Martell, Richard F., David M. Lane, and Cynthia Emrich. 1996. "Male-Female Differences: A Computer Simulation." *American Psychologist* 51: 157–58.

Martin, Patricia Yancey. 2004. "Gender as a Social Institution." *Social Forces* 82: 1249–73.

Massey, Douglas. 2007. *Categorically Unequal: The American Stratification System.* New York: Russell Sage Foundation.

McAdam, Douglas. 1982. *Political Process and the Development of Black Insurgency, 1930–1970.* Chicago: University of Chicago Press.

McCall, Leslie. 2001. *Complex Inequality: Gender, Class, and Race in the New Economy.* New York: Routledge.

McDonald, Steve. "Right Place, Right Time: Serendipity and Informal Job Matching." *Socio-Economic Review* 8(2): 307–31.

McDonald, Steve, Nan Lin, and Dan Ao. 2009. "Networks of Opportunity: Gender, Race and Unsolicited Job Leads." *Social Problems* 56(3): 385–402.

McTague, Tricia, Kevin Stainback, and Donald Tomaskovic-Devey. 2009. "An Organizational Approach to Understanding Sex and Race Segregation in U.S. Workplaces." *Social Forces* 87: 1499–1527.

Mendelberg, Tali. 1997. "Executing Hortons: Racial Crime in the 1988 Presidential Campaign." *Public Opinion Quarterly* 61: 134–57.

Meyer, John W., and Brian Rowan. 1977. "Institutionalized Organizations: Formal Structure as Myth and Ceremony." *American Journal of Sociology* 83: 340–63.

Milkman, Ruth. 1987. *Gender at Work: The Dynamics of Job Segregation by Sex During World War II.* Champaign: University of Illinois Press.

Miller, Seymour M., and Donald Tomaskovic-Devey. 1983. *Recapitalizing America: Alternatives to the Corporate Distortion of National Policy.* New York: Routledge & Kegan Paul.

Minkoff, Debra C. 1997. "The Sequencing of Social Movements." *American Sociological Review* 62(5): 779–99

Mong, Sherry, and Vincent J. Roscigno. 2010. "African American Men and the Experience of Employment Discrimination." *Qualitative Sociology* 33: 1–21.

Moreno, Paul D. 1997. *From Direct Action to Affirmative Action: Fair Employment Law and Policy in America, 1933–1972.* Baton Rouge: Louisiana State University Press.

Morris, Aldon D. 1984. *Origins of the Civil Rights Movements*. New York: Free Press.
————. 1999. "A Retrospective on the Civil Rights Movement: Political and Intellectual Landmarks." *Annual Review of Sociology* 25: 517–39.

Moss, Phillip, and Chris Tilly. 1996. *Stories Employers Tell: Race, Skill, and Hiring in America*. New York: Russell Sage Foundation.

Murphy, Raymond. 1988. *Social Closure: The Theory of Monopolization and Exclusion*. New York: Oxford University Press.

Nelson, Robert L., Ellen C. Berry, and Laura Beth Nielsen. 2008. "Divergent Paths: Conflicting Conceptions of Employment Discrimination in Law and Social Sciences." *Annual Review of Law and Social Science* 4: 103–22.

Nielsen, Laura Beth, and Robert L. Nelson. 2005. "Rights Realized? An Empirical Analysis of Employment Discrimination Litigation as a Claiming System." *Wisconsin Law Review* 2005: 63–711.

Nixon, Richard M. 1968. "Acceptance Speech, Republican Nomination for President." Available at: http://www.pbs.org/wgbh/americanexperience/features/primary-resources/nixon-accept68/ (accessed April 19, 2012).

Norgren, Paul H., and Samuel E. Hill. 1964. *Toward Fair Employment*. New York: Columbia University Press.

Norton, Michael, and Samuel R. Sommers. 2011. "Whites See Racism as a Zero-Sum Game That They Are Now Losing." *Perspectives on Psychological Science* 6: 215–18.

Nosek, Brian A., Frederick L. Smyth, Jeffrey J. Hansen, Thierry Devos, Nicole M. Lindner, Kate A. Ranganath, Colin Tucker Smith, Kristina R. Olson, Dolly Chugh, Anthony G. Greenwald, and Mahzarin R. Banaji. 2007. "Pervasiveness and Correlates of Implicit Attitudes and Stereotypes." *European Review of Social Psychology* 18: 36–88.

Olzak, Susan. 1994. *The Dynamics of Ethnic Competition*. Stanford, Calif.: Stanford University Press.

O'Reilly, Kenneth. 1995. *Nixon's Piano: Presidents and Racial Politics from Washington to Clinton*. New York: Free Press.

Ortiz, Susan Y., and Vincent Roscigno. 2009. "Discrimination, Women, and Work: Dimensions and Variations by Race and Class." *Sociological Quarterly* 50: 336–59.

Padavic, Irene. 1991. "The Re-creation of Gender in a Male Workplace." *Symbolic Interaction* 14: 279–94.

Pager, Devah. 2003. "The Mark of a Criminal Record." *American Journal of Sociology* 108: 937–75.

Pager, Devah, and Hana Shepherd. 2008. "The Sociology of Racial Discrimination in Employment, Housing, Credit, and Consumer Markets." *Annual Review of Sociology* 34: 181–209.

Parkin, Frank. 1979. *Marxism and Class Theory: A Bourgeois Critique*. New York: Columbia University Press.

Pedriana, Nicholas, and Amanda Abraham. 2006. "'Now You See Them, Now You Don't': The Legal Field and Newspaper Desegregation of Sex-Segregated Help Wanted Ads, 1965–1975." *Law and Social Inquiry* 31: 905–38.

Pedriana, Nicholas, and Robin Stryker. 2004. "The Strength of a Weak Agency: Enforcement of Title VII of the 1964 Civil Rights Act and the Expansion of State Capacity, 1965–1971." *American Journal of Sociology* 110: 709–60.

Penner, Andrew M., and Harold J. Toro-Tulla. 2010. "Women in Power and Gender Wage Inequality: The Case of Small Businesses." In *Research in the Sociology of Work: Gender and Sexuality in the Workplace*, edited by Christine L. Williams and Kirsten Dellinger. Bingley, U.K.: Emerald.

Penner, Andrew M., Harold J. Toro-Tulla, and Matt L. Huffman. 2010. "Do Women Managers Ameliorate Gender Differences in Wages? Evidence from a Large Grocery Retailer." Paper presented to the meeting of the International Sociological Association Research Committee on Social Stratification and Mobility (RC28), Haifa, Israel (May).

Petersen, Trond, and Laurie Morgan. 1995. "Separate and Unequal: Occupation-Establishment Sex Segregation and the Gender Wage Gap." *American Journal of Sociology* 101: 329–65.

Petersen, Trond, and Ishak Saporta. 2004. "The Opportunity Structure for Discrimination." *American Journal of Sociology* 109: 852–901.

Pettigrew, Thomas F., and Linda R. Tropp. 2006. "A Meta-analytic Test of Intergroup Contact Theory." *Journal of Personality and Social Psychology* 90: 751–83.

Pfeffer, Jeffrey, and Yinon Cohen. 1984. "Determinants of Internal Labor Markets in Organizations." *Administrative Science Quarterly* 29: 550–72.

Pfeffer, Jeffrey, and Gerald R. Salancik. 1978. *The External Control of Organizations.* New York: Harper & Row.

Pincus, Fred L. 2003. *Reverse Discrimination: Dismantling the Myth.* Boulder, Colo.: Lynne Rienner.

Piven, Frances F., and Richard Cloward. 1977. *Poor People's Movements: Why They Succeed, How They Fail.* New York: Pantheon.

Quillian, Lincoln. 1996. "Group Threat and Regional Change in Attitudes Toward African-Americans." *American Journal of Sociology* 102: 816–60.

Reed, Merl E. 1980. "FEPC and the Federal Agencies in the South." *Journal of Negro History* 65: 43–56.

Reskin, Barbara F. 1988. "Bringing the Men Back in: Sex Differentiation and the Devaluation of Women's Work." *Gender and Society* 2: 58–81.

———. 2000. "The Proximate Causes of Discrimination." *Contemporary Sociology* 29: 319–28.

Reskin, Barbara F., and Debra Branch McBrier. 2000. "Why Not Ascription? Organizations' Employment of Male and Female Managers." *American Sociological Review* 65: 210–33.

Reskin, Barbara F., and Patricia A. Roos. 1992. *Job Queues, Gender Queues: Explain-*

ing Women's Inroads into Male Occupations. Philadelphia: Temple University Press.

Ridgeway, Cecilia L. 1997. "Interaction and the Conservation of Gender Inequality: Considering Employment." *American Sociological Review* 62: 218–35.

Robinson, Corre L., Tiffany Taylor, Donald Tomaskovic-Devey, Catherine Zimmer, and Matthew Irwin. 2005. "Studying Race or Ethnic and Sex Segregation at the Establishment Level: Methodological Issues and Substantive Opportunities Using EEO-1 Reports." *Work and Occupations* 32: 5–38.

Roscigno, Vincent. 2007. *The Face of Discrimination: How Race and Gender Impact Work and Home Lives*. New York: Rowman & Littlefield.

Roscigno, Vincent J., Lisette Garcia, and Donna Bobbitt-Zeher. 2007. "Social Closure and Processes of Race/Sex Employment Discrimination." *Annals of the American Academy of Political and Social Sciences* 609(1): 16–48.

Roscigno, Vincent, and Donald Tomaskovic-Devey. 1994. "Racial Politics in the Contemporary South: Toward a More Critical Understanding." *Social Problems* 41: 585–607.

Royster, Deirdre A. 2003. *Race and the Invisible Hand: How White Networks Exclude Black Men from Blue Collar Jobs*. University of California Press26.

Ruchames, Louis. 1953. *Race, Jobs, and Politics: The Story of FEPC*. New York: Columbia University Press.

Sakamoto, Arthur, Goyette Kimberly A., and Kim ChangHwan. 2009. "Socioeconomic Attainments of Asian Americans." *Annual Review of Sociology* 35: 255–76.

Salancik, Gerald R. 1979. "Interorganizational Dependence and Responsiveness to Affirmative Action: The Case of Women and Defense Contractors." *Academy of Management Journal* 22: 375–94.

Schuman, Howard, Charlotte Steeh, Lawrence Bobo, and Maria Krysan. 1997. *Racial Attitudes in America: Trends and Interpretations*. Cambridge, Mass.: Harvard University Press.

Schwalbe, Michael, Sandra Godwin, Daphne Holden, Douglas Schrock, Shealy Thompson, and Michele Wolkomir. 2000. "Generic Processes in the Reproduction of Inequality: An Interactionist Analysis." *Social Forces* 79: 419–52.

Silverman, Leslie E. 2006. "Systemic Task Force Report to the Chair of the Equal Employment Opportunity Commission." Washington: U.S. Equal Employment Opportunity Commission (March). Available at: http://archive.eeoc.gov/abouteeoc/task_reports/systemic.pdf (accessed February 9, 2012).

Sitkoff, Harvard. 1993. *Struggle for Black Equality*. New York: Hill and Wang.

Skaggs, Sheryl. 2008. "Producing Change or Bagging Opportunity? The Effects of Discrimination Litigation on Women in Supermarket Management." *American Journal of Sociology* 113: 1148–83.

———. 2009. "Legal-Political Pressures and African American Access to Managerial Jobs." *American Sociological Review* 74: 225–44.

————. 2010. "Does Proximity Matter? Examining the Indirect Effects of Discrimination Litigation on Women's Managerial Representation." Unpublished Paper, University of Texas at Dallas.

Skaggs, Sheryl, Kevin Stainback, and Phyllis Duncan. 2012. "Shaking Things Up or Business as Usual? The Influence of Female Corporate Executives and Board of Directors on Women's Managerial Representation." *Social Science Research.* Available at: http://www.sciencedirect.com/science/article/pii/S0049089X 12000269 (accessed May 8, 2012).

Skrentny, John David. 1996. *The Ironies of Affirmative Action: Politics, Culture, and Justice in America.* Chicago: University of Chicago Press.

Smith, James P., and Finis Welch. 1977. "Black-White Male Wage Ratios, 1960–1970." *American Economic Review* 67: 323–38.

————. 1984. "Affirmative Action and Labor Markets." *Journal of Labor Economics* 2: 269–301.

Smith, Ryan A., and James R. Elliott. 2002. "Does Ethnic Concentration Influence Employees' Access to Authority? An Examination of Contemporary Urban Labor Markets." *Social Forces* 81: 255–79.

————. 2004. "Race, Gender, and Workplace Power." *American Sociological Review* 69: 365–86.

Smith, Tom W., Peter V. Marsden, and Michael Hout. 2011. *General Social Survey, 1972–2010* [Cumulative File]. ICPSR31521-v1. Storrs, Conn: Roper Center for Public Opinion Research, University of Connecticut/Ann Arbor, Mich.: Interuniversity Consortium for Political and Social Research [distributors], 2011-08 -05. doi:10.3886/ICPSR31521.v1.

Smith-Doerr, Laurel. 2004. "Flexibility and Fairness: Effects of the Network Form of Organization on Gender Equity in Life Science Careers." *Sociological Perspectives* 47(1): 25–54.

Spilerman, Seymour, and Trond Petersen. 1999. "Organizational Structure, Determinants of Promotion, and Gender Differences in Attainment." *Social Science Research* 28: 203–27.

Stainback, Kevin. 2008. "Social Contacts and Race/Ethnic Job Matching." *Social Forces* 87(2): 857–86.

Stainback, Kevin, and Matthew Irvin. 2012. "Workplace Racial Composition, Racial Discrimination, and Organizational Attachment." *Social Science Research* 41: 657–70.

Stainback, Kevin, and Soyoung Kwon. 2012. "Female Leaders, Organizational Power, and Sex Segregation." *Annals of the American Academy of Political and Social Science* 639: 217–35.

Stainback, Kevin, Thomas N. Ratliff, and Vincent J. Roscigno. 2011. "The Organizational Context of Sex Discrimination: Sex Composition, Workplace Culture, and Relative Power." *Social Forces* 89(4): 1165–88.

Stainback, Kevin, Corre L. Robinson, and Donald Tomaskovic-Devey. 2005. "Race and Workplace Integration: A 'Politically Mediated' Process?" *American Behavioral Scientist* 48: 1200–1228.

Stainback, Kevin, and Zhenyu Tang. 2012. "Female-Dominated Jobs and the Gender Wage Gap: Evaluating Gendered and Human Capital Explanations." Working Paper, Purdue University.

Stainback, Kevin, and Donald Tomaskovic-Devey. 2009. "Long-Term Trends in Managerial Representation for Black and White Women and Men in Private Sector U.S. Firms." *American Sociological Review* 74(5): 800–20.

Stainback, Kevin, Donald Tomaskovic-Devey, and Sheryl Skaggs. 2010. "Organizational Approaches to Inequality: Inertia, Relative Power, and Environments." *Annual Review of Sociology* 36: 225–47.

Stinchcombe, Arthur. 1965. "Social Structure and Organizations." In *Handbook of Organizations*, edited by James G. March. Chicago: Rand McNally.

Strauss, David A. 2001. "The Irrelevance of Constitutional Amendments." *Harvard Law Review* 114: 1457–1505.

Sutton, John R., Frank Dobbin, John W. Meyer, and W. Richard Scott. 1994. "The Legalization of the Workplace." *American Journal of Sociology* 99: 944–71.

Szafran, Robert. 1982. "What Kinds of Firms Hire and Promote Women and Blacks? A Review of the Literature." *Sociological Quarterly* 23: 171–90.

Taylor, Tiffany. 2010. "Supply, Demand, and Organizational Processes: Changes in Women's Share of Management in United States Workplaces, 1966–2000." *Advances in Gender Research* 14: 167–88.

Thernstrom, Stephen, and Abigail Thernstrom. 1997. *America in Black and White: One Nation, Indivisible.* New York: Simon & Schuster.

Tilly, Charles. 1998. *Durable Inequality.* Berkeley: University of California Press.

Tolbert, Charles M., and Molly Sizer. 1996. "U.S. Commuting Zones and Labor Market Areas: A 1990 Update." Staff paper AGES-9614. Washington: U.S. Department of Agriculture, Economic Research Service, Rural Economy Division.

Tomaskovic-Devey, Donald. 1993. *Gender and Racial Inequality at Work: The Sources and Consequences of Job Segregation.* Ithaca, N.Y.: ILR Press.

Tomaskovic-Devey, Donald, Arne L. Kalleberg, and Peter V. Marsden. 1996. "Organizational Patterns of Sex Segregation." In *Organizations in America: Analyzing Their Structures and Human Resource Practices*, edited by Arne L. Kalleberg, David Knoke, Peter V. Marsden, and Joe L. Spaeth. Thousand Oaks, Calif.: Sage Publications.

Tomaskovic-Devey, Donald, and Ken-Hou Lin. 2011. "Income Dynamics, Economic Rents, and the Financialization of the U.S. Economy." *American Sociological Review* 76: 538–59.

Tomaskovic-Devey, Donald, and Vincent Roscigno. 1996. "Racial Economic Subordination and White Gain in the U.S. South." *American Sociological Review* 61: 565–89.

———. 1997. "Uneven Development and Local Inequality in the U.S. South: The Role of Outside Investment, Landed Elites, and Racial Dynamics." *Sociological Forum* 12: 565–97.

Tomaskovic-Devey, Donald, and Sheryl L. Skaggs. 1999a. "Workplace Gender and Racial Composition and Productivity: An Establishment-Level Test of the Statistical Discrimination Hypothesis." *Work and Occupations* 26: 422–45.

———. 1999b. "Degendered Jobs?: Organizational Processes and Gender Segregated Employment." *Research in Social Stratification and Mobility* 17: 139–72.

———. 2002. "Sex Segregation, Labor Process Organization, and Gender Earnings Inequality." *American Journal of Sociology* 108: 102–28.

Tomaskovic-Devey, Donald, and Kevin Stainback. 2007. "Discrimination and Desegregation." *Annals of the American Academy of Political and Social Sciences* 609: 49–84.

Tomaskovic-Devey, Donald, Melvin Thomas, and Kecia Johnson. 2005. "Race and the Accumulation of Human Capital Across the Career: A Theoretical Model and Fixed-Effects Application." *American Journal of Sociology* 111(1): 58–89.

Tomaskovic-Devey, Donald, Catherine Zimmer, Kevin Stainback, Corre L. Robinson, Tiffany C. Taylor, and Tricia McTague. 2006. "Documenting Desegregation: Segregation in American Workplaces by Race, Ethnicity, and Sex, 1966–2003." *American Sociological Review* 71: 565–88.

Tsui, Anne S., and Charles A. O'Reilly III. 1989. "Beyond Simple Demographic Effects: The Importance of Relational Demography in Superior-Subordinate Dyads." *Academy of Management Journal* 32(2): 402–23.

U.S. Commission on Civil Rights. 1995. *Funding Federal Civil Rights Enforcement.* Washington, D.C.: U.S. Commission on Civil Rights.

Wakefield, Sara, and Christopher Uggen. 2004. "The Declining Significance of Race in Federal Civil Rights Law: The Social Structure of Employment Discrimination Claims." *Sociological Inquiry* 74: 128–57.

Western, Bruce, and Becky Pettit. 2010. "Incarceration and Social Inequality." *Daedalus* 193(Summer): 8–19.

Wilson, George. 1997a. "Pathways to Power: Racial Differences in the Determinants of Job Authority." *Social Problems* 44: 38–54.

———. 1997b. "Payoffs to Power Among Males in the Middle Class: Has Race Made a Difference?" *Industrial Relations* 43: 660–89.

Wilson, George, and Vincent Roscigno. 2011. "Race, Public Sector Reform, and Wages: Are African Americans Losing Their Occupational Niche?" Working paper, University of Miami.

Wilson, William J. 1979. *The Declining Significance of Race.* Chicago: University of Chicago Press.

———. 1997. *When Work Disappears: The World of the New Urban Poor.* New York: Vintage.

Wood, B. Dan. 1990. "Does Politics Make a Difference at the EEOC?" *American Journal of Political Science* 34(2): 503–30.

Wooten, Lynn Perry, and Erika Hayes James. 2004. "When Firms Fail to Learn: The Perpetuation of Discrimination in the Workplace." *Journal of Management Inquiry* 13(1): 23–33.

Index

Boldface numbers refer to figures and tables.

Abbott, Andrew, xxv
accountability, 290, 291–92, 303–5, 311
administrative support workers. *See* clerical and administrative support workers
affirmative action: Clinton administration, 157, 172–75, 261; Johnson administration, 85–86, 91, 92, 115; Kennedy administration, 51, 68–69, 71, 78–81, 108, 294; labor queuing theory, 194; legal challenges, 121, **165**; OFCCP compliance, 141, 153, 262, 264–65, 266, 314–15, 316; public sector implementation, 42; Reagan administration, 155; Republican Party's opposition, 126; reverse discrimination backlash, xxii, 121, 126, 311–13; Roosevelt administration, xxxi, 51, 65–66, 69; voluntary vs. nonvoluntary plans, 288
African Americans. *See* blacks, black men, black women
age discrimination complaints, **258**
agriculture, **47**, 48
Alba, Richard, 293–94, 307
Albemarle Paper Co. v. Moody, **120**
Alexander v. Gardner-Denver Co., **120**
antidiscrimination laws: Civil Rights Act (1991), 162, 164; Equal Pay Act (1963), 65, 69; Family and Medical Leave Act (1993), 156–57, 159, 160, 274; federal mandates before Civil Rights Act (1964), 64–73; limitations of, 4–6; Pregnancy Discrimination Act (1978), 122, 159–60. *See also* Civil Rights Act (1964); fair employment practice (FEP) laws
applications, employment, 284
ascription, bottom-up, 14, 277–78, 279
Asian Americans: employment segregation trends, 306; labor force composition, 38; labor market competition impact, 195, 196; labor queue position, 194; managerial jobs, **202, 203, 204, 205**; model minority status, 283; top labor markets for, **205**
Atwater, Lee, 156
Avent-Holt, Dustin, 18

banks, **225, 231, 243**, 275, 276
Baron, James, xxix, 13, 41, 62, 153, 285
Bielby, William, xxix, 41, 62
black men: discrimination claims, 27; educational attainment, **40**; EEO-1 reporting firm employment, **42,**

black men (*cont.*)
    51–52, 92–93; employment growth,
    94, **95**; employment segregation
    trends, 53, **54, 76,** 127–33, **168**; fed-
    eral contractor employment, 69, **70,
    72, 73, 80,** 142–44; government em-
    ployment, **43**; homogeneous work-
    places, **52**; labor force composition,
    38; labor market competition impact,
    195; occupational distribution, **52,**
    53, 96–99; Plans for Progress firm
    employment, 80–81; regional varia-
    tion in segregation, 55, **56**; sector
    variation in segregation, 55, **57, 215**;
    small-firm private-sector employ-
    ment, **44**; workplace integration, 95–
    96; workplace isolation, **32, 59, 72,
    76, 80, 103, 110, 133, 174**. *See also*
    good-quality job representation
black men-white men desegregation or
    segregation. *See* white men-black
    men desegregation or segregation
black men-white women desegrega-
    tion or segregation: in EEOC-report-
    ing firms, **71**; in federal contractor
    firms, **71**; during neoliberal era, **169**;
    organizational variation, 57, **58**; by
    political era, **170**; during pre-Civil
    Rights Act period (1966), **54, 56, 58,
    71**; regional variation, **56,** 185; work-
    place birth and death impact, **253**;
    workplace environmental context,
    256
blacks: civil rights advancement, xxvi;
    EEOC claim filings, 265; good job
    opportunities, 307–8; immigrants'
    impact on labor market opportuni-
    ties, 194, 208–9; incarceration rates,
    48; manufacturing employment, 213;
    racial discrimination experiences, 26;
    service sector employment, 213; top
    labor markets for, **203**; unemploy-

ment, 48. *See also* black men; black
    women; civil rights movement
black women: discrimination claims,
    27–28; discrimination lawsuits, 267;
    educational attainment, **40**; in EEO-1
    reporting firm employment, **42,** 51–
    52, 92–93; employment growth, 94,
    95; employment segregation trends,
    53, **54, 76, 80,** 118, 127–33, **168**; fed-
    eral contractor employment, **70, 72,
    73,** 145–48, 152; government employ-
    ment, **43**; homogeneous workplaces,
    52; labor force composition, **38**; labor
    market competition impact, 195–96;
    labor queue position, 194; occupa-
    tional distribution, **52,** 53, 96–99;
    Plans for Progress firm employment,
    80, 81; regional variation in segrega-
    tion, 55, **56**; as reverse discrimination
    beneficiary, xxii, 311–13; sector varia-
    tion in segregation, 55, **57, 218, 219**;
    small-firm private-sector employ-
    ment, **44**; workplace integration, 95;
    workplace isolation, **32, 59, 72, 76,
    80, 103, 110, 133, 174**. *See also* good-
    quality job representation
black women-white men desegrega-
    tion or segregation. *See* white men-
    black women desegregation or
    segregation
black women-white women desegre-
    gation or segregation. *See* white
    women-black women desegregation
    or segregation
Blalock, Hubert, 208
Blankenship, Kim, 341*n*2 (ch. 2)
Blumrosen, Alfred, 89, 90, 91, 108,
    341*n*2 (ch. 3)
Borjas, George, 208–9
bottom-up ascription, 277–78
branch plants, 57, **58,** 277, 335–36
Broschak, Joseph, 275, 276

Brown v. Board of Education, 67, 68
bureaucracy, 9, 285–86, 310
Bureau of Labor Statistics, 325
Burk, Robert, 68
Burstein, Paul, 5, 12
Bush (George H. W.) administration: Civil Rights Act (1990) veto, 164; desegregation trajectories, **170**; election (1988), 156; OFCCP regulation, **174, 175**
Bush (George W.) administration: desegregation trajectories, **170**; OFCCP regulation, **174, 175**; racial integration, 169

capitalism, 250
Carter administration: civil rights, 125–26; election (1980), 155
Castilla, Emilio, 285, 286–87
Catanzarite, Lisa, 187
CEOs (chief executive officers), 270, 294–95, 313
Cha, Youngjoo, 269–70, 289, 290
change, organizational, xxiii, xxix, 5, 10–16
Charles, Maria, 213, 217
Chen, Anthony, 64, 74
chief executive officers (CEOs), 270, 294–95, 313
Chused, Richard, 276
Civil Rights Act (1964): amendment (Civil Rights Act of 1991), 162, 164; amendments (proposed), 157, 164; enactment of, xxi; impact of, xxvi, 298–99; importance of, xxi; limitations of, 4–10; provisions, 85; Title IX, 137, 224; Title VII, xxi, 63–64, 88–89; votes by political party, 87. *See also* Title VII of Civil Rights Act of 1964
Civil Rights Act (1991), 162, 164
civil rights movement: advancements

of, 65–69; decline of, 123–26, 153–54; desegregation impact, xxvi; number of organizations, **122**; political parties' support, 87; protest events, 65, **123**
Civil Rights Restoration Act (1995), 157
civil service, 68, 119
Civil Service Reform Act (1978), 119
class-action lawsuits: defendant firms' characteristics, 255; desegregation effectiveness, 266–73; EEOC participation, 313; industry comparisons as baseline for segregation level, 241; during neoliberal era, 158, 166; settlements, 259, 290
clerical and administrative support workers: EEO-1 definition, 331; employment growth, **97**; federal contractor firms, 72, 114; race-gender group distribution, **52**
Clinton administration: affirmative action, 157, 172–75, 261; desegregation trajectories, **170**; equal opportunity, 167; Family and Medical Leave Act (1993), 156–57; gender desegregation, 169; good quality job representation, 171–72; OFCCP regulation, **174, 175**
Cockburn, Cynthia, 13, 274
coercive isomorphism, 11–12, 64, 90
cognitive biases, 21–25, 27. *See also* prejudice
Cohen, Lisa, 275, 276
Cold War, 65, 113, 294
college education: college graduates by industry, 224–27; credential-based screening, 19, 137–38, 235–40, 302; by race and gender relative to white men, 39–40, **41**
commuting zones, 328, 334
competition, labor market. *See* local labor market competition

competition theory, 189
competitive markets, 18
complaints. *See* discrimination complaints
compliance, regulatory, 64, 303–5. *See also* Office of Federal Contract Compliance Programs (OFCCP)
Congress: EEOC's power to file lawsuits, 87; equal employment opportunity leadership, 319–20
Congress of Industrial Organizations (CIO), xxvi
Connecticut v. Teal, **165**
contact theory, 189
contractors. *See* federal contractors
Corning Glass Works v. Brennan, **120**
corporate headquarters, 57, **58,** 277, 324–25, 335–36
corporations: defense against discrimination lawsuits, 260–61, 310; employment distribution analysis, 315–17; equal opportunity policies, 11; gender equality, 121–23; occupational and managerial desegregation, 284–85. *See also* human resources
Cotter, David, 303
County of Washington v. Gunther, **165**
courts, 17, 273, 305. *See also* Supreme Court
craft job representation: during early post-Civil Rights Act period, 96–97, 104–7; EEO-1 definition, 331; employment growth, **96**; federal contractors, **73, 112**; and industry credentialing, **239**; and industry employment growth, **239**; and industry relative income, 238, **239**; and labor market participation, 33–34; labor queues, 198; during neoliberal era, 171–72; during pre-Civil Rights Act period (1966), 61–62; race-gender

group distribution, **52**; regional differences, 186–87; during regulatory decade (1972 to 1980), 138–40; in states with FEP laws, **77**
credential-based screening: desegregation impact, 302; industry analysis, 235–40; professional jobs, 3, 35–36, 137–38; and statistical discrimination, 19
Crenshaw, Kimberle, 267
cultural differences, 209
culture, organizational, 8–10, 285, 290–91

data collection, for employment distribution analysis, 315–17
data sources, xxii, xxv, 225, 236, 326. *See also* Employer Information Reports (EEO-1)
defense industry, 65–66. *See also* federal contractors
deindustrialization, 37
Democratic Party, 87–88, 123–26, 155–57
demonstrations and protests, **123, 124**
departmentalization, 285
Department of Justice, Civil Rights Division, 317, 318, 319–20
desegregation. *See* employment segregation and desegregation
disability discrimination complaints, **258**
discrimination complaints: desegregation impact, 277; employer retaliation, 270–71; and formalization of human resource practices, 286; investigations of, 313–15; literature review, 26–28; during neoliberal era, 158, **162**; during regulatory decade (1972 to 1980), 119; sexual harassment, **162**; trends, 257–61
discrimination lawsuits: corporate de-

fenses, 260–61, 310; desegregation impact, 265–73; EEOC's power to initiate, 87, 119; effects of, xxii; employer retaliation, 270–71; gender discrimination, 121–22; number of, 259, 265–66; pregnancy discrimination, 159; during regulatory decade (1972 to 1980), 141. *See also* class-action lawsuits

disparate impact doctrine, 117, 120–21, 163

diversity programs: CEOs' commitment to, 313; desegregation effects, 14, 274–83, 291; diversity managers or committees, 288, 309; emergence of, 166–67; monitoring of, 313; training, 289

Dobbin, Frank, 11, 12, 14, 51, 69, 71, 78–79, 81, 82, 108, 109, 116, 153, 154, 159, 160, 166, 262, 265, 266, 272, 274, 277, 285, 287–90, 303, 309–10

Donohue, John, 266

downsizing, 287

Dukakis, Michael, 156

Dukes v. Wal-Mart, 164, **165**

duRivage, Virginia, 157

economics, discrimination definition and identification, 17–18

economy, shift from goods-producing to service-oriented economy, 37

Edelman, Lauren, 285, 303

educational attainment, 39–40

educational credentials. *See* credential-based screening

Edwards, Mark, 159

EEO-1 (Employer Information Reports). *See* Employer Information Reports (EEO-1)

EEO1-Analytics, 313–14

EEOC (Equal Employment Opportunity Commission). *See* Equal Employment Opportunity Commission (EEOC)

Eisenberg, Susan, 105

Eisenhower administration: civil rights, 67–68

elections, presidential. *See* presidential elections

Elliott, James, 277–78

employee hiring process. *See* hiring process

employees, EEOC's definition of, 325

Employer Information Reports (EEO-1): confidentiality, 323–24; coverage rates, 325; coverage scope, 324; data collection expansion, 318; data quality, 325–26; desegregation analysis, 28–36; employment counts, 324; employment distribution analysis, 316–17; employment in firms filing, 41–42; history of, 50–51; industry codes, 327–28; occupational definitions, 330–32; race and ethnicity measurement, 326–27; regional coverage, 44–47; scope of, xxii; sector coverage, 47–48; types of, 324–25

employer retaliation, 270–71

employment composition shifts, 94–95

employment discrimination: case law, xxvi; definition and identification of, 16–19, 117, 126, 163–64; prevalence of, 26–28; social closure theory, 20–21; statistical discrimination, 19–20; and stereotypical beliefs, 21–25; variability across workplaces, 25. *See also* antidiscrimination laws; discrimination complaints; discrimination lawsuits

employment distribution, 52–53, 96–99, 315–17

employment growth: in EEOC-reporting firms, 93–95; in high-skilled white-collar jobs, **98**; by industry,

employment growth (*cont.*)
224–27, 235–40; in white-collar jobs, 97; in working class jobs, **96**
employment segregation and desegregation: contemporary period (2001 to 2005), 26–28, 229–35, 241–49, 313; data sources, xxii, xxv, 225, 236, 326; early post-Civil Rights Act period (1966 to 1972), 84–117; EEOC case effects, 257–61; erroneous beliefs about, xxii–xxiii; future prospects, 320–21; historical legacy of segregation, xxv–xxvi, 7–10; introduction, xxi–xxxiv; key actors and mechanisms, xxviii–xxx; local labor markets, 181–210; methodology, 3–4, 6–7, 28–33, 36–39, 323–38; narrative approach, xxv–xxviii; neoliberal era, 155–77; organizational variation, 250–92; pre-Civil Rights Act period (1966), 50–83; regulatory decade (1972 to 1980), 118–54; research considerations, xxi–xxv; sector and industry analysis, 211–49; shift from national to local inequality regimes, 293–321
enforcement: after Equal Employment Opportunity Act (1972) passage, 119–21; congressional leadership, 320; during early post-Civil Rights Act period, 86–87, 89–92, 117, 119–20; effectiveness of, 257–61; future of, 313–18; targeting, 249. *See also* Equal Employment Opportunity Commission (EEOC); Office of Federal Contract Compliance Programs (OFCCP)
England, Paula, 303
environmental uncertainty. *See* uncertainty
Equal Employment Opportunity Act (1972), 117, 119

Equal Employment Opportunity Commission (EEOC): annual reporting requirements, 323; cooperation with OFCCP, 316; employment distribution analysis, 315–17; enforcement power, 87, 89–92, 117, 119–20; funding, 319; future of, 313–18; gender employment discrimination, 90–91; political influence, 86–87; Reagan budget cuts, 158; role of, 84; staffing levels, **316**. *See also* discrimination complaints; discrimination lawsuits; Employer Information Reports (EEO-1)
Equal Pay Act (1963), 65, 69
Equal Rights Amendment (ERA), 121
establishment reports, 324–25
exclusion, workplace, 51–52, 70, 92–93, 295
executive orders: 8802, xxxi, 51, 65–66, 69; 9346, 66; 9981, 66–67; 10479, 67–68; 10590, 68; 10925, 51, 68–69, 71, 78–81, 108, 294; 11246, 85–86, 91; 11375, 92, 115

fair employment practice (FEP) laws: adoption of, 74–75, 335; and craft production job desegregation, **105,** 106–7; employer resistance, 50–51, 64; and segregation trends, 75–78, 102–3
Fair Employment Practices Committee (FEPC), 65–66
Family and Medical Leave Act (1993), 156–57, 159, 160, 274
Faragher v. City of Boca Raton and Burlington Industries, Inc., v. Ellerth, **165**
federal contractors: EEO plan adoption, 12; employment growth, 95; gender discrimination, 91–92; Plans for Progress, 79–81, 82, 108–13, 116; segregation and desegregation trends, 69–73, 80–81, 93, 108–13, 116,

142–48, 262–64. *See also* Office of Federal Contract Compliance Programs (OFCCP)

federal district courts, 273, 305

federal laws. *See* antidiscrimination laws

federal regulation, 11–12, 313–18. *See also* enforcement

feminist movement. *See* women's movement

FEPC (Fair Employment Practices Committee), 65–66

FEP (fair employment practice) laws. *See* fair employment practice (FEP) laws

flexible work arrangements, 160–61

Ford, Gerald, 125

formalization of human resource practices, 15, 150–51, 153, 276–77, 284–91

Franks v. Bowman Transportation Co., **120**

gender discrimination: EEOC complaints, 257–61; pregnancy discrimination, 122, 159–61, 164; prevalence of, 26–28. *See also* employment discrimination; sexual harassment

gender employment segregation and desegregation: in competitive markets, 18; and departmentalization, 285; during early post-Civil Rights Act period, 85, 99–100, 115; EEOC's enforcement, 90–91; historical legacy, xxv–xxvi, 7–10; and HR practices, 150; during pre-Civil Rights Act period (1966), 51–58, 62; vs. racial segregation, 6–7; service sector variation, 213, 214–17; and women in managerial roles, 14

gender of employees, measurement of, 29

gender wage gap, 14, 25

General Electric Co. v. Gilbert, **120**, 122, 159

General Telephone Company of the Northwest v. Equal Employment Opportunity Commission, **120**

Gilmer v. Interstate/Johnson Lane, **165**

Giuliano, Laura, 275

Goldwater, Barry, 88

good-quality job representation: African Americans, 307–8; and discrimination lawsuits, 271–72; during early post-Civil Rights Act period, 104–8, 112–13, 114; federal contractors, **73,** 112–13; labor queues, 197–200; and local labor market group size, 191–93; methodology, 31–33; during neoliberal era, 169–72; during pre-Civil Rights Act period (1966), 59–62; regional differences, 185–88; during regulatory decade (1972 to 1980), 133–40; in states with FEP laws, 76–78. *See also* craft job representation; managerial job representation; professional job representation

government contractors. *See* federal contractors

Graham, Mary, 317

Griggs v. Duke Power, 117, 119–20

Grusky, David, 213, 217

harassment, 19, 27. *See also* sexual harassment

Harris v. Forklift Systems, Inc., **165**

Haveman, Heather, 275, 276

Hazelwood School District v. United States, **120**

Helms, Jesse, 157

Hermsen, Joan, 303

high-wage industries: desegregation, 21, 227, 229, 303; managerial representation, 238; resegregation, xxiii, 234; top twenty, **225**

Hill, Anita, 162
hiring discrimination, 27
hiring process: bias in, 25; formalization of practices, 15, 150–51, 153, 276–77, 284–91; job advertisements, 91, 121–22, 310; professionals, 137–38; recruitment strategies, 15, 275
Hirsh, Elizabeth, 258–61, 265, 267, 268, 269–70, 272, 277, 284, 289, 290
Hispanics: discrimination, 26, 305, 342*n*1 (ch. 6); employment segregation trends, 187–88, 305–6; labor force representation, 38, **308**; labor market competition impact, 195; managerial jobs, **202, 203, 204, 205**; top labor markets for, **204**
Hodgson, James D., 92
homogeneous workplaces, 51–52, 70, 92–93, 295
Horton, Willie, 156
hospitals, 284, 289
Hotchkiss, Julie, 317
House of Representatives, Civil Rights Act (1964) votes, 87
Huffman, Matt, 276, 277
Hultin, Mia, 14, 276
human capital, 17, 39–41
human resource managers: as EEO advocates, 274; by gender and minority status, **161**; role of, 309–13; white women, 15–16, 152, **161,** 166–67, 176
human resources: EEO practices and policies, 14–16, 148–53, 166, 266, 269–70, 284–91, 309–13; flexible work arrangements, 160–61; maternity leave, 160, 274. *See also* diversity programs; hiring process
Humphrey, Hubert, 123–24

immigrants and immigration, 182, 194–200, 208–9
incarceration, 48

income, and industry desegregation, 224–27, 235–40
income inequality, 21
individual-level discrimination, erroneous beliefs about, xxiii
industry analysis. *See* sector and industry analysis
industry data, as source for organizational policies and practices, 255–57
innovation, 311
institutionalized discrimination, 189
institutional isomorphism, 12–13
intergroup contact: during early post-Civil Rights Act period, 111; and local labor market competition, 189, 204–6; and managerial job representation, 291; and racial desegregation, 103–4; during regulatory decade (1972 to 1980), 131–33
internal labor markets, 12, 285
internal workplace constituencies, 13–14, 273–83, 299
International Union, UAW, v. Johnson Controls, **165**
investment industry. *See* security, commodity brokers, and investment industry
isolation, workplace: among federal contractors, 71–72, 80–81; during early post-Civil Rights Act period, 103–4; in EEOC-reporting private-sector workplaces, **32**; measurement of, 30–31, 58; during neoliberal era, 172, **174**; in Plans for Progress firms, 80–81; during pre-Civil Rights Act period (1966), 58–59; during regulatory decade (1972 to 1980), 131–33; and state FEP laws, 74–75

James, Erika, 268–69, 271–72
Jim Crow, 7, 188
job advertisements, 91, 121–22, 310

job mobility, 303
job representation. *See* good-quality job representation
Johnson administration: Civil Rights Act (1964), xxi; civil rights commitment, 88, 294; Executive Order 11246, 85–86, 91
Johnson v. Transportation Agency, Santa Clara County, **165**
judges, federal district courts, 273, 305
Justice Department, Civil Rights Division, 317, 318, 319–20

Kalev, Alexandra, 14, 153, 262, 265, 266, 272, 276, 287–90, 291, 311
Kanter, Rosabeth Moss, 14, 275, 281
Kelly, Erin, 262, 274, 287–89
Kennedy administration: civil rights, 51, 68–69, 71, 78–81, 108, 294–95; election (1960), 87
Kessler, Ronald, 26
Kmec, Julie A., 284, 285–86, 289
Koo, Soohan, 14, 287
Kurtulus, Fidan Ana, 277
Kwon, Soyoung, 287

Labor Department, 92
laborers and helpers, **52, 96,** 332
labor force composition, 37–39, 306–8
labor force participation, 48
labor market competition. *See* local labor market competition
labor queue approach, 182–83, 188, 194–200, 208, 307
Latinos. *See* Hispanics
laws. *See* antidiscrimination laws
lawsuits. *See* discrimination lawsuits
Leonard, Jonathan, 141, 264, 266, 275
Levine, David, 275
Little Rock Central High School, forced desegregation, 68
local inequality regimes: introduction,

xxiv; local labor market competition, 181–210; organizational variation, 250–92; sector and industry analysis, 211–49
local labor market competition, 181–210; introduction, 181–83; labor queue processes, 194–200; labor supply effects, 188–94; managerial representation, 201–4; methodology, 328, 334–36; regional differences, 183–88; top markets for white male overrepresentation, 206–8; white male exposure to intergroup contact, 204–6
Lockheed Aircraft, 79
Lorance v. AT&T Technologies, **165**
Los Angeles: ethnic-typed employment, 187–88
Los Angeles v. Manhart, **120**
low-wage industries: desegregation, 21, 227, 232, 235; managerial representation, 220, 224; resegregation, 234–35; top twenty, **226**
Lucas, Samuel, 16, 293

managerial composition, 276, 278–81
managerial diversity, 14, 274–78, 274–83, 291
managerial job representation: best and worst industries, 246–49; desegregation, 34–35; and discrimination lawsuits, 266–70; during early post-Civil Rights Act period, **106,** 107; federal contractors, **73, 112;** and formalized human resource practices, 15, 284; and industry credentialing, **239;** and industry employment growth, **239;** and industry relative income, **239;** and internal workplace constituencies, 13–14, 273–83, 299; labor queues, 197–98, 201–4; local labor market analysis, 201–4, 206–8,

managerial job representation (*cont.*) 209; during neoliberal era, 171; OFCCP regulation effects, 173–75, 263–64; during pre-Civil Rights Act period (1966), 60, **61**; race-gender group distribution, **52**; regional differences, 186–87; during regulatory decade (1972 to 1980), 134–35, 154; reverse discrimination, 311–13; in states with FEP laws, **77**; white male overrepresentation, 7, 206–8, **221**; workplace diversity impact, 274–83, 291

managers: EEO-1 definition, 330; employment growth, **98**. *See also* human resource managers

Massey, Douglas, 305

matching, manager-worker, 281–83, 291

maternity leave, 160, 274

McBrier, Debra, 15

McCall, Leslie, 194

McDonald v. Santa Fe Transport, **120**, 121

McDonnell Douglas v. Green, **120**

men: gender stereotypes, 23–24. *See also* black men; white men

mentoring, 275, 288–89

meritocracy, xxiii, 301–3, 310–11

Meritor Savings Bank v. Vinson, 162, 163, **165**

methodology: analytic strategy, 36–39; equal employment opportunity trends measurement, 28–33; introduction, 3–4; local labor market variation, 328; narrative approach, xxv; occupational-job mismatch adjustment, 333–34; race and gender comparison, 6–7; statistical modeling, 334–38. *See also* Employer Information Reports (EEO-1)

metropolitan areas, 328

Mickelson, K. D., 26

military, racial integration of, 66–67

Minkoff, Debra, **122**

minorities, human resource managers, **161**. *See also specific minority groups*

model minority, 283

moral leadership, 318–20

motive-based notion of discrimination, 163–64

multi-establishment firm reports, 324

narrative approach, xxv

National Organization for Women (NOW), 91, 121, 160

national origin discrimination complaints, **258**

Nielsen , Laura Beth, 26, 265

Nelson, Robert, 26, 265

networking, 288–89

new workplaces, 252–54

Nixon, Richard M.: civil rights, 124–25; election (1960), 87; election (1968), 123–24, 156

normative changes, 5, 12–13

NOW (National Organization for Women), 91, 121, 160

Obama administration: equal opportunity agenda, 319

Occidental Life Insurance. v. Equal Employment Opportunity Commission, **120**

occupational distribution, 52–53, 96–99, 315–17. *See also* good-quality job representation

occupational-job mismatch, 333–34

occupations, EEO-1 definitions, 330–32

Office of Federal Contract Compliance (OFCC), xxvi, 85–86

Office of Federal Contract Compliance Programs (OFCCP): compliance reviews, 141, 153, 262, 264–65, 266, 314–15, 316; cooperation with EEOC, 316; desegregation associated with regulation by, 173–75, 261–65; enforcement power, 119–20; establishment of, xxvi, 85–86; funding, 319; future of, 313–18; gender employment discrimination, 91–92, 154; political appointments, 87; Reagan budget cuts, 157–58; role of, 85–86, 314–15; staffing levels, **316**

Office of Government Contract Compliance, 67

Ohio Civil Rights Commission, 27

Oncale v. Sundowner Offshore Services, **165**

on-the-job training, 19–20

operatives: EEO-1 definition, 331–32; employment growth, 96–97; race-gender group distribution, **52,** 53

opportunity hoarding, 20–21, 137

O'Reilly, Kenneth, 156

organizational change, xxiii, xxix, 5, 10–16

organizational culture, 8–10, 285, 290–91

organizational theory, xxix, 9, 12, 16, 64, 223

organizational variation in segregation, 250–92; in 1966, 58, **58**; and EEOC enforcement, 257–61, 265–73; environmental impact, 255–57; human resource policies and practices, 14–16, 148–53, 166, 266, 269–70, 284–91, 309–13; internal constituencies, 273–83; introduction, 250–52; methodology, 337–38; and OFCCP regulation, 261–65; organizational birth and death impact, 252–54

Pager, Devah, 265

Pedriana, Nicholas, 90

performance reviews, 284, 285

personnel practices. *See* human resources

Petersen, Trond, 286

Pincus, Fred, 311

Plans for Progress (PFP), 79–81, 82, 108–13, 116

political advertising, 156

political issues: of early post-Civil Rights Act period, 87–89, 116–17; EEOC nominations, 86–87; of neoliberal era, 155–57

power, 11–12

pregnancy discrimination, 122, 159–61, 164

Pregnancy Discrimination Act (1978), 122, 159–60

prejudice: "contested prejudice," 16, 293; discrimination arising from, xxiii; employment decision impact, 25; and intergroup contact, 30, 58, 189; prevalence of, 22–24. *See also* stereotypes and stereotyping

presidential elections: 1960, 87; 1968, 123–24, 156; 1976, 125–26; 1980, 155; 1988, 156; 1992, 156–57

presidential nominees, EEOC, 86–87

Price Waterhouse v. Hopkins, 163, **165**

professional job representation: and credential-based screening, 33, 35–36, 137–38; desegregation, 15, 98; during early post-Civil Rights Act period, 107–8; equal opportunity, 224; federal contractors, **73, 112**; and industry credentialing, **239**; and industry employment growth, **239**; and industry relative income, 238, **239**; labor queues, 198–99; during neoliberal era, 171, **172**; during pre-Civil Rights Act period (1966), 60–61; race-gender group distribution, **52**; during regulatory decade (1972 to 1980), 135–38; in states with FEP laws, **77**

professionals: EEO-1 definition, 330; employment growth, **98**

profitability, 18
promotion discrimination, 27
promotions, 276, 284
protests and demonstrations, **123, 124**
psychological biases, 21–25, 27. *See also* prejudice
public-sector employment, 42–44, 317, 318, 319

quit rates, 275

race of employees, measurement of, 29–30
racial discrimination: EEOC complaints, 257–61; prevalence of, 26–28. *See also* employment discrimination
racial employment segregation and desegregation: during early post-Civil Rights Act period, 84–85, 100; vs. gender segregation, 6–7; historical legacy, xxv–xxvi, 7–10; during neoliberal era, 155–57; during pre-Civil Rights Act period (1966), 51–58, 62; in states with FEP laws, 74–78
racism, 320–21
Randolph, A. Philip, 65
Reagan administration: civil rights, 157–59; desegregation trajectories, **170,** 297; election (1980), 155; managerial representation shifts associated with OFCCP regulation, **175;** segregation shifts associated with OFCCP regulation, **174;** Supreme Court appointments, 163
reasonable cause, 259
recruitment strategies, 15, 275
Reed, Merl, 66
Reeves v. Sanderson Plumbing Products, Inc., **165**
Regents of the University of California v. Bakke, 121

regional variation in segregation, 44–47, 54–58, 100–102, 183–88
regulation, 11–12, 157–59, 313–18. *See also* enforcement
relative income, and industry desegregation, 224–27, 235–40
religious discrimination complaints, **258**
Republican Party, 87–88, 116–17, 123–26, 155–57, 296–97
research, congressional funding for, 319
resegregation: after Civil War, xxvii; among women, 110–11, 131, 146–47, 168, 217, 232–35, 245, 296; current problem, 313; future prospects, 320–21; industry variation, 229–35, 241, 242, **244,** 245, 249; manufacturing firms, 214; during neoliberal era, 168; during regulatory decade (1972 to 1980), 131, 146–47; sector variation, 217; trends, xxiii, xxvii–xxviii
residential segregation, 125–26
Reskin, Barbara, 15, 224
retaliation, employer, 270–71
reverse discrimination, xxii, 121, 126, 311–13
Robinson, Corre L., 323
Roosevelt, Franklin D., Jr., 91
Roosevelt administration: Executive Order 8802, xxxi, 51, 65–66, 69; Executive Order 9346, 66
Roscigno, Vincent, 27, 164, 286

Sakamoto, Art, 283
sales jobs: EEO-1 definition, 331; employment growth, **97;** race-gender group distribution, **52**
Schrage, Daniel, 153
scientists, 290
sector and industry analysis, 211–49;

EEO-1 coverage, 47–48; EEOC's capacity, 314; employment segregation and desegregation trends, 55–58; industry educational screening and desegregation, 235–40; industry growth and desegregation, 235–40; industry relative income and desegregation, 235–40; industry segregation and desegregation trajectories, 223–35, 301–2; introduction, 211–12; methodology, 336–37; sector segregation and desegregation trajectories, 212–23; within-organization segregation, 240–49

Securities and Exchange Commission (SEC), 318

segregation, employment. *See* employment segregation and desegregation

segregation, residential, 125–26

selection of employees. *See* hiring process

Senate, Civil Rights Act (1964) votes, 87

settlements, 259, 272, 277, 290

sex-based discrimination. *See* gender discrimination

sex of employees, measurement of, 29

sexual harassment: defined as gender discrimination, 122, 161–63; diversity training impact, 289; EEOC complaint filings, **162**; Supreme court rulings, 162, 163, 164, **165**; women's rights movement, xxvii

sharecropping, 45

shaming top firms for segregation and desegregation, 317–18

Shepherd, Hana, 265

SIC (standard industrial classification) codes, 224, 326, 327–28, **329**

Siegelman, Peter, 266

Silverman, Leslie, 314, 318

single-establishment firms: EEO-1 reports, 324; segregation and desegregation, 57, **58,** 60, 335–36

Skaggs, Sheryl, 209, 267–68, 269, 270, 272, 273

skilled jobs. *See* craft job representation

small firms, 43–44, 257

Smith, James P., 326

Smith, Ryan, 277–78

Smith-Doerr, Laurel, 290–91

social closure: desegregation, 104, 301–3; discrimination production, 27; educational credentials, 137; industry variation, 223–24; measurement of, 337; organizational variation, 285, 291, 301–3; processes, 20–21

social distance, 282–83, 291, 306. *See also* isolation, workplace

social movements, 11. *See also* civil rights movement; women's movement

sociology, discrimination definition and identification, 17–18

Southern Democrats, 87

Southern Strategy, 124–25, 296–97

state fair employment practice (FEP) laws. *See* fair employment practice (FEP) laws

statistical discrimination, 19–20

statistical modeling, 334–38

stereotypes and stereotyping: employment decisions influenced by, 21–25, 27, 28; persistence of, 293, 321; reduction of, 14, 30, 275, 291; and statistical discrimination, 19. *See also* prejudice

St. Mary's Honor Center v. Hicks, **165**

stock market, 269–70

Stryker, Robin, 90

Supreme Court: affirmative action, 126, 311; conservative judicial leanings (1981 to 2011), 163–66; disparate im-

Supreme Court: (*cont.*)
  pact doctrine, 117, 119–21, 163; gender discrimination, 85, 91, 154; pregnancy discrimination, 122, 159; racial segregation, 67; sexual harassment, 162, 163. *See also specific decisions*
Sutton, John, 12, 285, 303
Sweden: women's wages, 14
Systemic Gender EEO Scorecard, 317
Szulkin, Richard, 14, 276

Taylor, Tiffany, 213
teams, workplace, 291
Teamsters v. United States, **120**
technical jobs and technicians, **52, 98,** 330
temporary workers, 287, 325
Thernstrom, Abigail, 5
Thernstrom, Stephen, 5
Thomas, Clarence, 158, 162
Title IX of Civil Rights Act of 1964, 137, 224
Title VII of Civil Rights Act of 1964, xxi, 63–64, 88–89
tokenism, 281
Troutman, Robert, 80, 116
Truman administration: Executive Order 9981, 66–67

uncertainty: definition of, 10–11; during neoliberal era, 164; during pre-Civil Rights Act period (1966), 63–64; during regulatory decade (1972 to 1980), 121–22, 127, 139, 141–42, 153–54
unemployment rates, 48
unions and unionization, xxvi
United Steel Workers of America v. Weber, **120**

Vanneman, Reeve, 303
Voting Rights Act (1965), 125

wage gaps, 14, 25, 276, 306
Wall Street Journal: gender employment discrimination, 90–91
Wards Cove Packing Co. v. Antonio, 163, **165**
War Manpower Commission (WMC), 65–66
Watson v. Fort Worth Bank & Trust, **165**
Weber, Max, 9
Welch, Finis, 326
white-collar jobs, 97–98
white male advantage, xxii, 182, 238, 293
white men: EEOC-reporting firm employment, **42**; employment growth, 93, **94, 95**; federal contractor employment, **70, 72, 73,** 148; government employment, **43**; homogeneous workplaces, **52**; human resource managers, **161**; intergroup contact exposure, 204–6; labor force composition, **38**; occupational distribution, **52**, 96–99; reverse discrimination, xxii, 121, 126, 311–13; small-firm private-sector employment, **44**; workplace isolation, **32**, 58–59, **72, 76, 80, 110,** 131, **133, 174**. *See also* good-quality job representation
white men-black men desegregation or segregation: 1966 to 2005, **298**; and black male local labor market participation, **190**; in EEOC-reporting firms, **71**; in federal contractor firms, **71**; by FEP law status, **76**; industry variation, **228, 230, 231, 233, 237**; labor queuing process, 195–96; OFCCP regulation impact, **263**; organizational variation, 57, **58,** 242–45, **300**; in Plans for Progress firms, **80**; by political era, **170**; during pre-Civil Rights Act period (1966), **54, 56, 57, 58, 71**; regional variation, **56**; sector

variation, 55, **57, 220**; workplace birth and death impact, **253**; workplace environmental context, **256**

white men-black women desegregation or segregation: 1966 to 2005, **298**; and black female local labor market participation, **190**, 191; in EEOC-reporting firms, **71**; industry variation, **228, 230, 231, 233, 237**; OFCCP regulation impact, **263**; organizational variation, 57, **58, 300**; by political era, **170**; during pre-Civil Rights Act period (1966), **54, 56, 58, 71**; regional variation, **56**; workplace birth and death impact, **253**; workplace environmental context, **256**

white men-white women desegregation or segregation: 1966 to 2005, **298**; in EEOC-reporting firms, **71**; in federal contractor firms, **71**; industry variation, **228, 230, 231, 233, 237**; labor market competition impact, 195; neoliberal era, **169**; OFCCP regulation impact, **263**; organizational variation, 57, **58, 242, 243, 244, 300**; by political era, **170**; during pre-Civil Rights Act period (1966), **54, 56, 57, 58, 71**; regional variation, **56**; sector variation, **57**; and white female local labor market participation, 190–91; workplace birth and death impact, **253**; workplace environmental context, **256**

whites: immigrants' impact on labor market opportunities, 208–9; racial resentment, 320–21; racial stereotypes, 21–23

white women: discrimination claims, 27; discrimination lawsuits, 266–67; educational attainment, **40**; EEOC-reporting firm employment, **42**; employment growth, 94, **95**; employment segregation trends, 53, **54, 76, 80**, 118, 127–33, **168**; federal contractor employment, **70, 72, 73**, 144–45; government employment, **43**; homogeneous workplaces, **52**; human resource managers, 15–16, 152, **161**, 166–67, 176; labor force composition, 38, **38**; labor market competition impact, 196; labor queuing process and segregation from white men, 194–95; managerial representation by sector, 220, **222**; occupational distribution, **52**, 53, 96–99; Plans for Progress firm employment, **80**, 81; regional variation in segregation, 55, **56**; sector variation in segregation, 55, **57, 216, 219**; small-firm private-sector employment, **44**; workplace integration, 95–96; workplace isolation, **32, 59, 72, 76, 80, 110**, 131–33, **174**. *See also* good-quality job representation

white women-black men desegregation or segregation. *See* black men-white women desegregation or segregation

white women-black women desegregation or segregation: EEOC-reporting firms, **71**; federal contractor firms, **71**; by FEP law status, **76**; industry variation, 232–35; labor queuing process, 196–97; neoliberal era, **169**; OFCCP regulation impact, **263**; organizational variation, 57, **58, 243, 244**, 245–46, **300**; Plans for Progress firms, **80**; by political era, **170**; pre-Civil Rights Act period (1966), **54, 56, 57, 58, 71**; regional variation, **56**; sector variation, **57, 220**; workplace birth and death impact, **253**; workplace environmental context, **256**

white women-Hispanic women desegregation or segregation, 305

Williams, David, 26
Williams v. Saxbe, 161–62
Willie Horton ads, 156
women: gender stereotypes, 23–24; in
    management, 14, 15, 274–78; promo-
    tions, 284; skilled craft job exclusion,
    105. *See also* black women; gender
    discrimination; white women
women's movement: desegregation
    impact, xxvi–xxvii, 126, 296, 318–19;
    emergence of, 89, 118, 121; during
    neoliberal era, 160; number of orga-
nizations, **122**; pregnancy discrimi-
    nation, 160; protest events, **123**; ra-
    cial issues within, 131
Wooten, Lynn, 268–69, 271–72
working-class jobs, 33, 96–97, 303. *See
    also* craft job representation
workplace integration, 38–39, 92–96
workplace variation. *See* organiza-
    tional variation in segregation
World War II, 65–66

Zimbabwe, 8–9